ROSE HENDERSON

Rose Henderson

A Woman for the People

PETER CAMPBELL

McGill-Queen's University Press
Montreal & Kingston • London • Ithaca

© McGill-Queen's University Press 2010
ISBN 978-0-7735-3764-4

Legal deposit fourth quarter 2010
Bibliothèque nationale du Québec

Printed in Canada on acid-free paper that is 100% ancient forest free
(100% post-consumer recycled), processed chlorine free

This book has been published with the help of a grant from the
Canadian Federation for the Humanities and Social Sciences, through
the Aid to Scholarly Publications Programme, using funds provided
by the Social Sciences and Humanities Research Council of Canada.

McGill-Queen's University Press acknowledges the support
of the Canada Council for the Arts for our publishing program.
We also acknowledge the financial support of the Government of
Canada through the Canada Book Fund for our publishing activities.

Library and Archives Canada Cataloguing in Publication

Campbell, J. Peter, 1952–
     Rose Henderson: a woman for the people / Peter Campbell.

     Includes bibliographical references and index.
     ISBN 978-0-7735-3764-4

     1. Henderson, Rose, 1871–1937. 2. Feminists – Canada – Biography.
     3. Social reformers – Canada – Biography. 4. Pacifists – Canada – Biography.
     5. Feminism – Canada – History – 20th century. 6. Social movements –
     Canada – History – 20th century. 7. Labor movement – Canada – History –
     20th century. I. Title.

     HQ1455.H45C34 2011   305.42092   C2010-903870-3

This book was typeset by Interscript in 11/14 Garamond.

Contents

Acknowledgments

Biography, like any kind of history, is based on research, and there is a long list of individuals and institutions to thank for this life of Rose Henderson making its way into print. I would especially like to acknowledge Wendy Chmielewski and the staff of the Women's International League for Peace and Freedom Collection at Swarthmore College, Pierre Louis Lapointe of the Archives Nationales du Québec, Sylvie Grandin and her colleagues at the Hôtel de Ville, Montreal, Johanne Pelletier and staff at the McGill University Archives, Larry Black at the Centre for Research on Canadian-Russian Relations, Carleton University, Donald Nethery and staff at the Toronto and District School Board Archives, and Ellen Scheinberg and Laura Tipton at the Ontario Jewish Archives. I owe a debt of gratitude as well to the staffs of the Montreal Central Library, the Church of Ireland Representative Church Body Library, Dublin, Ireland, the General Register Office, Dublin, Ireland, the Archives of Ontario, the Canadian Jewish Congress Archives, Stauffer Library at Queen's University, the City of Toronto Archives, the William Ready Archives at McMaster University, the Thomas Fisher Rare Book Library, and Queen's University Archives.

The completion of my work has been greatly aided by two awards from the Fund for Scholarly Research and Creative Work (Adjuncts) pursuant to the Collective Agreement between Queen's University and the Queen's University Faculty Association. My thanks to John Dixon, Carolyn Falkner, Christine Overall, and Margo Paterson, members of the Sub-Committee of the Joint Committee for the Administration of the Agreement.

I have been encouraged along the way by friends and colleagues who have been unwavering in their support of my efforts to tell Rose

Henderson's story. At the same time I have benefited enormously from their questioning, pushing and prodding, which has compelled me again and again to reconsider what I was saying and why I was saying it. For research, advice, and encouragement I thank Joan Sangster, Will van den Hoonaard, Suzanne Morton, Marlene Macke, Annette Hayward, Selena Crosson, Nancy Butler, Gerald Tulchinsky, Larry Hannant, Nancy Forestell, James Naylor, Katherine McKenna, and Monda Halpern. I owe an especial debt of gratitude to Tamara Myers and Andrée Lévesque, who shared their knowledge and enthusiasm, as well as meaningful suggestions and criticisms. My work is much the better for their contributions.

I have benefited greatly from the ideas and information provided by Deirdre Bonnycastle, Rose's great-granddaughter. I hope that she comes away from my book with an even greater appreciation of the life and contributions of her marvellous great-grandmother.

One of the great benefits of publishing a second book with McGill-Queen's Press has been the pleasure of working with copy editor extraordinaire Maureen Garvie. Maureen has caught any number of inconsistencies and doubtful assertions; her imprint is all over the finished work. It has also been a pleasure to work with Joan McGilvray, Mary-Lynne Ascough, and Kyla Madden.

I am saddened by the fact that my father did not live to see my book come out, and gladdened by the fact that my mother will. She has been asking about Rose for some time now. My patient and faithful wife, Anna, can rest assured that from now on she will be the only woman in my life.

This book is dedicated to all those who carry on Rose Henderson's struggle for the dignity and humanity of the people.

Abbreviations

ACCL	All-Canadian Congress of Labor
CBRE	Canadian Brotherhood of Railway Employees
CLDL	Canadian Labor Defence League
CLP	Canadian Labor Party
CSA	Canadian Suffrage Association
CYC	Canadian Youth Congress
CTA	Catholic Taxpayers' Association
CRA	Congo Reform Association
CCF	Cooperative Commonwealth Federation
CCYM	Cooperative Commonwealth Youth Movement
EYWA	East York Workers' Association
ESC	Employment Service of Canada
GCIS	Girls' Cottage Industry School
ILP	Independent Labor Party
LEAO	Labor Educational Association of Ontario
LAWF	League against War and Fascism
MTLC	Montreal Trades and Labor Council
NCWC	National Council of Women of Canada
NLP	National Labor Party
NEP	New Economic Policy
OBU	One Big Union
OLP	Ontario Labor Party
PWA	Progressive Women's Association
SPC (OS)	Socialist Party of Canada (Ontario Section)
TDSB	Toronto and District School Board

TLP	Toronto Labor Party
TLCC	Trades and Labor Congress of Canada
UFO	United Farmers of Ontario
UWEFO	United Women's Educational Federation of Ontario
VOKS	Society for Cultural Relations
WILPF	Women's International League for Peace and Freedom
WJC	Women's Joint Committee
WPP	Women's Peace Party
WPU	Women's Peace Union
WUL	Workers' Unity League
YMHA	Young Men's Hebrew Association

Rose Henderson in an early 1920s *Toronto Star* photo, at the time of her trip to The Hague to represent the Canadian Section of the Women's International League for Peace and Freedom. *Toronto Daily Star*, 4 December 1922

The photograph of Rose Henderson that accompanied her "Britain Revisited" series of articles in the *Canadian Unionist*, August 1928 – February 1929. *Canadian Unionist*, October 1928

Rose Henderson as she appeared in a *Toronto Globe* photo in the fall of 1935, in the midst of her federal election campaign in Toronto's Parkdale riding. *Toronto Globe*, 12 October 1935

Minister of Labour Mackenzie King in December 1910, at the time of his consultation with Rose Henderson concerning the Opium Bill. William James Topley Studio fonds, Library and Archives Canada, accession 1936-270 NPC, item no. 115221, PA-027993

Ida Siegel, Jewish activist and Rose Henderson's colleague on the Toronto and District School Board in the mid-1930s. Ontario Jewish Archives, fonds 15, item 25

Rabbi Maurice Eisendrath, seated second from left; Dorothy Dworkin, prominent Jewish community activist; and Toronto labour mayor Jimmy Simpson, seated at right, in 1935. Ontario Jewish Archives, fonds 10, item 22

CCF leader J.S. Woodsworth speaking in 1935, when the party was struggling to establish itself as a social democratic alternative to the old line parties. J.S. Woodsworth Photographs, Library and Archives Canada, accession 1973-225NPC, C-055451

A HEROINE OF MINE

She was a high-born lady from the gentry on the land
She never had known poverty, but she seemed to understand
That her privilege depended on the labour of the poor

And she spent her life in working just to even up the score
She married a young lawyer and Chief Justice he became
She could have spent her whole life in the shelter of his name
But not for her the glory of reflections in the glass
She saw the vast injustice and she couldn't let it pass

She was an inspiration to the women of her time
And Jessie Street will always be a heroine of mine

She never had to work but still she fought for equal pay
And she fought for Aborigines to the silvertails' dismay
She was woman for the people, her commitment clear and strong
And she used her wealth and influence to help the cause along

She saw the waste of human life in wars that make men rich
Her work for peace was endless and they put her on the list
They branded her a traitor, called her communist and more
But Jessie's voice was never stilled against the crime of war

She was an inspiration to the women of her time
And Jessie Street will always be a heroine of mine

And Jessie your example helps us all along the way
Foundations that were laid back then we're building on today
The struggle isn't over, there are mountains still to climb
But the legacy you and your sisters left is our lifeline

You were an inspiration to the women of your time
And Jessie Street you'll always be a heroine of mine

Words and music by Judy Small ©1985 Crafty Maid Music

Judy Small's homage to Australian human rights activist Jessie Street (1889–1970) eloquently expresses the feelings Rose Henderson inspired in many who knew of her life and work.

ROSE HENDERSON

Introduction

At the 1 February 1937 meeting of Toronto City Council, Alderman Mrs Plumptre moved that "this Council record its expression of sincere sympathy and condolence to the daughter and sorrowing relatives of Dr. Rose Henderson, a member of the Board of Education for the past three years, who died suddenly on Saturday last, January 30th, following the delivery of an address on penal reform. The late Dr. Henderson was a prominent social worker and formerly Assistant to the Judge of the Juvenile Court in Montreal for seven or eight years, and keenly interested in the work of the Board of Education and also active in forwarding social reforms in Canada. Her loss will be deeply felt by the citizens of Toronto."[1]

Flags flew at half mast in Toronto schools, and Mayor William D. Robbins declared that they were to be lowered at other civic institutions as well.[2] At the meeting of the Toronto Board of Education on 4 February, the day after Rose Henderson's funeral, trustees and the audience stood in her memory for two minutes while a sheaf of red roses rested on her desk.[3]

It is a truism of Canadian public life that Canadians do not know their own history. The loss of memory of the life of Rose Henderson suggests that there is more than a little truth in the truism. The vast majority of Canadians have never heard of Rose Henderson, although that might be said of any number of important figures in Canadian history. The task at hand is to demonstrate that there was something compelling about Henderson, to convincingly argue that she is worth remembering after all this time. In order to do that, she needs to speak to us in our own day and age, to bring meaning to our lives across the intervening decades since her death.

I begin, I suppose, with the existential question – what do any of our lives mean? In our own day, how does one point to a movement, a piece of social legislation, an idea that one can attribute to Rose Henderson? If Tommy Douglas was the "Father of Medicare," of what was Henderson the mother? She did not succeed in making all homes a haven of enlightenment and caring; her tireless efforts in the peace movement did not end war; her work as an educator did not end schoolyard violence, bullying, and teen suicide. Her unceasing efforts to better the lives of young children notwithstanding, all over the world they continue to die in their thousands every day of hunger, disease, and neglect. In many respects it is difficult to argue that the world is a better place than it was on that day in January 1937 when Henderson died too soon.

Even if we look at Henderson in the context of the social reformers of her day, it is difficult to argue that she stands out in any definable way. Unlike Agnes Macphail, Dorise Nielsen, and Grace MacInnis, she never succeeded in being elected to a provincial legislature or the federal parliament.[4] She never led a political party or was appointed to the Senate, never headed a royal commission or had a public institution named after her. She is not with the Famous Five on Parliament Hill, and no first in medicine, education, or law is associated with her name.

Even within feminist historiography it is difficult to assess where she fits. In the early days of feminist biography, as Barbara Caine points out, the focus was on "the importance of individual women and their achievements."[5] The concern was with the leaders of major national and regional women's organizations and movements, notably of the suffrage movement. These biographies of "prominent" women, Joan Sangster argues, were important because they emphasized the shared struggle of women against patriarchy and the fight against the restrictive social conventions of their time.[6] In the 1970s and 1980s, when feminist biographies were being written in increasing numbers, it had not yet been established that Henderson was a "prominent" woman and worthy of serious consideration. In addition, the attention paid to "elite" women led to a counter-argument, that biographies of exceptional women marginalized the great majority of women in most historical contexts.[7] Bettina Bradbury, for instance, shifted the historian's gaze away from Sangster's focus, emphasizing the importance of writing about "ordinary women, rather than the relatively visible elite."[8] Henderson fits neither category, and both.

This book is an effort to shift our gaze away from a debate that, in the case of Henderson, at least, is not the most fruitful approach to understanding her life of social activism and the political culture in which she operated. Understanding her historical significance involves appreciating Barbara Taylor's argument that in the early decades of nineteenth century England it was a "utopian dream" to see women's liberation as part of a general process of social regeneration. According to Taylor, the dream died around 1845, and with it went "the ideological tie between feminism and working-class radicalism." After 1845, "sex oppression and class exploitation increasingly became viewed not as twin targets of a single strategy, but as separate objects of separate struggles, organized from different – and sometimes opposing – perspectives."[9] If the dream died in 1845, someone forgot to tell Henderson. Like Mary Wollstonecraft, she drew "a comparison between the political subalternity of women and that of the male working class."[10] In many ways, her life of social activism was a powerful evocation of the "ideological tie" between the liberation of women and the liberation of the working class. Henderson lived and worked in this broader spirit; her vision was of women and the working class transforming the world together. There were feminists in Britain, the United States, and elsewhere like Henderson, but in the Canadian context she had few, if any, equals.

The way in which Canadian labour and women's history has been written has made it difficult, if not impossible, to bring to light a life dedicated to the ideological ties between feminism and working-class protest. There is a definable difference in Canadian historical writing between a largely male-authored labour history and an overwhelmingly female-authored historiography of feminism and the women's movement. Henderson has maintained a presence in both literatures for more than a generation but has failed to find a home in either. She was too much a middle-class female social reformer to become a major figure in labour history, too much a leftist and labour activist to be considered a legitimate member of the pantheon of female heroes of the women's movement. The scorn that many male Marxists had for "bourgeois" women reformers in Henderson's own day has its echoes in the writing of Canadian labour history, and Canadian women's history is replete with condemnations of the sexism and misogyny of male-dominated socialist and labour movements that marginalized women and their concerns. Henderson has been praised and remembered in both literatures, but for all intents and purposes there is no body of literature on the ideological ties between the two movements that she was attempting to unite.

Understanding Henderson's life and legacy involves muddying the waters, pushing at the boundaries of labour and feminist history, questioning long-held assumptions and ideological predispositions. I will argue, even as a male labour historian, that in understanding her contribution, we must begin with Rose Henderson as woman and fully engage her maternal feminism. She did espouse the "cult of domesticity" and did believe that, in the best of all possible worlds, women should be in the home, raising their children in a caring, nurturing environment. She did not agree with working-class women leaving their homes and children to work in factories, but she fully understood why they had to do it. The radical element in her thinking derived from the fact that she knew that revolutionary changes had to take place in the capitalist system in order for women to fulfill their "natural" roles. This change for women was not going to come about without the assistance of men and the organized labour movement. The crucial point about Henderson's maternal feminism is that it led her to broaden, not narrow, her vision and led her to embrace, not reject, a male-dominated left and labour movement.

Understanding Henderson and appreciating her contribution means questioning the claim made by Canadian historians that being a maternal feminist, emphasizing the centrality of motherhood, involved the depoliticization of women. The implication is that focusing on the maternal role of women relegated them to the home, removing them from active and meaningful involvement in a male-dominated public sphere. I defend Henderson in much the way Kathleen Brown defends Ella Reeve "Mother" Bloor, the leading feminist activist of the American Communist Party. Brown notes that "some historians of both the Left and women in the United States have labeled Bloor a maternalist and de-emphasized her political importance by arguing that she essentialized and depoliticized women." Brown counters this argument by suggesting that "Bloor's deployment of motherhood, within the framework of Left politics, was not sentimentalist, essentialist, or naturalist, but instead part of her construction of a serious ideology about the need to reproduce life and culture humanely."[11] While not denying a "sentimentalist" element in Henderson's thinking, I would count her among those feminists who recognized "the gendered nature of every aspect of experience."[12]

The full significance of what Henderson was trying to do has been lost in the existing interpretations of her life and work. Two broad characterizations need to be questioned. The first is put forward by historians such as John Manley, who sees a progression from "pre-war 'maternal feminism' to fully-fledged political opposition to all aspects of women's oppression." The problem with Manley's formulation is that it portrays maternal feminism as something to get over, as a world view incompatible with a rigorous anti-capitalist politics. The position taken in this work is that Henderson's anti-capitalist politics flowed directly out of maternal feminism and is not comprehensible without it. By the 1930s her maternal feminism was not tying women to the home – it was insisting that women get out of the home and become immersed in the public life of the society, especially in the labour movement, the schools, and politics. For her, socialist activism was inconceivable without a leading role being taken by women.

This caveat notwithstanding, Manley is closer to the mark when he suggests that in the 1920s Henderson "began to question all restraints on the human development of women."[13] Carol Bacchi misses the mark when she argues that the First World War "dissipated the basis for philosophical idealism" that lay behind the women's reform movement.[14] In the case of Henderson, nothing could be further from the truth. As historians of the women's peace movement in the United States have pointed out, the philosophical idealism of the suffrage movement of the First World War period was transferred to the peace movement in the 1920s. Given the soul-destroying destruction of human life that had occurred in the trenches of France and Belgium, what force other than the love of a mother for her child could overcome western capitalist society's penchant for consuming its own young and bringing civilization to the brink of collapse? The maternal feminist generation of which Henderson was a part understood, in a way now seemingly lost to us, that war is always a war on women, always a war on children, always a war in which men run away from who they are.

The second categorization of Henderson that needs challenging is the distinction that is made between her ideas that were "socialist" and her ideas that were "feminist."[15] The weakness in this distinction is that in the life and work of Rose Henderson, it is often difficult, at times impossible, to make the distinction. She used the terms "mother" and "worker" interchangeably; she spoke of the historic role of women in much the same way that Karl Marx spoke of the historic role of the wage worker. She was as alive as any person of her generation to the forces driving women out of the home and into the workplace. She was a tireless advocate of the idea that the union movement was a crucial vehicle in improving the lot of working women, and while it is true that her vision was one shared with male Marxists of an idyllic female-based home life, it did not blind her to the reality of the lives of poor working women. We can dispute her vision, but we cannot question her understanding that creating a world of peace in which the home was a place of nurturing and caring meant the complete transformation of capitalist society and male domination.

Henderson was no saint; she accepted credit for things she did not do, and she did not always live up to her own high ethical standards. She was a woman who wanted to be in the public eye, and wanted the public to have a particular understanding of what she was doing and why she was doing it. She had, at times, an inflated sense of her own importance. She belonged to a generation of social reformers whose ideas came from the United States and Great Britain, who rarely developed a theory or implemented a reform that a historian can characterize as unique or originating in Canada. Even among Canadian social activists, she did not stand out as an innovative thinker. Yet there was something powerful, something compelling, and something genuine about her that made her more respected by the middle-class female reformers and male working-class radicals of her day than by later generations. In her life, if only for fleeting moments, she convinced middle-class feminists and male working-class radicals to see beyond the specificity of their own daily struggles to envision a world in which they would all be free together.

I

Montreal Beginnings

The early decades of Rose Henderson's life remain maddeningly mysterious; comparing and contrasting her own version of her early life with other sources merely adds to that mystery. We begin with an account of her early life as she related it to a reporter for the *Toronto Daily Star* in 1922:

> She is Irish ... She descends from certain plantationists, of the name of Wills, long a well-known Bristol family, now devoted to the profits of tobacco, and maybe at one time flourishing from the gains of the slave trade with Ireland, and, later, with the slave trade elsewhere, on which no insignificant ratio of the wealth of what was the second British city, has been founded ... Father Wills was the manager of a big department store in Dublin ... He spoke French, and used to entertain at home French salesmen who came to the store. He was as Irish in national affections as the most nationalist of them. Like the progenies of most plantationists, his family had become bone of the Irish bone, and flesh of the Irish flesh ... It's a great heritage to be daughter to such a man. At school, when Rose Wills heard the teacher say that the French were the natural enemies of the British, she protested, remembering the blessed courtesies of her home.[1]

While this account confirms Henderson's generally acknowledged Anglo-Irish middle-class origins, it raises as many questions as it answers. Why is her father not identified by his first name? Why is there no mention of her mother? Why did Henderson, at a young age, leave such a seemingly idyllic middle-class childhood for the anxieties and dangers of a trans-Atlantic crossing and an uncertain future in North America?

The sources compound the confusion rather than providing clarification. Rose Henderson died in Toronto on 30 January 1937, at the age of sixty-eight, according to her death certificate. The *Daily Clarion*, the paper of the Communist Party of Canada, stated at the time of her death that she was born in Dublin "some 65 years ago."[2] That the Communist Party's account may be the more accurate one is revealed by the 1891 and 1901 censuses of Canada. In the 1891 Census of Canada, "Rosina" Henderson was listed as being twenty-two years of age, indicating a birth year of 1869.[3] In contrast the 1901 census, identifying her as "Louisa" Henderson, gave her birth date as 14 December 1871.[4] This date cannot be confirmed, because the Irish birth registry has no record for a Rose Wills born on 14 December 1871. Given that the 1901 Canadian census reported that she came to North America in 1885, it is possible that some family trauma, perhaps the desertion or death of her mother, prompted a barely teenage Rose Wills to strike out on her own.

Switching focus to her father and her husband only deepens the mystery. Surprisingly, given the fact that Henderson claimed her father managed a Dublin department store, the *Canadian Who's Who* for 1936–37 identified her father as the Reverend George Wills. Yet the Church of Ireland Archives in Dublin has no record of a Reverend George Wills. The identity of her husband is equally shrouded in ambiguity and contradiction. The *Canadian Who's Who* for 1936–37 identified him as H.D. Henderson, and stated that he died in 1912. Other sources tell a dramatically different story. The 1891 Canadian census revealed that Rose's husband was Charles A. Henderson, born in the United States of Scottish parents. His age was given as twenty-one, indicating 1870 as the year of his birth.[5] But as we are rapidly learning, nothing is as it appears in the lives of Rose and Charles. The 1901 census indicated that Charles Henderson was born in Scotland, not the United States. His date of birth, 4 August 1868, made him two years older than indicated in the census of 1891[6] – a two-year age discrepancy, as in the case of Rose, but in the other direction.

When and where Rose Wills and Charles Henderson were married also remains a subject of speculation. The inference that they were married in Boston appears to be refuted by the lack of a marriage certificate in the Massachusetts State Archives. The *Toronto Daily Star* reported, without supporting evidence, that she spent her early married life in Boston.[7] The fact that her daughter, Ida, was born in Quebec on 25 November 1890 suggests that the time in Boston cannot have been long, if it happened at all.[8] Indeed, in 1920 the Quebec premier Lomer Gouin wrote that Henderson had "*une fille de 20 ans d'un légitime mariage.*"[9] Gouin's knowledge of her marriage would seem to indicate that she was married in Quebec.

Contrary to the date given in *Who's Who in Canada*, Charles Henderson died in Montreal's Royal Victoria Hospital on 15 January 1904.[10] Although he died in the middle of a brutally cold winter, during outbreaks of typhoid and diphtheria, hospital records give the cause of death as a cerebral haemorrhage. He was buried in the Mount Royal Cemetery on 16 January 1904, following a funeral service conducted in the family home at 84 Hutchison Street by J.W. Graham, minister at St James Methodist Church on St Catherine Street.[11] The funeral service being conducted by a Methodist minister indicates the first of several changes in the religious affiliation of Rose Henderson, an odyssey that began in the Church of Ireland and ended in the Society of Friends.[12]

As we approach Henderson's entrance into a long, impassioned, and influential life of social activism, the question arises as to the linkages between tragedy in her private life and her entrance into the public realm. Without private papers, only speculation is possible, speculation that suggests she dealt with her husband's death by becoming active in the public life of the society. The sudden death of her husband at a young age may have led her to seek some purpose in her life. While her private motivations for entering a life of social activism will remain hidden from the historian's gaze, we do have her own account of the process, as related to a Winnipeg journalist in the pages of the *Manitoba Free Press*, dated 30 April 1921:

When my husband died and my child had grown up … I found myself without occupation. I didn't even know what I did want to do. All I did know is that I had a profound love for children and a desire to serve them. One day a friend of mine who taught in a mission Sunday school in the slums of Montreal asked me to take a class there. I did so. Poor little atoms. My chief teaching concerned the inculcation of a prejudice in favor of clean faces and in trying to get them

warm and comfortable before they started out again. Presently my little friends would pipe up that 'Father' or 'Mother' would like to see
me. My social circle widened. I discovered that some of my new ac-
quaintances had a pleasing way of getting drunk and keeping drunk
from Saturday to Monday. Every so often the arm of the law would
reach out and gather them in, and not infrequently I would find myself at the police court, called in to help. At this police court I began
to be aware of the fact that little children were being brought up and
tried along with criminals, and sometimes housed with them. That
started me on the juvenile court agitation.

The chronology of events is difficult to delineate. Rose's husband died in
January 1904, and there is no evidence to suggest that she was involved in
social activism before his death. She may have been teaching in mission
Sunday schools in 1905–06, but her daughter, Ida, born in 1890, was hardly
"grown up" by this time. This may be a rationalization on Henderson's part,
or it may be that she did not begin her involvement with young people until
1908, the year Ida became "grown up" by getting married, at eighteen, to
William Robinson Bonnycastle of Louisville, Kentucky. As we shall see, the
evidence suggests that the earlier date is the more likely.

When Henderson began her work of social outreach, she was a middle-
class Anglo-Celtic woman of some means. Beginning in the early 1890s,
the Hendersons lived on Hutchison Street, running north from Sherbrooke
Street, a few blocks east of the McGill University campus. In 1891–92
they lived at 39 Hutchison Street, and by the turn of the century they had
moved to 84 Hutchison, where they resided when Charles Henderson
died in January 1904. In 1901 Charles Henderson, clerk, was making
$1,800 a year, roughly three times as much as a typical working-class
family in Montreal with several more children. The middle-class lifestyle
of the Hendersons in 1900 is revealed by the $320 of that $1,800 that
went to pay their rent.[13] The $320 speaks to their social status, but even
so that figure represents less than 20 per cent of Charles's total income in
an age before personal income taxes. All indications are that Rose was in
good shape financially following her husband's death, a standing that fa-
cilitated her life of public activism.[14]

She became a social activist in the midst of dramatic changes affecting
the economic, political, and social life of Quebec's largest city. As

industrial capitalism grew and diversified, the women and children who were her main concern continued to work as domestic servants but were increasingly drawn to the industries – cotton textiles and the garment, tobacco, and food industries – that provided Montreal with its distinctiveness as a Canadian business centre.[15] Young girls also looked after younger siblings while their parents were away at work. The young boys Henderson came in contact with worked in factories, sold newspapers on street corners, shone shoes, and worked as messenger and delivery boys.

Rose Henderson lived in the city described in Herbert Brown Ames's *The City below the Hill*, a path-breaking and still influential work published in 1897. Ethnically, Ames found a city divided by thirds into French Catholics, Irish Catholics, and English, Irish, and Scottish Protestants. They lived in the same city but in a real sense did not live in the same political culture. For anglophone Protestants living in the independent municipality of Westmount, the Irish in Griffintown and the poverty-stricken French Catholics living in the old quartiers of the city might as well have been in a different country.

Consideration of Ames's prescription for amelioration of the lives of the poor of Montreal reveals the extent to which Henderson was, and was not, part of the vision he sets out. He observes in his introduction, "There are among the dwellers of 'the city above the hill' not a few, we believe, who have the welfare of their fellow-men at heart, who realize that there is no influence more elevating than the proper home, who acknowledge that there is need for improvement in the matter of housing the working classes of this city, and who would be willing to assist any movement of a semi-philanthropic character having for its object the erection of proper homes for the families of working men. These persons are business men."[16]

Rose Henderson shared Ames's belief in the importance of the "proper home" in the moral uplift of the city's poor. Yet she was not a businessman and was not in a position to be improving existing housing or building new and better housing. Interestingly, given the emphasis she placed on environment in improving the lot of poor mothers and children, she did not focus her attention on the physical condition of the housing she encountered. Rather, her concerns for the cleanliness of young children had more to do with the conscientiousness of the mother and the cleaning of young faces and hands than it had to do with campaigning for better housing.

Poor quality housing was not her main concern, but it provided the setting for the lives of the working-class residents of Montreal she worked among. More than 80 per cent of Montreal's citizens were renters, not owners, and absentee landlords were the rule, not the exception.[17] In the working-class districts, poor sanitation – including open-pit toilets – overcrowding, damp, dirt, rooms without direct means of ventilation, lack of yards and open spaces, and lack or absence of sunlight were all commonplace. Ames's solution was model dwellings, which he claimed could be built "with reasonable hope of a fair return upon capital."[18] The Progressive reformers of the major American cities, whose work inspired him, were opposed to direct state involvement in housing construction. The aim of most housing reformers was to encourage workers to save enough to purchase a home; even Le Parti Ouvrier, on the left of Montreal's politics, favoured loans to workers to purchase housing rather than direct state involvement.[19]

Henderson worked in a political culture in which even social reformers like Ames believed that society could not "interfere with the inscrutable law of supply and demand to raise the workingman's wages."[20] Montreal was the "eight-months city," its dependence on a port that was frozen in four months of the year producing a working class in which only roughly 25 per cent of workers could count on year-round employment.[21] The $1,800 a year that Charles Henderson was earning at the turn of the century stands in stark contrast to the roughly $400 earned by factory workers on full employment.[22] Even with the wife earning the average female wage of $190 annually, the typical working-class couple could muster only one-third of the income of Charles Henderson.[23]

Rose Henderson shared with the other social reformers of her day a number of assumptions about the 20–25 per cent of Montreal women in the labour force. Louis Guyon, a chief factory inspector writing in 1922, sums up many of the prevailing attitudes of the first two decades of the century when he describes women working outside the home as "a true social heresy" – a woman outside her home was "a woman without a country." He then quotes a "learned sociologue" to the effect that the woman must be restored to the home if society is to avoid degeneration.[24] Although Rose Henderson shared these attitudes, she was more understanding of the realities of working-class life, realities that required teen-aged girls going out to work in order for the family to survive.

At the turn of the century Montreal was "the most dangerous city" in the western world to be born into. More than 25 per cent of children died before their first birthday.[25] Unsafe water, contaminated milk, and the continued virulence of diseases such as tuberculosis, diphtheria, and typhoid made Montreal a virtual game of Russian roulette for infants in working-class districts.

Paradoxically, the city that often seemed to care so little for the infant was more moved by the plight of working youth. Children were a major part of the workforce, and there was a marked concern among the city's philanthropists and social reformers that the impoverishment of children was reflected in their physical appearance. A female factory inspector, Louisa King, commented that children working in factories were often older than they appeared, and that typically children were smaller than the size of their parents indicated they should be.[26] After being employed by the Montreal Juvenile Court in January 1912, Henderson commented on the uniformly small size of the young girls and boys who appeared before Judge Choquet.

While hard data is difficult to come by, impressionistic evidence suggests that the boys Henderson worked with were not by and large the factory workers but rather the small army who lived much of their lives on the street as newsboys and delivery and messenger boys. In 1912 Guyon reported in the *Annual Report of the Quebec Department of Labour* that such boys could be seen "shivering on the street until eleven o'clock at night."[27] The Industrial Establishments Act of 1893 did not apply to the street trades, leaving the factory inspectors with no jurisdiction over these boys. Their contacts with the state were more likely to come through the Children's Aid Society or, as of January 1912, the Juvenile Court.

Henderson worked first as a volunteer with the Children's Aid Society and then as a paid probation officer with the Juvenile Court. While it is difficult to generalize about the education level of the children she came into contact with, typically they did not get beyond the third or fourth year of elementary school.[28] In theory, Protestant children were better off than French Catholic children, given that between 1897 and 1910 the Protestant School Commission received "roughly the same amount of municipal school tax as the Catholic Board," even though there were almost twice as many French Catholic children in the Catholic public system.[29] Yet it would be misleading to claim that conditions were significantly better in the Protestant system. There were not enough schools, and those that did exist were crowded. Jewish children had been given the legal right to attend Protestant schools in 1903, and the early twentieth century was a period of heavy Jewish migration to Montreal. As Terry Copp points out, enrolment in Protestant schools doubled between 1905 and 1915, and by the latter date 43 per cent of students were Jewish.[30] It is not clear, the concerns of Montreal's Anglo-Protestant elite notwithstanding, that the typical Protestant or Jewish child from a working-class background was getting a better education than his or her French Canadian counterpart.

What is certain is that by the beginning of the twentieth century there was a widespread concern in Montreal, shared by French Canadian, English Canadian, and Jew alike, with the increasing problem of juvenile delinquency. That concern led to agitation to create a court system specifically for young offenders. According to *Woman's Century*, the paper of the National Council of Women of Canada, the establishment of the juvenile court "owed much to the Montreal Women's Club. A Juvenile Court Committee to promote the movement for separate courts for juvenile offenders was formed in 1904, and later the Club gave financial support to the first probation officer in Montreal."[31] Given that the Montreal Women's Club was promoting a juvenile court the same year Charles Henderson died, scepticism is the healthy response to the claim made in the *Toronto Daily Star* that it was Rose Henderson who "pioneered the advocacy of juvenile courts."[32]

It does appear to be true, as the *Star* claimed, that Rose Henderson spent three months in New York observing the operations of the juvenile court there before lobbying the federal parliament in Canada for the implementation of juvenile courts.[33] When she was hired in 1912 as the non-Catholic probation officer by the Montreal Juvenile Court, the *Montreal Daily Herald* reported: "She studied in New York, Boston, Toronto, and Ottawa, and also studied in Europe, spending some time in Germany, in Hungary, in Copenhagen, where she observed the milk system in schools, in Norway and in Sweden. In spite of all that travel and instruction she still feels herself to be ignorant, and believes that she has a lot to learn."[34]

There seems no reason to doubt that at some point in this period Henderson did indeed undertake an extensive international study of juvenile courts, possibly funded by the Montreal Women's Club. In the March 1915 issue of *Woman's Century*, she published a piece entitled "A Knight of the Slums," based on her experiences at the Five Points Mission in New York. In the April 1915 issue, in an article entitled "The Need for a Woman's Court," she compared her experiences in the women's court in Toronto in September 1914 with her earlier experiences in New York.

A 29 November 1907 letter from Caroline Béïque to Prime Minister Wilfrid Laurier set out the plans of the Montreal Women's Club.[35] Béïque wrote, "Le Montreal Women's Club veut s'occuper cette anné de la question des Juvenile Courts, et après une entente avec quelques juges, va se charger de payer le salaire d'un Probation Officer, afin de faire une expérience pratique du système suivi aux Etats-Unis."

Béïque asked Laurier to write some lines approving of the principle of a special court for children.[36] In his reply, Laurier declined the request, pointing out that the project of establishing a juvenile court patterned after one in Colorado was presently being studied by the Department of Justice and that a law might be introduced in the current session. He argued that under the circumstances it would be inappropriate for him to take sides on the issue.[37]

In her memoir *Quatre-Vingts Ans de Souvenirs*, Béïque notes that as president of the Fédération Nationale Saint-Jean-Baptiste she was asked by the Montreal Women's Club to participate in the group gathering information concerning juvenile courts and that for about three years this group met weekly in her home. Their campaign involved *"une étude assez poussée de l'organisation de cours spéciales pour enfants."*[38] While no direct evidence has surfaced that Henderson was the woman asked to study juvenile courts in Europe and the United States, the circumstantial evidence suggests that it was her. The year may have been 1908, because in that year the occupant of Henderson's apartment at 69 Hutchison was a man by the name of Philip Steele.[39] Henderson's absence may be explained in part by the wedding of her daughter, Ida, to William Robinson Bonnycastle in the United States, but it may also be because she was on a fact-finding mission for the Montreal Women's Club. Again, no direct evidence exists that she was involved in lobbying the federal government during this process, but it is certainly not beyond the realm of possibility. As we will see, Henderson came to the attention of Mackenzie King during this period, and it may have been as a result of her juvenile court agitation.

The question of the responsibility for the Juvenile Delinquents' Act of 1908 and the setting up of the Montreal Juvenile Court is not easy to answer. On the national scene, the key players where J.J. Kelso, who established the Toronto Children's Aid Society, and W.L. Scott, who established the CAS in Ottawa.[40] As Tamara Myers points out, the fact that Kelso and Scott were active in Ontario has led to the neglect of the important role played by Montreal in the process.[41] Interestingly, Myers identifies the Fédération Nationale Saint-Jean-Baptiste, the Women's Christian Temperance Union, and the Local Council of Women as taking important roles in the agitation, but not the Montreal Women's Club.[42] If the Montreal Women's Club did indeed fund an international fact-finding trip by Henderson, an important element of the juvenile court agitation is missing in this version of events. On the other hand, Myers's national focus and broad-based understanding of the many individuals and organizations involved in the movement places Henderson in context, and quite clearly demonstrates that claims for her seminal role cannot be substantiated on the basis of the existing evidence.

The 1909 report of the Montreal Children's Aid Society also calls into question the assertion of a leading role for Henderson in the founding of the juvenile court system in Montreal. In 1909 the president of the Montreal Children's Aid Society was F.-X. Choquet, who would become the judge of the juvenile court when it began operations in 1912.[43] In his presidential report Choquet stated that one of the goals of the CAS was "to take the part of a friend to any children accused of offences against the laws of the Province, the City, or the Dominion, and to guard their interests in the court of justice." He added that "the object for which the Society exists cannot be properly attained until a law is passed by the Provincial Parliament to create juvenile courts, and appoint officers, and provide a proper place to which the younger children could be sent where they could be under such surveillance as would aid in their reform." He noted that in the past year "representations" had been made to the provincial government for the passing of an act in accordance with the federal act, but that an act was not passed in the last session. He also noted that the Society for the past year had employed a probation officer, who had enjoyed "great success." That probation officer, Marie Clément, stated in a report that in a juvenile court system the judge functioned as a "good father," and the probation officer as "the friend of the child." The city needed such a "special court and judge."[44] A vote of thanks was given to the Montreal Women's Club "for their generosity in paying the salary of the Probation Officer during the past two years, since the office was started."[45]

Henderson's involvement with the juvenile court agitation in Montreal established a pattern that would repeat itself throughout her life of political activism. On the one hand, in her own day she was credited in the left-wing press with single-handedly establishing the Montreal Juvenile Court, an unfounded claim that must be laid to rest. On the other hand, the work of francophone and anglophone feminists beginning in the 1970s is characterized by complete neglect of Henderson, even including work that focuses on the left, the women's movement, and child welfare reform in Montreal.[46] Henderson made a much more important contribution to the life of Montreal in the early years of the twentieth century than has been recognized.

She had certainly become a force in the public life of Montreal by 1910–11. In 1910–11, Bill 97, "An Act to Prohibit the Improper Use of Opium and Other Drugs," was making its way through the Canadian parliament. Spurred by the paranoia generated by fear of alleged drug use by the Chinese on Canada's West Coast, what was often referred to as the "Cocaine Bill" included a provision for which Henderson was given credit in the *Canadian Who's Who* for 1936–37. There the claim was made that she "succeeded in getting Parlt. to pass an amendment to the Drug Act, 1912, to prevent the sale of drugs except by doctor's prescription." The provision was in section 5/2 of the bill, but no convincing evidence has surfaced to prove Rose Henderson's leading role in its implementation.

There is, however, conclusive evidence that she was a major force in prompting the bill itself. Early in 1911 she appears in the diaries of Mackenzie King, at that time the minister of labour in the government of Sir Wilfrid Laurier. On 12 January 1911 King recorded, "I telegraphed Mrs. Henderson of Montreal, probation officer of Children's Society to come up. She gave me a startling account of extent to which cocaine habit is being developed among young children in Montreal, her story corresponds with police account."[47] It is unclear how Henderson had established enough of a reputation to be sought out as a consultant by the minister of labour, but there is no doubting the influence she was already exerting on the public life of Montreal, and on King. A week after his first entry King noted, "This morning we had a meeting of the Cabinet from 11 to 1. I was very busy before glancing over letters, many of which had to do with the Cocaine Bill. There has been a strong movement worked up in Montreal, and I have had letters from all kinds of sources. The little woman Mrs. Henderson deserves the greatest credit, she is back of it all."[48]

The letters King refers to have not been found, but a document in the file on the "Opium Traffic" in his papers contains short snippets from thirty-six letters. Most of them are from Quebec, with the great majority coming from Montreal. King was not exaggerating in saying that the letters came from "all kinds of sources." The writers were from the Protestant Ministerial Association of Montreal, the Montreal Women's Club, and the Young Men's Christian Association of Montreal. The letter of Alderman S.J. Carter quite clearly demonstrates Henderson's influence, as he writes, "In view of the awful havoc of the cocaine evil and the wide prevalence of the habit in Montreal, especially among the boys and girls, this proposed Bill is most opportune ... and I trust that your measure will pass." Carter's sentiments, indeed much of his vocabulary, were echoed by a number of other prominent Montreal residents.[49]

The letters reached across the ethnic and religious divide, as writers included Mayor James John Guerin, and Archbishop Paul Bruchési. Radical Anglo-Celtic feminist Rose Henderson and "arch-conservative" French Canadian Catholic Archbishop Bruchési shared a concern for youth that transcended their differences.[50] Since the publication of Hugh MacLennan's classic novel, it has become *de rigeur* to describe English and French Canada as "two solitudes," but the capitalism of the early twentieth century respected no such distinction. There were differences of emphasis; Archbishop Bruchési was part of a French Canadian elite concerned with the ubiquitous nature of "Protestant materialism" in a rapidly industrializing and modernizing North America.[51] For Henderson the issue was not that materialism had a religion but rather that capitalism was an economic system that put profit ahead of human needs. There was agreement, nonetheless, concerning the ills that industrial capitalism was visiting upon the youth of Montreal.

At this point in her life Henderson's critique of the failings of modern capitalist society drew more fully on Methodism than on Marxism. In the 1891 Canadian census both she and her husband were identified as belonging to the "Church of England," although her affiliation from childhood was more accurately Church of Ireland.[52] In the 1901 census, however, Charles was identified as a Methodist, not a member of the Church of England.[53] The fact that his funeral service was conducted in the Henderson home by a Methodist minister suggests that Rose had also converted. In all probability the "mission Sunday schools" she began teaching in were Methodist Sunday schools.

It is only possible to advance tentative arguments about Methodism's impact on Henderson. She entered upon a life of social activism at precisely the point that the mainline Protestant churches in Canada were uniting evangelism and social reform in an aggressive push to deal with the growing social problems besetting Canadian society. As Nancy Christie and Michael Gauvreau point out, there was tension within the Protestant denominations concerning the degree of interdenominational cooperation that was necessary, indeed desirable, to meet the challenges of a rapidly industrializing economy. S.D. Chown, first secretary of the Methodist Department of Temperance and Moral Reform, opposed the constitution of the interdenominational Moral and Social Reform Council of Canada organized in 1908, because it threatened Methodist autonomy.[54] If Henderson's lifelong unease with having to compromise her own ideas and actions in order to belong to political parties, reform organizations, and established religions is any indication, we can surmise that she was a supporter of interdenominational initiatives. The interdenominational character of the letters in support of the Opium Bill in 1910–11 also suggests that she was moving in interdenominational circles in Montreal's Protestant community.

The interdenominational movement in Protestantism took place in the context of a wider and more influential movement, inspired by the Protestant tradition but going beyond it. The influence of American Progressivism is difficult to pin down, but it is of paramount importance to locate Henderson's work with young offenders in the context of the Progressive Age. Perhaps the classic formulation is that of Robert Wiebe, whose *The Search for Order* posits the Progressive impulse as impelled by the shift from a small-town America of what he calls "island communities" to an urbanizing, industrializing America of corporations, corruption, and crime.[55] For Progressives, as Carol Bacchi puts it, "social disintegration was the fear and social order the goal."[56] The solution has been described by Christie and Gauvreau as "Christian progressivism."[57] For Henderson, part of the solution was a kind of spiritual renewal in the people, a renewed commitment to the teachings of the Nazarene. The companion piece of this spiritual renewal was the heavy emphasis on "scientific methods" that characterized the politics of Progressive reform in Canada as it spread from the United States in the early twentieth century. As a probation officer, Henderson was very much part of social work becoming a profession that characterized the response to the impact of industrial capitalism and its attendant ills. The strands of these two tendencies were deeply intertwined, and they are pulled apart only at the peril of the historian.

That said, it remains true that it is the emphasis on environment that is most readily identifiable, and Henderson, because she worked with children and poor working-class mothers, was drawn to the belief that their plight could be dealt with by changing their surroundings. American historian Robert Harrison points out that children were much more easily perceived as victims of their environment than were adults. A central objective of the Progressive Age was to give the poor, especially children, the opportunity to choose to do right rather than wrong. It was of paramount importance "to create a social and moral environment which was conducive to the raising of good citizens."[58] As Harrison points out, this extreme environmentalism was in some ways as reductionist as the emphasis on degradation of character, but it had the great advantage of promoting social activism.[59]

Henderson's ideas and actions reveal an intriguing relationship with the Progressive thought of her age. The influence of American Progressivism arrived in Montreal in its full impact with the creation in 1909 of the Montreal City Improvement League (CIL). "The very model," according to Terry Copp, "of a modern civic organization,"[60] the CIL was a co-ordinating body for existing organizations dedicated to city betterment. It took up the cry of Herbert Ames for model tenements and called for the creation of "garden cities." In 1912, the year Henderson began working for the Juvenile Court, the CIL secured the passing of an act to create the Metropolitan Parks Commission. While no direct evidence exists to suggest that Henderson was directly involved in the CIL or related organizations, she was affected by them, and her experience of them is revealing.

One of the CIL's lasting contributions before its demise at the beginning of the First World War was the City Improvement Plan. As part of the plan, as Terry Copp notes, "seeds were being distributed to children so that they could plant flowers in their back yards."[61] In the article in the *Montreal Daily Herald* on 27 January 1912 about the setting up of the Montreal Juvenile Court, the reporter related this story: "A little girl had obtained some seed, probably hay-seed. A block was loose in the sidewalk and she started her seeds growing in the earth beneath and put a stone over the hole so no one else should see it. Every day she would look to see how it was getting on. The neighbors did not know what she was doing. Mrs. Henderson stopped and asked what she had there, and she answered, 'Aw, go on, it's a park I'm growing.'"

Although Henderson presented this story to the reporter as evidence of the "inventive genius" of children, it seems almost certain that the child got the seed as part of the City Improvement League's "city beautiful" plan. Henderson was quite aware of the movement, noting that in London and New York, children had their own gardens where they grew vegetables to eat. In her view of the "inventive genius" of children, there is a compelling yet naïve belief in the ability of the poor and dispossessed to change a world run by powerful men and forces beyond individual control. There is little evidence to suggest that she was aware of that aspect of the Progressive Era that involved powerful business interests incorporating and co-opting the most radical of the Progressive demands.[62]

Her naïveté notwithstanding, the world in which she lived and worked was changing in significant ways. The long article in the *Herald* on the creation of the Juvenile Court evinced an understanding of the significance of the court and the fact that it signalled the entrance of women into the public life of society in new and significant ways. It noted that there were only three other women in Montreal with public offices: Dr Marion Hansford, medical school inspector, and Mrs Alonzo King and Miss C. Clément, government inspectors of factories. The hiring of Rose Henderson and a second woman, Marie Clément, as probation officers almost doubled the number of women in the city with public offices.

The article also noted a major transformation that had taken place in attitudes toward children. The new idea was that children were innately good, not bad, and should be guided, not punished. The new probation officers were introduced as "child-lovers." Henderson commented to the reporter, "The Juvenile Court is a place for formation, not for reformation, for sympathetic understanding and not for retribution. It is a guarantee

from the Government to give the children of the poor a fair show."
Women were better able to communicate with children, learn their se-
crets, and get them to acknowledge wrongdoing because women had the
"mother-heart," she said. Society had entered an age of dealing with causes, not effects, an age of understanding that criminality in children was
chiefly a result of environment. The issue was one of class: 'The children
of the poor are brought to court for stealing, and the children of the rich
and middle classes commit the same sins and are not brought to court."
She made a similar argument in a small book written during her years in
Montreal, *Kids What I Knows*: "It is man, not God who has created class
distinctions; has created rich and poor, learned and ignorant. Man through
his love of power and greed for gold has created poverty (the worst of all
crimes) and through the unequal distribution of wealth he has compelled
unequal opportunity."[63]

Henderson was a Progressive reformer in the sense identified by Henry
F. May: her life and work were "full of prophetic denunciations and last
stands for righteousness."[64] She was the female Canadian counterpart of
Richard Hofstadter's American "Man of Good Will," who did not join
organizations "to advance his own interests" but rather "would study the
issues and think them through, rather than learn about them through
pursuing his needs."[65] Like her fellow Progressives, her main weapon was
"the spotlight. Once the enemies were exposed, the people could deal
with them."[66]

She was convinced that once the people of Montreal and Canada became aware of the problems, and understood that the answers to fixing
those problems were at hand, they would act. Government legislation
was a key element in her social activism, but the ultimate resolution
could not come about by leaving in place the existing power structure. It
was the self-activity of ordinary men and women challenging the power
of the rich that would bring about an egalitarian society, a society not
possible without a revolution in human affairs.

2

Mothers and Children

In January 1912 Rose Henderson was appointed to the Montreal Juvenile Court as the probation officer for non-Catholic children. With this appointment she became one of a small group of women in Quebec's largest city with a high public profile. Heretofore, she has gone unnoticed in the historical literature on a city with a number of prominent women in suffrage and social welfare organizations, including the Fédération Nationale Saint-Jean Baptiste, co-founded by Caroline Béïque and Marie Gérin-Lajoie, the Local Council of Women, and the Montreal Women's Club. Montreal boasted Dr Grace Ritchie-England, the first woman to receive a medical degree in the province of Quebec, and Carie Derick, who in 1912 was the first woman to become a full professor at McGill University.

In August 1912, in a front page article in the *Montreal Daily Star*, Rose Henderson was quoted at length on Prime Minister Robert Borden's recent meeting with British suffragettes.[1] On 28 August, Borden met with a five-woman delegation of the Women's Social and Political Union in the Savoy Hotel, in London, England.[2] One of the delegates, Rachel Barrett, warned Borden that British suffragettes might start a militant campaign in Canada. Borden appeared to take this as a threat and stated that he would not be influenced "by any such tactics." Canadian women "were quite capable of looking after themselves," he said, and he and the Canadian government "were willing at any time to meet the women of Canada and discuss with them their needs." On the question of advocating the franchise for women, Borden described it upon his return to Canada as "a matter in which I have no concern. The power rests with the different provinces."[3]

Why the *Daily Star* interviewed Henderson instead of any of the more prominent women activists of the day is unclear, but it speaks to the fact that she had quickly become a "go-to" person for the anglophone Montreal media on issues related to women and suffrage.[4] Her comments on Borden's position are worth quoting at length:

> I should think that what he said will be a great stimulus to the women all over Canada, to gather their forces and send a deputation to wait on him. And if they do not, it will prove conclusively that the women of Canada are not yet awakened. I, for one, do not believe that they are yet politically awakened, or else they would not have waited thus [sic] long to send a deputation to Ottawa. I also believe that when the women of Canada are ready for suffrage they will not find a great deal of opposition. I have always found the Canadian men and members of Parliament, to whom I have spoken on the subject, sympathetic, broad, and intelligent.

Here Henderson anticipates late twentieth-century interpretations of the Canadian feminist movement. Carol Bacchi observes that "once it became clear that female enfranchisement was imminent, politicians from all shades of the political spectrum proved willing to introduce the legislation on the off-chance that the women might feel some sense of obligation to support their benefactors."[5] The notable difference between Henderson and Bacchi is in the imputation of motive, Henderson being more willing than the feminist of a later generation to credit male politicians with altruistic motives.

Early in her career Henderson evinced willingness to judge men on the basis of their thoughts and actions, not on the basis of who they were – including their class position. She was more disturbed by hypocrisy than by patriarchy, commenting: "The ballot to-day includes bad men and good men, men of all colors, and even dead men, excluding only paupers, idiots, criminals, minors, and – women."[6] She condemned the control that men had over women and the institutions and practices that kept them in thrall, but believed that at the end of the day it was the agency of women themselves that was the key to bringing about change. In winning the vote for women, there was no need to condemn men as a group; it was only necessary for women to fight for the rights they deserved.

Indeed, at this point in her life Henderson was much more scathing in her denunciations of bourgeois women than she was of men. While she did at times speak of women as a collective, at others she clearly distinguished working-class women from bourgeois women: "Even if the women of ease in Canada are anxious or not for the ballot, there is one hopeful sign, the working women of Montreal, at least, are wide-awake to the power and use of the ballot, for they are already using it in the various trade union organizations which are made up of both men and women."[7] Here she was being relatively mild in her criticism of bourgeois women; at other times she was much more biting. The year before, Olive Schreiner had published her classic work *Woman and Labor*, which contained three chapters on the "parasitism" of the bourgeois woman.[8] While conclusive evidence has not been found to indicate that Henderson read Schreiner's book, there is no questioning the shared point of view. The bourgeois woman who failed to act was the problem, not men. Indeed, Henderson saw working-class men as indispensable allies in the struggle for women's equality.

She was able to appeal directly to the labour men of Canada when she walked onto the national stage at the annual convention of the Trades and Labor Congress (TLCC) held in Guelph, Ontario, in September 1912.[9] She told the assembled delegates that she had come to speak on old-age pensions for mothers, saying she was at the conference "to speak in the interests of the voiceless and helpless children of the poor."[10] She began by speaking in support of votes for women, saying that men "have fought our battles long enough, and we want the ballot to help you to deal with the child problem. If any workman is opposed to giving the ballot to women it is because he does not know any better."[11] This is vintage Rose Henderson, coming at men from several angles, appealing to their compassion, acknowledging their chivalry, shaming them into doing the right thing.

Henderson was appealing to craft unionists, men who shared many of the attitudes commonly found among middle-class men, in particular the belief that a woman's place was in the home looking after her children. Henderson knew how to speak this language. Women who had lost the "breadwinner" could not be expected to care for their children as well as go out to work to earn the money to support them. The key was having good homes and mothers, not placing children in institutions.[12] The union movement, Henderson argued, had the history and traditions to do this, being responsible for "any of the comforts which we enjoy to-day."[13] Such reforms including "old age pensions, workmen's compensation, the rise of wages, factory legislation for children and the women of the sweat shops are the result of this great movement in which you are interested."[14] These changes came about through the unions, and were "something to be proud of."[15]

Henderson spoke the language of organized labour because she shared its most glaring contradiction – appealing to the state while remaining fearful of the potential corrupting power of its institutions. She was careful to point out that she was advocating a helping hand, not a handout. Experience showed, she argued, "that many necessitous mothers were able and willing to do their share towards their children's support when they were assured of some supplementary relief given at regular intervals."[16] She proceeded to a broad-ranging account of provisions for motherhood in Germany, Italy, Norway, Sweden, France, and Switzerland, at once heightening her credibility as an expert in the field and subtly suggesting to the delegates that it was time Canada caught up to the rest of the world. She provided data from the Swiss case, then moved on to Hungary, Denmark, and New Zealand. Addressing the American situation, she drew on the experiences of Missouri, Michigan, Oklahoma, California, and Colorado. She continued to shame and inform, while evincing the respect she had for Montreal's Jewish community, noting that the only institution she knew of in Canada trying to "subsidize motherhood" was the Baron de Hirsch Institute in Montreal, which "distributes a large amount annually among widows, orphans, deserted wives, insufficient earners, and the sick."[17]

Her approach to the overwhelmingly male assemblage was brilliant. Votes for women, she argued, would lighten the load of men, switching responsibility for the downtrodden and destitute of society onto the shoulders of women. The enlightened man, she argued, would recognize the advantages (and, we might add in hindsight, what man does not want women to think of him as enlightened?). As a maternal feminist, Henderson realized that the greatest fears of working-class trade unionists – male and female – were the breakdown of the home and the inability of male workers to provide for their families. In this one speech, she came as close as any social activist of her day to bridging the gap between a male-dominated labour movement and middle-class female social reformers. In the opinion of later generations of feminists, of course, she conceded too much, but we must marvel at her audacity, her insight, and her total commitment to uniting men and women in defence of the children of her society.

In March 1914 she took her campaign for mother's pensions to Ottawa, attending a meeting of the Social Service Congress of Canada. This first national Canadian congress on "the social question" was well attended by delegates from the Social Service Council of Canada, formerly the Moral and Social Reform Council, and by others including Prime Minister Robert Borden and former Prime Minister Sir Wilfrid Laurier.[18] Henderson's participation signalled her Christian Progressivism, and also the "hint of social gospel persuasion" noted by Richard Allen.[19] In her speech she argued that to "subsidize the dependent mother to carry out her parental duties in the home, is but putting our beliefs, which we admit to be right, into practical form, applying our Christianity."[20] J.S. Woodsworth could not have said it better.

We must pause a moment to recognize the similarities in Henderson's ideas to not just those of the leading advocates of the social gospel but also of the leading child welfare advocates. There was a marked similarity between Henderson's ideas and those of the Methodist J.J. Kelso, who founded the Children's Aid Society in 1891. Kelso advocated pensions for widowed mothers as early as 1904.[21] He argued that 40 per cent of juvenile delinquents came from homes where the mother worked outside the home because there was no male breadwinner.[22] Like Kelso, Henderson saw state intervention as aid to parents and a way to "promote the economic self-reliance of families."[23] Kelso's direct influence on her is unknown, but Nancy Christie's suggestion that in the early years of the twentieth century juvenile delinquency was the "guiding imperative" of the campaign for mothers' allowances demonstrates that Henderson's advocacy was very much part of an existing movement.[24]

It is true, however, that Henderson was recognized by her peers as bringing an immediacy to the issue that few other social advocates were capable of doing. She came to the Social Service Congress meeting in 1914 armed with the same breadth of knowledge of the movement for mothers' pensions that she demonstrated at the 1912 TLCC Congress, this time adding information about Japan. She also demonstrated that she was only willing to take Kelso's economic self-reliance argument so far,

pointing out that "to suggest putting money away for a rainy day out of a
salary not enough to clothe and feed a family, is not only farcical, but immoral and dangerous to the family and community."[25] The effort had to be a
serious one, requiring "a Dominion wide Mothers' Pension movement."[26]

Henderson also broke with many of her contemporaries on the question
of her vision of rural and urban life. The parochialism and xenophobia
that characterized rural and small-town Canada in Quebec as well as
English Canada was not part of her psychic makeup as a child of the city.
We do not find in her "the direct impress of the rural hinterland" that
Nancy Christie and Michael Gauvreau identify as characteristic of the
"progressive reform coalition" of which she was part.[27] Dr Peter H. Bryce,
for example, considered the rural environment healthier and was preoccu-
pied with the "degenerative effects of urbanized, industrialized society."[28]
Henderson too was concerned with degenerative effects, but her focus was
on the existing urban environment, not on the idealization of rural life or
on the attribution of degeneration to heredity. In her speech to the Social
Service Congress she commented: "When the support of the father is lost
the home is destroyed, the children are placed in different institutions
according to age and rule, and the mother is left childless. This is a real
cruelty to the mother and a terrible disadvantage to the children, and the
fact that poverty alone enforces these conditions is a stain on the nation."
There was no attribution of causation to heredity here: responsibility lay
with "poverty alone."

In the nature versus nurture debate, Henderson was decidedly on the
side of nurture. Yet she was part of a political culture in which the belief
in heredity was powerful, and it is inconceivable that she was not influenced by it, because it was all around her. As Angus McLaren points out,
one of the most influential speakers at the Social Service Congress was
Helen MacMurchy, described by McLaren as Ontario's leading public
health expert in the First World War period.[29] MacMurchy, an advocate
of the sterilization of the unfit, spoke at the Congress in favour of immigration restriction, raising the "spectre of hordes of the unfit being born
in Canada."[30] The way to deal with the "unfit" was to keep them out of
the country, and failing that, to prevent them from reproducing.

MacMurchy was a leading figure in the eugenics movement, as were many
other middle-class women activists of this period. The movement, founded
by Francis Galton (1822–1911), who believed "in the predominance

of heredity over social environment,"[31] had a profound influence on the thinking of Canadian social reformers, and Henderson was not immune to its influence. In her speech to the Social Service Congress she provided detailed data from the United States to argue in favour of the various Fund to Parents Acts in states such as Illinois. Under this law, she pointed out, "the mother is hired by the State to bring up her own children in her own home, under natural and normal conditions, thus preventing the children and mother eventually becoming a charge on the State by degenerating into incompetents, and at half the cost to the tax payers that it takes to bring them up in institutions."[32] What set her apart from MacMurchy is that she did not believe that mothers and children *were* degenerates as a result of heredity, or ethnicity, but that they could *become* "degenerates" as a result of poverty. Instead of calling for sterilization, she asked the state for something else. Her solution was disarmingly simple yet strikingly insightful: the state should initiate payments to mothers that would alleviate the poverty that led them and their children to become charges on the state.

Henderson did not simply idealize the home, because the class component of her analysis led her to a more sophisticated argument. "We must realize, no matter what our prejudices are, that home life for the masses has been almost destroyed by our modern industrial conditions," she maintained. "It is no use talking about the sacredness of home unless we consider shacks and overcrowded tenements sacred."[33] She was constantly in the homes of the poor of Montreal, and those homes did not lend themselves to idealization. She did share with Kelso a desire to make young people contributing members of society, but the society they would contribute to would be rid of the rich, the powerful, and the hypocritical who controlled capitalist societies. She commented, "We pension Royalty, noblemen, statesmen, judges, civil servants, industrial magnates, army and naval officers, all in receipt of good salaries during their lives. Is there any reason why our widowed mothers with young children should not be pensioned? Thirty-three bishops and archbishops in the House of Lords in England draw large pensions for practically doing nothing but opposing progressive measures introduced for the amelioration of the lot of the poor."[34]

Whatever conservative elements there were in her thinking, the radical component of her vision was central to her critique. Her perspective remained based in class: "Can there be any crueler or more unhuman [sic] or unchristian way of dealing with a mother than to separate her from her children through no fault of her own, with only poverty as our excuse?" She then pointed out that one of the "greatest grievances" of abolitionists in the United States was "the separation of the children from their mothers," thereby creating an analogy between slave mothers and the working-class mothers of Montreal.[35]

The question that arises from Henderson's activism on behalf of mothers' pensions is whether or not, as Nancy Christie suggests, the compelling need was "to uphold the breadwinner ideal."[36] Christie argues that "organized labour endorsed government assistance to widowed women to keep them out of the workforce and from lowering the standard male wage."[37] The problem, at least in Henderson's case, is that she did not believe it possible for a worker in industry to truly be a "breadwinner." As she stated at the Social Service Congress: "Men to-day do not earn enough to belong to their unions, much less to save money."[38] As her speeches to the TLCC conventions demonstrate, her focus was not on the "breadwinner" but rather on labour's collective responsibility for the health of mothers, the sanctity of the home, and the future of the children.

Here we see one of the most interesting aspects of Henderson's world view. Unlike Kelso, she did not blame men for the situation of the family. Kelso criticized fathers who failed to live up to their responsibilities, and placed the blame for marriage breakdown on men.[39] In her 1912 speech to the TLCC, she instead put the blame on low wages: "The average wage in Canada is a little over $400 for the male workers and for women approximately $200 per annum. With such low wages it is almost impossible for the worker to pay union dues, much less insurance dues. Industrial accidents are on the increase and there are hundreds of men who cannot endure the sight of their children suffering because of poverty. This condition leads to the constant nagging by the mother, and the result is that the husband becomes a wife deserter."[40]

The quick and easy response to Henderson's position is to decry her blaming of the victim, and her attendant failure to condemn male irresponsibility. An alternative response is to recognize that it is refreshing, indeed inspiring, to see a woman recognizing that the suffering of children causes the suffering of the father as well as of the mother. There can be no doubt that in a society predicated on the idea that any man who was unable to provide for his family was a failure, if not a degenerate, wives did constantly "nag" husbands, and desertion, while not a valiant option, was preferable for some men than the continual confronting of their own inadequacy. We can dismiss Henderson as a conservative or a reactionary, or we can recognize the depth of her perception. She saw mothers and children as victims – precisely why they needed to be provided for by the state – but she understood that working-class men were victims as well. For her, the "breadwinner ideal" had little meaning in a society in which the great majority of workers were forced to live in poverty, and both men and women were victims of a cruel system.

The breadwinner ideal was also irrelevant in the case of widows. The literature on mothers' pensions is confusing, because at the time the terms "mother" and "widow" were used interchangeably. We see the phenomenon in an article entitled "Treatment of Widows Is Anti-Christian," from the 5 February 1915 edition of the *Toronto Daily Star*, reporting a talk Henderson gave to the first annual meeting of the Ontario Women's Franchise Association at Willard Hall in Toronto. In her talk she declared that the treatment of widows in Canada was "anti-human, anti-social, and anti-Christian," and argued that from "every point of view mothers' pensions are necessary, economic, patriotic, and humane." She then returned to speaking about widows and orphans, going so far as to suggest that they were "the foundation of the nation."[41] They were so because providing for them would prevent the criminality of youth that undermined that foundation. By focusing on widows, she contributed to the trend, as the First World War progressed, toward mothers' pensions increasingly becoming known as widows' pensions, which were justified on the basis of women rendering specific services to the state.[42] In the process the state demanded greater "moral surveillance" of these women, not really Henderson's intent. Her intent was to make the home the foundation of the nation, and in this sense she was in line with the thoughts of working-class widows themselves, who preferred remaining in the home to care for their children in lieu of going out to work.[43] In the process, however, working-class mothers and widows lost a degree of independence to increasing state involvement, which Henderson had hoped would be the vehicle of greater freedom of action for them.

For Henderson, the state became a surrogate for the absent father, because she believed that when "the support of the father is lost the home is destroyed."[44] She was one of the "Canadian social feminists" who was "at the forefront of new definitions of political economy, in which ... the State was no longer considered an abstraction separate from its citizens."[45] Indeed, it was the man who in a sense became the abstraction. Given the unquestioned belief of the period that a woman without a man was in a very real sense less than a full human being, it is instructive that nowhere did Henderson suggest that the solution for mothers who had lost their husbands was to find another man. It is possible that she perceived the sudden traumatic death of her own husband in January 1904 as a kind of desertion, but a desertion that could not be blamed on him. For all her middle-class privilege, she was able to relate to working-class women whose husbands had died, deserted them, or once the First World War began, enlisted.

Although we are never likely to know for certain, it may be that Henderson's conflicted attitudes toward working-class mothers reflects how she felt about her own role as a mother whose daughter left home at a young age. On the one hand, she maintained that children being taken from the mother and placed in an institution was "through no fault of her own," and that it was invidious to blame the mother for the deterioration of the home. Yet in her daily work at the Montreal Juvenile Court, she often did hold the mother responsible for neglecting her children, failing to budget properly, and not providing a nurturing home life. In the spring of 1919, she would go so far as to suggest that if she had the power, she would "prohibit" mothers from working outside the home.[46]

During the First World War the "guiding imperative" of mother's pensions ceased to be concern with juvenile delinquency and became concern with the breadwinner ideal and national economic efficiency. The family, as Christie argues, was "no longer an essentially spiritual, maternal-centred entity but rather primarily an economic unit dominated by the male wage earner."[47] Henderson fought for the family as a "spiritual, maternal-centred entity" and lost. Yet in the process she redefined both patriotism and the meaning of the nation in an attempt to make the home the focal point of Canadian society. Patriotism, as she redefined it, became the desire to remove the stain of child poverty from the nation: "We believe that the child is the nation's greatest asset, and that patriotism, morality and good citizenship are born and nourished in the home, that the child to grow up to be normal, useful and self-respecting, must have his life and training in the home and the community, by his mother."[48] Henderson

was not among the many middle-class feminists who wanted "less generous benefits" that would motivate mothers to seek part-time work, notably domestic service.[49] She was in general agreement with male trade
union leaders who wanted "generous benefits" that would keep women in
the home, although she differed from them in focusing on the future of
the child, not on preserving the breadwinner ideal.

Henderson is a long neglected yet pivotal figure in our understanding
of first wave feminism, because she was one of the few direct links between the activities of the children's aid societies and juvenile delinquency on the one hand, and the campaign for mothers' pensions on the
other. Few women of her generation were taken seriously by the male-
dominated trade union movement, and that movement did take
Henderson seriously. Not many women of her generation had her breadth
and depth of experience that ranged from the poverty-stricken homes of
the Montreal working class to the halls of justice. Given that breadth, it
is not surprising that the historian is able to ferret out inconsistencies in
her ideas and discrepancies between her theories and her practices. Were
it otherwise, she would not have been human.

Was Henderson on what Christie calls "the more progressive wing of
maternal feminism?"[50] The answer is yes if we look beyond Henderson's
classic maternal feminism to see a class analysis that was more insistent
and more biting than that of most of her female compatriots. It is also yes
if we recognize that, while concerned about the degeneracy of the "race,"
she blamed poverty, not ethnicity or heredity. The answer to the question
is no if we judge her by a later feminist politics that sees the celebration
of the woman as caregiver in the home as validating patriarchy and restricting women to the private sphere. It is also no if we isolate her criticisms of working-class mothers who were uneducated in the ways of
providing for their children; as Linda Kealey points out, Henderson was
"strongly shaped by maternal feminist convictions shared by middle- and
upper-class women reformers of the day."[51]

Within a month of her March speech to the Social Service Congress,
Henderson provided further evidence that she did not always believe that
the plight of the working-class mother was "no fault of her own." In April
1914, she, along with Judge Choquet and clerk Owen Dawson of the
Montreal Juvenile Court, gave testimony before the Select Committee
looking into the use of cigarettes. On 16 April, Judge Choquet told the

enquiry they "certainly ought to hear Mrs. Henderson. She has had great experience, is a hard worker and a very clever woman." Henderson testified five days later on 21 April, stating that "the smoking of cigarettes among the young is one of the most pernicious and terrible things that we have met. The children who come in there [the juvenile court] are many of them absolutely lacking in mentality, having no ideas of moral conduct." Challenged as to cigarettes being the cause of this condition, Henderson affirmed that cigarette use "certainly stunts the growth of the child." Her solution was to pass legislation prohibiting the smoking of cigarettes until young people were at least eighteen years of age.[52]

Her testimony provides striking evidence that in her day-to-day work as a probation officer she did not put into practice the claim she made at the Social Service Congress that the behaviour of the poor mother came about through "no fault of her own." The parents of children who smoked, she stated, "are very ignorant of the duty of motherhood or fatherhood, and the consequence is they are not fitted to guide their children; they simply do not know any better."[53] Yet asked about the impact of poverty, she replied that it "certainly has an effect because when the father and mother are out of work and there is no food in the home it lowers the moral fibre of the children."[54] We see here how quickly she shifted responsibility from blaming the mother for the lowering of children's "moral fibre" to blaming the environment – a common pattern in her thought.

In the phrase "moral fibre," we see a noun describing a physical property, and an adjective describing an ethical or philosophical world view. It is not possible to exaggerate the importance of understanding Henderson's commitment to the essentially Lamarckian idea that environment, in this case the slums of Montreal, perpetuated immoral behaviour through the physical reproduction of children by mothers degenerated by their physical surroundings.[55] While no evidence has surfaced to draw a direct link, there is a strong similarity between Henderson's thinking and that of Charlotte Perkins Gilman, the influential author of the classic feminist utopia *Herland*. In Henderson's thought we see the same impassioned belief that a "race" of super-children – all female in *Herland* – could be developed on the basis of a radically improved environment. Henderson did not agree with Gilman's vision that this required the removal of men, but she did believe that it required both recognition of poverty as the root cause and the increasing assumption by women of responsibility for ameliorating their own lives.

Henderson was asked by Mr Kyte of the Select Committee if women's societies in Montreal had "taken up the question of cigarette smoking by society women." In response to a question about reclaiming these women, she said, "I do not think they need to be reclaimed. I think any woman, grown to womanhood, with plenty of money, would think it a great impertinence to be told she should not smoke." She then appeared to contradict herself. The questioner pointed out that young boys smoked because of the example set by members of all classes in Montreal society. Asked if it would not be a good idea for women's societies in Montreal to lead a "crusade" against society women smoking, Henderson replied, "I think it would be a very good thing." Mr Barnard then got to the point: how was it possible to demand that people of any class stop smoking? Henderson's answer is difficult to interpret, but it is based in her characterization of poor women, who allowed their children to smoke "on account of ignorance." [56] She stated that if a poor mother felt that her children were being corrupted, she would be more likely to listen. The society woman, on the other hand, was intelligent, informed, and responsible for her own actions.

This seeming contradiction in Henderson's testimony speaks to the complexities of moral reform agitation in early twentieth century Canada. Henderson was herself conflicted, clearly uneasy with telling even upperclass women how to live their lives, yet wanting to correct their behaviour because of the negative influence it had on young people, especially where "bad habits" such as cigarette smoking were concerned. She was hesitant to criticize upper-class women for smoking, because they knew better, but working mothers needed to be shown the error of their ways. Once again we see her caught on the horns of the same dilemma: she disliked the impact the upper classes were having on the working classes and the poor, but her inclination was clearly to emphasize the extent to which the disadvantaged were responsible for their own situation. Her solution was to give them enough state support to get them back on their own two feet. In this sense, her solution was difficult to distinguish from that of J.J. Kelso, and was strikingly similar to the rationale adopted by politicians and civil servants who supported mothers' pensions as a way of alleviating poverty-stricken families without rewarding "laziness" and immoral or undisciplined behaviour.

The interpretation of the *Canadian Cigar and Tobacco Journal* was that in her testimony Henderson "harrowed the feelings of the committee. She

said that in her work she had found that children using cigarettes exces-
sively were undersized and were mentally and morally deficient. Even
without the advantage of Mrs. Henderson's observations, one would hardly have contested such a statement and a special committee of Parliament
seems an expensive way of getting at such self-evident facts."[57] The point,
of course, is that at this time the health impacts of cigarette smoking
were not self-evident in Canadian society, even where adult smokers were
concerned. Henderson had not thought through the implications of her
at-times contradictory positions on cigarettes, but she was both more
aware of the problem, and more willing to seek solutions, than the vast
majority of her fellow citizens.

By now we can see that there are no easy characterizations of Henderson's
ideas and actions, no late twentieth or early twenty-first century categories of academic analysis into which we can conveniently fit her. What we
can infer, in the absence of evidence allowing more forceful conclusions,
is that we are dealing here with a middle-class woman who was moving
in the direction of socialism, but who evinced the ongoing influence of
laissez-faire liberalism. In many ways she was a soul at war with itself,
struggling to find a balance between an ethos of personal responsibility
and an ethos of state support.

As we have noted, in her work as a probation officer with the juvenile
court Henderson believed that the court was extending "maternal rule" to
the public life of the society. Henceforth juvenile delinquents would be
treated with mercy, not punishment, as befitted a court guided by mother
love. As Tamara Myers points out, however, Henderson's role was not
without its contradictions. She was critical of working-class mothers who
worked outside the home; the point of her advocacy of mothers' pensions
was to enable mothers to remain at home. On the other hand, she believed that "poverty and weak, ill-prepared mothers produced juvenile
delinquents." She "upheld a model of bourgeois propriety and scientific
child rearing as a panacea for troubled youth." She "invoked a maternalist
rhetoric that at once demanded the state take more responsibility for
maternal and child welfare and denounced working mothers."[58] Myers
concludes that one might expect a greater sense of "gender solidarity"
from a maternal feminist.[59]

The equivocations in Henderson's defence of women and girls notwithstanding, she did evince greater gender solidarity than Myers suggests.

She did not go out of her way to attack men, but neither did she absolve them of responsibility. In her advocacy of women's courts, she observed that it is "pathetic, often heartrending," to see young girls in court for the first time losing "the last vestige of modesty and self-respect" before "a gaping, curious, leering crowd of men." Too long, she said, "women have borne the brunt and the stigma of immorality, too long they have been forced to maintain the virtue and purity of the race alone ... It remains with women to change this false conventional idea of morality and make men equally responsible with women for the morality and health of the race."[60] This is no clarion call for the destruction of patriarchy, but it is a forceful appeal for the end of a centuries-old double standard.

Nor did Henderson accept marriage as an institution beyond critique. Her position began with the double standard applied to female prostitutes, arguing that it was "no more natural for a man to be immoral than it is for a woman ... immoral men must suffer equally with the immoral women or both must go free." Getting to the heart of her society's hypocrisy, she argued that the "fallen man" is "a greater menace to the race" than the "fallen woman." Women, she pointed out, were expected to marry immoral men and save them, but those same people would be scandalized by the idea that men should marry immoral women and save them. That would indeed be "a revolution in the world of marriage."[61]

Yet it is true, as Myers points out, that Henderson's work at the juvenile court "permitted access only to band-aid solutions within individual families, not a revolution."[62] In a sense she was living the double life of many maternal feminists of her day, combining the pragmatism demanded by her job with the idealism she was able to express as a political activist and public speaker. If we return to the speech she gave to the Social Service Congress in March 1914, we find her arguing that "There is a freedom about home, school and community life which is absolutely necessary to the development of the child. Through this environment the child must evolve in order to try out and strengthen his character and overcome weaknesses and meanness, which he can only discover in free exchange with other children. This valuable and necessary part of his training he is deprived of if shut up in an institution."

Sincerity, fellow-feeling, insight, and empathy are but a few of the characteristics that can be identified here, spoken by a woman of enormous compassion, idealism, and commitment. But Henderson was a probation officer, and probation officers deal with real human beings, in real-life situations, in a world in which tough decisions are made and ideals get lost in the shuffle. As a probation officer, she was faced with an insoluble dilemma: how was it possible to put young juvenile delinquents back in homes that she felt had caused the problem in the first place? Mothers were often part of the problem and, as Myers points out, Henderson rarely assigned an appropriate level of responsibility to the father. For her, the home was an environment, and the "delinquent" mother was part of that environment. A state institution was often the preferable alternative. Henderson appears to have been able to convince herself that the state cared in a way that the errant mother did not, and therefore she did not hesitate to recommend incarceration as the solution for her young clients.

For Henderson, reform schools and other state institutions served as stopgaps until a transformed society could provide homes that nurtured healthy, happy, and educated children. In 1911 the Girls' Cottage Industrial School (GCIS) was opened as a Protestant alternative to the Catholic reform school. Conceived as a training school, the GCIS was described as a "home." It was, as Myers points out, "an experiment in surrogate family life," a fact that in all probability reconciled Henderson to incarcerating her young charges in apparent contradiction of her stated desire to keep them in the home.[63] She and the female social reformers of her day did not create the environment in which they worked, and the choices they had to make were limited and rarely ideal. The contradiction in Henderson's work at the Juvenile Court was real, but it was not resolvable in the social milieu in which she worked.

Although a product of her Anglo-Celtic Protestant background, Henderson was not isolated in English-speaking Montreal, shut off from the French Canadian and immigrant worlds around her. While there is no body of evidence to suggest that she made immigrant Montreal families one of her central concerns, we cannot think of her as typical of a generation of middle-class Anglo-Celtic female reformers who were at best anti-immigrant, at worst blatantly racist. She was not caught up in the typical middle-class Anglo-Saxon concern with Catholic and Jewish immigration, leading to the spectre of "race suicide." While evidence of her attitudes are thin, we can turn to a talk she gave on Friday, 17 March 1916, to the Young Men's Hebrew Association, entitled "What We Can Do for the Immigrant." Her speech was described in the Jewish press as a "stirring, sincere, revelation. It is not too much to say that the audience was enthusiastic to a high degree for the excellent oration."[64] Given such praise, we can only conclude that what Henderson said was anything but xenophobic.

By way of contrast, many of her contemporaries were blatantly racist, anti-Semitic, and anti-immigrant. Reverend John G. Shearer, a Presbyterian minister and Henderson's ally in the campaign against opium use among Montreal's youth, was general secretary of the Lord's Day Alliance from 1899 to 1906. A vehement defender of Sunday observance, Shearer was also vehemently anti-Semitic.[65] Dr C.K. Clarke, Canada's most famous psychiatrist in the First World War period, espoused what Mariana Valverde calls "frankly fascist views" on the immigration of Jewish children.[66] Emily Murphy, the first female magistrate in the British Empire and one of the Famous Five, exhibited in word and picture her deeply racist attitudes about black and Chinese men allegedly using opium to seduce white women.[67] We explore Henderson's contradictory legacy on race, with a focus on her fear of black male sexuality, at a later point. For now, we focus on how unusually free she was of anti-Semitism in a social reform movement in which it was a significant element of the Anglo-Celtic middle-class world view.

Henderson was in much closer touch with the Jewish community in Montreal than the great majority of her contemporaries, anglophone and francophone. Her job as a probation officer made her responsible for Jewish children in Montreal. Lyon Cohen and Maxwell Goldstein were representatives of the Jewish community on the Juvenile Court Committee (Non-Catholic) who acted as advisors to her. Cohen was a successful businessman and philanthropist, a co-founder with Samuel Jacobs of the *Canadian Jewish Times*. President of the Baron de Hirsch Institute and Shaar Hashomayim, he became a key figure in the Canadian Jewish Congress following its creation in 1919. Goldstein, a lawyer, campaigned for Jewish rights and was the founding president of the Federation of Jewish Philanthropies of Montreal in 1917.[68] In all probability it was through the aegis of Cohen and Jacobs that Henderson became, starting in February 1914, one of the most prominent non-Jewish figures in the pages of the *Canadian Jewish Times* as a speaker to Jewish organizations.

In February 1914 she spoke to the YMHA on the topic "Elements of Jewish Interest in the Juvenile Court." She outlined a plan for the creation

of a Jewish organization interested in the work of the court, composed of
men and women from the various Jewish societies. Such an organization
would be of the "utmost assistance" in counteracting, "by advice and by
sympathy with our poverty-stricken little brothers and sisters, the evil
influences of sordid and dismal surroundings on the moral character of
these helpless children." Henderson also alerted her audience to the "ur-
gent necessity" of a Jewish representative on the school board. The writer agreed with her that Jews in Montreal needed a committee or society
to "take our juvenile defaulters under its own wings and deal with them
with the understanding and compassion by which their own people can
best help them."[69]

On 29 January 1915 Henderson again spoke to the YMHA; her topic
this time was "The Social Message of Maeterlinck's Drama of the Blue
Bird." In a 27 January 1912 *Montreal Daily Herald* article about the opening of the Montreal Juvenile Court, the idea that children were innately
good, not bad, and should be guided, not punished, was introduced with
reference to Maurice Maeterlinck's *Blue Bird*, a play that Henderson lectured on into the 1920s. Speaking in January 1915 before "the largest
audience assembled this season in the series of Friday Night Talks," she
argued that "Maeterlinck's message is one of optimism; one of happiness;
one of a new order of things; one for the return to a state of society where
the cardinal virtues will not stalk about blindfolded, but all this is to be
obtained at the cost of a continuous struggle on the part of the valiant in
human-kind." The playwright's message is brought home by the dia-
logue he placed in the mouths of "two delightful children."[70]

The message she was referring to emerges in the play's first scene, set in
a woodcutter's cottage. The family is poor, but the presentation of family
life is idyllic. The two children, Tyltyl and his sister, Mytyl, awaken on
Christmas Eve. Tyltyl tells his sister that Father Christmas will not be visiting them, but he will be coming to "the rich children." Looking out their
window, they see a party taking place in a neighbouring house. Mytyl is
astonished by her brother's assurance that the children next door are not
hungry and have enough to eat every day. Enter a fairy, who asks the children to find the blue bird, who will make her very ill daughter happy. In
the course of their conversation with the fairy we learn that the children
have no shoes and that they have three dead brothers and four dead sisters.
The fairy tells them that they will see their brothers and sisters when they

go through the Land of Memory on their way to finding the blue bird. On their journey they encounter "The Happiness" and "Maternal Love."[71]

In the final scene Mummy Tyl scolds the children for sleeping in, saying that she "mustn't let them grow up idle."[72] When the neighbour, Madame Berlingot, comes in, the children think she is the Fairy Bérylune. Her daughter is sick, and she wants Tyltyl's turtledove, which is now much bluer than before the children went on their journey. Tyltyl exclaims, "Why, that's the blue bird we were looking for! ... We went so far and he was here all the time![73] He gives the bird to the neighbour, who returns shortly with her daughter, now cured and clutching the "blue" bird in her arms. In the end, the dove escapes, and Tyltyl addresses the audience members, asking them to return it if they find it.

Maeterlinck's attraction for Henderson, I think, is revealed by Otto Heller, who notes the playwright's influence on Ralph Waldo Emerson, Emmanuel Swedenborg, and Henrik Ibsen, on whom Henderson also lectured. Maeterlinck appealed to a woman who fervently believed it possible to morally and ethically regenerate human society. She, like him, can be understood "as an ardent advocate of practical action while at the same time a firm believer in the transcendental."[74] She could relate to him as a prophet of "modern mysticism" who "holds to the faith that a more highly spiritualized era is dawning, and from the observed indications he prognosticates a wider awakening of the spellbound soul of man." Heller adds: "The revival of interest in the metaphysical powers of man which expressed itself almost epidemically through such widely divergent cults as Theosophy and Christian Science, was indubitable proof of spiritual yearnings in the broader masses of the people. And it had a practical counterpart in civic tendencies and reforms that evidenced a great agitation of the social conscience."[75]

Heller points out that as Maeterlinck's career progressed, joy increasingly became a "richer mine" than sorrow.[76] His outlook was "more and more optimistic," residing in "a calm and serious realization of what is lastingly beautiful, good, and true. A person's attainment of this beatitude imposes on him the clear duty of helping others to rise to a similar exalted level of existence."[77] Whatever the tragedies in her life, Henderson too spent it attempting to raise the dispossessed of her world – women, children, and workers – to a more exalted level of existence.

Her spiritualism, revealed in her passion for Maeterlinck's play, is further evidenced by the fact that she was one of the early Bahái's in Canada, at least since 1911, if not earlier.[78] When and how the Bahá'i faith came to Canada is difficult to establish, although it seems certain that it had reached Montreal by the early 1900s. One of the key links in the spread of the faith to Canada was William Henry Jackson (1861–1952), personal secretary to Louis Riel at the time of the Northwest Rebellion in 1885. Jackson, born into a Methodist family in Wingham, Ontario, moved to Prince Albert, Saskatchewan, in 1881 and sympathized with the Métis in their struggle with the Canadian government. Captured on 12 May 1885, Jackson was committed to an insane asylum but escaped to the United States. He changed his name to Honoré Jaxon, converted to Catholicism, and became active in the labour movement in Chicago. In 1897 he became a Bahá'i, and spoke in Canada on the faith in 1907 before returning to the United States. He died in New York in January 1952.[79]

It is not known if Henderson met Jaxon when he came to Montreal, but her commitment to the faith was revealed in the 1911 Canadian census, where her religion was listed as Bahá'i, following previous identifications as Church of Ireland and Methodist. Almost certainly she attended the talks given by Abdu'l-Baha, son of the Bahá'i faith's founder and its leader when he came to Montreal in 1912.[80] She was certainly influenced by May Maxwell, the most important Bahá'i in the city, who had visited Abdu'l-Baha in the United States in the late nineteenth century.

We get a sense of why Henderson would be drawn to the faith from a letter Maxwell sent to the Bahá'i paper *Star of the West* in 1912: "As the great work of preparation for the coming of Abdul-Baha is going forward everywhere, it may be of interest to know of the progress in Montreal and of the widespread change which is taking place in Canada. This change has covered a period of several years, in which old, dead systems are giving way to new social and political groups, old, crystallized forms are dissolving in the radiance of the broad, generous ideas of the new age, and personal power and authority are giving place to principles of justice and truth, to a higher conception of human brotherhood."[81] It is not difficult to see links between these sentiments and those in Maeterlinck's *The Blue Bird*. Henderson too believed that a new age was dawning, one in which the collective principles of justice and truth would replace the dog-eat-dog ethos and individualism of industrial capitalism.

At the same time as she began her career as a probation officer at the Juvenile Court, a job that involved making daily pragmatic decisions about the lives of young offenders, she was embracing a faith that promised a future of universal brotherhood and peace. In Henderson we see the melding of two powerful tendencies of the age, the metaphysical and the practical. As Robert Fowler points out in his biography of Carrie Chapman Catt, this dual tendency, so easily dismissed as contradictory, was actually part and parcel of the consciousness of first wave feminism. Not to see this linkage is to fundamentally misinterpret who these women were, what their lives were about, and what their legacy is to us.

An Anglo-Celtic woman of Protestant background, now converted to the Bahá'i faith, was not as out of place speaking to the Young Men's Hebrew Association as we might think. Much has been written about the messianic tradition in Jewish thought; many writers have described the Jews as a nation of dreamers. As Gerald Tulchinsky points out, in the Montreal of Henderson's time, among East European Jewish immigrants from Russia or Eastern Europe the messianic impulse was as likely to be channelled into socialism as into advocacy of the creation of a Jewish state in Palestine.[82] Socialist, Zionist, or socialist Zionist Jewish Montrealers went about the pragmatic concerns of making a living by day, dreaming of a Jewish state or a socialist society by night. The message of Maeterlinck's *Blue Bird* was one they understood and appreciated, as they appreciated the passion and honesty of the teller. There is no need to claim that Jews in Montreal felt some kind of deep emotional bond with Henderson, or she with them, to appreciate the fact that words, feelings, and ideas crossed the boundaries of identity and touched them both.

There was a cultural and religious gap, but there is no gainsaying that Henderson had an impact upon Montreal's Jewish community. At the end of July 1915 the *Canadian Jewish Chronicle* published an article by A.J. Livinson on the founding of the Jewish Big Brothers' Association, making reference to Henderson.[83] Livinson noted that the association, formed in the latter part of 1914 with a leading role being taken by Dr S. Vineberg, had been handicapped by lack of funds. It had not been possible to establish a Jewish Boys' Club Room "in one of the Yiddish streets," yet the association was accomplishing "much good" with its limited funds. Livinson continued: "It might also be mentioned in this article that the members of the Association have been honored by hearing two addresses by Mrs. Rose Henderson, Probation Officer of the Juvenile Court. In the person of Mrs. Henderson, the Jewish community recognizes one who is a dear friend; and, indeed, the labours of the Association have been encouraged by her timely words of advice."[84]

On 19 October 1915 Henderson spoke to the Jewish Big Brothers' Association in the YMHA Hall on St Urbain Street. Dr Vineberg presided.[85] In its report on the meeting the *Chronicle* related that Henderson "told the members of the excellent work a Big Brothers organization could do in connection with the Juvenile Court. The plan of work had been tried in all the large American cities and had everywhere proven a success. Jewish Big Brother work in Montreal will undoubtedly lower the now growing percentage of Jewish juvenile delinquents."[86] Henderson was speaking to the concerns of the Federation of Jewish Philanthropies and the Jewish Big Brothers' Association, which believed that Jewish juvenile delinquency was indeed becoming a more serious problem.[87]

Her talks to Jewish audiences provide us with the full range of her interests, and there is no indication that she considered Jewish Canadians to be "exotic" or interested in different topics on the basis of religion or ethnicity. In the fall of 1915 the *Canadian Jewish Chronicle* published an upcoming lecture series that she was to give to the Young Women's Hebrew Association: on 2 November 1915, she was speaking on Maeterlinck's *Blue Bird*, or "The Right of the Child to Life in its Fullest"; on 16 November 1915, *The Doll's House* by Ibsen, or "The Revolt of Woman"; on 30 November 1915, Galsworthy's *Mob*, or "The Martyrdom of the Prophet and Leader"; on 14 December 1915 George Bernard Shaw's *Getting Married*, or "Conventional Hypocrisies"; on 28 December 1915 Margaret Illington's *Kindling*, or "A Woman's Right to Love and Motherhood"; on 12 January 1916, "World Peace," or "The Futility of War."[88]

While the sum of these talks reveals the breadth of Henderson's cultural knowledge, *Kindling* and *A Doll's House* are of special significance.[89] They tell us that in the theatre she sought out female characters who exemplified her conception of the proper role of the woman and mother. It tells us that she kept abreast of the latest developments in the theatre and also in the movie industry; in 1915, *Kindling* was released on film, directed by Hollywood legend Cecil B. DeMille, but without Margaret Illington in the lead role.[90] In the play, Illington portrayed a working-class woman in a tenement on the east side of New York, a woman who was "redeemed by her longing for motherhood."[91] By way of contrast the heroine of *A Doll's House*, Nora Helmer, leaves not only her husband but her children. Ibsen's resolution was so controversial that he wrote an alternative ending in which Nora stays in the relationship for the sake of the children.[92] Henderson's attraction to these two plays reveals the classic contradiction at the heart of her generation's feminism; as Melanie Phillips observes, they "wanted women to be independent of men; and yet they could not reconcile such economic independence with the demands of motherhood."[93] Without the actual texts of Henderson's talks on these two works, it is impossible to know her interpretation of them. Her choosing them reveals, however, that she was aware of her feminism's contradiction, but the body of her work suggests that, like her female compatriots, she never fully reconciled it.

By 1916 she was well known in Montreal, not just to the anglophone community but to the francophone and Jewish communities as well. Her work was attracting attention beyond the city and the province, as an article on the Montreal Juvenile Court in the March 1916 issue of the *Canadian Municipal Journal* attests. In the article Henderson observed that "there are people who still cling to the old idea of the inherent wickedness of mankind, and corporal punishment as the only cure. This idea belongs to the dark ages, a time when men held in the hollow of their hands the lives of their wives, children and dependents. Fortunately for the race, especially the children, men and women are arising everywhere and proclaiming a new doctrine, culled from the great university of life." She continued: "We are beginning to realize that crime has its origin chiefly in something outside rather than inside human beings, that our social conditions are manufacturing crime just as it creates disease. In no place is this fact brought out more plainly than in the Juvenile Court. Here we see children the victims in nine out of ten cases of either present or transmitted environment, suffering from a social disease, a moral sickness which has its roots sunken deep into the body politic."

Her idealism here is striking; she argued that nine out of ten juvenile delinquents, when asked by Judge Choquet not to re-offend, did not re-offend: "nine times out of ten the promise is kept; and instead of an embittered, resentful, embro criminal, there goes forth a young citizen inspired with new ideals of self-respect, and responsibility towards himself, the community, his home and parents; a citizen saved to the state." She added that the Juvenile Court was "the extension of maternal rule into the larger life of the community."[94]

Her use of the term "embro" to describe the criminal evinces the Canadian left's fascination with the theories of Herbert Spencer. In the Socialist Party of Canada at this time it was common to describe someone beginning to understand the socialist position as an "embryo" socialist. As Ian McKay persuasively argues, Spencer's world view convinced a wide range of Canadian leftists "not only that society was *like* an organism, but also that in many respects it actually *was* an organism."[95] For Henderson, young people "evolved" into criminals, or they "evolved" into self-respecting, contributing members of society. Her use of the term "transmitted environment" alerts us to the fact that she, like future Canadian Prime Minister Mackenzie King, was a Lamarckian.[96] Lamarkianism was a godsend for social activists like Henderson, because it assured them that the reformation of society did not depend on individuals changing their behaviour – the essential change needed was in the environment in which they lived. And who better to change this environment than enlightened, determined, morally upstanding maternal feminists making their presence felt in public life?

Henderson was a champion of the leading role of women in the labour movement, as well as in the middle-class reform movement, as she demonstrated when she addressed the annual convention of the Canadian Trades and Labor Congress in Toronto on 28 September 1916. As in her first appearance before the convention four years earlier, the mutual respect she had for labour, and labour had for her, was much in evidence. In introducing her, President James Watters "made reference to the excellent work Mrs. Henderson had accomplished in the interests of the children" of Montreal; Henderson responded by noting the inspiration she always got by attending meetings of "the great Parliament of Labor."[97] In her speech, she was at her subtle best, commenting to the assembled delegates, "I am sorry we haven't a body of women as large as this. All our legislation, even to the shedding of blood, has come through our men. On the other hand, if it were not for the women, many men would scab and go back to work when they should continue the fight for improved industrial conditions." In the space of two sentences, she managed to affirm the virility of working-class men while at the same time claiming that the real backbone in the labour movement belonged to the women. Through a brilliant juxtaposition of praise and blame, she both appealed to the "manliness" of working-class males and insisted that they recognize the contributions of neglected working-class women. She was an artist at work.

This is not to deny, however, the very real ambiguities and contradictions in her politics of class. Her use of the word "scab" suggests that she identified with a male-dominated working class with its hatred of the strikebreaker almost universally attributed to Jack London, author of *White Fang*, *The Call of the Wild*, and the socialist classic *The Iron Heel*. On the other hand, her statement, "Let us put men in power to represent the cause of humanity and not the privileged interests," echoes the sentiments of the Progressive movement in the United States and is not in the words of a class-struggle Marxist.[98] That said, her expression "the cause of humanity" is not so much anti-Marxist as it is firmly in the tradition of the utopian socialists of the early nineteenth century who sought, in Engels's words, to emancipate "all humanity at once."[99] For Henderson, emancipating all humanity meant forging a meaningful alliance between women and working-class men.

By the fall of 1916 she was increasingly moving into the orbit of organized labour, where in the coming years she would earn a reputation as a radical. Whether or not that reputation was merited is another issue, and we need to contextualize it. In October she began publishing articles in *The Labor World/Le Monde Ouvrier*, the paper of the Montreal Trades and Labor Council. In the November issue her column announced the first session of the Montreal People's Forum, to be held at the Technical School on Sherbrooke Street East. She addressed the history of open forums and traced their "ancient origin" to the Greeks and Romans, going so far as to claim that in "Egypt and even in Ireland they were the centers of veritable intellectual orgies." Given the perception of Henderson as a radical in the late war period, her views on the open forum are worth quoting at length:

The forum, as the name indicates, stands for open discussion and the hearing of all sides of questions often tabooed on other platforms, questions relating to the life and welfare of the people and nation generally. It aims to gather in that large body of men and women, whose thoughts, while often disagreeing with the established order of things, are nevertheless a decided contribution to the sum total of progress and changing thought of the community. People of all nations and religious beliefs find here a common meeting ground, a

sense of brotherhood and democracy foreign to most churches. The
millionaire and the artisan will get each other's point of view in a way
not possible in a factory, office, or shop and will in most cases find
that their points of similarity are much greater than their points of
difference on the vital things of life.

In such a forum, she went on to say, the "Methodist and trade-unionist
will meet with the anarchist, and find that he too is human like themselves, seeking to get the best he can out of life, and not the intense bomb
thrower, thirsting after their money and blood as they were led to believe
him to be."[100] She then changed focus, presenting the people's forum as a
venue where the "aims, ideals and grievances" of labour could be heard.
She believed that once anti-union people heard about the "objects and
ideals" of labour, they would drop their prejudices and support the movement.[101] As an advocate of persuasion, not class struggle, she genuinely
believed that middle- and even upper-class people could be swayed to
support the aims of the working-class movement. She did not believe that
the ideas of individuals could be "read off" their class position.

Henderson would move to the left in the late war period, but in the
midst of the First World War she was not a Marxian socialist; she was
willing to judge people on the basis of their behaviour, not their objective
class position. In the open forum she saw a place of freewheeling discussions where even millionaires and anarchists could come to understand
each other – a far cry from the Marxian socialism of members of the
Socialist Party of Canada. On the other hand, there is the clear implication in her attitude that people who were anti-union were wrong and
people who were pro-union were right. In the context of the open forum
it was possible for every point of view to be freely expressed, but in the
final analysis, labour had to win out.

The contradictions in her position on class had counterparts in her attitudes toward middle-class female reformers. In her first article in *The
Labor World/Le Monde Ouvrier*, she launched a scathing critique of the pa-
ternalism of the society woman. A working-class woman with six children whose husband had gone off to war had recently had a "Lay Visitor"
who suggested feeding her children boiled rice, beans, and cabbage soup
as a way of economizing. Henderson sarcastically presented the society
woman's cost-cutting measures as the self-evident solution to a problem

that had befuddled "our politicians, economists and house wives." Noting
that she herself had "inherited a generous missionary spirit and an insatiable desire for passing good things along," she dismissed the society
woman thus: "There are women who are dead, but not yet buried, living
in a dream world of their own making, far, far away from the reality of
things: with servants to wait on them, motor cars to carry them around,
no children to tire or vex their sensibilities, and men folk to work, and
scheme, to supply the necessary cash to make their life a sweet symphony
from birth to death as far as natural things are concerned. How can these
women be expected to understand the condition of the masses?" Society
gave these "idle women" the right "to go into the homes of other women
less fortunate, at all and any hour of the day or evening, to ask questions
of the most private and insolent nature, to give advice to mothers whose
very existence and the existence of their families absolutely depend on
their industry, economy and wise management."[102]

To what extent was Henderson aware of the hypocrisy of her analysis
here? As Myers points out, in her capacity as a probation officer she was
constantly filling out forms describing in detail the lives of the young juvenile delinquents with whom she worked. She was going into the homes
of the poor at all hours, asking all manner of questions; she was condemning
the mothers of young girls for not staying home, not being good mothers,
not making good use of the resources available to them. Here she credited
working-class women with the "industry, economy and wise management"
that in her work as a probation officer she so often claimed they did not
have. One gets the sense that she was aware of the contradiction, because
amidst her searing criticism she acknowledged that the "aim and object" of
these society women – teaching knowledge of hygiene and training in
thrift and morality – was laudable, thereby acknowledging that this was
something she herself did. To "keep well the nation's childhood" was the
"very basis of civilization." The problem in her eyes was that these women
knew nothing of what they preached. Certainly Henderson had a greater
knowledge of the lives of the poor than the average Montreal socialite, but
it does not change the fact that she was more like the women she was attacking than she cared to admit. In her speeches to the annual convention
of the Trades and Labor Congress, she was seeking to divorce herself from
society women, striving to establish her credibility as a middle-class
woman who truly understood the needs of the labour movement.

In that effort she was largely successful. It may be true, as Nancy Christie suggests, that in the context of Canadian political culture as a whole there was no "powerful female figure" in the campaign for mothers' pensions.[103] It is also true that in the minds of many male trade unionists in Canada, Rose Henderson was precisely that: She linked the labour movement's call for state intervention to safeguard the breadwinner ideal with the call of the middle-class women's movement for increased state intervention to prevent family breakdown, and she did so in a powerful and direct way that is difficult to attribute to any other social reformer of her day.[104] In the process, she faithfully reflected the desires of working-class women, who were "often the fiercest advocates of the interventionist state."[105] In part she was able to do this because she gendered the state as female. There was no doubt in her mind that in the long run the male-dominated state with its attendant wars, exploitation, and poverty would cede the future to motherhood.

3

Revolt and Repression

Understanding Rose Henderson's political activism in the late First World War period requires a melding of English and French Canadian history, as well as a melding of the histories of female moral reform and the left. Her life brings together ethnic, class, religious, and gender issues in a manner difficult to assess in any other approach. As an anglophone resident of Montreal, she transgressed the two solitudes, working with and influencing both francophone women in the moral reform movements and male francophone socialists and trade unionists. In increasing our knowledge and understanding of her political activism in this period, we increase our knowledge and understanding of Quebec and Canadian history, and also of the fate of the left in a province traditionally neglected in anglophone historical works.

For all the divisions between English and French Canada, by late 1916 and early 1917 an area of agreement was emerging in opposition to the increasing likelihood that the Borden government would implement conscription.[1] Opposition to the Conservative government – and then the Unionist one elected in December 1917 – was shared by English and French Canadian liberals and socialists. In English Canada, as Terry Copp points out, registration, conscription, war profiteering, and the abuses of the War Measures Act broadened support for independent labour politics and the appeal of radical socialism.[2] In Quebec, however, the situation was markedly different: "The Liberals had placed themselves squarely in opposition to precisely these issues and the wonder is that any form of labour political activity was possible in the province."[3]

Rose Henderson was one of the reasons why labour political activity was possible in Montreal. By 1916–17, she was making a name for herself as an outspoken proponent of the cause of organized labour. In her column in the journal of the National Council of Women of Canada (NCWC), *Woman's Century*, she brought the message of labour to liberal women in an article about the September 1916 annual convention of the Trades and Labor Congress. Referring to this "brotherhood of men" which dealt with "the very basic laws of life," she drew a stark picture of organized labour as men and women on the verge of starvation, fearful of becoming "involuntary objects of charity" and losing their self-respect. She lauded the concern of male craft unionists for the fate of poor women and children, a fate linked to their own: "They are vitally concerned with child and woman labour – knowing from bitter experience, that everyone who sells their labour power below a certain point, lowers the standard of life for all. Women and children, being unorganized, can be exploited more easily, they work for lower wages, which in turn, result in the deterioration of the nation at large. For this as well as other reasons, the congress is working towards the final abolition of child labour as it exists, to-day."[4]

We are given here a revealing look into Henderson's politics. At this point in her life, she hardly seemed like a woman who would become a forthright exponent of the One Big Union in 1919, an organization whose members regularly and vitriolically denounced the TLC and its leadership. She was much too sanguine in her appreciation of the TLC's concern with women workers; as Canadian labour and feminist historians have amply demonstrated, the TLC at best dragged its feet, at worst was actively hostile to the organization of women workers.[5] It is difficult to tell if Henderson really believed what she was saying, or if this was a view of the TLC directed specifically at the members of the NCWC, who were lukewarm at best toward organized labour. Whatever we think of these "Rose-coloured glasses," we must continue to be impressed by her relentless, compelling ability to draw the lives of working-class men, women, and children together in a critique of existing capitalist society.

In typical fashion, Henderson ended by putting the onus back on women. She asserted "that every women's trade and craft in this dominion should be organized and ready to send its delegate to represent and voice its needs and aspirations." The very fact she felt that women workers had trades and crafts signalled her ability to surmount the gender prejudices of her political culture. These women, she stated, "need not wait for a Moses or a Shepherd to lead them out of the wilderness, they must seek and work for their own emancipation, or continue to be drudges and chattels, underpaid, over-worked, and of secondary importance." Of working women, she concluded, "organized labour cannot afford to be without them."[6]

Early in 1917 she made the Montreal papers as an exponent of a federal labour party. On 3 March 1917 the *Montreal Daily Star* reported on the talk she had given the night before to the YMHA, in which she explained the need for a labour or people's party. Britain, Australia, and New Zealand already had such parties, she said, representing "the people" as opposed to "the interests." A labour party was needed to push for the nationalization and municipalization of public services. In New Zealand the state provided milk to the poor, an example "of what the people could do when they had a party of their own." In Canada the situation was different: the provincial and federal governments were only interested in the "big interests."[7] The *Montreal Gazette* carried essentially the same report, noting Henderson's assertion "that the only hope for the Canadian people getting a square deal from the Government was to form a real people's party which would elect enough independent men to Parliament to prevent any group of interests swaying legislation in its own favor."[8] In the spring of 1917, Henderson's world remained the world of the Progressive, the world of "the people" versus "the interests," a world in which it was still possible for one of Canada's leading feminists to call for the election of "independent men" to office with no apparent consciousness of the potential contradictions.

Yet at the Ottawa convention of the Trades and Labor Congress in the fall of 1917, she demonstrated an increasingly radical edge, challenging labour men to be uncompromising in their advocacy of the working class:

If it is audacity you need, then be audacious, bold and daring and in proportion will you get your just reward. Labor is the tree of existence, and upon your shoulders rests responsibility and so far as you are free, organized and do not cringe and beg, your power will be recognized, your dignity asserted, and you will get your just reward. You hold the key which opens the door to life, but not only your own life but the lives of all those who depend upon you. You build the mansions and live in shacks in which the master refuses to house his horses and dogs. This is what you get for producing the world's wealth.

Until you men stand up unafraid and unashamed you will be treated in this way.

She then signalled a dramatic change in her thinking from the days in 1912 when she spoke so glowingly of the men in Parliament who could be convinced to act in the best interests of women seeking the vote. Now, as far as most of the "men in Parliament to-day" were concerned, she said, "I wouldn't give [them] a pound a week. They couldn't hold a job. And yet these are the men you have sent to Parliament ... it is only when all the workers of the world unite, we will have a world of peace ... You not only want to organize industrially but politically. You should send your own men to Parliament for it is impossible to expect that the men now there can understand your problems and deal with them. I should think the last few years would open your eyes."[9] While we cannot pinpoint the exact reason for the shift in her thinking, the American entry into the First World War, war profiteering, scandals, and what Canadian labour considered Prime Minister Borden's betrayal on the conscription issue cannot have failed to impel her in a more radical direction.

The conscription issue was one of the factors in the creation of the Canadian Labor Party (CLP) by the Trades and Labor Congress in the fall of 1917. A Montreal local was organized, and at a meeting on 12 May 1918, members elected Joseph Métivier as president of the new party. The importance of women in Montreal's labour politics was indicated by the fact that Bella Hall was elected second vice-president, and Rose Henderson was elected corresponding secretary.[10] Henderson's election was significant, given that no evidence exists in her articles or correspondence that she could write in French. Substantially more than half the executive members of the Montreal local of the CLP were francophone, and it speaks to the respect that francophone labour leaders and socialists had for Henderson that she occupied this position.

That respect extended into English Canada. Two weeks after she became corresponding secretary of the CLP's Montreal local, she travelled to Niagara Falls, Ontario, where she was a guest speaker at the 16th Annual Convention of the Labor Educational Association of Ontario (LEAO), held on 24–25 May. The LEAO was first organized in Woodstock, Ontario, in 1902 and held its First Annual Convention in 1903.[11] At the 15th Annual Convention of the LEAO, held on 24 April 1917, the delegates unanimously threw their support behind the creation of branches of an independent labour party.[12] On 2 July 1917, the founding convention of the Independent Labor Party (ILP) was held.[13] James Naylor describes the LEAO as "a loosely organized provincial federation of labour" that "spearheaded the campaign for the Workmen's Compensation Act."[14] At the 1918 convention, delegates strongly endorsed the recommendation of the executive "that the convention take steps towards the more thorough organization of the woman workers of the province," and "the incoming Executive was instructed to act with the least possible delay."[15] The lead in organizing women workers was taken by Minnie Singer and Joseph Marks, editor of the *Industrial Banner*.[16]

At the LEAO's 1918 convention, Henderson shared the speaker's platform with Ella Reeve Bloor, who was in the process of becoming the legendary labour organizer Mother Bloor.[17] Hamilton's *Labor News* described her as "one of the foremost women in the United States in the organizing of women workers"; at the convention she "commended the Canadian workers for organizing an Independent Labor Party."[18] While the *Labor News* made no mention of Henderson, the *Industrial Banner* was fulsome in its praise of her, stating that she "has endeared herself to the workers of the Dominion by the keen interest she takes in the welfare of the nations' children and her undisguised admiration for the organized labor movement of our country."[19]

In her talk Henderson demonstrated the dialectical nature of her thinking that had few parallels on the Canadian left at that moment in time. She had enjoyed her visit, she said, "but I am going to be honest with you to tell you plainly that some of the delegates were talking pure bosh when they claimed the workers should be more patriotic ... Just think of it, after three years of the most gigantic struggle in the history of the world, when the workers who have to make the greatest sacrifices, who have to bear the burdens and the cost of the war, and have to face death on the battle line, are told they ought to be more patriotic ... It is the workers who are the real patriots."[20]

It was highly unusual in this period for a socialist in Canada to recognize that workers and soldiers were the same people. In the rhetoric of Canadian Marxists in the Socialist Party, for example, this was almost never done; workers who became soldiers were symbolically turned over to the cause of the capitalists, militarists, and politicians. The delegates at Niagara Falls were commenting on the workers still in Canada, while Henderson was thinking about those workers on the battlefield, melding their dual identities, and in doing so holding on to their sacrifice and their humanity.

Henderson's other theme at the convention was women, noting that what working women needed was "not so much a minimum wage as a minimum life." She emphasized that women's struggles were not separate from those of men: "You have had your struggle for years but we women are just entering the kindergarten of labor and you must help us, not only because we are your sisters but for your own sake and to protect the rights and privileges you have won as the result of years of toil and anguish, endeavor and sacrifice. We must join our forces and co-operate together and march together to attain the emancipation of the toiling masses."

From an early twenty-first century feminist perspective, Henderson's reference to the "kindergarten of labor" and plea for the help of labour men has a supplicatory quality. We are reminded of the long-standing debate about the Canadian suffrage movement and the extent to which leading suffragists used this kind of language as a political tool, and to what extent the sentiments were internalized. There is no self-evident conclusion to be drawn, and the same is the case with Henderson. In any event, the more important issue is that she had a way of melding the struggles of women and children with the struggles of labour to organize that broke down barriers and advanced "the cause of humanity." We can certainly see the impact of her rhetoric on Joseph Marks, who shortly after the 1918 convention wrote: "As was stated by Mother Bloor and Mrs. Rose Henderson ... the great problem that Labor has to face, not only in the near future, but right here and now, is that of the organization of the Democratic womanhood of the nation."[21]

In the fall of 1918 Henderson addressed the annual convention of the Trades and Labor Congress in Quebec City, calling on the male delegates to "open wide the doors" to the participation of women in politics and industry. Freeing women from domestic slavery, she said, was the "last link in the chain for the emancipation of the workers of the world."[22] Again she was representing the struggle for the emancipation of working-class women as an integral part of the struggle for the emancipation of the working class, and her inclusiveness extended to recent immigrants. Shifting to address the recent Orders-in-Council directed at "enemy aliens," she objected to the term: "In the great world of capital there is no such word as alien. The workers of the world must realize that there can be no such word in our ranks as alien."[23] Here we see her entering into a world view that allied her with Canadian Marxists, who argued that the capitalist was the only alien.[24]

By 1918 Henderson had her own column, "Case and Comment," in the *Labor World* and was being described as a speaker "whose authority on Labor problems is throughout the whole American continent."[25] At the same time she was an important figure in the National Council of Women of Canada, a quintessentially "bourgeois" organization closely allied with the Liberal Party.[26] For a brief period in 1915, she was the associate editor of the NCWC's paper *Woman's Century*, and for the rest of the First World War period she was a regular contributor to it. For a time she had two columns in *Woman's Century*, "Juvenile Court," and "The Cradle and the Nation." As late as August 1918 she was highly thought of by the paper's editor, and even her forthright emulation of the British Labour Party and its plans for the "socialization" of British society after the war did not cause her to be shunned. Yet there clearly was a line, and Henderson virtually disappeared from the pages of *Woman's Century* in 1919.[27] Her forthright defence of organized labour estranged her from the National Council of Women in much the same way that her socialism estranged her from the Bahá'í community.[28]

Henderson was not a Marxist who advocated class struggle politics, but caution must be exercised in accepting John Manley's characterization of her socialism as of "the Independent Labour Party ... evolutionary type."[29] In the Special Number of *Woman's Century* of September 1918, Henderson criticized labour's narrow focus on wages: "If ... labor is content to go on from day to day seeking only an increasing wage, thinking only of the immediate needs of a small section of the working class, recognizing class interests, rather than social interests, then the outlook for the future is not bright.[30] Rather than conforming to the "bread and butter" unionism of the American Federation of Labor and the Trades and Labor Congress, she was deeply committed to what a later generation would call social unionism. Labour, she believed, was impelled to reach beyond its own interests, bound to fight against poverty, discrimination, and exploitation in all its forms. She dreamed of a transformed world, a world that all who believed in it could help to build. Hers was not a class struggle vision in the classical Marxist sense, but a revolutionary vision it was nonetheless.

During the war years she was establishing her credentials as a working-class hero, but her standing as the labour revolt of 1919 approached must be contextualized. By the end of the war she had attracted the attention of leading Unionist politicians and become part of the very state structure she so forcibly condemned. She accepted an appointment to the Employment Service of Canada (ESC), a "national network of labour exchanges jointly financed and administered by the federal and provincial governments," created 23 December 1918 by Order-in-Council 3111.[31] The ESC's original purpose was to deal with an acute shortage of farm labourers. Its focus, however, quickly became the demobilization of returned soldiers. As "a broadly representative advisory council," it was to report to the federal government on ways to prevent unemployment.[32] The provinces had "complete authority over the establishment and operation of employment offices," but the system was administered by the federal government in Ottawa.[33]

The key role in placing Henderson on the council may have been played by Newton Rowell, the leading Liberal in Borden's Union government. Rowell, a Methodist, was a temperance advocate, and like Henderson an admirer of the "New Liberalism" of David Lloyd George. Henderson had little to oppose in Rowell's postwar plans for "state social insurance, subsidized low-cost housing, an eight-hour working day, worker participation in management, and higher taxes on wealth."[34]

At the conference of the ESC held in Ottawa on 12 May 1919, Henderson attended as a representative of the Department of Labour. On 13 May she expressed herself as "strongly in favour of the abolition" of private employment agencies. She also felt that employment offices "should exercise the greatest care in the placement of the child worker." During the election of officers, she was appointed to the committee of the Handicapped and Juvenile Division delegated to work out a plan to be submitted to the next ESC meeting.[35]

As James Struthers points out, federal officials saw the ESC "as a necessary response not simply to demobilization but to the consequences of an industrial society as well."[36] Prime Minister Robert Borden was no social reformer, but he did believe "in enhancing the bureaucratic efficiency of government through civil service reform and more direct state regulation of the economy."[37] Politicians such as Newton Rowell had become convinced that employment was an industrial, not just a reconstruction, problem.[38]

Henderson's work with the ESC led to her even greater involvement with federal institutions. On 4 May 1918, Order-in-Council 1034 had created the Labour Sub-Committee of the Reconstruction and Development Committee. In February 1919 Labour Minister Gideon Robertson recommended that six new members be added to the committee, including Rose Henderson. On 17 February 1919 the additions to the committee were ratified by Order-in-Council 337. Robertson noted in his letter to the Governor General in Council that the new members had already attended several meetings, but it is not known if Henderson was one of them.[39] Within months, however, the state's perception of her would change dramatically, and she would go from being a sought-after consultant to being a dangerous radical and threat to the security of the Canadian state.

It is unlikely that Henderson attended all or even most meetings of the ESC and the Labour Sub-Committee of the Reconstruction and Development Committee, given that she spent some two weeks in St Catharines, Ontario, in February 1919 campaigning for the Independent Labor Party. In the election, ILP candidate W.E. Longden was in a tough fight against Conservative incumbent Fred Parnell, born into a local farm family that had been in the district since 1783. Parnell, well off and well liked, was expected to sweep to victory in the traditional Conservative Party stronghold. The Liberal Party was not running a candidate against Parnell, and a number of prominent Liberals were supporting him. According to the *Toronto Daily Star*, the election was expected to be "a walk-over."[40]

Longden was an unemployed returning soldier, a machinist who belonged to the International Association of Machinists. Young and lacking in political experience, he had a chance in a riding that the redistribution of 1914 had made largely industrial, in which the combined returned soldier and labour vote promised to threaten the Conservative stranglehold on the riding.[41] The provincial ILP realized the possibilities, and was making great efforts on Longden's behalf. Speakers included Allan Studholme, the veteran labour member from East Hamilton (1906–1919); Walter Rollo, who would sweep Hamilton West in the 1919 provincial election; Hamilton controller Harry Halford; Mayor Malcolm MacBride of Brantford; and ILP provincial secretary Joseph Marks.

The reportage in the *Toronto Daily Star* reveals the extent to which attention was drawn away from the male "heavyweights" in the campaign to the burgeoning involvement of women. The *Star* noted with evident surprise that women "are proving to be an actual factor in the fight." The wives of working men and soldiers "are throwing themselves into the contest with a determination quite new to St. Catharines politics."[42] The *Industrial Banner* noted: "Women's meetings are being held every afternoon during the week and other meetings addressed by men and women in various localities in the riding are being held every night, and sometimes two and three in a single evening."[43] According to the *Star*, Henderson was speaking in the evenings and also conducting an afternoon series of meetings for women.[44] Her "quiet, earnest manner and a pleasant personality" had "apparently built up a large following."[45] On 10 February one of these meetings was scheduled for the ILP Committee Rooms, "but such a crowd came that a hall six times the size had to be used." Hundreds of women came, many with babies in tow: outside the hall "was an array of baby carriages and go-carts." The women were determined not just to vote for Longden but also to work for him. According to the report, at the meeting "the issues of 'labor' and 'the returned soldier' ran so closely together that they merged and became almost indistinguishable."[46]

Henderson's impact was indisputable and her ability to mobilize women virtually without parallel, yet her dynamism and outspoken nature also proved to be a distraction. In reference to the major ILP figures campaigning for Longden, the *Star* commented that Henderson was "stirring up more controversy than any of them."[47] In his speech, the Honourable T.W. McGarry "asked why St. Catharines people should be advised by a woman from Quebec."[48] At a Conservative meeting on 11 February 1919, a Mrs W.A. Cameron echoed McGarry's criticism by taking a swipe at Henderson: "We don't want any red flag waving in this country," Cameron was quoted "in reference to the statement that a woman organizer from Quebec was active in the interests of W. E. Longden."[49] Agitators like Henderson should "go back where they came from."

On the evening of 13 February 1919 Henderson spoke at the "monster meeting" in support of Longden at the Grand Opera House. In her speech she felt compelled to respond to a second attack by T.W. McGarry to the effect that she "had gone up and down in Quebec preventing boys from doing their duty." She then demonstrated why it was dangerous taking her on in public debate: 'If I had the time, I could make him swallow his words ... In my own immediate family every man has given his life but one, and he has been wounded. Why couldn't Mr. McGarry himself go to the war? But I suppose he was too busy here."[50]

In the process of detailing the admittedly intriguing campaign of vilification of Henderson, it is easy to lose sight of the significance of this moment. The mobilization of women that took place in St Catharines in February 1919 was the result of a conjunction of events that would not be repeated in the coming years. Women in Ontario had acquired the vote in April 1917 and the federal vote in May 1918, and there can be no denying the impact at the provincial level in the St Catharines by-election.[51] The conjunction of high unemployment and returning Canadian soldiers left a bad taste in the mouths of the soldiers and their wives: they had not suffered for four long years to be reduced to poverty in peacetime. This unusual situation almost put Longden in office, but on election day he lost by the extremely narrow margin of 174 votes.[52]

Henderson unquestionably made a major contribution to Longden's campaign, and she could take much credit for the positive result. On the other hand, it is possible that she was not as effective as she might have been because she was unwilling, or unable, to set aside her own agenda in the cause of electing the ILP candidate. On 13 February 1919 the *Star* reported: "Invading the Parnell stronghold of Grantham last night W. E. Longden and his supporters were treated to the first real opposition that has marked any of the campaign meetings, but emerged from the fray with flying colors. Mrs. Rose Henderson fairly captivated her audience, and was accorded a magnificent reception following her clear enunciation of the principles for which labor was fighting and her insistent demand for the abolition of child labor."[53] Henderson's ambivalent impact derived from the fact that she used the campaign to advocate a much needed reform, the abolition of child labour, in a context in which the "winning" issue was the travails of returning soldiers in a period of high unemployment. Yet even on this issue her legacy was ambiguous, because the anti-Quebec attacks she provoked reminded bigoted St Catharines voters of the lower enlistment rates in Quebec. Conservative supporters were able to use Henderson as a whipping boy, offsetting at least to some extent the female voters she mobilized and the pro-labour sentiment she aroused.

The by-election campaign also revealed the ongoing contradictions in Henderson's class politics. On the one hand, she argued during the campaign that the ILP was "not a class movement, but includes all who labor either with hand or brain and who wish to join."[54] Yet in her 13 February speech, she appeared to be speaking to the working-class members of the crowd: "Vote for the Labor party which puts men on their feet, making them capable of standing alone without the aid of the political crutch of any one else. Oh! That I could make you realize your power. You build the railways, but you often have to hobo it on the brake beams. You have conquered in the industrial field. Now you must conquer on the political platform."[55]

In 1919, even when Henderson was as radical as she was to be in her life of political activism, it remains problematic to argue that class was her central category of analysis and understanding. Once again, we must recognize that she more often judged people on the basis of what they said and did than on the basis of who they were. This approach extended to members of the middle and upper classes, who were as welcome at an open forum as were anarchists and labour men and women. As the labour revolt of 1919 approached, she remained as much a Progressive and a utopian socialist as a Marxist.

In late March 1919 the Union government of Sir Robert Borden, worried about increasing industrial unrest in the country, appointed the Royal Commission on Industrial Relations to travel across Canada to take the pulse of labour. Commonly referred to as the Mathers Commission after its chair, Judge Mathers, the commission heard 486 witnesses in twenty-eight cities between 26 April and 13 June.[56] Gregory Kealey argues that the commission was "defiantly challenged" by Canadian workers appearing before it, making the labour revolt of 1919 a nation-wide phenomenon. It is true that Henderson, in her testimony in Montreal on 29 May 1919, challenged the commissioners by stating that in Montreal "there are certainly the makings of a great revolution."[57] She did claim that in the current situation "the real revolutionist is the mother – not the man. She says openly that there is nothing but Revolution."[58]

Kealey's citing of Henderson's words must be understood in the context of the debate that took place among Canadian labour historians in the early 1980s. The debate's centrepiece was a 1977 article by David Bercuson in which he argued that the labour radicalism of 1919 arose from local conditions related to wages and working conditions that made worker protest deeper and more widespread in western Canada than eastern Canada.[59] In his response to Bercuson's "western exceptionalist" position, Kealey accused him of being the historian "most guilty" of overstating the case for "a unique western working-class militancy."[60]

Kealey's assiduous research has demonstrated the extent of working-class revolt in eastern Canada and effectively challenged the "western exceptionalist" perspective. It is also true, however, that Bercuson was justified in asking how widely this sentiment was shared by the workers of Montreal, and in arguing that Kealey was attempting to fit the evidence into a Marxist framework.[61] Bercuson asked an important question: is it accurate "to treat women as part of the same working-class culture as men?"[62] Kealey's interpretation of Henderson's remarks do not take into consideration the fact that she was positing the private female realm of the mother, not the public realm of the male wage worker, as the birthplace of revolution in Montreal. Henderson's gender, class position, and type of employment all distinguished her from the majority of Canadian wage workers.

That said, it would be equally erroneous to swing too far in the opposite direction and depict her maternalism as embodying the essential conservatism of left-wing politics in Quebec. Stereotyping Quebec workers as "conservative" has, as Geoffrey Ewen argues, disguised the fact that during the national labour revolt there was "an unprecedented level of strike activity that revealed a remarkable degree of solidarity" in Quebec.[63] In spite of opposition in the province to women working outside the home, "efforts to recruit women and to encourage their participation in labour organization reached a new peak in 1919."[64] Henderson was one of the women swept up in the fervour that accompanied the creation of the One Big Union, and the promise of working-class unity that it entailed. With the Winnipeg General Strike still in progress, within days of her appearance before the Mathers Commission, the Montreal local of the Canadian Labor Party met to debate support for the OBU. Recording secretary Ulrike Binette introduced the following motion: "Qu'il soit résolu que l'assemblée de Montréal du parti ouvrier national approuve le principe de la 'One Big Union' comme représentant les intérêts de la masse industrielle."[65] Of particular note is the fact that, in a 30–21 vote on supporting the OBU in principle, all of the female members identified – Henderson, Larocque, Mendelsohn, and Boulay – voted in favour.[66] It was a revealing moment, as these four women represented the unity of English, French, and Jewish Montreal that Henderson herself so well exemplified.

Her involvement with the One Big Union would prove to be of short duration, but it would be long enough to change the course of her life. In the early hours of Dominion Day 1919, she became a target of the police searches being carried out across the country. Her apartment was raided and her papers confiscated.[67] Under the direction of Chief Bélanger, 130 constables, armed with special warrants signed by Judge F.-X. Choquet of the Montreal Juvenile Court, raided offices and homes including Henderson's Apartment 18, 210 Milton Street, and her office at 209 Champ de Mars. At two AM the officers returned to police headquarters with "about a ton of newspapers, booklets, journals, correspondence and telegrams," as well as leases, passports, registration cards, and marriage certificates. According to the *Montreal Gazette*, the confiscated items would "give the authorities much valuable information linking up the activities of the 'red' element in Winnipeg with Montreal, between which two cities there has been apparently a regular exchange of Bolshevik correspondence."[68]

The next day Chief Bélanger wrote to Edmond Décary, president of the administrative commission at Montreal City Hall, identifying the thirty individuals and organizations whose homes and offices had been raided. He emphasized that socialist literature was found in both Henderson's residence and her place of work. Noting that she occupied *"une position de confiance"* at the Juvenile Court and was in constant contact with young people, Bélanger suggested that the attention of the authorities should be drawn to this fact.[69]

On 8 July 1919 Décary wrote to Premier Lomer Gouin, including a copy of the report sent to him by Chief Bélanger.[70] The premier's office replied on 11 July, stating that the matter would receive *"toute notre attention."*[71] On the same date Gouin's office received a letter, likely from Deputy Attorney General Charles Lanctot, in which the writer referred to the seized documents as *"littérature anarchiste"* and *"littérature socialiste,"* noting that the search warrants (*mandats*) were brought from Winnipeg by a Sergeant Smily, and were *"visés"* by Judge Choquet. The writer emphasized that socialist literature was seized at Henderson's office as well as at her home, suggesting – not without cause – that she had been engaged in left-wing activities while at work. Lanctot advised Gouin to write to

Ottawa or Winnipeg to obtain a copy of the documents seized from Henderson. Lanctot said that he awaited Gouin's advice, and stated: "Nous pourrons après agir en pleine connaissance de cause en ce qui regarde Mademoiselle Henderson."[72] Gouin replied from Pointe-au-Pic on 13 July 1919, approving Lanctot's suggestion.[73]

In mid-July 1919 Lanctot wrote to the minister of justice in Ottawa, saying that in "view of the duties performed by Rose Henderson, we have an interest in taking communication of the documents seized at her residence and at the court. I would therefore request you to be good enough to give the necessary instructions to have copies sent to us."[74] On 22 July 1919, the acting deputy minister of justice, Stuart Edwards, wrote to Lanctot stating that as "these searches were conducted at the instance of the Manitoba Government," he was forwarding Lanctot's letter to the attorney general of Manitoba.[75] On 8 August 1919, Deputy Attorney General John Allen of Manitoba wrote to Lanctot, enclosing a copy of a 31 July 1919 letter sent to him by Alfred J. Andrews, the lead prosecutor in the trials of the Winnipeg Strike defendants.

In his letter Andrews noted that five of the documents seized from Henderson, including *The Communist Manifesto* and Robert Blatchford's *Merrie England*, were prohibited by order-in-council. Andrews also noted that they had letters written by Henderson to R.B. Russell[76] concerning the One Big Union, and an article co-written by Henderson entitled "Money" that was confiscated from Russell's residence and the OBU offices in Winnipeg. Andrews offered to send Allen copies of these documents.[77] Lanctot, having received a copy of a letter Allen sent to Andrews on 31 July 1919, wrote to Andrews on 21 August 1919, saying he would be "very much obliged" if Andrews would provide his office with copies of the Henderson documents.[78] On 8 September 1919 Andrews wrote to Lanctot, enclosing copies of the letters Henderson sent to Bob Russell.[79] On 13 September Lanctot wrote to Henderson, asking "whether you are the signatory of these letters and document."[80] Unaware that she was on vacation in the United States, Lanctot sent a telegram on 18 September 1919, saying his office had received no response from her and that the attorney general "insists upon an immediate answer."[81]

It is difficult, indeed impossible, to tell if the actual content of the seized documents was a significant factor in the eventual loss of Henderson's position at the Juvenile Court that December. The document containing the fullest exposition of a radical critique was the article entitled "Money." It was co-authored by a woman named Manita Johnson, about whom little is known. She had published a series of articles in Cotton's Weekly, January–March 1909, under the title "Suggested Means of Abolishing Poverty." The editor claimed the articles were written "a number of years ago" and commented that Johnson became a member of the Socialist Party of Canada in December 1908.

"Money" was dated 12 January 1913.[82] Given that Russell was not well known when the treatise was written, and that Henderson may not even have known who he was before the end of the war, it was likely sent to him in late 1918 or early 1919. Presumably the atmosphere of the building labour revolt of the 1917–19 period revived her interest in the article.

The most intriguing aspect of "Money" is that it actually sets out a blueprint for a socialist economy. The socialist future it envisions is based on a population of 90,000, in which 60,000 people are non-workers, 4,000 people work in administration, education, and so on, 10,000 people work in private enterprise, and 16,000 work in social production.[83] The working day is five hours. The currency in this socialist society is measured in time, because time never varies, and the result is an economy in which the few are unable to manipulate the basis article upon which all forms of exchange are based. In this society there is an actual "labour time currency" that is measured in hours, minutes, and seconds. According to Johnson and Henderson, labour time currency is superior to one based on gold because labour time never decreases in value, as even gold can. The worker, therefore, is never cheated and is always able to purchase commodities equivalent to the value of his labour time. In this socialist economy, technological innovation that results in the lowering of the time of production leads to cheaper commodities, not to increased profits.

It is not possible to know how many lawyers, politicians, and civil servants in Winnipeg, Ottawa, and Montreal actually read "Money." We do know that it was A.J. Andrews, lead prosecutor in the Winnipeg Strike Trials, who most thoroughly went through the mass of documents confiscated in Winnipeg and the rest of the country;[84] if any lawyer, politician, or government official read "Money" and was influenced by it, it was he. Perhaps it is not surprising, therefore, that in his summation following Russell's trial, Andrews acknowledged that the immediate intent of the Winnipeg General Strike was not revolution. He insisted, nevertheless, that "some day" in the future the radicals of 1919 intended to overturn the government.[85] The "constructive programme" of socialism set out in Henderson and Johnson's treatise may have been one of the reasons why opponents of the Winnipeg General Strike, notably Andrews, believed that the labour revolt of 1919 was motivated by the desire of revolutionary socialists to create a socialist society at some point in the future.

The series of events leading to Henderson's resignation from the Montreal Juvenile Court continued to play out in the fall of 1919. On 30 September 1919, while she was still away in Cleveland, Charles Lanctot wrote to Judge Choquet of the Juvenile Court. Lanctot reported that Henderson had failed to respond to the letter of 13 September and the telegram of 18 September. This letter indicates that over the course of more than two weeks Lanctot did not bother to get in touch with Choquet to find out why Henderson was not responding. In his letter, Lanctot reiterated the long-standing accusation against her: "Ces documents renferment, à notre sens, des choses qui démontrent que Mademoiselle Rose Henderson n'a pas les qualités voulues pour surveiller la conduite de jeunes enfants. Cela étant et vu sa négligence à nous répondre nous vous demanderions de bien vouloir lui suggérer de transmettre sa démission. En cas de refus, le Procureur général se verra dans l'obligation de la démettre." Here he added to the charges against Henderson, noting her lack of responsibility in failing to respond, compounding the negative influence she was having on young people.[86]

Three days later, there was a dramatic escalation of the stakes involved. On 3 October, J.H. Edgar, honorary secretary of the Imperial Order Sons of the Empire, wrote to Premier Gouin, reporting on a resolution unanimously adopted at the organization's meeting on Wednesday, 1 October 1919: "That the English speaking juvenile officer employed in Montreal, in view of her pronounced and oft-repeated Bolshevistic utterances, be removed from office and replaced by the widow or mother of some soldier who fell in action during the War of 1914–18."[87] The next day, 4 October 1919, Gouin forwarded the letter to Attorney General Taschereau, saying: "Il s'agit probablement de Mme Henderson."[88]

A flurry of correspondence followed on 6 October 1919. Henderson sent Lanctot a telegram, saying she was writing a letter immediately. Choquet wrote to Lanctot, saying that Henderson had arrived back at her office from vacation. Lanctot wrote to Henderson, saying that she had been suspended because "papers of a compromising nature, bearing your name, were found in the possession of several people."[89] Henderson wrote a long letter to Lanctot as the follow-up to her telegram. Lanctot wrote to Choquet, enclosing a copy of the letter he sent to Henderson. Lanctot wrote to J.H. Edgar of the Imperial Order Sons of the Empire, telling him that "action was taken to-day."[90] Lanctot wrote to M. le Greffier at the Palais de Justice, asking him to suspend Henderson *"avec perte de traitement."*[91]

Henderson wrote to Lanctot on the letterhead of the Parti Ouvrier du Canada, Section de la Province de Québec, Assemblée de Montréal. Her name was at the top, identifying her as corresponding secretary, while President Joseph Métivier's name was in the upper right-hand corner. The letterhead was almost as intriguing as the contents. Why did Henderson use it and not that of the Juvenile Court? By doing so, she was telling Lanctot that she was functioning as corresponding secretary of the Labor Party while at work, thereby compounding Lanctot's earlier charges that her left-wing ideas were influencing the young people she was working with, and that she had been acting irresponsibly. In a hurry to respond to Lanctot, did she simply grab the nearest paper? Or was she deliberately thumbing her nose at the provincial government, in essence daring Lanctot to fire her for her political activities?

Again it is difficult to assess the extent to which Lanctot was aware of Henderson's activities and the politics of the Parti Ouvrier. As we have seen, the 7 June 1919 issue of *Le Monde Ouvrier* reported that the Montreal local of the Canadian Labor Party had approved the One Big Union in principle. This was not exactly a ringing endorsement, but it certainly tied Henderson to Russell and the OBU. Lanctot may also have known that in July the Parti Ouvrier had vigorously protested against the raids on "de braves citoyens coupables seulement de croire encore à l'idéal de la justice et de la liberté."[92]

Given the letterhead, one of the arguments Henderson made in the letter is difficult to understand. She wrote: "I do not belong to any party for the reason I can not accept all their doctrines and reserve the right to reject what is not to my mind good." What can she possibly mean? Was she acting as the corresponding secretary of the Labor Party without actually being a member of the party? Or by "party" did she mean the Liberal, Conservative, or Unionist parties? The issue is further confounded by the fact that she went on to characterize herself as a good Quebec Liberal: "Sir Wilfred's gospel was unity of the peoples and before he died he laid down the principle that before we could hope for peace in Canada the best in liberalism and Labor must come together and unite politically I believed this and worked accordingly." Following an attack on the Union government, Henderson said: "I can never forget the province of Ontario during my campaigne there on behalf of Liberalism. I had would you [sic] want to be ruled by "Catholic "Ignorant" slacking" [sic] slow Quebec? Hurled at me everywhere and this gov. was responsible through its press and posters for it." She concluded: "I shall continue no matter what your decision to lay the ugly spector of hate and dis-cord created by this Gov at Ottawa against Quebec on all occasions. I have lived in this city all my life and have learned to love it at all times I will try to serve to the best of my ability."[93]

To say the least, she was playing fast and loose with her own history and the nature of her political beliefs. In her St Catharines campaign she was speaking on behalf of the Independent Labor Party candidate, not on behalf of "Liberalism." As historians of labourism in Canada have pointed out, there was a powerful legacy in the ILP, tracing its roots to Gladstonian liberalism in Victorian England, but Henderson's reference to large-L liberalism distorts the nature of her involvement.[94] No doubt she found herself defending Quebec while campaigning in Ontario, and there is no question that elements of her politics could be reconciled with Laurier's liberalism. Yet she was also asserting a misleading connection to the city of Montreal and a misleading allegiance to the province and its government. Her claim of living in Montreal all her life is difficult to reconcile with her Dublin childhood. She prided herself on being a woman of integrity, but it is difficult to read this letter and not conclude that in the course of its writing her integrity received a few blemishes.

On 12 November 1919 Judge Choquet wrote to the solicitor general, reminding him that on 7 October the office had informed him that Henderson had been suspended from her duties, and that in the meantime no one had been named to replace her. Choquet wanted to know if the suspension was "définitif." He informed the attorney general that Section 25 of the Juvenile Delinquents' Act required the nomination of such an officer.[95] The next day Taschereau replied, telling Choquet that Henderson had asked for an interview and that it was necessary to wait several days before making a decision.[96]

At this time Henderson wrote an interesting note to Samuel Jacobs, first elected as a Liberal to the federal parliament for the riding of Cartier

in December 1917.[97] (It was Jacobs who, in 1912, drafted an amendment
to the Juvenile Delinquents' Act requiring that a full effort be made to
place Jewish children in the care of Jewish institutions or with Jewish
families before placing them in the care of Protestants or Roman
Catholics.) The note is undated but was likely written in the period of
Taschereau's correspondence with Choquet in mid to late November.
Referring to her upcoming meeting with Taschereau, Henderson informed
Jacobs that she had "waited patiently day after day & week after week as he
promised to be here." Unfortunately, she now had to be away and asked
Jacobs if he would meet, phone, or write to Taschereau on her behalf.[98]

The existing sources do not reveal if Henderson or Jacobs ever met with
Taschereau. In the end, Henderson tendered her resignation to Taschereau
on 13 December 1919. The letter suggests that the resignation was a
disturbing experience for her; it was addressed to "Charles Taschereau,"
the deputy attorney general's first name, and the attorney general's last
name. She stated in her letter: "I have much regret that we could not
come to some understanding."[99]

How are we to understand Henderson's dismissal from her job at the
Montreal Juvenile Court? Was this state repression of a left-wing radical,
a part of the story of the suppression of the labour revolt of 1919 and the
trial of the Winnipeg strike leaders? It is tempting to believe that A.J.
Andrews influenced the attorney general and deputy attorney general of
Quebec to pursue Henderson's dismissal from her job as part of the national campaign against the radicals of 1919. As Tom Mitchell points
out, however, the "state repression" thesis faces some serious problems.
The zeal of federal and provincial politicians and civil servants for the
prosecution of the radicals was far from uniform, and had waned dramatically by the time Henderson was suspended in early October 1919. As
Mitchell notes, "Andrews complained to Meighen that provincial authorities had no intention of proceeding with prosecutions in any of the sedition cases."[100] The Winnipeg prosecutions were spearheaded by Andrews
and the Citizens' Committee of 1000, meaning that "the 1919 seditious
conspiracy proceedings in Winnipeg were private prosecutions under-
taken by the Citizens' Committee of 1000, authorized by the Attorney
General of Manitoba, and paid for by the federal Department of Justice."[101]

The evidence points strongly to the conclusion that Attorney General
Taschereau was reluctant to remove Henderson from her position, taking

more than two months to do so even after she had been suspended. The timing of her dismissal suggests it was heavily influenced by the intervention of the Imperial Order Sons of the Empire. At the end of the war, French Canadian Liberal politicians such as Taschereau were sensitive to charges of disloyalty to the empire, especially on the heels of the widespread and often vicious attacks on French Canada's enlistment contribution to the war. For Taschereau, the charge of disloyalty, in combination with Henderson's left-wing activities and influence on youth, was enough to cause him to act. Henderson was repressed by the state, but non-state actors and her conducting of labour party business from her place of employment played more than negligible roles in her eventual dismissal.

That Henderson had so often defended and spoken highly of Montreal's trade unionists was no guarantee that they would stick with her through thick and thin. Long before the final resolution in December 1919, the mainstream labour movement was rushing to distance itself from the "Bolshevistic utterances" the Imperial Order Sons of the Empire had accused Henderson of making. Within days of the raid on her apartment in July, the Montreal Trades and Labor Council was referring to "Bolsheviks" as "sly dealers" and "crooks."[102] The anger that Montreal trade unionists felt about the way in which Henderson had been treated during the raid on her home did not translate into full acceptance of her socialist ideas or radical labour politics.

What sets Henderson apart from Bob Russell and his fellow radicals on trial in Winnipeg is that she was not actually charged with seditious conspiracy. In a sense, therefore, in spite of the fact that she was not put on trial and imprisoned, being removed from her job at the Juvenile Court was a greater travesty than the trial and incarceration of the Winnipeg Strike leaders. The distinction does not appear to have been recognized on the Canadian left, but that did not prevent news of the repression she endured in Montreal from spreading throughout English Canada in the labour press. It gave her a powerful cachet, a cachet she parlayed into great influence on the Canadian left as the labour revolt of 1919 shaded into the politics of survival in the 1920s. In English Canada her long record of work with mothers and children that had first brought her to national attention at the 1912 meeting of the Trades and Labor Congress was reinforced by her dismissal from the Montreal Juvenile Court. Perceived as a victim of a repressive state, in English Canada she took on the status of a gallant hero of labour's cause and the British heritage of liberal freedoms.

4

Working-Class Hero

The response to Rose Henderson's dismissal from her position at the Montreal Juvenile Court provides fascinating insights into the Canadian political culture of the early 1920s. Far from becoming a pariah among trade unionists, feminists, and social reformers, she became a celebrity of sorts, one of the most popular and sought-after speakers and political activists in the land. There were those, of course, who condemned her, but many others were quick to rush to her defence. She became a working-class hero to much of the mainstream labour movement in English Canada in the early 1920s, and her reputation among female social reformers showed few signs of waning. Even among prominent civic and provincial politicians, her reputation flourished.

A month to the day after she resigned her position at the Montreal Juvenile Court, an article appeared in the *Toronto Globe* describing an address she gave to the Club for the Study of Social Science at the Margaret Eaton School in Toronto on 12 January 1920. Reading the report of what she said, it is difficult to envision the "Bolshevik" who so disturbed the sleep of Canadian politicians and business leaders in 1919. Speaking of postwar labour unrest, she was quoted as saying: "It is folly ... to say that it is the radical element which is responsible. The causes of the present unrest are deep and fundamental." As in the pre-war period her message was more Progressive than Marxist, arguing that working-class men were asking for greater participation in government, not its overthrow. The problem was not government per se but rather the fact that there were too few educated working men participating in government, because working men did not have the "political education to fit them for casting the ballot."[1]

Henderson's experience of the labour revolt of 1919 had not changed her belief that women and workers were responsible for their own subjugation. To a significant extent, she argued, government "rests on the ignorance and prejudice of the masses." She did argue from class; she insisted, as she had always done, that her audience recognize that working-class people suffered more severely from the abuses of power and corruption than did the middle and upper classes. She was attacking the hypocrisy of a society that forced a larger percentage of working-class children into industry and led to more working-class children appearing in Juvenile Court and the increasing "problem" of the working-class girl.[2] Of course, Henderson was calling for the uplift of the Canadian working class while appealing to audiences who were largely middle class. This was an old dilemma reaching back to the utopian socialists of the early nineteenth century, traceable through the British Fabians and the politics of the moral and social reform movements of the pre-First World War period. It was a dilemma that Henderson, if we can judge on the basis of the existing sources, never fully recognized or confronted.

On 13 January 1920, the day after she spoke at Margaret Eaton School, she was feted at the King Edward Hotel at a luncheon given by the Big Sisters' Association. Identifying those in attendance reveals quite starkly the problem with portraying Henderson as a victim of state repression and a pariah in the political culture of Canada. The head table guests included His Worship the Mayor Tommy Church (1870–1950), mayor of Toronto from 1915–1921, Controller R.H. Cameron, and Alderman Maguire. Other guests included Mrs Roebuck, almost certainly the wife of Arthur Roebuck (1878–1971), a Liberal politician and labour lawyer who served as Ontario attorney general in Mitchell Hepburn's government from 1934 to 1937. The board of *Woman's Century* was well represented; in attendance were editors Jesse Campbell MacIver and Constance Hamilton, and secretary-treasurer Mrs J.B. Laidlaw. The Independent Labor Party was represented by Dorothy Glen, the ILP's literature agent in the early 1920s, at the same time that her husband, Andrew, was an executive member.[3] Also present was Adelaide Plumptre, wife of Henry Pemberton Plumptre, who became the rector of St James Cathedral in Toronto in 1909. The Plumptres moved to Toronto from Montreal, where Adelaide was a member of the Local Council of Women and in all probability knew Rose Henderson. Plumptre was secretary of the Canadian

Red Cross between 1914 and 1920.[4] The resolution of thanks was moved by Judge Hawley Mott of the Toronto Juvenile Court and seconded by President Burton of the Big Brothers' Association.[5]

It is striking that someone from Quebec, not a prominent politician or business person, and a woman no less, was able to attract this kind of attention in Tory Toronto in 1920. In this vein, it is also striking to see that the 14 January 1920 article in the *Toronto Evening Telegram* referred to Henderson as "Judge Henderson" no less than seven times.[6] A month after losing her position as a probation officer of the Montreal Juvenile Court, she had been elevated to the position of judge of that very court. It would be a mistake to dismiss this as media hyperbole; while working at the Montreal Juvenile Court, Henderson was routinely described as an "assistant judge," an appellation the media would use even after her death. She came to Toronto to make "her plea for an assistant woman judge in Toronto's Juvenile Court."[7] If she conveyed to the Toronto media that she was a judge in Montreal, she misrepresented her position, but she did so in the name of a greater good. She believed that it was absolutely necessary for young girls in juvenile courts to have female support and guidance, and even for a woman proud of her personal integrity, this must have seemed a defensible stretching of the truth.

Following the luncheon, Henderson gave a talk to the Big Sisters' Association at Sherburne House. As reported in the *Globe*, her topic was school reform, which she contextualized by pointing out the role that a "united womanhood" would play in "the regeneration of the world." According to Henderson, one "great field of activity" was the school, where up until now there had been a "man-made curriculum, which left the child unfitted for the tasks of life." Women knew better what children needed in school, and must use their influence to implement "the sanest possible curriculum." She ended by saying, "What a few are doing to-day, to-morrow a great army of women will do when they know and understand."[8] Here, early in 1920, we have Henderson setting the stage for the primary involvement of the last years of her life as a trustee on the Toronto Board of Education.

In this talk we see laid bare the apparent contradiction that has characterized Henderson's feminism since its earliest days. On the one hand we have an argument that "mothers" should be in the home, and on the other, that "women" should be stepping into the public realm, educating themselves, becoming "a great army" to sweep all before it in its campaign to save the schools, reform government, and clean up the mess created by men. The question, of course, is how could she advocate these positions at the same time? Are mothers not women, and women mothers?

The similarity here with the thought of Mary Wollstonecraft is notable. For more than two hundred years, commentators on Wollstonecraft's classic work, *A Vindication of the Rights of Woman* (1792), have observed a fundamental contradiction in Wollstonecraft's view of women. Wollstonecraft affirmed that marriage and motherhood were the principal callings of women, with the implication at least that these were "natural" callings. At the same time, she sought to break down the division between the private and the public spheres, to make women, through the acquisition of knowledge and rational thought, fit companions for men. As Gregory Claeys points out, for Wollstonecraft the "special contribution" that women made to the public good was "the education of virtuous youth."[9] This was precisely Henderson's view of the special contribution of women. No evidence has surfaced proving that she read Wollstonecraft, but the similarities are so striking that it is difficult to believe that she did not. Interest in Wollstonecraft revived with the rise of the suffrage movement in the late nineteenth and early twentieth centuries, and it seems likely that Henderson read Wollstonecraft or one of a number of books about Wollstonecraft that emerged at this time.[10]

There was a contradiction in Wollstonecraft's and Henderson's thought, but it is not as incomprehensible as one might think. The mother was an educator, and the domestic sphere had a profound impact on the public realm. Mothers were part of the army of women Henderson spoke of in Toronto on 13 January 1920. She believed that mothers were an integral part of the public sphere even when they were not physically present; they did not need to leave the home in order to play their part. Their knowledge, their understanding, their passion, their commitment to the creation of a world without war lived on through their husbands and children. Like working-class men, of course, they had to be educated in order to fulfill their role as guides and teachers, to realize their potential, and to make that "special contribution" that only mothers were capable of making. A later generation of feminists would find the argument that women needed to be "fit companions of men" a disturbing concession to patriarchy, but it was an argument Henderson had been making in the labour movement since 1912. To be "fit" was to be educated, and there were men in the world who needed to learn to be the "fit companions" of women.

If our understanding of Henderson's standing in the Canadian political culture as a whole is in need of revision, the same must be said of her standing in the labour movement. Her identification with labour radicalism and the One Big Union in 1919 must be placed in the context of her long-term relationship with Canada's labour movement. Her involvement with the OBU was of short duration; by 1920 her focus was on independent labour parties, reflecting her advocacy in the special edition of *Woman's Century* in September 1918 of a British-style labour party. Her campaign on behalf of W.E. Longden in the St Catharines by-election in February 1919 made her well known and admired among English Canadian trade unionists and supporters of independent labour politics. Her support for the OBU notwithstanding, she had maintained good relations with the mainstream labour movement since 1912, and it was not difficult for her to establish credibility in English Canada as an advocate of independent labour politics.

In the years 1919–21, Henderson, a woman of middle-class birth and upbringing, became a hero to a male-dominated working-class movement that prided itself on its masculine defence of the working class. She blurred what Stephen Penfold calls the "discursive opposition of masculine and feminine,"[11] becoming what he calls a "masculine class actor" by launching a "virile" defence of workers, women, and children; yet when she was attacked by ideological opponents, she took on the persona of a "damsel in distress" to many male trade unionists and labour politicians.[12] For a time her credibility as a defender of labour overcame concerns about her radicalism, and male trade unionists, ILP politicians, and socialist editors rushed to her support.

She became a working-class hero – for, but not of, the Canadian working class. The police raid, and the high-handed manner in which she was treated, made a martyr of her. The raids helped solidify her standing as a victim of a repressive state, a position amplified by the fact that she was a woman. Most male trade unionists and socialists in this period believed that women should be at home raising the children and looking after the household, but when push came to shove, they were able to see beyond their own prejudices to recognize a woman who was making as big a contribution to their cause as any man. There were ominous signs, however, that the future would be problematic. The anger that Montreal trade unionists felt at the raid on Henderson's home did not mean they accepted her more radical ideas. They were coming to a woman's defence as much or more as they were demonstrating their agreement with her ideas. While their admiration for her was genuine, it was conditional; there were boundaries beyond which she could not go.

On 5 March 1920 the *Industrial Banner* published an article entitled "Mr. Workingman, Listen!" in which the unidentified author called on workers to throw their support behind the Independent Labor Party. The author, who was Henderson, described the ILP's mandate: "It exists for the purpose of broadening and making Parliament more representative of the working people, who represent the largest portion of society. It seeks to create, through education, pamphlets and public meetings, a sane, intelligent public opinion. It aims to train men and women from the ranks of labor for Parliament and administrative positions. It aims to establish for the first time in history a Parliament representative of the masses to deal with the interests of all the people and not those of the privileged few."[13] Already Henderson was evincing the essentially social democratic political stance that would compel her to support the Cooperative Commonwealth Federation in the early 1930s. Her rhetoric, support for the Soviet Union, and vision of a radically transformed society continued to cause alarm in both labour and capitalist circles, but she remained committed to change that was "intelligent and constitutional."[14]

By the late winter of 1919–20 her message and reputation had spread beyond her home province; in March 1920 the *Industrial Banner* described her as "this gifted woman of the common people."[15] By early April the paper was touting her as a potential ILP candidate in North-East Toronto. Her "great reputation" and "great work" were causing even prominent Liberals and Conservatives to say they would work for her.[16] The *Banner* was encouraging ILP locals to bring her in as a speaker because she always produced "splendid results," and "a visit from her will not fail to rouse enthusiasm among the members of the branches visited and to secure the enrolling of new recruits."[17]

In early April 1920 the *Banner* published her article "On the Land and in the Factories." This was the more radical-sounding Henderson, condemning the treatment of returning veterans by a government that "has broken every promise made to them during the war." The sole aim of the government "should be to administer the nation in the interests of the people instead of in the interests of the trusts and plutocracy." Radical rhetoric – but once again we see her employing the language of American Progressivism, not the language of Marxist revolution. The "plutocrats, through press and pulpit and school, control the three sources of the people's information, and a mob mind is the result; there is no place in the world for the individual thinker." The Marxist influence that can be found in her thought had not dimmed her Protestantism and belief in the centrality of the individual conscience. For her, the only bright spot in the face of the "coming storm" was the Ontario Farmer-Labor government elected in Ontario on 20 October 1919, which she described as a "moral protest against the mob and anarchy of a trust-governed, spineless set of political jumping jacks at Ottawa and elsewhere." The "toilers of the land and factory" were uniting to relegate the "old parties" to the "rubbish heap where they have ages ago belonged."[18]

Adherents of the ILP thrilled to her biting condemnation of the "old line" parties, and by the early spring of 1920 she was in northeastern Ontario campaigning in a federal by-election on behalf of Angus McDonald, who would succeed in entering Parliament as a member of the ILP. In Temiskaming she found herself on the hustings in competition with Arthur Meighen and other Unionist heavyweights, vying for the votes of the area's workers and farmers. Meighen, soon to be prime minister, wrote to a Miss A.H. Clayton of Listowel, Ontario, informing her that Major E.F. Pullan, the Conservative candidate in the Temiskaming by-election, had told him that Premier E.C. Drury of Ontario had sent a congratulatory telegram to Henderson, in which he called her "the rose of the North."[19] Where Henderson was concerned, there was chivalry everywhere one turned.

Such chivalry regarding Henderson made its way onto the floor of the House of Commons in Ottawa. As part of his attack on the One Big Union, George B. Nicholson, member for Algoma East, rose in the House on 27 May 1920 to draw attention to a letter written by "Mistress Rose Henderson" to R.B. Russell. In his speech Nicholson implied that Henderson had been sent to Temiskaming in aid of Angus McDonald's ILP candidacy by Progressive Party leader T.A. Crerar.[20] Four days later Crerar denied the allegation, pointing out that he had never met Henderson.[21] The next day McDonald rose in the House to quote *Hansard*, where Nicholson had claimed that Crerar "entrusted the campaign in

Timiskaming" to Henderson. McDonald, calling Henderson "an estimable lady," also denied that the OBU played any role in his campaign.[22]

As this exchange was taking place in the House of Commons, Henderson was travelling to Nova Scotia to campaign on behalf of the newly formed ILP there. She began with an address to the Local Council of Women in Halifax on 27 May 1920. The 4 June issue of the *Citizen*, the paper of the Halifax Trades and Labor Council, was practically the Rose Henderson edition. Half a dozen reports detailed her recent involvement in Temiskaming and her impact in Nova Scotia. According to the *Citizen*, this "Remarkable Woman" had "won the hearts of the workers of Halifax." Described as "a Florence Nightingale" and "a Joan of Arc," she was praised as "the premier Labor woman of Canada." In Temiskaming, she was "a host in herself, going into all parts of the extensive riding and campaigning with a fervor and energy that was one of the most outstanding features of the dramatic campaign." In Halifax she was having an equally dramatic impact, setting forth "powerful truths" in "eloquent and effective language."[23]

Quickly, however, Henderson's campaigning for the ILP, and her advocacy of labour, was sidetracked by the response of some members of the Local Council of Women, who were shocked by her politics. On 11 June the *Citizen* attacked the "barefaced snobbery … of certain portions of the Women's Council of Halifax." The Halifax society was composed, according to the paper, of "climbers" and "would-be aristocrats" who failed to appreciate Henderson's selfless dedication to the cause of labour, the poor, mothers, and children.

At this point one must sound a note of caution. First of all, the NCWC was the organization Henderson herself had been associated with, and written for, for a number of years during the First World War. The *Citizen*'s attack cannot mislead us into thinking that it involved a left-wing analysis on the part of organized labour in Halifax. The writer commented that the Women's Council "probably did good work during the war," although it may have been "over-zealous in behalf of the war."[24] The Halifax Trades and Labor Council was far from endorsing the Marxist-based critique of the Socialist Party of Canada, or the anti-war politics of SPC members and other socialists who became supporters of the One Big Union and the Communist Party. The article's implication that the war should have been supported, but not too zealously, also failed to match Henderson's own impassioned condemnation of the death, destruction, and profiteering involved in the conflict.

Opposition within the Local Council of Women notwithstanding, Henderson continued her speaking tour of Nova Scotia. There were ups and downs. In New Glasgow on 2 June she impressed the audience with her "powerful eloquence, splendid delivery, and forceful logic."[25] But turnout was low when she spoke at the Greenvale Assembly Hall in Dartmouth, causing the *Dartmouth Independent* to charge that Dartmouth citizens should be "heartily ashamed of themselves."[26] On the other hand, she had a "triumphant march" through the industrial centres of Cape Breton, where once again she was "heralded as the premier Labor woman of Canada."[27] In Sydney Mines on 8 June she "proved conclusively before she advanced very far in her well reasoned address ... that she is in a class by herself on the public platform."[28]

This praise notwithstanding, organized labour continued to exhibit an ambiguous attitude toward Henderson's social activism. When she left Cape Breton for Pictou County, she spoke at the Orange Hall in Westville on 21 June 1920. Having praised her speaking style, the *Workers' Weekly* observed that it was "the most compelling, irresistible social power on earth, a good woman pleading and working for the welfare of the unfortunate and the downtrodden." Henderson may have been respected as "a living dynamo of political economics and an encyclopedia of knowledge in many volumes," but she was still very much a woman whose impact and effectiveness were seen as a function of her gender.[29] Yet this "good woman" was also acting in a definably "male" way. *The Citizen*, commenting on her impact in the Nova Scotia capital, observed that she "brings a virile gospel of love and service such as has never been told before in the halls of Halifax."[30] While her "virile gospel" was vaguely unsettling to male trade unionists, it was downright threatening to many middle-class women. When she spoke at the Strickland Theatre in Trenton, some of the "so called society ladies were heard saying that Mrs. Rose Henderson was nothing but a Bolshevik of the worst type."[31]

Leading federal officials were also menaced by her muscular moral suasion. In August 1920 the Department of Labour published a pamphlet entitled "Information Respecting the Russian Soviet System and its Propaganda in North America," an attempt to counter what it considered the dangerous propaganda being disseminated by L.A.C. Martens, "plenipotentiary representative" of the Peoples Commissariat of Foreign Affairs of the Soviet Union operating out of New York.[32] Prepared by Gideon

Robertson, the labour minister, the pamphlet was approved by Arthur Meighen. On 29 July, Robertson enclosed a copy to Colonel Cortlandt Starnes, assistant commissioner of the Royal Canadian Mounted Police, presenting it "as counter-propaganda to the socialistic revolutionary movement in Canada." In his reply Starnes suggested a couple of improvements, including one that would establish "a wider connection between the Soviet Bureau and the O.B.U."[33] Included in the pamphlet was a letter Henderson had sent to Bob Russell at the time of the founding of the One Big Union, a letter in which she concluded by saying: "So you see I was in O.B.U. before I was a Socialist or Bolsheviki."[34]

On 28 August 1920 the *Canadian Labor Press*, a fervent defender of the international trade union movement, and vehement opponent of the OBU, trumpeted its vindication in a front-page article. Quoting Henderson's letter in full, the paper smugly concluded that it had been right all along that the OBU was "part of the campaign of Lenine and Trotsky."[35] In response, *The Citizen*, in a front-page article entitled "Why Rose Henderson Is Bitterly Assailed," declared that throughout the country "workers are up in arms against this new conspiracy to discredit and persecute a woman who is giving her life in the cause of the children and the working men and women of this country."[36] The paper singled out the *Canadian Labor Press* as sharing the politics of the Conservative Party, and rejected the charge that support for Henderson indicated that the Halifax Trades and Labor Council was being taken over by the One Big Union.[37]

Gideon Robertson's direct attack on the OBU, and indirect attack on Henderson, incurred the wrath of Malcolm M. MacBride, one of the eleven members of the Independent Labor Party elected to the Ontario Legislature in 1919.[38] During the 1920 election campaign in Nova Scotia, MacBride spoke in Halifax and Dartmouth. Henderson had met him in February 1919 in St Catharines, when both spoke in support of the ILP candidate.[39] MacBride, the mayor of Brantford, had a "highly personal" political style and had been known to praise Conservatives and attack socialists.[40] At one point he told the *Toronto Globe* that Gideon Robertson was a "contemptible coward" for attacking Henderson.[41] MacBride called her "one of nature's noblewomen," and condemned the Conservatives for "stooping to attack Canadian womanhood."[42]

In rushing to Henderson's defence, MacBride was not defending the OBU, or Henderson's own revolutionary vision of a transformed human

future. Grandstanding aside, his response was consistent with the responses of other labour leaders and male trade unionists who sought to
rescue a damsel in distress but not to endorse her more radical ideas.
When Henderson transgressed established gender boundaries in her "virile" defence of downtrodden workers, women, and children, it was not
only middle-class women but male trade unionists who condemned, or at
least distanced themselves from, her "Bolshevik tendencies."

By the time the controversy hit, however, Henderson had already
moved on.[43] In early September she was in Vancouver, calling for working-class self-reliance and self-respect as key elements in progressing beyond the capitalist state and the wage system.[44] On 10 October 1920, she
gave a talk on her experiences at the Montreal Juvenile Court to the
Vancouver Labour Church. The argument was familiar; economic conditions were responsible for creating juvenile delinquents, and members of
the ruling class got away with their crimes while the poor were "merci-
lessly" punished.[45] By November she was in Nanaimo, campaigning on
behalf of T.A. Barnard, the candidate of the Federated Labor Party in the
British Columbia provincial election. The BC *Federationist* reported on a
mass meeting at which she spoke after the candidate, keeping more than
a thousand people in "rapt attention" for an hour and forty-five minutes.[46] Mounted Police surveillance of Henderson tended to confirm her
impact on West Coast audiences, describing her as a "regular fire-brand,"
but there is little indication that the speeches she was giving at this time
were considered a serious threat to the Canadian state.[47]

The spring of 1921 found Henderson in Winnipeg, where the
Manitoba Free Press ran a feature article on her under the headline "Labor,
Women and Politics." Describing Henderson as "one of the outstanding leaders in the Labor ranks today," the article continued: "Her burn-
ingly sincere interest is not of the ticketable variety, but is sunk deep in
her sympathy with the struggles of humanity. One may or may not
agree with her diagnosis of the case, but one must recognize that she is
closely in touch with a class long inarticulate, the women of the manual
labor strata, and to a certain extent anyway she is in a position to voice
their attitude." The expression "not of the ticketable variety" hearkens
back to Henderson's letter to the attorney general of Quebec, when she
stated that the independence of her views ruled out belonging to any
political party.[48]

On 11 May 1921 she addressed a "large gathering of women" in the Board of Trade building in Winnipeg, on the subject "Woman: Power, Plague or Plaything." She touched on familiar themes that she would touch on again. She discussed woman as drudge, woman as plaything, and woman as plague, tracing the latter designation to the Bible, ancient saints, and church dignitaries. Society's focus on upper-class women had left little time to focus on the working-class women, the drudges of the sex. Things were changing; the working-class woman, "under the pressure of her conditions," had begun to think. As the wife of a working man, she was "the slave of a slave," but she had begun to fight for her emancipation and that of her children.[49]

In the fall of 1921 Henderson ran as a labour candidate in the federal riding of St Laurent-St Georges in Montreal. Given this election's historic significance for Canadian women, it has received astonishingly little attention from feminist historians. Henderson was the only female candidate east of Toronto, where Harriet Dunlop Prenter ran and was defeated in Toronto West. Henderson paid the price for her support of the One Big Union and the widespread perception that she was a "Bolshevik." She ran against Conservative candidate C.C. Ballantyne, appointed minister of fisheries and marine in 1917, and Liberal candidate Herbert Marler, Montreal-born notary and fuel administrator for the province of Quebec in 1917–18. Henderson did poorly, garnering only 506 votes out of a total of nearly 13,500.[50]

Her poor performance is not surprising given the lack of support from sources one might expect to be sympathetic. In the period leading up to the election, and in the issues covering the election, there was not a single acknowledgment in *Woman's Century*, the *Canadian Jewish Chronicle*, or the *Labor World/Le Monde Ouvrier* that she was a candidate. She had burned her Quebec bridges with the mainstream women's movement and labour movement in the cauldron of 1919. More surprising is her abandonment by the *Chronicle*, which had been fulsome in its praise of her and her advocacy on behalf of Montreal's Jewish community throughout the First World War period. The *Chronicle*, now edited by Ida Seigler, supported Conservative candidate C.C. Ballantyne, and the Jewish Women Voters' Association arranged to have Ballantyne, not Henderson, speak to Jewish women.[51]

It seems a minor incident in the broad sweep of Canadian history, but Henderson's election defeat of 1921 bears many meanings. Resort to class and gender is problematic; the "capitalist press," the *Montreal Gazette*, for example, recognized the significance of her candidacy, while the women's and labour movements did not. Ethnicity is equally unreliable, given that *Le Devoir* – the paper of virulent anti-feminist Henri Bourassa – gave her more coverage than the English-language women's and labour press.[52] In a sense, she was a greater threat to maternal feminists and trade unionists than to the anglophone and francophone middle classes of Quebec.

At this crucial moment in the making of Canada, Henderson went down to ignominious defeat. Lacking direct confirmation of her reasons for running, it can only be surmised that she appreciated the significance of the election and sought to make at least a symbolic gesture on behalf of Quebec and Canadian women. That gesture was rebuffed by her erstwhile allies, because she had committed the unpardonable sin of being a "Bolshevik," a perception that we have seen was a gross distortion of her actual political ideas. The neglect of her gesture speaks to the narrowness of mind that too often characterized a left and a women's movement that prided themselves on being more tolerant and open-minded than their conservative foes.

Henderson's poor showing in the 1921 federal election, and apparent alienation from Montreal labour, the Jewish community, and middle-class women's groups did not seriously damage her appeal in Ontario. Early in 1922 she gave a series of six lectures in Toronto under the auspices of the Independent Labor Party and the Women's International League for Peace and Freedom (WILPF). Her involvement with both organizations confirms Thomas Socknat's point that over the course of the First World War "the pacifist initiative had passed from the old coalition of progressive reformers to a developing realignment of pacifists with the political left."[53]

It is difficult to tell if Henderson's talks were part of a single, coordinated lecture series, or if there were two sets of talks organized separately by the ILP and WILPF. In any event, she gave talks that appealed to different audiences; one lecture series on "the revolutionary tendencies of the modern drama" began on 2 February 1922 with a talk on Maeterlinck's play *Blue Bird*. In this talk under the auspices of the WILPF, Henderson scorned happiness derived from the possession of wealth and lauded "the simple pleasures which be at hand in everyday life, the beauties of nature and the friendship of those around one."[54] This sentiment sounded like

Emerson or Thoreau, and it is difficult to imagine it having the same appeal to a male, working-class audience as to a middle-class female audience. It is more likely that a majority of the nine hundred people who attended her talk on 5 February 1922 under the auspices of the ILP on the Paris Peace Conference, "The Failure of Peace Conf.," were working-class men.[55] In all probability Henderson's critique of western capitalism's exploitation of a defeated Germany resounded more fully with a male working-class audience than did her analysis of the work of Maeterlinck.

By 1922 Henderson was still admired in labour circles, but the ringing praises of the 1919–21 period had been muted. In late February 1922, ILP leader John W. Buckley wrote to Andrew Glen and his wife, Dorothy, who looked after the party's literature committee. Buckley expressed his regrets at being unable to meet Henderson due to his wife's illness. He was "looking forward to meeting Mrs Henderson," who was staying with the Glens.[56] The Central Executive Report of the ILP submitted at the annual convention in Toronto on 21 October 1922 included an account of Henderson's activities on behalf of the ILP that year. The report noted that the party "was fortunate in having the assistance of Mrs. Rose Henderson" over the winter, and that she "addressed several meetings, and did other good work for the Party."[57] This was a far cry from the peons of praise that issued from the pens of labour and socialist editors a short year before, and suggests that her impact on the Canadian left had waned.

While in Toronto in early 1922, Henderson signalled a shift in her thinking that presaged her activism in educational circles in Toronto in the 1930s. On 8 March 1922 she spoke to the Home and School Council in the Administration Building of the Toronto Board of Education on College Street. Her call for a "national school system whereby the people would be educated to a higher ideal of parentage" was "presented in simple, forceful language, and created a profound impression." She urged "that the curricula of the schools be so altered that children be taught the science of life, the science of bodily health, and the fact that they were the architects of future generations." The shift here from the home to the school is significant.

Once again Henderson's analysis warns against facile characterizations of her as a socialist or radical leftist. Her concern was not with exploiting capitalists, but rather with two types of women who were the "millstones about the neck of civilization." The first type "was the woman drudge, leaden-footed, leaden-brained, mentally stunted and undernourished, who brought into the world children even worse than herself." The second type "was the vapid, insincere caricature of a woman; the woman with money and leisure for education, culture and mental and spiritual development, but who was found at every dance, half-clad, seeking unsatisfying pleasures – a mere parasite of no earthly use to society or to herself."

The critique of the narcissistic society woman, a constant theme in Henderson's thought, is no surprise; her searing critique of the poverty-stricken mother, on the other hand, appears intemperate, patronizing, and arrogant. Yet she cautioned that delinquent parents "should not be too hardly condemned until it was known in what environment they had spent their own childhood." The clear implication was that the locus of educating children needed to shift from the home to the school. Children needed to be educated to be better parents, "so that when they became parents their children would fill the place of a weaker generation that would pass away."[58] It was easier, she suggested, to create a healthy environment for educating children to be better parents in the school than in the home.[59]

Henderson's politics now were clearly not the revolutionary politics she was identified with in 1919. Modern social conditions, she argued, "were opposed to healthy marriage, morality and parenthood." Changing the "very face of society" did not involve working-class protest or revolutionary action, but rather parents getting together and agitating for change that would sweep away "the present hampering, demoralizing conditions." The agent of transformation for Henderson tended to change, depending on the audience she was speaking to and the subject under consideration. In the context of a presentation to the Home and School Association, the agents were parents and schools, not the working class. From all appearances, the necessary change could come about within the existing system, without a revolutionary overthrow of the ruling class.

Henderson was a working-class hero in English Canada in 1919–21, genuinely revered and respected by working-class men and women as a tireless advocate of the downtrodden and dispossessed. She was welcomed into the house of labour and given a prominent seat at the table. But she had to mind her manners: there were lines she could not cross, stances she could not take. Genuine respect for her was compromised by working-class chivalry, which had more to do with protecting the person the BC

Federationist called this "pleasant-appearing, persuasive little woman" than it had to do with defending her right to be a radical.[60] As Nellie McClung famously said, "Chivalry is like a line of credit. You can get plenty of it when you do not need it."[61] By 1922, Henderson had begun to move her focus away from the working class to the role of women in the education system and the peace movement. In the process, her standing in a male-dominated labour movement began to slip, and her lustre began to dim.

The Russian Revolution, and formation of the underground Communist Party of Canada in the spring of 1921 dramatically changed the face of the Canadian left. It left the Rose Hendersons of the world in an anomalous position as leftists who supported the Soviet Union and were perceived as "Bolsheviks," but who decided not to join the Communist Party of Canada. Nor did Henderson decide to join when Canadian Communists organized the above-ground Workers Party in February 1922. In the year of the formation of the Workers' Party of Canada, she found herself falling between the cracks of Canada's left politics. She did not, like Harriet Prenter, become a member of the Worker's Party, and therefore was suspect in communist circles. Her support in 1919–20 for the One Big Union left a lingering stain in the minds of supporters of the Trades and Labor Congress and craft unionism in Canada. The Independent Labor Party was in decline in Ontario and the Maritimes, and Henderson had become the champion of a labour politics whose promise was fading. The existing evidence suggests that she herself felt the changing times, and her attention shifted from the Canadian context to international events. We now move to a chapter in her life about which we know so little but that gives us new insights into a decade that was so crucial as the inheritor of the hope and despair of the First World War generation, and the precursor of the upheavals of the Great Depression of the 1930s.

5

An International Life

Rose Henderson was convinced to the marrow of her bones that the working class and women of the world had learned the lessons of the First World War – indeed, that they emerged from that war with a renewed commitment to the creation of a world of peace, a world of plenty, a world in which children could grow to adulthood in a nurturing environment free from the evils of militarism, corruption, and greed. To believe that they had not learned these lessons was beyond the realm of possibility. There was now a beacon in the world that made this optimism possible – the Soviet Union. Henderson resolutely defended it from all comers and criticisms. Yet she resisted any desire she might have had to join the Communist Party, reflecting perhaps her desire to maintain the freedom of the independent thinker. She would relinquish a great deal of that freedom as a member of the Cooperative Commonwealth Federation in the 1930s, but in the 1920s she retained the spirit of the radical that makes it so difficult to pin an ideological label on her. In the 1920s she, like the decade itself, was searching for self-definition, seeking to be her own person in a world so profoundly shaped by the decade that came before, setting the stage for the momentous decade to follow.

In the early 1920s Henderson launched a life on the left in Great Britain and Europe that has heretofore been unknown. In the process of exploring it we come to an appreciation of the ways in which her international travels forged her world view and influenced her activities in Canada in the inter-war period. The evidence is episodic, and the historian must exercise caution in attempting to make sweeping generalizations about Henderson's ideas in this period, and the meanings that can be attributed to them. Yet by making our theme interlocking hierarchies of power – class, gender, ethnicity, race, and leaders and followers – a revealing portrait of Henderson's often conflicted but always insightful perspective comes into view.

The ambiguities and contradictions of Henderson's activism in the 1920s began in her involvement with the Self-Determination for Ireland League of Canada and Newfoundland. Henderson always claimed that her father, although Anglo-Irish, was an Irish radical, and that she had inherited his spirit. Prior to 1921, however, there is little evidence that she took much notice of Irish affairs. With the emerging civil war that erupted in 1922 in the wake of the Easter Uprising, she became more directly involved.[1] According to the *Canadian Annual Review*, Rose Henderson and Miss Katherine Hughes were leading supporters of lead organizer Lindsay Crawford.[2] Crawford, born in County Antrim in 1868, was an Irishman Henderson could identify with, a Protestant nationalist who sympathized with tenant farmers and the working class. In 1905 he had called on Irish Protestants and Catholics to unite. In 1910 he emigrated to Canada, having been expelled from the Independent Orange Order, a radical breakaway group from the official order that Crawford himself had founded.[3] In Toronto he published *The Statesman*, a vehemently anti-British newspaper.[4] No doubt Henderson was attracted to Crawford because he insisted that the conflict in Ireland was based in economic conditions, not in religious sectarianism.

Some seven hundred delegates attended the organization of the Self-Determination for Ireland League as a national society in Ottawa on 17 October 1920. The chief speakers included Armand Lavergne, widely believed to be Wilfrid Laurier's illegitimate son.[5] A letter from the Irish nationalist icon Eamon de Valera was read, thanking the Canadian people on behalf of the Irish people for their support. Crawford was elected president, with nine provincial presidents as vice-presidents. One of two resolutions "condemned any attempt to curtail the rights of the French language in Canada."[6] In the evening Harriet Prenter spoke on behalf of the league and the Independent Labor Party. Katherine Hughes did not address the delegates, but she had spoken at the first convention of the Quebec provincial branch of the league in Quebec City on 29 August 1920.[7]

Henderson did not attend either convention, but there is evidence to suggest that she was in British Columbia during this period, acting as a representative of the league. In mid-October 1920, at the time of the

Ottawa organizational meeting, she gave a talk on Sinn Fein to an open forum.[8] Her advocacy continued through the winter of 1920–21, and she gave her last talk, "The Cause of Anarchy in Ireland," before heading back east.[9] The titles of her talks permit only speculation concerning her message, although her 11 February 1921 open forum speech, "Violence or Solidarity," suggests that she was advocating Catholic-Protestant unity in the face of British imperialism.[10] The pride she expressed in her Irish nationalist father would suggest such an interpretation is warranted.

At a Montreal conference of the league, 5–7 November 1921, five hundred delegates were in attendance. "Several thousand persons" attended the public meeting on Monday, 7 November, in the Monument National.[11] Henri Bourassa, who claimed he had upheld the cause of Ireland for thirty years, provided a spirited affirmation of the ability of the Irish to govern themselves. Bourassa expressed great admiration for Sinn Fein, which he identified as leading the rebirth of Ireland. He denied that the conflict was mainly religious and "declared that the great religious fervor of Catholic Ireland would be but greater security for the Protestant minority against injustice."[12]

Exactly what role Henderson was playing at this time, and what her ideas were about the ideas of the organization, remain unknown. The mystery is deepened by a Mounted Police report on her activities in British Columbia in the fall of 1920, which stated: "Mrs. Henderson has also actively interested herself in the affairs of the Self Determination for Ireland League at this point, but the [12] best authorities say she is not very conversant with the question."[13] If true, this observation suggests that Henderson's interest in Irish affairs was of recent vintage. As someone born in Ireland and with a reputation for being "well posted" on a wide range of public issues, she may have felt a need to inform herself better on the Irish situation. A report in the *Toronto Globe* in late winter, 1922, announced her impending trip to Great Britain and Europe to attend a conference of the Women's International League for Peace and Freedom. The notice added that on her trip she "hopes to make a study of Irish conditions."[14]

Assessing the significance of Henderson's "Irish episode" is no easy task. The historian is hard pressed to find any other evidence of her impact, apart from the acknowledgment of her role by the *Canadian Annual Review*. John W. Boyle, in his treatment of Robert Lindsay Crawford, recognizes Katherine Hughes as the "provisional organiser" of the Self-Determination for Ireland League of Canada and Newfoundland, but there is no mention of Henderson.[15] We see here a pattern for Henderson that will be repeated in the 1920s – intense involvements of short duration, but the motivations for getting involved, and for ceasing involvement, lost to the historian's gaze.

In Scotland and Ireland, Henderson wrote articles and sent them back to Canada to be published in the *Maritime Labor Herald* and the *One Big Union Bulletin*. In the summer of 1922 she was staying in a hotel in Glasgow where she encountered a young Irish businessman and his family fleeing the violence in their homeland. In her article "The Irish Question," written in her role as special correspondent for the *Maritime Labor Herald*, she quoted the young man as saying that he was in favour of the "co-operative commonwealth." The young man, who she later learned was a "prominent free stater," had opinions remarkably similar to her own. He told Henderson that the "parasites" must go, and that the Irish people would elect splendid representatives who would bring in progressive measures "for the inevitable good of all the people." Asked if the Irish people feared the Bolshevists, he replied that the "black and tan" held more terrors than Lenin and Trotsky.[16]

Henderson's next article, "The Civil War in Ireland," appeared in the *Maritime Labor Herald* on 16 September 1922. In her analysis she spoke to the Irish situation itself, but her real purpose was to use that situation to communicate the international significance. Drawing on the Canadian working-class reality of the unemployment of the postwar period, she cited the statement made by the chairman at a workers' meeting the previous evening to the effect that there were 6,000 people unemployed in Cork.[17] She moved on to overcrowding, stating that 21,000 families in Dublin were living in one-room tenements. There was no money to remedy these injustices, yet "for military purposes nothing is lacking." Ireland needed, according to Henderson, men who knew "more of economics and less of politics." Ireland, like all nations, needed more statesmen, not politicians and militarists.

Although Henderson was speaking of an Ireland in the midst of a civil war, she saw the same problems there that she saw in Canada – too much spending on the military and not enough on social needs: "The world is cursed, the peoples are wasting away from famine and disease, the causes of which are secret diplomacy, political intrigue and an insatiable desire for power and wealth on the part of the few. This power will and must be broken or civilization must sink down to the depths of animalism." In such a situation, she believed, the youth of Ireland would not repeat the mistakes of their fathers; they would "recognize their foolishness," understand "who and where their enemies are," and act.[18] Irish workers, women, and youth, like their Canadian counterparts, would not fail to see the problem and have the courage to do something about it. An Ireland wracked by vicious civil war confirmed for Henderson the same lessons she had learned in nearly twenty years of social activism in a more privileged Canada.

Given that she was acting as a "special correspondent" for the *Maritime Labor Herald* at this time, it is not clear why her next article on Ireland, "Ireland and Its People," appeared in the *One Big Union Bulletin* on 28 September 1922. Written in Dublin, it deepens the mystery concerning Henderson's origins, because the article betrays not a single sign that she was writing from the city of her birth. She stayed with a landlady, not with relatives. The weaknesses of her politics, and perhaps an echo of the opinion expressed in Canada that she was not knowledgeable on the Irish question, was revealed in her praise of Arthur Griffith. Born in Dublin in 1872 of Welsh parents, Griffith is generally credited with being the principal founder of Sinn Fein. A journalist, he had been acting president of the Irish parliament in 1919–20 while Eamon de Valera was in the United States, and president of the Irish parliament from January to August 1922. Henderson was in Ireland when Griffith died on 12 August 1922, and she described long line-ups of people waiting to see his body. Griffith, she said, was "the one man with any claim to statesmanship" of all the Irish politicians.[19]

Her analysis is both insightful and shallow. In light of her close relationship with Montreal's Jewish community in the First World War period, an association that would continue in Toronto, her lauding of the anti-Semitic Griffith as a leading statesman rings hollow, especially when Griffith's praise of Czar Nicholas II of Russia and Kaiser Wilhelm of Germany is added to the portrait. In addition, Henderson's praise of Griffith not only slighted other "statesmen" such as de Valera and Michael Collins but left no place of honour for heroes of the Easter Rising such as Patrick Pearse and Roger Casement. Faced with the violence of civil war, her belief in "constitutional" action and her aversion to conflict in human affairs came to the fore. She did link the struggle of the Irish people to the struggle of the British working class, but in the final analysis fell back on faith in the character of the Irish people: "There is sufficient virility of thought, morality, native sense and humanity in Ireland to ere long put an end to her intriguing politicians responsible for this senseless civil war, always the most useless and horrible of all wars, for it leaves only a heritage of hate from generation to generation."[20] She saw the future of Ireland, but she relied on the native good sense of the common people to prevent it from happening.

The second major focus of Henderson's international life of the early 1920s centred on conditions in Britain in general and the state of the British Labour Party in particular. Her association with the British labour movement has been misrepresented by a claim made by Martin Robin in 1968 that has led to endless repetition of false claims about her origins. Misreading an article on the second convention of the Independent Labor Party held in Toronto on 18 April 1919, Robin claims that Henderson joined the ILP in Great Britain in 1893 and was there when the ILP affiliated with the Labour Party in 1900. The woman he identifies as Henderson was actually Rose Hodgson, who was on the executive of the Ontario Independent Labor Party at the time of the convention.[21] This mistake is the reason for John Manley's claim that Henderson "had many years experience in the British Independent Labour Party before emigrating to Canada around 1910."[22] When the British ILP was organized in 1893, Henderson was in Montreal caring for her three-year-old daughter.

Her interest in the British Labour Party emerged out of her labour activism in First World War Montreal and was signalled in her article "Labor, Capital and the War," which appeared in a special issue of *Woman's Century* in September 1918. In the article she called the recently announced platform of the British Labour Party one of the "most fundamental and statesmanlike documents ever given to the world since the Magna Charta." Contemplating the Labour Party document had renewed her confidence that organized workers, unorganized workers, women, and sympathetic members of the middle and upper classes would unite to create a better world. For her, this "manifesto" got to the root of the evils of society and created a path for humanity. She had no problem with the British Labour Party's accommodations with capitalism, because she believed that the divisions between capital and labour must be overcome, else fighting the war would have been for naught. Sounding for all the world like Mackenzie King, she sought "a more definite understanding between labor and capital." Capital must have "a broader social vision and a greater humanitarian viewpoint," while labour must reach beyond the trade union setting to meet "the larger needs of the community" and to work with the unorganized as well as the organized.[23] This was no call for class warfare; like the utopian socialists, Henderson was calling for all humanity to be liberated, a cause that did not exclude sympathetic members of the capitalist class.

At its best, Henderson's call for the liberation of humanity embraced workers of colour. This inclusiveness emerged in the campaigning she did in the fall of 1923 for the British Labour Party in the riding of Battersea North. She campaigned in the London riding for Shapurji Saklatvala, elected as a Communist Party candidate in 1922. In the 1923 election Saklatvala was campaigning with Labour Party support.[24] According to Henderson, "the workers of Battersea have set an example to the workers of other lands in so far as they have demonstrated in a concrete way that their advocacy of internationalism is no mere theory with them. This example may well be followed by labor elsewhere." Her writings on race are worth quoting at length:

Racial prejudices and religious bigotries have been and still are two of the hardest to break down. Fed and fostered as they are by a class who themselves know no class or race distinctions in their economic and political relationships, these prejudices have proven to be most power-ful weapons in their hands for conquering and destroying the labor movement, and the election of an Indian labor M.P. to the Mother of Parliaments is pregnant with hope for the future possible unity of man-kind … This election is a symbol of the unity and struggle of the working class. East and west have joined hands in a common cause. East and west are one in their suffering and slavery. As members of one family, heirs to a common heritage, they must rise or sink together.

She expressed tremendous respect for Saklatvala, who "has renounced all honor except the honor of serving the working class." She added that as "an internationalist it was good to be there and lend a hand."[25]

When compared with the male leftists and maternal feminists of her day, on the race question Henderson was impressively open minded. Yet these positive racial attitudes must be placed in the broader context of the racial prejudices she shared with the great majority of Anglo-Celts of her day. The complexities and contradictions of the racial dimension of her internationalism emerge from her admiration of E.D. Morel (1873–1924). The son of an English mother and a low-ranking French civil servant father, Morel grew up on "the edge of poverty" in England and France.[26] He left school at the age of fifteen and worked for the Liverpool-based shipping company Elder Dempster. Initially, as a shipping clerk in the Liverpool office, Morel celebrated the commercial aspects of the trade, but gradually became alarmed at the elaborate network of fraud, corruption, and brutality he found himself part of. He awoke to the realization that he was complicit in a system of forced labour in the Belgian Congo, dealing with what he himself described as "a secret society of murderers."[27]

In 1903–04, he organized the Congo Reform Association (CRA) to campaign for justice in the Congo. He enlisted the support of a prominent group of journalists, clergymen, politicians, businessmen, and aristocrats, and the CRA attracted more than a thousand people to its first meeting in Liverpool on 23 March 1904.[28] By 1908, according to Catherine Cline, he was "literally dictating the Congo policy of the British government."[29] By the outbreak of the First World War he had become the western world's most admired defender of the rights of black Africans.

There was another side to E.D. Morel's racial attitudes. On 10 April 1920 he published an article in the *Daily Herald*, Britain's leading left-wing daily, in which he claimed that many rapes had been committed by over-sexed, syphilitic black troops stationed in occupied German territories by France.[30] The article caused a sensation in left-wing circles, and Morel followed up the article with the publication of a pamphlet, *The Horror on the Rhine*. The first two editions of five thousand copies sold out in less than a month, and by April 1921 there were eight editions.[31] Robert Reinders believes that Morel's campaign was "spent" by the summer of 1921,[32] but a month before his death in November 1924 the *Maritime Labor Herald* published a report from London decrying the "sex situation in Germany where France is using colored troops to keep the white population subjugated."[33]

It would be comforting to be able to say that Henderson, fired by internationalism, working-class unity, and love of her fellow human beings, repudiated Morel's racist campaign. The reality is that she embraced some of its most racist aspects. In her widely disseminated pamphlet *Woman and War*, published shortly after Morel's death, she claimed in a section entitled "How France Prepares for Peace" that the power of France "rests upon a black basis." This was, she wrote, "one of the most menacing and sinister facts of history ... Is Europe to be dominated by Africa, are the blacks to be trained to subdue and enslave the white peoples?" Then she wrote: "Supposing friction were to arise between England and America? (not at all impossible), how would Canadian mothers feel to see the negroes of the south sent into the industrial centers to protect the interests of the United States. This would be merely war tactics, exactly what is happening now in Europe."[34]

In order to understand Henderson's support for Morel's campaign, both her personal and political lives must be entered into the equation. She knew Morel, a man she described as "a comrade of rare intellect, rare spiritual gifts and personal charm."[35] Morel, she said, "heard the cry of his dark-skinned brothers for liberty, for justice, alike with his white-skinned brother; to him the struggle was equally noble, equally important. The tears of the dark-skinned woman and child did not fall in vain. He felt alike with her the anguish born of commercial barbarism and sought to dethrone it." He believed in "the oneness of all people."[36]

There can be little doubt that Morel's personal appeal to Henderson was a factor in her embracing his most racist attitudes. In *The Horror on the Rhine*, he asked his readers to imagine the situation being reversed, to put themselves in the situation of the German people. How would the citizens of Great Britain feel if Germany stationed black troops in the West Country, south Wales, or the lowlands of Scotland?[37] Henderson took Morel's analogy and ran with it, asking how Canadians would feel if black American troops were stationed in Montreal, Toronto, Winnipeg, and Vancouver.

Her response to Morel's campaign must be contextualized. Morel emphasized that he was indicting French militarism, not the black troops.[38] How could these troops, he asked, fail to "yield to temptations from which European occupying troops are certainly not exempt?"[39] As a pacifist who was jailed during the First World War for his beliefs, Morel was critiquing capitalistic imperialism and what it did to its unwitting victims, including black troops in Europe. That said, he considered the rape of white women by black men a more heinous crime than the rape of white women by white men. His language was worthy of a late nineteenth-century racist in the American South, creating a monstrous image of armed blacks who, "their fierce passions hot within them, roam the countryside" in search of helpless victims.[40]

While in England, Henderson was very much part of the left-wing political culture that nurtured Morel, a culture that believed the French intent was "to humiliate and to insult" the German people.[41] Claude McKay, writing in response to Morel's 10 April 1920 article in the *Daily Herald*, got to the heart of the matter when he wrote that British socialists "were fearful that the French militarists intended to destroy the nascent German republic and with it the power of the Social Democrats – the white hope of the Second International."[42] British leftists feared that the collapse of the German republic "would severely damage the cause of international socialism."[43] This belief, on the part of Henderson and Morel alike, was part of an all-encompassing critique of the Treaty of Versailles and the League of Nations as ill-disguised attempts by international capitalists to exploit a defeated and poverty-stricken people.

Distasteful as it might be, it is really no surprise that middle-class white women of Henderson's generation, including left-wing women, took up Morel's campaign. Within days of the publication of his *Daily Herald* article, the National Conference of Labour Women met in London and adopted a resolution calling for the withdrawal of African troops from Germany.[44] Initially even the Women's International League for Peace and Freedom, one of Henderson's many involvements, supported Morel, although they became more critical as time went on.[45] Henderson held on to Morel's fear-mongering, in part because of his personal influence. She also held on, ironically, because in the early 1920s she was more radical than many of her left-wing feminist contemporaries, more vehement in her denunciations of capitalist imperialism. That vehemence made it almost impossible for her to resist Morel's characterization of black male sexuality as an instrument of the capitalist war machine. Unquestionably, her position on black troops in Europe was racist, and she failed to come to grips with the malevolence of the "white" hierarchy of power. She ultimately traced male violence against women to capitalism and war, not to race – an evasion, yet an analysis with more truth to it than later generations of anti-racist thinkers would recognize.

After the First World War Henderson had a vision of human society that was guided by hope, but one that at times brought her to the brink of despair. Writing from Great Britain in March 1923, she is revealed at perhaps the most bitter moment of her life: "Silk hatted gentlemen, and jewelled bedecked women flit past in handsome motors driven by mechanics dressed in the liveries of slaves, who perforce must waste their time helping to entertain useless parasites, mere mountains of flesh, arrogant monopolists of the people's goods and lives – the product of a society so putrid that if not buried soon will poison the entire body politic and destroy us all." The "masses are jailed, bludgeoned, starved and ravished, and only the masses can stem the headlong plunge of civilization to its doom." She then more directly addressed the abuse of women than was the case before the war: "Men take the lives of women upon short provocation. They use and abuse and push them [to] one side as if so much human scrap."[46] Driven by the spectre of a western world controlled by monopoly capitalism and marching down the road to yet another devastating war, her critique of the ruling class – bourgeois women included – was now intertwined with a more explicit attack on patriarchy than had characterized her pre-war thinking. She understood very well that hierarchies of power were mutually reinforcing.

It will come as no surprise to readers by now accustomed to the vagaries of Henderson's world view that she continued to be as quick to praise men as to blame them. At the same time as she was condemning black troops in the Rhineland and greedy and corrupt leaders, she turned to principled, honest leaders to guide the working class to a better world. In the summer of 1923 she published several revealing articles on legendary mine leader Robert Smillie in the OBU *Bulletin* and the *Maritime Labor Herald*.[47] She met Smillie for the first time at the Edinburgh Labour Party conference in July 1922, having learned about him through Keir Hardie. Describing Smillie as "a fighter and always the champion of the weak," firmly rooted "in the soil of proletarian culture," she added:

Bob is not deluded, nor does he delude the workers into believing that their emancipation can be achieved solely through the ballot box. He knows that the real power of British Imperialism is no longer in Westminster, but is outside in the banks and trusts who can and will when needed, call to their assistance the combined forces of reaction

and terrorism ... He ever keeps in mind the facts and horrors of South
Africa, India, Egypt, Ireland and Mesopotamia, and he knows that
when Indian villages, Egyptian meetings, defenseless old men,
women and children are bombed and harried by machine guns and
airplanes the suffering is just as great and the crime as unforgivable as
if it had happened to the Scotch, English or Irish working class.

Here we see Henderson at her internationalist best, refusing ethnic and
racial distinctions and justifications, exposing the brutality of British imperialism in all its forms. The problem, of course, is that Morel had inspired her to adopt rather different racial attitudes, and the difference
speaks to the fact that a kind of hero worship at times blunted her critique and weakened her analysis.

We see her reliance on the good individual in her praise of Smillie: "He
understands perfectly that there are fundamental principles upon which
all capitalist governments rest imicable [sic] to interests of the people
which must be changed before any good can accrue to the people. ... he
has unbounded faith in the ultimate victory of the people over exploitation and bondage, a faith always born to the incorruptible leader. He has
heard not only their cries of despair, but in the silent midnight hours the
triumphant shouts of the hosts of Labor marching toward the rising sun
of their emancipation."[48] As the history of labour and socialism so eloquently attests, there have been few "incorruptible" leaders, and the "rising sun" of labour emancipation has often been clouded over. Henderson's
admiration for labour leaders such as Smillie inspired some of her most
powerful rhetoric and analysis, but also blunted her creativity and willingness to seek solutions that went beyond reliance on individual leaders
and the idealism of the working class.[49]

Near the end of the article we find the beginnings of Henderson's critique of the British Labour Party that would appear in the Canadian labour
press in the fall of 1923. Smillie, she said, "does not believe that the Labor
Party as it is now constituted can be the ultimate goal of Labor. He regrets
that the Labor Party has now become the excommunicators of the minority not altogether agreeing with it, especially as this minority is an ever
growing one and of the working class ... He recognizes the fact that
there are strong elements outside the party which must be brought in
and weak elements inside which must be strengthened or cast out."[50] In

all probability "the minority" she referred to was made up of Communist Party members, and there is a clue here as to why she would shortly take a trip to the Soviet Union: a desire to defend communists associated with the brutalities of the Bolsheviks being reported in the mainstream press at the time. She saw Smillie as above the partisan politics she so disliked, and that made her wary of joining political parties in which she would be forced to compromise her beliefs. In the process she distinguished between "good" leaders and "bad" leaders. Certain that she knew which was which, she was not shy, as a Canadian, to prescribe the necessary changes required on the part of British labour.

On hierarchies of power within the left, on the nature of leadership, Henderson's politics was an ever-shifting kaleidoscope of opinions. On the one hand, she echoed many a statement made by members of the Socialist Party of Canada on leadership: "Labor must be true to principles first and to leaders only in as far as they are the spokesmen and expression of these principles. Blind trust and dependence on leadership has been the curse of Labor many, many times."[51] On the other hand we have her fulsome praise of Robert Smillie not two months before, leaving us wondering how she could condemn "leadership" and praise leaders at one and the same time. In part, the answer lies in her belief that she had the ability to distinguish "leaders" who were true to their principles from those who were not. Worthy individuals she encouraged to be "leaders," while the unworthy she condemned as part of a more general critique of leadership.

In September 1923 the *One Big Union Bulletin* ran her three-part series on the British Labour Party.[52] In her second article, which focused on Ramsay MacDonald, she identified a Labour Party leader who was part of the problem of leadership. The issue on which she assessed his performance was "the rape of Germany, a crime which will go down to history as the most heinous ever committed by any nation." MacDonald had been presented with a unique opportunity "to enunciate fearlessly the principles and ideals upon which a true internationalism and civilization must rest, of taking a bold stand against conquest of peoples and territory, of showing the difference between the old civilization and ideals which plutocracy seeks to strengthen and maintain, and that for which the Labor movement, the world over, dreams and sacrifices in order to establish. He had the opportunity of tearing the mask off the whole horrible intrigue of capitalism now reducing millions for their own economic interests to a condition of savagery." Instead, he had missed an opportunity to give Europe "a tremendous moral lead."[53]

Having decried the baneful effect of dependence on leadership in her first article, she took MacDonald to task for failing to take a stronger leadership role in speaking out against the humiliation of a defeated Germany. Then, anticipating the rise of the Nazis and anti-Semitism, she went on:

Millions of women and children welter in hunger, disease and im-morality. Hate, hopelessness, religious and racial prejudices are con-suming the hearts and minds of millions, they beg, they pray ... The subjection of millions of workers next door to Britain, beaten down to a coolie standard of living, is hourly bringing the crisis nearer to the English working man. Will the British leaders rise to the occasion or will they follow the policy and the tactics of the leaders who have failed so tragically and ignominiously in Europe?[54]

Her third article in the *OBU Bulletin* series was a response to a recent speech that MacDonald had given at the closing of parliament. According to Henderson, it "was certainly not the pronouncement expected from a lead-er of the working class":

Reparations are a refutation of all that labor stands for, reparations must come out of the mouths, off the backs, out of the homes, lives and necessities of the German women and innocent children for gen-erations to come. Reparations will go into the pockets of profiteers. They will not benefit the workers of the victorious nations, on the contrary, they will curse and impoverish them in proportion to the amount received by their masters. The moral principle is wrong. How can the loss of the millions of the flower of the nation's manhood, de-stroyed in the war, be repaired? The broken lives, diseased bodies, be repaired? How can the homes wrecked, the children made fatherless, and the women whose lives have been crushed be recompensed? It is wrong because in principle it puts all the blame for the war on Germany. Facts since the war have proven all the nations participated in causing war. Why then should labor uphold in any way the atro-cious lie of Germany being the only culprit.[55]

Here was Henderson at her insightful best, recognizing the true victims of reparations, seeing the victimization of German women and children as the product of interlocking gender, class, and ethnic hierarchies of
power. She failed at times to bring the full breadth and depth of her own
critique to bear on the world's injustices, but when she did, few feminists
and socialists of her generation did it better.

She continued her critique of leadership in an *OBU Bulletin* article on
4 October 1923 entitled "The Collapse of Leadership," stressing the dialectical relationship between leaders and the rank and file of the labour
movement. She lamented that, given the opportunity produced by the
Russian Revolution and the events of 1919, "the collapse of leaders in the
Labor and Socialist movements will go down to posterity as one of the
most tragic events in history." Returning to her critique of the postwar
settlement, she condemned the Treaty of Versailles as "the charter of
death" and dismissed it and the League of Nations as "capitalist subterfu-
ges" that "have strengthened the bonds of serfdom on the necks of the
workers more securely." Capitalism, she argued, had learned lessons that
labour had not: "While the capitalists did not hesitate to discard their old
war leaders, Labor still retains the same men with their old psychology,
who apparently have learned nothing through the war and most of whom
from all appearance are busy hitching the labor wagon to the chariot
wheels of mammon, rather than unloosing the chains."[56]

In a left in which the role of leaders and the role of the rank and file were
so often discussed in isolation, Henderson maintained her focus on the
dialectical relationship: "The masses must learn their own power and realize there is little hope for them until there is an intelligent rank and file
movement, capable of dictating to leaders instead of being led by them."
The failure of leaders was not a moral or ethical failure of the individual
personality. All left-wing leaders, from social democrat to communist,
were guilty of petty nationalism and political prejudices. This weakness
was not a function of a particular left ideology but rather a failing generated by the inability to really understand that leaders could only be as effective as the people they were leading. She concluded: "New times need
new men, bold of courage, broad of vision, tolerant of racial and national
differences. Men with but one purpose, that to unite the workers of the
world. Unity is the only rock, the only hope for future action and
progress."[57] The hierarchy of power within the left, like the hierarchy of

power within capitalist society, was the creation of an uneducated working class that had failed to unite in changing the world. A new working class with a bold agenda would produce new leaders.

In December 1923 or early 1924, Henderson went to the Soviet Union, probably leaving from Great Britain. She travelled by way of the Ruhr, where she experienced the poverty and destitution of the German people that made her an outspoken critic of the Versailles Treaty, the League of Nations, and the Allies. Although no details of the trip have been uncovered, speeches she gave about her experiences and articles she wrote when she returned to Canada indicate that much of her time was spent in shelters for children orphaned by the civil war that followed the Russian Revolution of 1917.

By the summer of 1924 she was back, and that fall she was one of the most sought after speakers in Canada on the subject of the Soviet Union. On 19 September 1924 a letter to the editor, written by one "B.M.S.," appeared in the *Labor Statesman*. The writer provided the kind of praise of Henderson that characterized the labour press in the 1920–21 period, claiming that in her years at the Montreal Juvenile Court she was "practically the assistant judge." It was Henderson who convinced the Trades and Labor Congress of Canada to make widows' pensions an issue "from one end of Canada to the other." It was her, "through her investigations into the ravages of cocaine amongst the children of Montreal, who succeeded in getting MacKenzie [sic] King, the then Minister of Labor, to put the amendment to his opium bill restricting its sale to young people." The writer then quoted Tom Moore, president of the Trades and Labor Congress, to the effect that Henderson "has done more than any other woman for the women and children of Canada." The letter ended with the kind of testament to Henderson's influence that one almost never finds concerning a Canadian radical activist: "I have been a worker for the Liberals all my life until I heard her. Now my all goes to Labor, and there are hundreds like me."[58]

By all appearances, Henderson's trip to the Soviet Union had done little to sully her reputation. One week after this letter to the editor appeared in print, Henderson's article "Old Russia – The Causes of the Revolution" appeared in the *British Columbia Federationist*.[59] Citing Gorky's recently published memoirs that presented pictures of the old and new Russia, she concluded that it was "the first time in the world's history that the people of any nation have been able to achieve their economic freedom." On Sunday, 28 September 1924, she spoke to a capacity crowd at the Royal Theatre in Vancouver on "Russia Today under a Workers' Government."[60] According to the BC *Federationist*, her talk was "one of the most interesting and enlightening that the workers have had the opportunity of hearing for some time regarding Russia," and they listened with "rapt attention."

In a second article in this series, "The Significance of the Russian Revolution," Henderson began by assuring her audience that there was no "bolshevist gold" behind her efforts. She stated that she was not a guest of the government, "a fact which left me free to get and give my facts as best I could – absolutely free, influenced by no one." She mocked the hysteria of the western media on "barbarous, irreligious Russia where bloodthirsty bolshevists grow long teeth and longer hair, where women and children are nationalized and divorces may be obtained with less trouble than it takes to obtain a dog license." Having dismissed western condemnations of the Soviet Union, however, she did not go to the other extreme and claim that Lenin and the Bolsheviks had created a socialist utopia.

Her understanding of how a socialist society would come about in the Soviet Union drew more fully from her own world view than it did from actually existing conditions in the Soviet Union. Socialism would come into being because it was a "powerful belief on the part of the masses," a perspective consistent with her ongoing affirmation of the necessity of change from below. For her, the Soviet Union was not being run on the basis of democratic centralism or the militarization of labour but rather "the principles of the sermon on the mount." She did not go so far as to portray Lenin as a Christ-like figure, but there was a pronounced "meek shall inherit the earth" tone to her analysis.[61] The fact that she was alive to the many problems still facing the Soviet Union did not change the reality that being there had been a kind of religious experience for her.

In the next instalment, "Women and Children under Soviet Rule," she began the analysis with her longstanding belief that "the human race can rise no higher than its source, the mother," a "biological truth" no one realized more than Lenin. "No statesman," she wrote, "in the most advanced democratic nation has done as much to liberate woman as Lenin did in the first year after seizing power." Under the czar, hundreds of thousands of Russian women had been forced into prostitution, "that most monstrous of all social horrors." Lenin had removed "every restriction limiting the sphere of woman." She quoted Lenin on the replacement of "the system of petty housekeeping" with a "socialist large-scale economy." She noted that the Soviets were implementing the complete sexual equality of women in people's restaurants, crèches, and kindergartens. Lenin, she concluded, was not one of the "intellectuals and the half-baked communists who do not concern themselves sufficiently with the welfare and importance of woman."[62]

In reality, the situation in the Soviet Union differed in important ways from the one that Henderson relayed to her audience. Lenin's New Economic Policy (NEP) had been adopted at the Tenth Party Congress in 1921, which saw a revival of private trade and the re-forming of a private sector in industry.[63] By the time of the Eleventh Party Congress in 1922, social welfare advocates were already protesting NEP's impact on women and children. As state spending was curtailed, and payment for all public services, including daycare, became necessary, thousands of children's institutions closed down or became overcrowded. Single working mothers were particularly hard hit; unable to work because they had no daycare, many watched helplessly as their children ran away to join the "*besprizornost*," or street children.[64]

While Henderson was in the Soviet Union, the number of children's institutions continued to decline, but the story she told was dramatically different. She reported that she had visited many of the "special colonies for the study of child culture as well as for agriculture." The progress made in gathering up the street children of the czarist period and the children made homeless by the deaths of three million Russian men during the war had been "nothing short of marvellous." Russian courts recognized that if either parent had rights to children over the other in divorce cases, it was the mother whose rights were stronger, based on the realization that "home life is better than institutional life for the children." Contrary to the lies being spread by the western press, the Soviet courts recognized the home as "the foundation of all civilized life." Henderson turned the stereotype on its head: far from being the destroyers of the home and motherhood, the Bolsheviks were their protectors. Having demonstrated that she was a clear-headed, insightful critic of gender and class hierarchies of power in the western left and western society as a whole, Henderson effectively declared that they did not exist in the Soviet Union.

She concluded this article: with women "emancipated and free to work out the destiny of Russia, co-operatively with men, and to add their spiritual and moral force, who can predict what the Russian nation may not achieve, and what her women may not symbolize to the rest of the world in the years to come?"[65] Again echoing Mary Wollstonecraft, Henderson saw Soviet women becoming the "fit companions" of men; as she had at times done in the Canadian context, she was close to arguing that it was women, not the working class, who were the motive force for the creation of a new society. The home, not class struggle, was her starting point. Even in her analysis of Soviet society, her maternal feminism remained as central to her vision as when she started to work at the Montreal Juvenile Court.[66]

In "The Resurrection of Religion in Russia," she defended the Bolsheviks for confiscating the wealth of the Orthodox Church and returning it to the people: "Religion – what lies, what intrigues, what bloodshed, and persecution have been committed in thy name ... The cloak of religion has served to cover up political intrigue and economic conquest so long that the mind of every honest thinker questions and is skeptical of, the entire system of organized religion." She added that it "would make a long chapter to set out half the numberless barbarities, the infamous and autocratic politicus [sic] of repression which were countenanced and supported even in this century by the ecclesiastical hierarchy."[67] The Bolsheviks had every reason to be brutally repressive but had in reality shown remarkable restraint in their attacks on organized religion. She described the Soviet government as non-sectarian but not irreligious. Religious institutions were open. Jews were "for the first time participating in all civil and government activities" and had "absolute religious freedom." The Quakers, Methodists, and Baptists had already created "great religious movements." Henderson's defence of the Soviets is worth quoting: "The government of Russia has been referred to as 'atheistic.' That there are thousands in Russia who are bitterly opposed to organized religion is only to be expected, and only too true, but because there are thousands who refuse to enter churches, and who scoff at supernatural religion, is this any proof that the people of Russia are irreligious and the government atheistic?"[68]

She then argued that just because there were rationalists, atheists, and agnostics in Canada and the United States, it did not mean that the people living there were "irreligious" and the government "atheistic." She saw the Bolsheviks attacking the hypocrisy of organized religion while safeguarding the rights of the people to practise their own faith in their own way.

While not all of Henderson's observations on this score were accurate, they contained more truth than the numerous news stories in the capitalist media that portrayed the Bolsheviks as waging a campaign of extermination on organized religion. It is true that the Decree on the Separation of Church and State of 20 January 1918 led to widespread looting of churches and terrorizing of the priesthood.[69] Whether or not there was a "war against religion" from 1921 to 1925 is open to interpretation.[70] Marx had opposed atheists "who attacked God with religious fervor," and Lenin did not insist on atheism as a condition of membership in the Bolshevik Party.[71] Post-revolutionary attacks on churches and priests were not necessarily party sanctioned; often "the defilers were simply hooligans."[72] Between 1917 and 1929 some 6 to 8 per cent of Orthodox churches were destroyed or converted to other uses, while at the same time new ones were being built.[73] In fact, some observers of the situation believed that church attendance was rising in the early 1920s.[74] This is not, of course, to deny that the ultimate goal of Lenin, Trotsky, and other leading Bolsheviks was the eventual eradication of religious belief in the Soviet Union, but rather to affirm that in some respects Henderson's perceptions on the ground were not entirely blinkered by ideological conviction.

The last article in her Russia series, "Education and Art under Soviet Rule," appeared on 24 October 1924. She began by claiming that in the Soviet Union workers for the first time in history "hold in their hands the education of their own children." Workers in other nations "are already aware that their children are not being educated; but are being converted into human phonographs, recording the ideas and psychology of their future masters, who are more intent on keeping them subservient in mind and body than that they should think and act for themselves in unison with changing world conditions." Under Lenin, education had become "the right of all, and not a class privilege ... The parasite is anathematized, the man of toil honored, the crime of war and its capitalistic background is emphasized, not its glories, and peace is held to be the greatest need and the ultimate goal of mankind." The world Henderson had dreamed of for fifteen years was unfolding before her eyes.

It is important at this point to stand back from Henderson in the mid-1920s to assess her world view and the impact she was having on the Canadian left. Without doubt she had been inspired and emboldened by the Russian Revolution, and her rhetoric reflected her new-found sense of confidence. The great deeds being done by the Russian working class, however, had thrown the western working class into a new light, and in many ways it was found wanting. The danger was heightened by the fact that western capitalists had found new ways to enslave the working class, and a more powerful media had ways of duping the workers into accepting the degradation of their everyday lives. This perspective emerged in "'R.U.R.' Drama of Exceptional Merit," published on 31 October 1924 in the *British Columbia Federationist*. The article was a review of the play *Rostums Universal Robots* by Karel Capek.[75] According to Henderson, the play "pictures vividly, where industrial efficiency, machine production, greed for profits, and power to enslave large masses will lead, if the profit system is not controlled." She concluded: "The modern robot can learn two lessons from this remarkable play, the first being that eventually the robots acquired sense enough to unite nationally and internationally as capitalists are doing to-day; and, secondly, that all the time their emancipation rested within themselves."[76]

In her review of Capek's play Henderson was using a new medium to explore old themes. Her reference to the "modern robot" echoed earlier critiques by Canadian Marxists of the unthinking workers incapable of understanding the "robotic" state into which capitalists and their minions had forced them. In a period in which both Stalin and Hitler were coming to power, the message had a heightened meaning and new urgency. Yet, like the members of the Socialist Party of Canada, Henderson could not believe that the working class would fail to see the evil and overcome it. For all her condemnations of the working class's blindness, she continued, like Marx, to believe in the self-emancipation of the workers – and women – of the world.

On 12 December 1924 the *British Columbia Federationist* published Henderson's article "Industrial European Situation." In evidence was her increasingly apocalyptic vision: "A great and ever-growing multitude of a once sturdy race is slowly and surely decaying, rotting from above from lack of vision and ignorance of the changing world, surfeited in luxury and enervated through idleness, and rotting from below – because of poverty, enforced idleness, lack of opportunity to express their creative instincts." The fault lay with the "cunning criminals who sit in the seats of the mighty – the munition and food profiteers, press and church lords and mantling kings." Typically, she ended the article by stating that the very same masses who were in such dire straits "are educating themselves, and are organizing their own movements to obtain truth, emancipate and lift humanity up."[77]

This is as close to the "real" Rose Henderson as we are likely to get, the woman who on the one hand saw a world threatened on every side by great dangers, but on the other hand was totally committed to the belief that the women and workers of the world would take up the challenge of creating a world of peace and justice. There could be no rest for a woman with this way of looking at the world, because the threats always seemed to be greater than the willingness or ability of women and workers to confront them. Henderson did not focus on any one of the major hierarchies of power in capitalist society but rather on them all. The result was a life of unceasing struggle.

How was she perceived in an ideologically divided Canadian left in the mid-1920s? To answer that question, we need to be aware of the ways in which her identity and ideas were being presented, indeed twisted, by labour officials and the working-class press. An interesting case study emerges from her article "International Unity Workers Forging the Needed Weapons" in the 30 January 1925 issue of the *British Columbia Federationist*. This article was reprinted in the *Labor World*, the paper of the Montreal Trades and Labor Council, on 28 February 1925, under the title "International Unity." The cutting of the latter part of the title is of more than passing significance. Henderson's original title evoked the armed struggle of the Russian Revolution and was unacceptable to labourists who favoured peaceful, parliamentary reform. So did Henderson, but she was not willing to speak against the Bolsheviks or abandon the necessity of the self-emancipation of the working class in the process. Generally speaking, there was more fear of the Bolsheviks and a greater willingness to believe the worst about them in Montreal than in Vancouver; the *Labor World* version was cut, starting with a paragraph in which Henderson railed against the "lies and misrepresentations" of the Soviet Union in the western press. Also missing was a second paragraph on the links between peasant movements in Mexico and the Soviet Union.

While it is only possible to surmise why this paragraph was taken out, a likely reason is the concern of a "responsible" trades and labour council leadership with Henderson's celebration of revolt from below and international labour solidarity that could not be controlled by safe and sane labour leaders like themselves. Labour leaders in Montreal were not opposed to all forms of international labour unity, including ones involving the Soviet Union, but they were wary of revolt from below in a way that Henderson never was.

The amount of time Henderson spent on the prairies and in British Columbia in 1924 and 1925 suggests that she found the West a more congenial setting than Montreal for her post-Soviet trip message. In the winter and spring of 1925 she continued to speak and agitate in British Columbia. On 20 March 1925 she published an article entitled "Workers' Children" in the *British Columbia Federationist*. In it she made an observation that is well worth looking at closely: "Tomorrow labor will realize that the greatest influence for education, for progress or reaction, are the mothers of the race, who, in their ignorance, have been down through the ages the real bulwark of the ruling class, and, realizing this fact, labor will glorify, not the slave of the kitchen, but the woman, free and intelligent, taking her place beside him, co-operating in every department to make earth a fitting abode for their offspring."

In this one sentence we find Henderson's vision, a powerful vindication of the republican motherhood she found in the Soviet Union. Yes, women had historically been mired in ignorance, but they would become conscious of the fact and arise. Yes, women had a "natural" role as mothers, but no human activity was closed to them. Yes, they were to become "fit companions" for men, but only to the extent that men became fit companions for women. Yes, the working class would triumph over the ruling class, but at the end of the day the victory would be as much or more a victory for women as for workers.

Henderson's travels in the mid-1920s, combined with an absence of evidence that she was gainfully employed, suggests that she had an income source linked to her deceased husband or other family members. As we will see, she may already have owned or been the beneficiary of rental properties in Toronto, although these do not appear to have been substantial enough to fund international travel and a series of lecture tours across Canada. Following her stay out West, she had returned to Montreal by the end of April 1925. On Sunday, 26 April, she spoke at an Open Forum in Montreal under the auspices of the International Association of Machinists. Her topic was "The Changed World Conditions between Capital and Labor."[78]

The end of May 1925 found her in Winnipeg, where on Sunday, 31 May 1925, she spoke at the Central Labor Church in the Labor Temple. In her speech she continued her critique of the postwar settlement, arguing that "the Peace Treaty is merely another method of carrying on the same war to achieve the selfsame objectives." Prior to the war, the "kings of finance" realized that the ranks of international labour "must be divided and their cause overthrown." Once the financiers had set the workers of one nation to fighting against those of another, the task became dividing the workers within nations. This was accomplished by buying off the leaders of the labour movement; labour leaders who refused to be bought were "stigmatized, imprisoned, or shot outright." The Versailles Treaty and the Dawes Plan were about the passing of "financial hegemony" from Germany to Britain, France, and the United States. If the German workers could be "crushed down," the debasing of workers in other lands would necessarily follow. Only Russia had been able to defy the "capitalist plot."[79]

The harsh critique of capitalism and the postwar settlement that characterized her Winnipeg talk did not reveal the full character of Henderson's thought in the mid-1920s. In 1924, when she returned to Canada from the Soviet Union, one of her first involvements was as director of the Summer School of Social Science held at West Summerland on Lake Okanagan in British Columbia, from 24–31 August. The school, now in its second year, was founded by the Theosophist Jack Logie. In addition to her role as director, Henderson was the main lecturer, giving four talks over the course of the week: "New Human Values," on Sunday, 24 August; "The Co-operative Commonwealth or Industrial Serfdom – Which?" on Monday, 25 August; "Russia, Yesterday and To-day under a Workers' Government," on Saturday, 30 August; and "Art and Education in Russia," on Sunday, 31 August. One of the other speakers was George Weaver, who gave a talk on "Music as a Public Utility," a title with distinct Bellamyite overtones.[80] The mornings were taken up with classes on economics and social welfare; Henderson's imprint was revealed by the Children's Story Hour held at 3:00 PM, followed by boating, bathing, and other forms of recreation.[81]

Henderson returned as director the following year from 16–30 August
1925. Speakers for this third annual Summer School included Henderson,
Dr W.J. Curry, George W. Weaver, R.H. Neelands, and George F. Stirling.[82]
The manager once again was its founder, Jack Logie.[83] According to the
Canadian Farmer-Labor Advocate, visitors were expected to arrive "from
Winnipeg to Seattle."[84]

In a personal account of the 1925 session that took place in this
"California of Canada," Curry described the log cabin as a centre of art
and handicraft "where the shade of Wm. Morris might revel in ecstasy."
In the afternoons "an hour or so was given to the children when the plas-
tic mind of youth was impressed with some plain, yet interesting, and
vital truths of working class philosophy." Henderson "specialized on this
work with marked success." Curry wrote of Logie: "The afternoon before
we said goodbye, Jack had a large assembly of boys and girls of all ages
reclining on the grass under the shade trees, where in view of the sunlight
throwing shadows of mountain bluffs, and majestic pines and cotton-
wood in the Lake, he, in picturesque language told Indian legends, and
stories of the myths, and miracles, and battles of the Indians of the Valley,
who are now rapidly vanishing before the onslaugh, [sic] and blight which
accompanies civilization."[85]

It is difficult to pin down Henderson's relationship with Logie and her
commitment to Theosophy. Theosophy, literally meaning "god-wisdom,"
is based in the idea that all religions contain truth and play a role in leading human beings to greater perfection.[86] Theosophy's conception of universal brotherhood includes not only all peoples, regardless of race, creed,
or colour, but also the natural world. We can be certain that Henderson
was sympathetic to Logie's critique of the "blight which accompanies
civilization," but there is no evidence to suggest that the plight of in-
digenous peoples was one of her concerns.

Yet her relationship to Theosophy was more than cosmetic, because she
continued her relationship with Theosophists in Toronto in the 1930s.
When she died in 1937, the Theosophist journal noted that she "fre-
quently spoke on Theosophical platforms."[87] Given that she had also
been a Bahá'i, and given her obvious love for Maeterlinck's play *The Blue
Bird*, we see that her trip to the Soviet Union and vitriolic denunciations
of western imperialism, war, and anti-Bolshevism had done little, if anything, to dampen the spiritual quest that had characterized her life to this

point. Theosophy was part of that spiritual quest, but caution must be taken in attributing W.J. Curry's and Jack Logie's celebration of nature to her; she has left no evidence that the location of the Summerland School cast a spell on her, or was a factor in keeping her coming back. Given that there is no evidence of her returning in 1926, we might surmise that she was rather like Lenin, her life the knowledge and struggle that came no matter where she was living and working.

While in British Columbia during the summer of 1925 Henderson published a series of articles in the "Woman's Department" of the *Canadian Farmer-Labor Advocate*. It is not possible to tell if she created the column or the column was created for her. In her first article, "Canadian Women, Awake!" she provided one of her more revealing portrayals of the relationship between the women's movement and the trade union movement. She pointed out the many women's organizations in existence, from Women's Labor Leagues to Birth Control Leagues, then noted that many of the women in these organizations were neither socialists nor communists.[88] Yet, they "are nevertheless far in advance of many of the old type of trade unionists, inasmuch as they are showing themselves not content with merely passing resolutions and discussing ways of obtaining a little higher wage, shorter hours and a few moral reforms." Women, by way of contrast, were dealing with "the problems inherent in the social structure." The key was education: "The ignorance of the working class, particularly the backwardness of the mother, is the greatest enemy of Labor's progress today. Therefore, the woman [sic] are recognizing that their chief concern is to educate themselves and their children to find the cause of their miseries, and become an intelligent force in the political and economic issues facing the welfare of their families." The future, Henderson said of woman, was "hers to mould to her desires."[89]

Henderson believed that at some point in the future working-class women, having educated themselves, would take control of the welfare of their families but without abandoning their role as mothers. As in the First World War period, no role was attributed to men in extricating women from their situation. In fact, Henderson had become more critical of male trade unionists, suggesting that women were capable of overcoming the causes of their oppression themselves rather than in partnership with male workers. Yet the concern that women would become estranged from their role as mothers seemed to permeate her thinking in this period. In this sense, she was anticipating a debate that would be at the forefront of women's issues in the late twentieth century: how women could "have it all," motherhood and a career.

As we have noted in relation to Henderson's involvement with Summerland, she cannot be associated with the celebration of the rural that Carol Bacchi suggests was typical of the suffragists of the First World War period.[90] Yet having written an article on working-class women for the 10 July 1925 issue of the *Canadian Farmer-Labor Advocate*, Henderson followed it up the next week with an article entitled "The Woman on the Farm" that suggested the future might belong to rural, not urban working-class, women. Her focus on working-class women notwithstanding, she could not possibly have spent as much time as she did in western Canada in this period without being struck by the vitality of farm women's organizations. She saw the farm woman as "beginning to emerge from her rural captivity" to take her place on school boards, agricultural associations, and the farmer press.[91] "Heretofore ignored or held in disdain by the city woman," Henderson wrote, the farm woman "bids fair to lead and teach the latter in the more fundamental principles of politics, economics and education." Farm women "have taken a long step in advance of the city women. Inarticulate although most of them are, their organizations are growing by leaps and bounds in every province and their influence is being felt as a power to be reckoned with."[92] Not to claim that Henderson did not mean everything she said, but the argument had few precedents in her writings, and hereafter she devoted little attention to rural issues or rural women.

Her brief focus on farm and working-class women speaks to the fact that she tended to be influenced by where she was and by the nature of her audience. Her position appears to suggest that in the mid-1920s her critique of capitalism flowed from gender, not class. Capitalist civilization (in other contexts, she suggested that this concept itself was a contradiction) had "failed because of its own inherent contradictions." It had failed because man "cannot hope to be free nor intelligent while woman remains backward and in subjection." While any number of influences may have been behind her statement, it certainly evoked utopian socialist Charles Fourier's claim that "the extension of women's privileges is the general principle for all social progress," and Karl Marx's observation that everyone "who knows anything of history knows that great social revolutions are impossible without the feminine ferment."[93] Henderson added: "In our plans for the betterment of the working class, let us hold in mind the place and power of unfettered woman, and not the timid, mental cripple that slave societies have produced."[94]

In "Woman and Marriage," Henderson spoke of "the girl of the new day." Young girls had "gone out to work and have found themselves quite able to do the work and to take care of themselves, consequently their whole outlook and attitude on life and to the family is changed." The "girl of today is content to be neither doll, dunce nor drudge"; she "reads and reasons for herself." Marriage "means giving up her freedom"; for the working class wife, motherhood is "often a sorrow if not a curse." Henderson was not guilty of a blind idealization of motherhood and marriage, being fully cognizant of the fact that the working-class reality of motherhood was much bleaker than even her own middle-class idealism would suggest. She argued that the "greed of competition has entered the home and commercial greed, grasping for cheap labor, has broken woman's chains and set her thinking."[95] Not only did Henderson recognize the oppressive impact of the intertwined hierarchies of gender and class power on working-class women; she also realized that if working-class women could see through that alliance, the outcome was potentially revolutionary in its implications.

Yet her optimism concerning "the girl of the new day" was not warranted by the actual situation of post–First World War Canadian women. As Veronica Strong-Boag points out, neither the feminists' "bold predictions of social justice and a fair deal for all" or the anti-feminists "dire forecasts of social breakdown and a world turned topsy-turvy" came to fruition in the 1920s and 1930s.[96] There was "no great discontinuity with the past," and a break with the past was central to Henderson's vision of the postwar world.[97] Her undoubted abilities as a social commentator and critic of the world around her were aided, and at the same time distorted, by her fervent belief that the world was moving in the direction that she wanted it to move. A later, much more cynical world may stand in awe of her passion and fervent desire, but shakes a collective head at her inability to fully come to grips with a world so capable of, and intent on, crushing her most cherished ideals.

In "Woman's Traducers," one of her more widely reprinted articles, Henderson decried "the diabolical gospel of woman's sin and inferiority" that had been preached for centuries, adding that it "has not only cursed and crushed the woman, but has crushed the race through making of her offspring not men and women, but warped imitations of what they should be." She included Martin Luther, whom she quoted, among "the wise-acres of the past, who were intolerant of any idea of women's equality, her right to political or economic emancipation, or her protection as wife and mother."[98] In the final analysis, she continued to look to women, not men, for the solution to the problem. In her last article in the series, "A Real Henry Dubb," she recounted a conversation with a worker who told her that the labour papers did not need a woman's page: "I gasped, for a moment, but as I looked into his honest face and earnest appeal, I realized he was mouthing his masters' philosophy and didn't know it." Rather than launching into a tirade about the ignorance of men, she concluded that there were "Sister Dubbs who likewise block the road to freedom."[99] In the mid-1920s she continued to evince that compelling ability to look beyond "human nature," beyond heredity, beyond the gender stereotypes of her day to ask why working people believed the things they did. For her, men blaming women or women blaming men was not the answer. The answer was understanding why people believed what they believed, and who it was that wanted them to believe these things.

The historian must resist the temptation to come to the conclusion that in the mid-1920s Henderson abandoned her broad-based critique of hier-archies of power for an argument that gender was more important than class or race. She wrote her series of articles for the *Canadian Farmer-Labor Advocate* at a particular moment for a particular purpose, and it must be understood in the broader context of her political thought in the 1920s. It remained the case that she retained her marvellous ability to critique all forms of oppression and to advance the commonalities of struggle.

According to Henderson, not just men and women but farmers and workers as well needed to be working together. On Saturday, 19 September 1925, she was nominated as the Labor Party candidate in the riding of New Westminster, British Columbia, and she set out her campaign ideas in an article entitled "Immediate Requirements: Farmers and Workers Must Unite against Oppressors." Her focus on farmers at least in part de-rived from the mixed rural and urban character of the New Westminster riding. She had clearly been reading up on farm exports and demonstrated a knowledge of Canada, England, Denmark, and Australia. Anticipating

many of the major reforms of the future, she called for the creation of a
National Bank, insurance against crop failure, and health services "at the
lowest possible fee." She suggested the need for Canada to regain control
of its own finances from American domination; Canada could not pay off
its national debt because it was busily paying off the interest on it. Something
must also be done about the "menace of unemployment." The "tragedy" of
the returned soldier "calls for an investigation of the whole system of pensions and land settlement." She argued that the $100,000 being spent on
cadet training might be better spent on old age pensions and subsidies to
dependent mothers. She ended by noting that Agnes Macphail was elected
by the farmers of Ontario in the 1921 federal election and suggesting that
the farmers of British Columbia "show themselves as wise in their day."[100]

Henderson's election pamphlet began with a message to the electors of
New Westminster, in which she called for farmers and workers to "stand
unitedly together" to "blaze a new trail towards a saner form of government and better conditions for all." She noted that in her "17 years of
public national service" she had fought "for the rights of the people first."
Her message was followed by a section called "DO YOU KNOW," in which
her use of satire is striking. For example, she asked, "Do you know that
Premier Mackenzie King says that the Hon. Arthur Meighen is not fit to
govern, and Would-be Premier Meighen says that Mackenzie King is not
fit to govern. They are both right." Moreover, "the Liberals and Conservatives
have been spending $3,000,000 a year on Marine and Fisheries, and less
than one million a year to protect the people's health. It is safer to be a
Canadian Fish than a Canadian Citizen."[101]

Humour, sincerity, and innovative ideas were not enough to win the
election, although she polled a respectable 3,315 votes, 22.4 per cent of
the total. Her percentage of the total vote was highest amongst the BC
labour candidates: Wallis Lefeaux polled 10 per cent of the vote in
Vancouver Centre; John Sidaway polled 11.9 per cent in Vancouver-
Burrard; Alf Hurry took 17.9 per cent in Vancouver South; and W.J.
Curry polled 18.5 per cent (incomplete) in North Vancouver. Given that
all the other Labour candidates were male and well-known figures on the
British Columbia left, Henderson's showing as an Eastern Canadian
woman is a remarkable accomplishment.[102]

Following her election defeat in New Westminster, she returned to
Montreal, where she once again became active in Jewish circles. On

Thursday, 18 March 1926, along with former Montreal mayor Médéric
Martin and several city aldermen, she addressed the Second Annual Civic
Night of the Dufferin Educational Society at the Commercial High
School on Sherbrooke Street West.[103] A number of resolutions were
passed and forwarded to the executive of the city council. These resolutions called for votes for women in municipal elections and the right to
hold municipal office; improvements to Mount Royal Park and open air
bathing for children; creation of a domestic night court; a town planning
programmer for the city of Montreal; free milk stations for the poor; better city administration; identification of voters at elections; and the addition of Jewish books to city libraries. Henderson "successfully upheld"
the resolution on votes for women in municipal elections proposed by
Sarah Miller.[104]

In the spring of 1926 Henderson began one of her more obscure yet
intriguing involvements, with the Society for Cultural Relations between
the Peoples of the Dominion of Canada and the Union of Soviet Socialist
Republics. A clue regarding her reasons for becoming involved in the
organization may be found in the 27 March 1926 issue of *Labor World*,
which contained her article entitled "Impressions of Count Ilda Tolstoy's
Address on Russia." Tolstoy, the son of Leo Tolstoy, spoke in Montreal on
Monday, 22 March 1926. According to Henderson, his talk was attended
by an "audience of women" expecting to hear about the life and literature
of his father, but instead they were treated to "a tirade against the present
Bolshevist regime." She criticized Tolstoy's claim that Bolshevism was
doomed, saying that Soviet trade with the outside world was increasing
each year and that there was "a good deal of life in the Bolshevist corpse."
Tolstoy attacked the Bolsheviks but "not once did he speak of the robbery,
the cruelty, the tortures and oppression under the Czars regime, or its responsibility for the revolution." Henderson concluded: "Count Tolstoy's
message is belated, prejudiced, and not calculated to foster good will, peace,
and justice between nations. The principles for which his father stood, and
would no doubt if living today, champion the fight of the Russian people for
their emancipation from the horrors of the Czars regime."[105]

If her response to Tolstoy's speech is any indication, at this time
Henderson was looking for a way to improve relations between Canada and
the Soviet Union and to continue the defence of Lenin and the Bolsheviks
she took up following her return from the Soviet Union. By all

appearances, the Society for Cultural Relations was a rather strange choice for doing that. The man behind the society appears to have been one Colonel H.J. Mackie, who was working in Moscow as a contact for Canadian business organizations and working through the USSR Society for Cultural Relations with Foreign Countries (VOKS). Mackie corresponded regularly with Madame Kameneva, president of VOKS, and her general secretary, F.V. Linde.[106] According to J.L. Black, Mackie founded the Society for Cultural Relations in Toronto in 1926, but Henderson's correspondence suggests that the original local may have been in Montreal, the offices located at 375 St Catherine Street West. The society's first general meeting was on Thursday, 1 April 1926, at Montreal's Ritz-Carleton Hotel.[107] On 3 May 1926 Henderson wrote to Madame Kameneva: "Just a word of greeting from the S.C.R. and to say we have had our first public meeting and that it was counted a great success. I hope by next autumn to have a strong organization, and to be able not only to break down much prejudice but to be able to make vital contacts between organizations in Canada and Soviet Russia."[108]

Henderson delved into her work as the society's secretary with her usual zeal. On 2 June 1926 she wrote to Madame Kameneva, telling her that she had sent reports of the school systems in various Canadian provinces, "which I hope will be of service to you in getting a report for the Educational Conference in Paris this sumer [sic] of which you have written."[109] The reports contained information about dropout rates, cost per student, teacher training, salaries, Catholic and public schools, numbers of students, and curriculum in the education systems of Ontario, Quebec, Manitoba, and British Columbia.[110]

One of Henderson's tasks as secretary was to provide letters of introduction to Canadians visiting the Soviet Union. On 29 April 1926 acting president Thomas Parsons wrote to Madame Kameneva, introducing Mr and Mrs Mac Williams of Winnipeg, "who are visiting Soviet Russia in the interest of education and general social conditions." Mrs Williams was identified as "the first and only woman member of the Council of the University of Manitoba and also President of the University Women's Club." The letter was also signed by Henderson.[111] In the fall of 1926 Parsons sent a letter of introduction to Madame Kameneva for Dr Jack Byers, a Western Canadian "veterinary expert" who was visiting the Soviet Union and was "desirous of studying recent progress in his profession." The letter was again signed by Henderson.[112]

We are only dealing here with two letters of introduction, but they take us back to a time when even non-communist Canadians considered the Soviet Union a source of new ideas and a country that Canadians could learn from. A letter Henderson wrote to Madame Kameneva, likely in late October or early November 1926, also evoked this relationship:

> In order to further the work of our Society we are wondering whether it would be possible to borrow a few representative posters dealing with hygiene, child culture, agricultural, and other topics in order to form the basis of an exhibition which we hope to hold this winter. We should be also very glad of any suggestions you could make, whereby we could get in touch with typical novels, dramas, musical compositions by post-revolutionary writers and artists. Would you also through your department take all possible steps to let us know as soon in advance as possible when any authors, professors, lecturers, musicians, artists, or technical experts are visiting this side of the Atlantic, in order that we may extend to them our hospitality, and give them an opportunity of telling us of advances in their special line in the U.S.S.R.[113]

A response was sent on 27 November 1926 by S. Trevos, the Anglo-American reference correspondent, and I. Korinetz, general secretary of VOKS. They told Henderson that posters and books were being collected, as well as novels, dramas, and musical compositions by post-revolutionary writers and artists. They wanted to know how big the exhibition would be and if it would be open to the public.[114] A letter of 14 December 1926 stated that VOKS was proposing to send nine hundred to a thousand books, as well as novels, musical pieces, and posters. The letter indicated that Henderson had not replied to the letter of 27 November and that VOKS was waiting to hear from her before proceeding.[115]

Following the correspondence of 1926, the records become rather silent about Henderson's involvement with the society. Whatever the reason, her involvement lagged, and the reports of the Anglo-American Section indicated displeasure with her lack of involvement. The report for 1930 indicated that she was still involved in some capacity, because the report written by the secretary of the Anglo-American Section, I. Amdur, revealed that Henderson had written a letter of introduction for Berta

Hamilton, who was to visit "social institutions" in the Soviet Union. Amdur was clearly frustrated with Henderson, calling her "the one-time Secretary of the one-time Canadian SCR."[116]

The December 1930 report of the British Society for Cultural Relations contained a section on Colonel Mackie, described as the chairman of the Canadian section "when our Society in Canada existed." At this point Mackie himself was claiming that the SCR in Canada still existed. He noted that Henderson was still "in touch with it." The demise of the SCR may, as the report suggests, be a function of the fact that Mackie was paying many of the expenses, including Henderson's salary, and may have come to the conclusion that the advantages did not justify the cost. Amdur, on the other hand, was of the opinion that the Canadian SCR no longer existed.[117]

In the late fall of 1926 Henderson began a series of articles that appeared on a regular basis in the *One Big Union Bulletin*, a commitment indicating she was even then far from concentrating full time on the SCR. Initially, the *Bulletin* serialized her pamphlet "Woman and War," beginning on 4 November and ending on 2 December (discussed in some detail in the next chapter). The serialization was immediately followed by a series of articles beginning on 9 December 1926 and ending on 2 June 1927. This series is the most complete she ever published, and one of the reasons behind its extensiveness is most certainly the fact that the *Bulletin* was able to pay her relatively well.[118]

The series began with a Rose Henderson classic entitled "Woman, the Backbone of Capitalism," and ended with an enquiry into the state of Canadian womanhood entitled "What's the Matter with Us?" In the former, she was at her dialectical best, declaring that "just as woman is today the very buttress upon which the whole system of exploitation is nourished and maintained, so tomorrow she must constitute the foundation upon which the new social order will rest."[119] Her idealism notwithstanding, the latter article despaired of the fact that nine years after the end of the First World War, Canadian women "have not as yet awakened to the danger of another world war." Comparing Canadian women unfavourably to women not just in Europe, the United States, and Australia, but also in India, China and Japan, Henderson predicted that unless they awakened to the impending danger, "ere long a great sorrow will wring their hearts."[120] As she did in her days in Montreal on the topic of the great strides in dealing with juvenile delinquency taking place in other countries, she attempted to shame Canadian women into action by bringing them face to face with what she considered the greater richness of women's activism in other countries.

In her articles on young people, she evinced both great concern for youth and a tremendous sympathy that blamed their rebellion on their elders. Young people were right to question authority, because their elders had broken faith with them and left a legacy of debt, poverty, disease, and national hatred. She viewed the revolt of youth as "a healthy rather than an unhealthy sign of the great changes taking place."[121] Likewise the modern girl was "a product of the times in which she lives, moves, and has her being." She "has learned that she is not inferior to the male" and that she "can be self-supporting, and as efficient, provided she gets the same opportunity as her boy companions." Alive to the hypocrisy she had inherited from the Victorian Age, the modern girl dared to "kick holes in the paper partition between what is termed 'moral' and 'immoral,' 'good' and 'bad.'" The modern girl, Henderson concluded, "is with us to stay."[122]

In this series Henderson continued to evince her marvellous ability to link women and the labour movement, gender, and class. She concluded her piece on the modern girl: "Life for the modern girl is a revolutionary period of transformation from an old to a new and a better civilization. Herein lies a mighty force for the Labor movement, if only labor wakes up."[123]

Labour men must realize that they needed to fully incorporate women into the labour movement, because by doing so they would create a power that would overturn the capitalist system and allow women to be mothers in the truest sense. Henderson evoked her vision: "Man's world is shrinking, while woman's world is enlarging, as a result of capitalism. There is no use telling her to go back to her home – this also is changed and broken up through Capitalism. When she returns, it will be to a different home, on a different status, on terms of an equal partnership, not as an inferior and a drudge. She will be mother, wife, teacher, and companion in the truest sense of these terms."[124] Here again Henderson demonstrated her powers as a dialectical thinker, recognizing – perhaps consciously, perhaps not – the core of Marx's argument that the creation of a socialist society involved both the realization and the destruction of capitalism. In her vision of women's future, she evoked Marx's insight, melding the

gender and class components of her world view in a way that has few
equals in Canadian history.

The impression that Henderson's focus at this time was not on the
SCR is further confirmed by her letter in May 1927, two weeks before
her series of articles ended in the *OBU Bulletin*, to Violet McNaughton,
editor of the "Mainly for Women" page of the *Western Producer* since
1925.[125] Henderson stated that she would be free to take on speaking
engagements beginning in September through to the spring of 1928 to
farm women and youth and in churches. She also offered to write a series
of articles for the *Western Producer* "at the usual rates that you pay your
writers."[126] Notwithstanding the fact that the letter was sent from the
SCR's Montreal offices at 375 St Catherine Street West, Henderson's wish
to be paid for her articles suggests that whatever she was being paid by
Colonel Mackie as SCR secretary was not enough to live on. In the event,
she did not end up writing articles for the *Western Producer*.

In the period 1927–29 little evidence of Henderson's activities and
movements has been uncovered. We do know that she returned to Great
Britain, from where she wrote a series of articles for the *Canadian Unionist*,
the paper of the All-Canadian Congress of Labour, between August 1928
and February 1929. In her continuing assessment of the British Labour
Party, she revealingly spent much of her time praising Keir Hardie, arguing that if he were alive he "would bitterly denounce much of what passes
to-day for labour policy and politics." As in the past, she saw both reason
for despair and reason for optimism concerning the party, and left open
the party's trajectory for the future to decide.[127] She was inspired by the
socialist summer schools being conducted by the Independent Labor
Party, seeing them as a factor in the British working class "growing more
intelligent and more restive." She concluded, as she had so often done in
the past, by attempting to goad Canadian labour into action, asking when
would it "try out this splendid means of educating the workers?"[128]

In Great Britain, she spent time in Wales, where she helped to feed and
clothe destitute miners and their families. In her explanation of the situation of the Welsh miners, she demonstrated keen insight into their
plight, caused by a combination of the flooding of British markets in
Europe with the cheap German coal demanded as part of the country's
war debt, and the failure of British mine owners to keep up with
changing technology. Henderson decried the apathy of the British public

and the in-fighting in a Labour Party that was too consumed by attempts to oust Communist Party members to respond effectively to the dire needs of the Welsh miners. Her solutions were radical, including nationalization of the mines and the redistribution to the homeless of lands held by the gentry and aristocracy.[129]

Not surprisingly, she asserted that, as hard as the lot of the Welsh miner was, "the life of the miner's wife is harder still." She described their condition as "appalling" and said she scarcely knew how to convey the "conditions and scenes" she witnessed in the Rhondda Valley. The suffering of the women "could be described only by a Hugo or a Jack London." Then, turning as she often did to youth, she decried their "mental, physical and spiritual decay." "I have seen," she related, "strong youths weep and heard bitter youths curse the day they were born." The culprit was the capitalist system, "grinding and crushing all that is best in a noble race."[130] The solution was for the men and women of the working class who had helped to build this system to take up the task of ending it.

There is, as Susan Mann Trofimenkoff points out, a temptation to identify activist women of Henderson's generation with "flightiness."[131] Henderson did not have a "single direction" in her life, and it is true that she was involved "in hundreds of things at the same time."[132] Her desire to evade orthodoxies and to maintain her personal integrity is laudatory, but it means that she refused to make the kind of accommodations necessary to leave the legacy of Communist Party leader Tim Buck, or Trades and Labor Congress president Tom Moore, or social democratic leader J.S. Woodsworth. That identification with one party, or movement, or ideological tendency has escaped Henderson, and her legacy has suffered for it.

The inchoate nature of her organizational life was paralleled by her broad-based social analysis that sought to tear down all the major hierarchies of power that controlled the capitalist society in which she lived. She sought to defend all oppressed peoples, but in any given situation, ethnicity appeared more important than gender, class appeared more important than ethnicity, and gender at times appeared more significant than either. Given her approach, the easy response is to condemn her inconsistencies and contradictions, to dismiss her as a confused thinker who too often allowed sentiment and bias to override the "scientific" approach that she always claimed for her work.

But the great weakness of Henderson's approach was also its great strength. She defended the oppressed because they were oppressed; she did not need to think about identity, or whether class was more important than gender, or vice versa. Distinguishing the women, children, and poor of Germany from the war machine of the German leadership and the aims and activities of the country's capitalists came easily to her. In a defence of "women," she had no difficulty condemning bourgeois women who lived off the avails of capitalism. In a defence of "workers," she had no qualms about attacking trade union leaders who sold out the rank and file of the labour movement and legitimated the capitalist hierarchy of power.

Henderson was as broad-minded as any socialist or feminist of her day, and that broad-mindedness led her to make glaring mistakes in contradiction of her own socialist and feminist principles. It also led to marvellous insights and analysis, and to a striking ability to see the cause of the downtrodden of the world in a single, vivid picture. Few Canadians of her generation so insistently, so insightfully, and so intelligently laid bare the contradictions of patriarchy and the capitalist system, and so consistently united working class men, working-class women, and their middle-class allies in the common cause of creating a future without poverty, prejudice, and war.

6

War and Peace

War and peace were the themes within which Rose Henderson advanced her ideas concerning women, children, and the working class in the decade following the First World War. War was capitalism's evil offspring and the inevitable outcome of a male-dominated world. Peace would come when the immorality of militarism was replaced by the morality of international motherhood. Of necessity, peace required a change in the thoughts and actions of men in the world, just as suffragists had argued that votes for women required a change in the outlook of the men who controlled the Canadian political system. As Carol Bacchi points out, suffragists "had hopes of reforming the entire male population. The purity issue aroused them to display a certain degree of sex antagonism, uniting them in a sisterhood of sorts against men."[1]

Henderson was in, but not entirely of, this sisterhood. In 1914 she was elected vice-president of the Canadian Suffrage Association (CSA) for the province of Quebec.[2] The CSA was created in 1906 by Augusta Stowe Gullen, daughter of Dr Emily Stowe, out of the awkwardly named Dominion Women's Enfranchisement Association. Stowe Gullen enlisted the support of Flora Macdonald Denison and Margaret Gordon, who comprised a "feminist" leadership of "outspoken defenders of women's rights."[3] Henderson was part of this sisterhood, and she was a defender of women's rights, but caution must be exercised in arguing that she was antagonistic to men in the First World War period. As we have observed, she was attempting to enlist the support of male trade unionists, not antagonize them. In her September 1912 speech to the Trades and Labor Congress convention, she told the assembled delegates that women "want the ballot to help you to deal with the child problem" – not because it would signal the realization of women's equality in the public realm.

Indeed, if any aspect of Henderson's thought stood out as suffragist, it was that women themselves were responsible for winning the vote, and that male politicians, once confronted, would step aside and allow women to enter the political realm. In her September 1918 article in the *BC Federationist* entitled "Woman and the War," she commented on women achieving the vote in federal elections, noting that only a small minority of women actually fought for it. She observed of the women who fought for the ballot that "the masses of women at no time, and at no place, were with them, so that it would be wrong to conclude that woman's political emancipation came about solely through their own efforts and desire for freedom." But the war was changing all this. Women had been wrenched from the home and ensconced in the factory. They "developed a strong sense of independence" and cast aside every "moral restriction, convention and ordinary safeguard." Women now had a "right to their own lives, and to come and go as they please."[4] The question was whether or not the mass of women would take advantage of this new-found freedom and, by implication, how men would respond to it.

Henderson's positing of the liberation of women was juxtaposed by a determinism that appeared to counter her emphasis on agency. Women were awakening and becoming more politically active, but they had been "thrown" into politics. They remained the "weak link in the industrial chain, the mill stone which will not allow labor to rise." Women would be impelled by the "moral force lying dormant" within them to become activists. This moral force would be of particular importance in the peace movement; because women, as mothers of the race, had a compelling reason to end all wars.[5] Like the Marxian socialists of her generation, Henderson could not allow herself to believe that women, like the working class, would fail to act on the knowledge of their "historic mission" to end war and bring peace.

The onus remained on women, as it had when suffrage was the issue, but the carnage of the First World War and a passionate desire that such a war never happen again caused a subtle but significant shift in Henderson's thinking. Far more was at stake when the issue was ending war than when the issue was votes for women. The arrogance, stupidity, and inhumanity of men was much more in evidence in a world that day after day revealed how little had been learned in the "war to end all wars." In the 1920s Henderson did not make peace her only campaign, just as she had not made suffrage her only campaign during the First World War. It is true, however, that this campaign revealed a passionate and visceral animus to a male-dominated world that had rarely surfaced in her earlier activism.

By the mid-1920s her deep and abiding commitment to ending war led her to support the Women's Peace Union (WPU), described by Frances Early as a "separatist absolute pacifist group" that was much smaller and less influential than the Women's International League for Peace and Freedom.[6] The Canadian-founded, American-based WPU espoused non-resistance, made universal disarmament its one issue, and opposed the League of Nations. Harriet Hyman Alonzo, historian of the WPU, points out the organization's "refusal to address women's issues."[7] Given Henderson's long history of involvement with women's issues, especially related to child welfare, mother's pensions, and the labour movement, her involvement with the WPU appears to suggest a quixotic turn away from her dedication to the cause of women and children in the pursuit of absolute pacifism.

The appearance disguises a different reality. Putting through an amendment to the American Constitution outlawing war involved an interesting melding of the principled and the pragmatic that characterized feminist pacifists of Henderson's generation. Like Carrie Chapman Catt, Henderson faced the dilemma of "the reconciliation of her intense idealism with an overwhelming pragmatism."[8] Her involvement with the WPU suggests that rather than identifying the organization as being on the "left" of the peace movement, it is more fruitful to understand absolute pacifism as one of a number of feminist pacifist attempts in the 1920s and 1930s to meld idealism and day-to-day activism. Henderson was quite conscious of the relationship, wondering if "the new age now winging its way into the minds and souls of mankind the world over" would come about through a moral force transformation, or through women demonstrating "a genius for reforms and legislation tending toward human betterment."[9] Harriet Alonzo has brilliantly looked beyond the apparent contradiction by observing that Henderson and other absolute pacifists were pursuing "the utopian end of the possible."[10]

Henderson's involvement with the WPU was preceded by her early peace activism with the Women's International League for Peace and

Freedom (WILPF).[11] The WILPF developed out of the Women's Peace Party (WPP) organized by Jane Addams and other feminist pacifists in January 1915. The official position of the WPP was not to commit or condone violence even in self-defence.[12] The American entry into the First World War created a crisis in the party, and its membership had declined from 25,000 to one hundred by the time the party re-formed in 1919 as the United States Section of the Women's International League for Peace and Freedom.[13] Although divisions existed within the WILPF, in general its members were more supportive of "virtuous wars" than were members of the Women's Peace Party. The WILPF was not a single-issue organization, engaging as it did in a number of causes, including the abolition of cadet training and opposition to militarism in school textbooks.

In Canada, Laura Hughes, Elsie Charlton, and Alice Chown were founding members of the Women's Peace Party.[14] Chown, best known for her autobiographical work *The Stairway*, echoed Henderson's thinking when she said that non-resistance "is only possible to men and women whose faith in this being a spiritual universe is strong," and that pacifists "have glimpsed the coming world ideal."[15] There are powerful echoes here of Henderson's description in her September 1918 article of the "new humanity" and the "new age" she believed would emerge from the First World War. As a socialist she placed greater emphasis on the economic causes of war than many feminist pacifists, but she shared the "unshakeable cosmic optimism" of liberal feminists and supporters of "virtuous wars" like Chapman Catt.[16]

Even before its transition to the WILPF, the WPP had suffered a serious blow. On 12 September 1918 Elinor Byrns, Caroline Lexow Babcock, Katherine Devereaux Blake, and Fanny Garrison Villard had resigned from the New York branch of the WPP and organized the Women's Peace Society (WPS). Byrns and Babcock would be the key organizers of the WPU in 1921.[17]

The founding of the WPU was a joint American and Canadian venture. While Linda Schott attributes the idea to Byrns and Babcock,[18] Harriet Alonso reveals that it was Christine Ross Barker, a Canadian member of the WILPF, who in June 1921 initiated the holding of a general conference in Niagara Falls, Ontario.[19] Out of the conference, held 19–21 August 1921 with Byrns as chair, came the Women's Peace Union of the Western Hemisphere which, as the name suggests, hoped to unite the non-resisters of the United States, Canada, and Latin America.[20]

Henderson had begun her involvement with the WILPF prior to the organization of the WPU. In the fall of 1916 Harriet Prenter reported to WILPF headquarters that Henderson had "fifty women ready to join a group" in Montreal.[21] The chairperson of the WILPF in Canada, Laura Hughes Lunde, had written to Emily Greene Balch from Chicago on 7 November 1919: "I talked over the whole proposition with Mrs. Rose Henderson of Montreal, Ass. Judge in the Juvenile Court there, a very sane & well balanced woman & one whom the workers love & trust. She said she thot [sic] for the present it would be better to try & get Canadian members for the English Ass. until we had enough women to get an organization that would count & be able to do active work. And she knows Canada as well as any woman there."[22]

No evidence has surfaced to suggest that Henderson, although an idealist and supporter of non-resistance, ever organized a branch of the WILPF in Montreal in either 1916 or 1919–20. Her willingness to do so may have been affected by the state of disarray of the Canadian wing, apart from the fact that she was isolated to some extent by being in French Canada. Laura Hughes Lunde's letter indicates that there were serious problems in the WILPF's Ontario wing. She made no secret of her feelings about Prenter, commenting that she "has gotten such a reputation for being under hand etc. that no one will join anything she is in. I was warned long ago to keep away from her."[23] Barbara Roberts suggests that Prenter may have attempted to subvert a radical study group that Hughes Lunde was organizing during the war.[24] Linda Kealey suggests that Hughes Lunde and Prenter were engaged in "an intense rivalry over leadership of the Toronto women's peace group."[25]

The conflict notwithstanding, both women appear to have been in agreement on the importance of enlisting Rose Henderson. By 1920, with Hughes Lunde now based in Chicago, Prenter took the lead in pursuing her. Writing to Balch on 13 January 1920, Prenter reported on the election in Ontario of a farmer-labour government, and the trial in Winnipeg of those "magnificent men" charged with seditious conspiracy.[26] She continued, "We are enlisting the support and sympathy of many members of our 'Independent Labor Party' in the W.I.L. work. We invited some of the leaders to bring their wives to a meeting last week

– we had some twenty five or more, and it is beginning [sic] of a big work among the different Labor groups in this city ... I have the promise of Mrs. Rose Henderson of Montreal that she will <u>at once</u> form a group in that big city – it will be a larger group than Toronto, and in Winnipeg we will have another headed by the splendid wife of one of the strike leaders, F. J. Dixon – he is member of Parliament for centre Winnipeg."[27] Balch wrote to Hughes Lunde that she had received two letters from Prenter that led her to conclude "that things seem decidedly looking up and that Miss Rose Henderson seems to be cooperating."[28]

Henderson may not have succeeded in organizing a functioning local of the WILPF in Montreal, but she spoke on behalf of the organization in Ontario. Prenter's January 1920 letter to Balch had described the increasing cooperation that was taking place in Ontario between the Independent Labor Party and the WILPF. We have also already noted Thomas Socknat's point that Henderson and Prenter were part of a developing alignment of pacifists and the political left.[29] In the fall of 1921 Prenter was a member of the ILP's Literature Committee, directed by Andrew Glen and his wife, Dorothy.[30] The series of six lectures that Henderson gave in Toronto in early 1922 under the auspices of the WILPF and the ILP provides further evidence of the relationship.

The left-wing political scene in Toronto changed dramatically with the organization of the Workers' Party while Henderson was in the city. The Workers' Party, the "open, legal arm" of the Communist Party, met in convention 16–22 February 1922.[31] Henderson does not appear to have commented on its formation, although it may have had an impact on her thinking about the WPU and the WILPF, but Prenter's opinions may provide a window on Henderson's ideas.

On 24 March 1922 Prenter wrote to Balch, commenting on the WPU, the WILPF, and the formation of the Workers' Party: "I did not join the Peace Union, when we met at Niagara Falls last year, it is impossible for <u>me</u> to refuse to help <u>any</u> war, I will of course refuse <u>all aid</u> to any Capitalist war, but one is too good an economist (though not so wonderful, at that) to ever dare to take such a pledge. Besides, I am deep in the Labor Movement, as member of "The Workers' Party of Canada" – a Communist, to the horror even of some of the w.i.l. group, and it was tragic to me, to see and hear those delightful women, at the Falls, passing their resolutions, and, apparently unconscious, that <u>they</u> – as a class – <u>mattered not</u>

at <u>all</u>, or at least very slightly, and how they calmly ignored the great underlying – economic – reasons for <u>all</u> wars!!"[32]

In the absence of a verbatim account of the Niagara Falls conference, it is difficult to test the validity of Prenter's argument that the WPU overlooked the importance of class and economics in relation to war, but it is certainly open to question. It must be remembered that Byrns, who chaired the Niagara Falls meeting, was more concerned with the economic causes of war than were many American feminist pacifists. For Prenter, as a newly minted communist, however, that level of concern was not enough – and it may not have been enough for Henderson. Given the absence of evidence that she was involved in the WPU in the early 1920s, and the fact that she spent much of the period outside North America, ideas about her opinions must remain speculative. But we can say that she was not yet ready to embrace absolute pacifism.

She made the transition to supporting the absolute pacifist position of the WPU in the same period in which her trip to the Soviet Union produced some of her most pro-socialist, anti-capitalist rhetoric and positions. It is a challenge to understand how she transferred her thinking about revolution and the working class to her thinking about women and peace. What links the two aspects of her politics is the centrality of agency and education, and in particular the need for a mental revolution. Women and workers both had to undergo this revolutionary transformation, and when they did, capitalism would be overthrown, war ended, and the new age of peace established. Her thinking was idealist, indeed millennial, although the heaven she envisioned was a heaven on earth. Like liberal feminist pacifists, she believed in a moral force guiding human destiny, a belief that rubbed shoulders with, but never quite embraced, the class struggle element of her politics.

It was in the mid-1920s that Henderson's critique of war and advocacy of peace became most pronounced. The 20 February 1925 issue of the *BC Federationist* contained an ad for her pamphlet "Woman and War," which had "just recently been printed" by the Federated Labor Party.[33] The pamphlet was based on her series "Woman and the Game of War" currently being run in the *Federationist*. It would be republished under the pamphlet title "Woman and War" in the OBU *Bulletin* in 1926. The name change is intriguing, but it is not clear if Henderson or the editor of the *Federationist* made the change, or indeed what it signified.

In "Woman and the Game of War" we get Henderson's ongoing setting of responsibility on the women of the world. She argued that soldiers should "demand that the women of the world search out the causes of war, where the germs of war are hatched and nurtured, and having found the source of the disease, join with the mothers of every land to wipe from the face of the earth war – the senseless, loathsome, diabolical game of war."[34] Eradicating war must be done every bit as thoroughly as eradicating disease. And if there was no room for half measures in fighting disease, there could be no room for half measures in the peace movement.

The instalment published on 27 February 1925 in the *Federationist* reveals that Henderson was studying in some detail the most recent developments in military weaponry. She was well versed in the development of chemical weapons and germ warfare. She was reading the *Army and Navy Gazette*, and employing information generated by the United States Chemical Warfare Service. She noted: "All governments are spending huge sums experimenting in laboratories with a view to making poison gas, lethal acids, high explosives, more deadly, to be dropped on innocent defenseless women and children from dragons of death, poluting [sic] the sky as their murderous bodies glide through the air."[35] With images that remind us of Guernica and Hiroshima, her powerful evocation of the brutality of modern war makes us wary of too lightly dismissing her as a naïve dreamer. There is an eyes-wide-open engagement with the politics of power here that must be made part of the totality of her critique of capitalism, war, and the arrogance of men.

It is in this context that we must understand her shift from the WILPF to the WPU. Her reasoning is set out quite clearly at the beginning of "Woman and War": "So far, peace societies have dealt with the problem of making an end of war from the sentimental point of view. They have attempted to tame the beast of militarism with honeyed words – approaching it in a 'diplomatic way' – courting the approval of 'leading citizens' and being scrupulously careful not to 'antagonize' and always loudly proclaiming their loyalty to the 'Empire,' the 'Republic,' or whatever form of government prevails in the country they live."[36] We must ask if Henderson, in this critique of the WILPF, had herself let go of the "sentimental point of view." Even if we acknowledge that "sentimental" and "moral" are related but different, we must question her belief that militarism would be checked by a "moral force," that moral force being a

"league of mothers."[37] We can agree with her that mothers, unlike nations, know no bounds; a league of mothers is possible where a league of
nations is not. But she leaves us with little sense of how this league would
come into being, let alone accomplish its goal of ending war.

In September 1925 Henderson united her two great passions, women
and peace. In the pages of the *Canadian Labor Advocate* she commented on
the number of peace conferences being held around this time, pointing
out that these "Peace Conferences" might better be called "Conferences to
Ensure War." Charging that women hitherto had "had no say as to peace
or future wars," she rose to rhetorical heights unusual even for her: "Their
tears, and the blood of their sons have washed away the foundations of
civilization as we used to know it seven years ago. Tear stained, blood
dripping, a charred and blackened Mars, a civilization unfitted to survive
by weight of its injustice and corruption is now whirling to its doom, and
out of its ashes is arising a new idealism and power which will lay the first
solid foundation for peace and international good will."[38] It is as if she
believed that the mere recognition of the importance of women would
bring an end to war, commenting: "There can be no peace until the oneness of humanity is recognized." She ended on an optimistic note, saying
that "women the world over are taking matters in their own hands and
are beginning to march forward in an effort to conquer the forces of dark-
ness now ruling and destroying mankind."[39]

Given her idealism, it is not surprising that she found the largest and
most influential women's peace organization, the WILPF, to be lacking.
By 1926 she had become a supporter, if not an actual member, of the
WPU. In June 1921 Christine Ross Barker, in the context of suggesting
the general conference in Niagara Falls that led to the WPU's creation, had
held up the peaceful relationship between Canada and the United States
as a model for the new organization.[40] This was important, because it
served as the justification of the WPU's single cause in the late 1920s and
1930s, a constitutional amendment outlawing war. The amendment,
written by Byrns and Babcock in 1923, was introduced in Congress every
year from 1926 to 1939.[41] The sponsor of the amendment was Lynn
Joseph Frazier, a Republican senator from North Dakota,[42] who first
introduced the amendment on 23 April 1926.[43]

It is at this point that Henderson became more actively involved in
the activities of the WPU. On 6 March 1926 Babcock wrote asking her to

be a Canadian representative on the WPU's International Advisory Committee.[44] Babcock wrote again on 6 April, making the same request. On 12 April Henderson wrote to Elinor Byrns from 375 St Catherine Street West in Montreal, explaining that the flu had kept her from responding sooner. She indicated that she would "gladly act" on the international board. In response to Byrns's enquiries about her pamphlet "Woman and War," Henderson said she would send it to her. She noted that 10,000 copies "have been published and sold without trouble and more are being asked for all the time."[45]

In this letter Henderson described her estrangement from the WILPF, which she began with in the early 1920s and would return to in the 1930s in Toronto. Employing the ever-present biological metaphor, she told Byrns:

> I am sure that Canada is ripe for a strong peace League. The Womans I.L. for Peace & freedom is headed every where by such compromisers that it is dying of its own inertia A new League must come into being and we must link up on this Continent.
>
> I agree almost entirely with Dr. Hinkle it's a base contradiction of all that is human for mothers to hand over their bearded babes to slaughter, and in the interests of profiteers – and when women once grasp the cruel abominable deception played upon them by men – war will quickly cease.[46]

On the bottom of the page Babcock wrote: "perhaps this is the reason she is thought to be a communist." This characterization, emerging as it did from a critique that was more gender based than class based, bears witness to Henderson's identification of class and gender radicalism. To take a radical position on the oppression of women was to be a "communist," not a radical feminist. It confirms what we have already noted about Henderson's internationalism, that she had a striking ability to convey the mutually reinforcing nature of gender and class hierarchies of power.

Babcock replied on 20 May 1926, informing Henderson that Byrns had shown her Henderson's "interesting letter." She informed Henderson that Frazier's amendment to the Constitution outlawing war had been introduced in the US Senate in April. She inquired: "What are the legal steps that would have to be taken to disarm Canada?"[47] Henderson, in her response, informed Babcock that she had consulted a member of parliament and "a prominent lawyer." It was possible, she wrote, but highly unlikely, that members of parliament would refuse to provide funds for the maintenance of the military for the coming year. Any amending of the constitution would have to be by statute of the British Parliament, and since Canada "has no power over her foreign policy it follows that when Great Britain is at war Canada is at war and I have no doubt that so long as Canada is a Colony these statutes will remain." Henderson continued in the vein of her 12 April letter, commenting: "It is criminal the way in which women who ought to know better are harnessing not only our boys but our girls also, for the 'next war.' I have made two trips from coast to coast Lecturing on Peace – but it seems but a drop in the Ocean of prejudice and ignorance."[48]

The women who "ought to know better," one presumes, were in the WILPF, but Henderson's continued focus on education and raising the consciousness of women clearly indicates that the WPU's campaign for an amendment to the Constitution, which the organization pursued untiringly, courageously, and without success until the outbreak of the Second World War, was not where her heart lay. By the early 1930s she would once again be speaking under the auspices of the WILPF.

Babcock replied to Henderson's "extremely clear letter" with two questions indicating that it was not so clear after all: "1. Do your provincial legislatures submit a referendum to the voters asking them to memorialize Parliament for an amendment to the Constitution, or does that movement come from the voters themselves? 2. When you say that the majority of the Canadian people in each province must desire an amendment to the Constitution, do you mean a majority of those voting or a majority of the voters?"

Babcock's questions, and her references to "the Constitution," indicated that she had an American conception of the relationship between the provinces and the federal government, a conception that lingered into 1930. Babcock also had little understanding of the weakness of the WPU in Canada, asking Henderson if "the movement there" was focusing on the refusal of appropriations to the army or on a constitutional amendment.[49] Henderson responded on 6 July, saying that the demand would have to come from the voters in each province (not really answering Babcock's question), which would necessitate a long campaign of education. It would then have to proceed through the provincial legislatures, House of Commons, Senate, and Imperial Parliament.[50]

In the midst of this correspondence with the WPU, Henderson wrote to Mackenzie King in July 1926 as the King-Byng constitutional crisis unfolded in Canada. She congratulated King on his stand against the governor-general's refusal to dissolve parliament:

> Your stand is the only one any self respecting man could follow. If men in high places throw constitutionalism to the winds what are we to expect from the dispossessed and unenlightened, and by what divine decree ... can we claim the right to throw into jail those who have lost faith in constitutional methods? I hope and trust – yea – I believe you will uphold in face of all abuse the ideals for which your ancestor fough [sic] and suffered and emerge from this scrimmage in the battle against re-action successfully. I am not of your politics but in the interests of Justice fair play and Constitutionalism? I know where my vote will be cast and any others I can influence outside of course of where a Labour candidate is running.[51]

This is a complex paragraph, full of ideas that appear to be at odds with many of Henderson's stated beliefs in other contexts. In part the explanation lies in the timing; she was writing to King at the very moment she was exploring the possibility of constitutional change leading to the ending of war preparations in Canada. It was an intriguing moment in which her desire for radical change and continuing adherence to the principles of British parliamentary democracy engaged in a strange dialectical dance.

The dance becomes even stranger when we factor in the possible role of the Communist Party. In 1925 Tim Buck, at this point the Communist Party's trade union secretary, published articles in the March issue of *Workers Monthly* and the 21 March 1925 issue of *The Worker*, advancing the position that Canada was still a colony of the British Empire.[52] In these articles, he set out the difficulty of amending the British North America Act, the reality that Henderson was trying to communicate to the leadership of the WPU. While no direct evidence has surfaced, it is entirely possible that Henderson knew about Buck's position, suggesting that her praise of King may have been more communist inspired than liberal inspired. Buck, in his 1970 work *Lenin and Canada*, noted that the demand for Canadian independence "was acclaimed by many people, particularly among middle class radicals."[53] In all likelihood one of those middle-class radicals was Henderson. As Norman Penner points out, however, Buck's position was quite similar to the position being taken by middle-class radicals such as J.S. Woodsworth; indeed Buck may have picked the idea up from them. Henderson may have been influenced by Buck, by Woodsworth, or by both men.[54]

The relative neglect of the 1920s in Canadian labour history has served to downplay the significance of events such as the left's response to the King-Byng Affair and the larger question of Canada's political and economic status. Henderson is an important window into this critical moment; her involvement with the WPU, the influences on her thinking from Buck to Woodsworth, and her ambiguous relationship with Prime Minister Mackenzie King all warn us against facile conclusions and easy categorization of left tendencies. What is "communist," what is "social democratic," and what is "liberal" at this moment in time is charged with ambiguity and contradiction. It is a moment, and a decade, that the life of Henderson suggests is worthy of greater study and more nuanced understanding.

King replied to Henderson the next day, saying "how pleased" he was to get her letter and commenting: "You may, I think, count on my being prepared to face all the approbrium[sic] and abuse which is certain to be heaped upon me in my effort consistently to maintain the constitutional ideal which I believe to be the only safeguard of the people's liberties and of the future freedom of our country. I am glad to know that in this great endeavour I may rely upon your generous and powerful aid."[55]

Henderson appeared energized by King's praise, writing to Babcock in November: "I am glad to say that there is a splendid move amongst the younger generation for peace in this Country, and my endeavours will be directed towards a greater unity with the Movements in the U.S.A. There have been many series of articles on peace appearing in the Farmer and Labor press all tending to awaken the minds of the people. I am personally speaking and writing on peace on every and all opportunities."[56]

On 23 December she wrote again to Babcock, saying that the editor of the *OBU Bulletin* had written to ask for permission to serialize the pamphlet "Woman and War." She observed: "It seems it has aroused an unusual amount of interest through out western Canada – and he has asked me to

write a series to follow up – so this I am sure will lead to Ideals of peace.
I am giving a series of lectures and of course I always bring in the Ideals
of peace the question of war."[57]

The serializing of "Woman and War" in the *Bulletin* began on 4 November
1926, and continued with instalments on 11 November, 18 November,
25 November, and 2 December. The following week the *Bulletin* announced
that the OBU Literature Department had copies of the "Woman and War"
pamphlet at ten cents each, reduced price for quantities. The "follow-up"
series of articles by Henderson then began on 9 December 1926 and ended
on 2 June 1927.

Babcock wrote to Henderson on 31 January 1927, apologizing for not
responding sooner to her last two letters. She told Henderson that the
hearing for the peace amendment was scheduled for Saturday, 22 January,
in the Senate Judiciary Committee Room in Washington, DC, and
hoped that Henderson would be able to attend.[58] Babcock wrote again
on 28 March 1927, indicating that she had sent a copy of the report of the
hearing before the Senate Judiciary Committee in January. She was "extremely sorry that you were not with us," and reported that the amendment "has been up for discussion at two different meetings of the
Committee." She ended the letter by asking if Henderson would "be at
Chautauqua or any other point in the United States" in the summer, because it "would be so nice to meet you."[59] Three days later Babcock sent
Henderson a telegram, asking her to "wire … or interview Canadian officials" about the opening the next day of the international bridge, and to
send the report to the Montreal papers.[60]

The papers of the WPU do not contain Henderson's responses to these
letters. Her next letter to Babcock, dated 21 March 1930, indicated that
the focus of the WPU's Canadian activity had shifted slightly from a peace
amendment to the British North America Act to the broader goal of
amending the act itself. As in 1926, Henderson said she had consulted
members of parliament and friends, finding out that there was no attempt, "and not likely to be," to amend the BNA Act. She continued, "We
have however secured the right within the last few years to say independ-
ently of the 'Mother Country' whether we as a nation shall or shall not
enter into any war declared by Gt Britain so this is a step in the right direction and I have not the slightest doubt that we will see ere long even a
greater measure of independence as 'Young Canada' is a very diferent [sic]

proposition from the old, Peace is being preached continually we have a few stalwarts in our Federal House who keep the ideal always in front, I do want to see greater cooperation between the Canadian and American women we should and must move together in reality – we are more nearly one in all our approach to life than with the women over seas."[61]

Babcock's response of 27 March 1930 indicated an almost complete failure to understand Henderson's points. Babcock asked if the BNA Act could be amended, seemingly oblivious to Henderson's answer of six days earlier. In spite of the fact that Henderson had explained that constitutional amendments could only be passed by the British Parliament, she asked again if Canada must "wait for action by the British Parliament?" On 1 April, Henderson made the point yet again, that "so long as our last court of appeal still rests with the Imperial Parliament we must submit any change in the 'British North American [sic] Act' to that Tribunal." She ended the letter with yet another restatement of her point: that "like yourselves we cannot make war illegal without changing our Constitution or what we call the 'B.N.A.' Act, then whatever we say must be O.K. by the Imperial Parliament."[62]

Babcock wrote apologetically on 5 August 1930 that the hearing on the amendment had taken place on 12 April, but that the printing of the report had been "shockingly delayed." In the meantime the Senate sub-judiciary committee had reported unfavourably. She added: "I have been rereading your kind explanatory letter of March 21st from which I gather that an amendment to the 'British North American Act' having pressing [sic] your Parliament would have to be submitted at Westminster. How grand if Canada were to give them this lead and present such a motion before Great Britain herself disarmed!"[63]

At this point Henderson must have been exasperated by both the failure of the peace amendment to get a hearing before the Senate and Babcock's continuing difficulties in grasping the constitutional relationship between Canada and Great Britain. Yet her efforts may not have been entirely in vain. Harriet Hyman Alonso points out that between August 1926 and January 1927 the WPU "wrote letters to foreign embassies in the U.S. and in other countries asking the diplomats if they knew the procedures in each respective country for making war illegal and abolishing the armed forces."[64] Given the timing, it is reasonable to assume that Henderson's information about the constitutional relationship between

Canada and Great Britain alerted Byrns and Babcock to the need to learn more about the situation in other countries. Henderson was also one of the reasons why "the unarmed peaceful border with Canada remained a chief WPU propaganda point."[65]

In November 1930 Henderson was accepted into membership by the Society of Friends in Toronto. In a sense this was a "spiritual" turn in her search for peace and suggests disillusionment with her experiences in the WPU. As a Quaker, she served on the Friends Service Committee, working with the Peace Committee on creating a Toronto Peace Council. Now in close personal contact with fellow Quaker and WILPF member Berta Hamilton, she became involved in the campaign against militarism in education and cadet training in the schools. Her turn to spirituality can only be understood in tandem with a return to the more pragmatic side of her peace activism. By becoming a Quaker, she became part of a long and genuine tradition of opposition to slavery, the fight for women's rights, and peace activism. In Quakerism she found companions who sought to live as they believed. In the Society of Friends she could practice "spirituality in action."

In the end, Henderson could not resolve the paradoxes of absolute pacifism and returned to association with the feminist pacifists and feminist causes of her earlier days. The belief in a moral universe and women's special mission in ending war, and the passionate conviction that humankind would undergo a revolutionary transformation in its way of thinking, united socialist pacifists like Henderson with liberal pacificists more than it divided them. In January 1934 Henderson spoke at a celebration organized by the League of Nations Pioneers to celebrate the fourteenth anniversary of the League of Nations. She addressed the young audience, "emphasizing the horror and futility of war. She recounted some of her experiences in a postwar trip through Germany, impressing upon her audience the sorrowful conditions prevailing among innocent children denied the happiness which is their right."[66] Given her increasing involvement with the education system, including being elected a trustee to the Toronto Board of Education in January 1934, it is not surprising that she moved away from absolute pacifism to a more direct engagement with the WILPF and issues such as cadet training that had a direct impact on young people.

We end where we began, with paradox. In her 21 March 1930 letter to Babcock, Henderson insisted that Canadian and American women "must move together in reality." It is a telling phrase, indicating that she was fully cognizant of the extent to which the peace movement in the female mind had not made its way into the world of human agency. In order to return to that world, she had to let go of at least one dream: an amendment to the American Constitution outlawing war. She sacrificed this direct confrontation with a male-dominated state to re-engage a female world of mutuality. It meant, in reality, that Henderson the socialist was now often in the company of middle-class women who opposed her class politics but who shared her idealism, her passion for change, and her faith in the internationalism of mothers.

Toronto Beginnings

Exactly why Rose Henderson moved to Toronto after some forty years of residence in Montreal is not known. Arriving just as the Roaring Twenties were about to lose their roar, she moved into a property on Montrose Avenue she had owned since 1912.[1] She was first listed as its proprietor in the *Toronto City Directory* for 1928, although her travels in Great Britain in that year suggest that she spent little, if any, time living in it. She lived at 337 Montrose Avenue, while renting out apartments 339, 339A, 341, and 341A. Montrose Avenue is in the Annex, bounded on the south by Bloor Street, on the west by Christie, on the north by Dupont, and on the east by Yonge. When Henderson moved to Toronto, it was in the federal riding of Toronto West Centre, whose voters in the federal election of 1930 would make the Liberal candidate Samuel Factor the first Jew from Toronto to be elected to the House of Commons.[2] The predominance of the Jewish population in the area is reflected in the names of her tenants, who by the mid-1930s may all have been Jewish.

Henderson was paying off a $7,000 mortgage held by the Canada Permanent Housing Corporation that she had taken out on 5 April 1926. It appears that this mortgage allowed her to discharge on 31 May 1926 another held by an Alfred R. Cameron.[3] The rent from the four apartments likely gave her an income of $150 a month, or $1,800 a year.[4] Her mortgage payments were likely in the region of $750 a year; allowing $300 a year for taxes, repairs, and other expenses, that left her with an annual income from property of some $750.[5]

At least until 1932, when she turned ownership of the Montrose Street property over to her daughter, Ida, she would have been able to live frugally largely on rental income. It seems unlikely, however, that she could have travelled in Canada and internationally without additional income, perhaps an inheritance from her or her husband's side of the family or both. Her financial dealings in the late 1920s may have made it more viable to live in Toronto than in Montreal without taking paid employment. She was a champion of organized labour, but she also appears to have been a rather astute businesswoman.

The Toronto that Henderson moved to was leaving behind the prosperous 1920s and entering the Great Depression. Ernest Hemingway had come and gone from the city; the author of *For Whom the Bell Tolls* and *The Sun Also Rises* had published more than 170 articles in the *Toronto Daily Star* between February 1920 and January 1924.[6] Temporarily gone was anarchist Emma Goldman, who was in the city from 1926 to 1928 on one of several sojourns there. She would return in the mid-1930s and die there in 1940. Maple Leaf Gardens, the house that Conn Smythe built, was under construction on the corner of Church and Carleton Streets.

Henderson moved to a province not long removed from the political "revolution" in 1919. That "revolution" saw the election of forty-five members of the United Farmers of Ontario (UFO) who, in alliance with eleven independent labour candidates, governed Ontario until June 1923. Then on 25 June 1923 the government of E.C. Drury was soundly defeated, with Toronto returning ten Conservative members to its ten ridings. In part the defeat was a product of divisions between farmer and labour members of the Ontario legislature, in part a reaction to the fact that between 1919 and 1923 the provincial budget doubled, and in part a reaction to Drury's rigorous enforcement of the Ontario Temperance Act, passed by the Hearst Conservatives in 1916.[7] In a plebiscite on 23 October 1923 Ontario voters "upheld prohibition by the slenderest of margins," leaving Ontario Conservatives looking for ways to ease up on the restrictions. The resulting compromise was beer with a 4.4 percent alcohol content, which the government claimed was not intoxicating.[8] To appease temperance advocates, the regulations prohibited the stand-up bar in Ontario.[9] Liquor drinkers, who deigned to consider beer with such a low alcohol content as alcohol in any meaningful sense, did not have long to wait; as of 1 June 1927 Torontonians were able to legally purchase the hard stuff.[10]

The man who replaced E.C. Drury as Ontario premier, G. Howard Ferguson, was an Orangeman and United Empire Loyalist. He was instrumental in fortifying the political culture of Toronto in the 1930s that Henderson spent much of her time fiercely combating. As Randall White observes, Ferguson had "a genuine taste for the noble imperial civilization of the British Empire." He served as his own minister of education; in this capacity "he boosted the dosage of imperial indoctrination that local schoolchildren had been receiving since the late nineteenth century. Under his authority *The Ontario Readers' Third Book* was published in 1925 by the T. Eaton Company; on the first page was a Union Jack, accompanied by the motto "ONE FLAG, ONE FLEET, ONE THRONE."[11] At the same time, however, Ferguson was in tune with the commercial revolution going on as New York replaced London as the world's leading financial centre. Following the defeat of the Farmer-Labour government, in Ontario there was "a fresh engagement with the commerce of the continent, but also a fresh engagement with the romance of the Empire."[12]

On the surface, it appeared as if Toronto was as Tory and British as it had always been, an impression reflected in the political life of the city. In the provincial election held on 1 December 1926, Ferguson's Conservatives won seventy-four of the 112 seats with 56 per cent of the popular vote. All fifteen Toronto ridings returned Conservatives.[13] In the provincial election on 30 October 1929, the Conservatives won ninety-two seats and 57 per cent of the popular vote; again, the Tories took every seat in Toronto. As Randall White points out, Toronto Toryism and allegiance to the British Empire was alive and well into the 1920s, with "its own mass base ... collective memories, populist pedigrees, and popular voices."[14] In the provincial and federal elections of 1921, 1923, 1925, 1926, and 1929, the Conservative Party, the political voice of allegiance to the British Empire, won every Toronto seat.

The Orange Order was still a formidable presence in Toronto's political culture, but there were signs that its grip was beginning to loosen. The challenge to Orange Order dominance got a boost in 1924 with the election as mayor of William Wesley Hiltz, who defeated Orange candidate Tommy Church, elected to the major's office every year from 1915 to 1921. Hiltz only served one term, defeated by Thomas Foster in 1925 with the backing of the Orange Order, indicating that Church's defeat in 1924 did not indicate a sea change in attitude toward the Order and the

British Protestant establishment it represented. That impression was affirmed when Foster won again in 1926 and 1927, but in 1928 he was defeated by Sam McBride by a "majority" of more than 15,000 votes. This time there was no missing the message, and the *Globe* observed that McBride's victory represented "a revolution in public feeling."[15]

That victory reflected more profound changes in the city; the reality on the streets was that by 1931 Toronto had become notably less British. The census of that year revealed that almost 20 per cent of the city's population had non-British origins. Almost 11,000 Torontonians were of French origin; there were more than 13,000 of Italian origin, 9,000 Germans, almost 8,500 Poles, 5,000 Dutchmen, almost 4,500 Ukrainians and nearly 3,500 Finns. The African and Asian communities showed little growth from the census of 1921.[16]

But the decline of the influence of the Orange Lodge and the blunting of the overt anti-Catholicism of the nineteenth century can in no way be equated with a dramatic decline in the commitment of Toronto's Protestants to their faith. In 1925 the Congregational Union, the Methodist Church of Canada, and roughly 70 per cent of the Presbyterian Church accomplished a church union envisioned since before the First World War. Thus was created the largest Protestant denomination in Canada. The first service of three was held in Toronto's Mutual Street Arena on 10 June 1925 – a Wednesday. Each service was attended by 8,000 persons, who lined up on the sidewalk waiting to get in. Members of the United Church immediately became a force to be reckoned with in the institutional life of the city. In the early 1930s the education system that Rose Henderson became deeply involved with was dominated by members of the United Church and the Anglican Church, the latter still the single largest religious group in the city.[17]

Given Henderson's ongoing relationship with Jews in Montreal, it comes as no surprise that this relationship continued in Toronto. She entered a left political culture in which Jews played a crucial role. After church union in June 1925, Jews comprised the fifth largest religious group in Toronto, trailing only the Anglicans, United Church members, Presbyterians, and Catholics. Toronto's Jewish population, near 35,000 in 1921, had become more than 45,000 by 1931. In the 1920s and 1930s Jews comprised a higher percentage of the population of Toronto than at any time before or since. We get some sense of the importance of the Jewish presence by realizing that in the early 1930s there were four times as many Jews in Toronto as Italians. By the 1920s, as Randall White notes, Jews "had become the largest and most influential pioneer of cultural diversity" in Toronto.[18] Joseph Singer became Toronto's first Jewish alderman in 1919. Future mayor Nathan Phillips was elected an alderman in 1924. Stephen Speisman argues that Jews "were reasonably successful on the municipal scene," in a period in which it was generally the case that "a seat on the Board of Education was considered the logical stepping stone to a political career." Samuel Factor was elected to the Toronto Board of Education in 1923, then went to City Hall; he was elected to the House of Commons in 1930. John J. Glass began his career by getting elected to the Board of Education in 1928, progressed to the position of alderman, then served as a Liberal member of the provincial legislature from 1934 to 1943.[19]

While there was no shortage of anti-Semitism in Toronto, as elsewhere in Canadian society, attempts were underway to break down the divisions and promote understanding. In the public life of Toronto in the 1920s there were "numerous incidents of continued good relations" between Jews and non-Jews. On 18 November 1924 the *Toronto Daily Star* reported that on the "Canada Night" held at the King Edward Hotel by the Toronto Lodge of B'nai B'rith, "Jews and Gentiles, Catholic priests and Protestant ministers ... orangemen and knights of Columbus, stood together." Ferguson's Conservative government began to fund Mount Sinai Hospital in 1925.[20] The rabbi of Holy Blossom Synagogue spoke to a number of non-Jewish organizations, and ministers were invited to speak at Holy Blossom. In 1928 Rabbi Isserman and the Reverend E. Crossley Hunter of Carleton Street United Church exchanged pulpits.[21]

The extent and severity of anti-Semitism in Toronto as the Great Depression began is a matter of dispute. Randall White argues that "in the grim times of the early 1930s the city was too broad-minded to embrace any overtly racist politics."[22] The key word may be "overtly"; Speisman points out that discrimination against Jews in employment continued into the 1930s. Jews "were denied leases to apartments in the better residential areas and were excluded from numerous hotels and resorts in the district surrounding the city."[23] Gerald Tulchinsky contrasts the "legally enforceable restrictive covenants" preventing Jews from buying property in certain areas of the city with the fact that some Jews were still able to achieve "modest upward mobility."[24]

As in Montreal, Henderson's relationship with the Jews of Toronto was meaningful and ongoing but not what one would call close. She was in constant association with prominent Jewish activists, notably Rabbi Maurice Eisendrath of Holy Blossom Synagogue and Ida Siegel, a fellow member of the Toronto Board of Education and associate in a number of social reform and left-wing organizations. Again as in Montreal, however, Henderson does not appear to have had any formal ties with the Jewish community, and her own religious views remained anchored in her Protestant roots. Yet through her relationships with Jewish activists in Toronto, we gain important insights into both the closeness and the spaces that existed between Jews and non-Jews in 1930s Canada.

Henderson moved to Toronto in the late 1920s with continuing ties to the mainstream Protestant churches and their adherents. The *Star* reported on 5 October 1929 that she was visiting with Dr and Mrs James L. Hughes. Henderson's connection with the couple is worthy of investigation, though no evidence has been found of their actual relationship. Hughes was the brother of Sir Sam Hughes, the minister of the militia in the First World War, relieved of his duties by Prime Minister Robert Borden late in 1916 as a result of the scandal involving the poorly performing Ross rifle. James Hughes was born in Durham County, Canada West, on 20 February 1846. He was Irish and French on his mother's side, on his father's descended from a Welsh family that went to Ireland with Cromwell.[25] There can be little doubt that as someone with a "plantationist" background he was someone with whom Henderson could identify. That identification extended much beyond religion and ethnicity. In 1891 he became president of the central Toronto Suffrage Club.[26] In 1895 he published a pamphlet entitled *Equal Suffrage*, in which he refuted arguments against granting the franchise to women. According to Catherine Cleverdon, Hughes argued from the Bible so effectively that "he ended any further serious debate on the religious aspect of the question."[27] Carol Bacchi cautions against seeing him as a "progressive" on the issue, pointing out that he was willing to grant women the vote because it did not involve abdicating their role as wives and mothers for any length of time.[28]

Henderson's ideas on education while she served as a trustee on the Toronto Board of Education in the mid-1930s evinced Hughes's unmistakable influence. Appointed inspector of schools in May 1874, he almost immediately set out to put his imprint on the city's education system. He introduced the kindergarten system and brought Ada Mareau from the United States to become the country's first kindergarten teacher. Ada also became his second wife and the mother of Laura Hughes, Henderson's associate in the Women's International League for Peace and Freedom. In spite of the fact that the Hugheses were pillars of the establishment and Henderson was a "dangerous radical," a common interest in women's suffrage, the education of youth, and social reform transcended the differences.

The argument, however, can only be pushed so far. Henderson and James Hughes were supporters of the temperance movement, critics of corporal punishment in the schools, and believers that where children were concerned, cleanliness was next to godliness. On the other hand, Hughes was a fervent imperialist and the man who began the public school cadet movement. In the 1920s he was honorary colonel of the cadets of Toronto.[29] It may be that Hughes never came into conflict with Henderson over the issue, but as we shall see, her opposition to cadet training in the schools, as part of her more general opposition to imperialism, militarism and war, left little room for agreement.

Henderson's pacifism ensured that moving to Toronto put her in ongoing contact with the Society of Friends. There were connections in her past with the Society of Friends; E.D. Morel's mother and wife, for example, were Quakers. When she was in Wales in 1928, distributing food and clothing to starving Welsh miners and their families, she spent some three weeks at a Quaker guest house in the Rhondda Valley called Maes-Yyr-Haf.[30] The Quaker faith was a good fit with her pacifism, and becoming a Quaker made sense for someone who had been a Bahá'i and retained Theosophist sympathies. On 19 October 1930 the minutes of the Toronto Monthly Meeting of Friends record that Henderson "made application for membership. The meeting was very happy to welcome her into the fellowship."[31] She quickly became an involved and valued member of the society,[32] one of eleven delegates appointed to the Quarterly Meeting held in Toronto on 29 November 1930.[33] In December 1930 the minutes record her interest in setting up a Literary Club, and it was left with her to form such a club.[34]

In January 1931 the report of the annual meeting revealed that she was now a member of both the Peace Committee and the Committee on Religious Education.[35] In March the Toronto Monthly Meeting recorded that "Rose Henderson will visit Girls Club."[36] In April 1931 she was chosen as one of sixteen delegates to attend the Quarterly Meeting, held in Toronto on 9 May 1931.[37] At the Newmarket Monthly Meeting on 7 May 1931 she was appointed one of the delegates to attend the Yearly Meeting at Coldstream and report back to the next Newmarket Quarterly Meeting in September.[38]

It was as a lecturer on women, children, drama, and the peace movement, and within a year as a Quaker, that Henderson made herself felt in Toronto as the Great Depression took hold. The *Star* took note of her presence in the city by carrying an interview with her in the fall of 1929. The writer noted that in the past Henderson had put herself in the shoes of the people and worked in laundries and textile and candy factories, thereby establishing her working-class credentials. Ironically, given that Henderson was speaking within days of the stock market crash, the *Star* caught her in an upbeat moment, claiming that civilization was getting better, in part because youth "are finding themselves."[39] Here she echoed opinions about youth she expressed in the articles in the *OBU Bulletin* in 1926–27, asserting the willingness of youth to throw off the conventions of their parents in the cause of making the world a better place.

The first lecture series Henderson gave as a Toronto resident (at least the first that comes to light in the daily press), concerned not labour, mother's pensions, juvenile delinquency, or the peace movement, but sexuality. On Tuesday, 5 November 1929, the *Star* reported that her series of lectures on "The Biology and Psychology of Sex" would begin the following day at the King Edward Hotel.[40] Almost exactly two years earlier, on 24 November 1927, Emma Goldman had given a lecture entitled "Sex – A Dominant Element in Life and Art."[41] There is no way of knowing how many nervous Torontonians made the connection, but they cannot have been reassured by the title of one of Henderson's talks, "Parenthood, Accident or Design?"[42] This lecture series marked her as beyond the pale of mainstream Christian thinking of the time.

There is little further trace of Henderson in the public life of Toronto until the following November. We do know that she attended the memorial service for Ada Hughes held at Knox College Chapel on 26 January 1930. The main speaker was Dr Augusta Stowe Gullen, whose characterization of Mrs Hughes as "primarily an educationist" and someone who "saw the home as a great factor in the child's life and the mother as a constant teacher and inspiration" could as easily have been said about Henderson.[43] Henderson spoke about Ada Hughes's greatness of vision and recognition of the child as the bearer of new ideals, echoing the sentiments about youth she had expressed in her November 1929 interview with the *Star*. Of note is the fact that another speaker was Christine Ross Barker, Henderson's compatriot in the Women's Peace Union.[44] The presence of both women at the funeral service suggests their trajectory away from absolute pacifism and reconciliation with the mainstream women's and peace movements.

Henderson emerges again on 6 November 1930 as the *Star* reported that she had spoken to the Hebrew Maternity Aid Society the day before at the King Edward Hotel, at a talk given by Rabbi Maurice Eisendrath entitled "Our Economic Morality." By now it was evident to leftists and other social activists, if not to Prime Minster R.B. Bennett and opposition leader W.L.M. King, that the Depression was not a typical downswing in the capitalist economy. In his talk Rabbi Eisendrath supported unemployment insurance as a "temporary palliative" to deal with the mounting unemployment crisis. He did not agree that unemployment insurance would "encourage shiftlessness and reduce labor's dignity." Henderson, described as a "sociologist" and "former assistant judge" of the Montreal Juvenile Court, supported the rabbi in a discussion she led after his talk. She moved on from his talk, arguing that women would get unemployment insurance put through. When women used their intelligence and developed a social conscience, they would "no longer vote politicians into office but social engineers."[45] A decade after the First World War, there were still powerful echoes in her position of the Progressive era, a continuing belief in the role of experts and their greater fitness than politicians to deal with social problems.

The coming together of Rabbi Eisendrath and Henderson provides an opportunity to further explore the role of Toronto's Jewish community and the interconnections with non-Jews. Eisendrath was the rabbi at Holy Blossom Synagogue, which dated back to September 1856. In 1920 Holy Blossom attached itself to the reform movement in the United States, inviting Rabbi Barnett R. Brickner to be rabbi. According to Stephen Speisman, orthodoxy was "effectively dead" at Holy Blossom by the end of the 1920s,[46] and the arrival in 1929 of Rabbi Eisendrath ensured the continuation of the trend.[47] He "stressed the rationalistic, ethical and universal aspect of Judaism," and believed "that traditional ritual was a bane to the modern Jew and must be discarded."[48] In the early 1930s he became well known in Toronto as a supporter of progressive causes, activism that brought him into contact with Henderson. Religious difference notwithstanding, the two shared a belief in the rational, ethical, and universal and an antipathy to the stultifying effect of tradition.

Henderson's appearance at the Hebrew Ladies Maternal Aid Society early in her days in Toronto is significant because it put her in contact with Ida (Lewis) Siegel. The object here is not to claim that the relationship between Henderson and Siegel is more historically significant than that between Henderson and any of dozens of female activists in Toronto, but rather to elucidate a problem in the historiography. That problem, which Bahá'í historian Will van den Hoonaard aptly calls "biographical zoning," results from a focus on identity that obscures relationships that cut across ethnic and religious lines.[49] One of the tasks in bringing Henderson's life and activism to light in Toronto of this period is to bring down the curtains obscuring the interactions of Jewish and non-Jewish leftists. She and Ida Siegel, to use one example, were part of a political culture that only functioned as well as it did because differences of identity were surmounted and common causes found and fought for.

Siegel came by her social activism honestly.[50] Her mother took the lead in organizing the Toronto Hebrew Ladies' Aid Society, which offered a wide range of services to the poor. They were provided with coal and cash for groceries. Recent immigrants were helped financially and funeral expenses covered. The ill were helped with hospital expenses and visited in their homes, where food was prepared and housecleaning looked after. The society helped Jews go into business for themselves by helping to fund the purchase of horses and wagons for peddlers, for example.[51]

Mrs Lewis's daughter Ida was active from a young age. In 1899, as a teenager, she organized the Daughters of Zion, the first Zionist youth organization in the city.[52] She organized a girls' sewing club in 1903 that developed into a Zionist Sunday School.[53] The woman that Speisman calls "the ubiquitous Ida Siegel" organized a group of young girls in "Shomrai Shabbos"; after Theodore Herzl died, she persuaded the club to change its name to the Herzl Girls. In 1916 she was one of the lead organizers of the Federation of Jewish Philanthropies of Toronto.[54]

Ida Siegel led a number of young women in organizing a Hebrew Ladies' Sewing Circle in 1906. In 1907 the organization became the Hebrew Ladies' Maternity Aid and Child Welfare Society. The society "sought to provide new mothers and their infants with medical care, domestic assistance, linen, milk and food, as well as with luxuries such as fresh fruit and sweets which might not otherwise be available. It also assured entry of the public health nurses into the homes of the Jewish poor by accompanying them and acting as interpreters."[55] In the 1909–10 period, as president of the Hebrew Maternity Aid Society, Siegel became involved in the Local Council of Women. The Council "had recently begun to establish pasteurized milk stations throughout the working-class areas of Toronto." Siegel and Dorothy Goldstick "organized a women's auxiliary to the Jewish Dispensary, which then undertook to operate a milk depot in the Ward with financial assistance from the Local Council."[56] At roughly the same time Henderson had become involved with the Montreal Local Council of Women, and so the two shared an interest in providing milk to poor, working-class children that extended from the pre-First World War period to the mid-1930s.

In this same period Siegel "proposed the establishment of a mothers' club at Hester How (Elizabeth Street) School, where parents and teachers could meet to discuss the welfare of the children." She also founded a Jewish girls' club that met on Saturday afternoons at Hester How. Siegel was well respected at the school because the Maternity Aid Society was providing needy children there with milk and clothing. According to Speisman, the mothers' club that Siegel founded at Hester How "later grew into a city-wide Home and School Association with no Jewish connections."[57]

The claim of direct evolution is misleading, however. According to Kari Dehli, the creation of the Home and School Association in 1916 under the leadership of Ada Mary Brown Courtice "brought together Home and School clubs, mothers' clubs, and art leagues associated with a number of Toronto schools, as well as individual members."[58] No doubt the Hester How Mother's Club that Siegel organized was one of them, but it was just that, one of them. Also misleading is Speisman's claim that the Home and School Association had "no Jewish connections." Organizationally this is true, but it disguises the fact that Siegel continued to be involved with the Home and School Council in the 1930s in her capacity as a trustee on the Toronto Board of Education. In both organizations, she was in regular contact with Henderson.

As we look more closely and directly at Henderson's life and activism in the Toronto of the 1930s, we need to keep in mind Siegel and the relationship between Jews and non-Jews. By the time Henderson was elected to the Toronto Board of Education for 1934, Siegel had been elected several times. She was not prevented by the ethnic hierarchy of power in Toronto the Good from getting elected to the board, but her success was made possible by the same gender stereotype that made Henderson's election possible – the association of women with maternal duties, the care of children, and education. Women were "fit" to deal with children and education, much less "fit" to deal with the affairs of state. Henderson was Anglo-Celtic, and Siegel was "ethnic," but they shared the challenge of overcoming the belief that biology "fitted" them to be educators but not politicians. They were breaking new trails, and breaking them together, but there were many rivers to cross.

This is not to suggest that Henderson's ideas on modern youth, birth control, sexuality, and women in public life were meeting with unalloyed hostility in the Toronto of the early 1930s – far from it. As a case in point, we might look to her series of lectures on George Bernard Shaw's *The Intelligent Woman's Guide to Socialism and Capitalism* given in the fall of 1930. Three years earlier, from October to December 1927, Emma Goldman had given a series of eighteen lectures in the city. Interested persons could subscribe to the full series for $4, or pay $.35 per talk;[59] two of the talks were on Shaw. It is entirely possible that Henderson knew about Goldman's talks and was building on her legacy, although lecturing on Shaw was a common practice among North American leftists and feminists of the time.

Described as a "lecturer and sociologist," Henderson spoke on successive Thursday evenings at the King Edward Hotel. The *Star* reported the cost for the full series of six lectures as two dollars, with individual lectures being fifty cents.[60] The second talk, under the auspices of the Women's International League for Peace and Freedom, was on 13 November 1930.[61] On Sunday, 16 November 1930, Henderson gave the third lecture on the topic "Bernard Shaw, The Rationalist."[62] She gave the fourth talk in her series, "The Money Market and World Collapse," on 27 November 1930. By now the price of admission had fallen from $0.50 to $0.35.

The absence of press reports suggests that the last two lectures in the series may not have been given. Like Goldman before her, Henderson knew that it was virtually impossible to make a living as a lecturer. Goldman "complained constantly" about small audiences and at the end of her series came to the conclusion that she could no longer "make a living for herself through lecturing in Canada."[63] Henderson was not Goldman, but in Toronto of the late 1920s and early 1930s Goldman did not cut a much more imposing public figure than Henderson. Henderson was able to lecture on many of the same topics, charge a similar admission, and have comparable success. It should also be remembered that Goldman was lecturing at the height of 1920s' prosperity, while Henderson was making a similar attempt after the crash of 1929.

Henderson's public image as a radical belies many of her involvements in the early 1930s. Her ongoing efforts to establish herself as a credible candidate for the Toronto Board of Education was a process characterized by contradiction. On the one hand, she would eventually be elected as a CCF candidate for the 1934 term, making her the most left-wing member on the board; on the other hand, the process of getting elected meant moving in middle-class circles, notably in middle-class women's organizations, and making herself known to and accepted by parents in her ward. How calculated this contradictory effort was is difficult to assess, although the existing evidence suggests that she knew what she had to do in order to get elected and was willing to do it, her reputation as a radical notwithstanding.

The kind of standing Henderson enjoyed as a social reformer in the period leading up to her election to the Toronto Board of Education is revealed at a gathering in the Bloor Street United Church organized by the Women's International League for Peace and Freedom on 31 May 1931. The speakers were Professor C.B. Sissons of the University of Toronto, Member of Parliament Agnes Macphail, Jane Addams, the now seventy-year-old honorary president of the WILPF, and Henderson. In her speech Henderson decried the "capitalistic influence upon education," which curbed "freedom of teaching and speech" in Canadian universities and resulted in the students not getting a "broad education." She provided details on the capitalist directors of McGill University and the University of Toronto, her contentions being "upheld" by Macphail in her speech.[64] Yet later that year, Henderson sought to become a board of education trustee, a position requiring her to work within the system in the company of prominent Toronto conservatives and capitalists. If she was bothered by the inconsistency, she never addressed it in her public utterances.

The significance of Henderson's campaign for a position on the 1932 Toronto Board of Education is revealed at a "civics" meeting at the library of the Oakwood Collegiate Institute Club on Thursday, 10 December 1931. As a new candidate for the board, she spoke briefly, and is recorded as stating "that the school was the cradle of the nation."[65] In this simple statement, with the momentous change of one word, Henderson evoked the crucial link between first and second wave feminism that has garnered so little attention from feminist historians. The school, she declared, had now replaced the home as the cradle of the nation. This shift represented a watershed in her thinking and that of the maternal feminists of her generation. The home had not been abandoned, but it had lost its dominant position, a telling reflection of the fact that Canada's female activists had made a powerful entrance into the public life of Canadian society, ever-present prejudices against women notwithstanding. In the school, Henderson declared, the women of the world could effect the revolutionary change that had for so long been impossible to effect from the home.

She was unsuccessful in her first attempt to be elected to the board. It is tempting to attribute her loss to prejudice against women and the labour movement, but it may just as easily have been a function of a first effort by a woman who was not a native of the city.[66] She was not discouraged and made a second attempt the following year. Apart from records of her involvement with the Toronto left, only bits and pieces of information exist concerning her activities in 1932 before her second campaign for the board in early winter. She continued her work with the Society of Friends, work that may have involved setting up a Peace Library in the meeting house.[67] While active as a Quaker, she continued to criticize the mainstream religious denominations for refusing to allow workers' organizations to hold meetings in their churches, a decision she said was costing them members.[68] She was not anti-religious; indeed, her criticisms were aimed at getting religious believers to live by their principles, an outcome that would have the effect of making the churches stronger, not weaker.

She was now speaking on a regular basis in churches, as she had been doing since the 1920s. Was this trajectory genuine, or was it at least in part political opportunism? Her decreasing criticism of the mainstream

Protestant churches raises other issues related not just to her political and religious beliefs but also to her qualifications. On Saturday, 29 October 1932, the *Star* carried a notice of a talk to be given by "Dr. Rose Henderson": for the first time, she was credited with a PhD. The problem with this claim is that no evidence has been found, after extensive searching, to indicate that she had such a degree. Indeed, no evidence has surfaced that she ever attended university. All references to her having a PhD fail to say where she got it. Having already failed once to gain a seat on the board of education, and facing questions about her qualifications as a trustee, was she falsely claiming to have a PhD in order to heighten her credibility? As we shall see, her claim did not go unchallenged.[69]

In her second campaign for the board of education, Henderson spoke out against cadet training in the schools. Why she chose to focus on this issue is not known, but it does reflect her reconciliation with the WILPF, which had been campaigning against cadet training since its early days. She may also have been hoping to build on the work of Agnes Macphail, who took the issue to the House of Commons and "began an annual campaign to end cadet training by reducing federal expenditure to one dollar."[70] Instead of being trained to kill, Henderson argued, children "should be taught the sacredness of human life, the ideals of peace, the interdependence of nations and the brotherhood of man."[71] On 28 December 1932 she spoke at the West End YMCA; opposing cadet training in the schools, she "advocated spending on recreation and actual needs of the children, rather than on teaching children to prepare for war."[72]

Henderson was unsuccessful in her second bid to become a trustee on the Toronto Board of Education, but two developments that took place during her 1932 campaign pointed toward better days. Her campaign against cadet training struck a nerve, and when she struck a nerve, opponents often struck back by trying to counter her passion and idealism by questioning her facts. On 31 December the *Star*'s editorial page reported that Trustee Menzies of Ward Five had challenged the figure Henderson was using for the cost of cadet training. The figure, which she had taken from the *Star*, she had confirmed at the school offices. The paper commented: "We fancy that most people will agree with Mrs. Henderson that $106,000 is a lot of money to take out of the pockets of the people for a rather doubtful purpose."[73]

By the winter of 1932–33 Henderson had a powerful ally in the *Star*, which was making a concerted effort to portray her in a positive light. On 29 December, at a meeting at Harbord Collegiate at which every candidate was interrupted and heckled, she was forced to defend her qualifications to sit on the board.[74] The *Star* took the opposite tack, pointing out that she "did much of the pioneer work that made it possible to have mothers' pensions and juvenile courts in Canada."[75] The paper's support was not enough to get her elected, but it cannot be argued that she lost because she faced a uniformly hostile Toronto press. The *Star* put a positive spin even on her defeat, commenting that she "would have given Trustee Menzies a closer race in Ward 5 if Dr. Caroline Brown had not split the vote with her."[76]

Following this second failed attempt at a board seat, Henderson spoke on a number of occasions to Home and School Associations, often on the topic of youth. While it is does not appear that she ever occupied an official position on the parent body or with any of the local associations, she worked closely with Home and School Associations throughout the mid-1930s and regularly spoke to them. Her focus on youth reflected trips she took to Europe to study youth movements there, although the exact number of trips and their duration is not known. Her peace activism was ongoing and was reflected in her association with the League of Nations Society and its youth wing, the League of Nations Pioneers. Her attitude toward the League of Nations had clearly changed since the days when she decried it as a handmaiden of the capitalist system.

Without the actual texts, it is only possible to provide the flavour of the talks she was giving to Home and School Associations in the winter, spring, and summer of 1933. On Wednesday, 8 February 1933, at the regular monthly meeting of the Palmerston Home and School Club, she gave an "inspiring address on 'European Youth of To-day in Regard to World Friendship.'"[77] On 4 April 1933, she was the main speaker at a meeting of the John Ross Robertson Home and School Association, her subject being "Personal Contact with the Youth Movement in Great Britain and Europe."[78] At the closing session of the Essex Home and School Club on 18 May 1933, she spoke on "the peace movement among youth of many lands."[79] At "a joint meeting of Davisville School staff, senior scholars and parents," she told "the large gathering" about the "development of the Youth Movement in European countries, and described demonstrations in favor of universal peace witnessed during her travels."[80] These talks often brought her together with other prominent feminists and peace activists. On 1 June 1933 she gave a short address to the League of Nations Pioneers, Toronto Branch, at the YWCA. Ida Siegel also spoke, and Alice Chown of the Women's League of Nations Society was in attendance.[81]

In the fall Henderson became involved, if briefly, with the Women's Political Action Association of Canada, which met, according to the *Star*, at the "Russian restaurant on Hayden St." on 6 November 1933. At this meeting Henderson was elected to the "legislative committee," which included among its members Mrs Harris McPhedran and Baroness de Hueck.[82] Baptized Russian Orthodox, de Hueck converted to Roman Catholicism in England in 1919. Archbishop McNeil of Toronto hired her to spy on ethnic organizations and the Communist Party, and de Hueck began submitting weekly reports to him as of October 1931.[83] In 1932 she submitted a ninety-five page document detailing the activities of the Communist Party and the ways in which the party's propaganda was misleading unsuspecting immigrants.[84] In 1933 McNeil used this study as a springboard for his pamphlet *The Red Menace*. Baroness de Hueck and Mrs McPhedran encouraged women of all religious denominations to go into the homes of the immigrant poor to offer support and understanding as a means of heading off sympathy for the Communist Party. In addition, the two women, along with Catholic reformer Helen McCrea, opened a Russian restaurant, the Tachainick, as a means of providing employment, taking people off the relief rolls, and shoring up the self-respect that would keep them from becoming communists.[85] This was the restaurant at which Henderson joined the Women's Political Action Association.

At first glance, it indeed seems a strange association for Henderson to have. Baroness de Hueck was an unlikely colleague, but Henderson could not have known about her clandestine activities. Henderson was certainly in favour of helping women, immigrants, and the poor, which appeared to be the association's goal. At the meeting, she cannot have disagreed with Mrs McPhedran, who stated: "The time has come for women to free themselves from the domination of men in politics ... because most men who seek to use women's organizations politically are mere politicians and not statesmen." All her life as a social activist Henderson had been calling for fewer "politicians" and more "statesmen" in Canadian public life. The association also revealed that it would "work at once for improvements in existing social legislation such as mothers' allowances and old age pensions."[86] Both these statements could easily have been made by Henderson.

It is difficult to assess the meaning of this one meeting, because no other reference to Henderson's association with this group has been found. It may be, given the talk about mother's allowances and old age pensions, that the meeting was directed at Henderson, although it is not immediately evident why de Hueck and McPhedran would be interested in her. Henderson was now actively working for the CCF and was in constant contact with members of the Communist Party. It may be that de Hueck and McPhedran perceived her as someone who could be convinced to abandon her radical ways, although this speculation must remain what it is – speculation.[87]

In summing up Henderson's work in the education field, the historian must resist the temptation to declare that gender had become more meaningful to her than class. This chapter has so far focused on her work as an educator with women and children in Toronto, but in reality it took place in tandem with her work with the left and the labour movement. Her associations with middle-class politicians and social reformers notwithstanding, she continued to critique capitalism from a working-class perspective.

Henderson played an important role on the Toronto left in the early 1930s, a role that emerges grudgingly from the historical record. She has remained in the shadows of J.S. Woodsworth, Agnes Macphail, Tim Buck, and James Simpson, even of less well-known figures such as Toronto and District Trades and Labor Council president J.W. Buckley, East York Workers' Association leader Arthur Williams, and Labor Party of Ontario president Arthur Mould. Yet Henderson was a key figure in the events leading up to the creation of the CCF and the debate within labour and left groups in Toronto as to the desirability of sinking their identities into what quickly became the flagship of Canadian social democracy. It is a history of enormous complexity, and Henderson's role adds to that complexity, but it also opens up new avenues of investigation and clarifies issues that are difficult, if not impossible, to understand without an appreciation of her role. Her activism as a member of the CCF with strong links to the Communist Party and its leading members enriches our understanding of the Toronto left in the 1930s.

The emergence of the CCF was not pre-ordained; other outcomes were possible, and Henderson initially fought for one of those outcomes. In the early 1930s she was vice-president of the Toronto Labor Party (TLP). Understanding the history and politics of the TLP requires an understanding of the history of the Canadian Labor Party and the split that occurred in its ranks in 1927. The CLP was organized in 1917 as an initiative of the Trades and Labor Congress of Canada. It ran a number of candidates in the federal election of that year, but none was elected. In Ontario the organizing convention was not held until March 1918, at which time 381 delegates met in search of working-class unity. More than half the delegates represented trade unions, with most of the others representing the Independent Labor Party and the Social Democratic Party.[88] The Ontario CLP remained inactive until it re-emerged in 1921, with metal trades leader Harry Kerwin as president, Mary McNab as vice-president, and James Simpson as secretary.[89] The ILP perceived the organization as a direct challenge to its dominance of the labour political movement in the province, while the CLP wanted "to maintain a united front" with the ILP.[90] Following the ILP's disastrous showing in the 1921 federal election, its decline and the increasing appeal of the CLP were much in evidence. By 1923 the CLP was claiming it had replaced the ILP as the leading party of labour in Ontario. The fact that it comprised an uneasy alliance of reformist and revolutionary socialists notwithstanding, the CLP was growing in size and influence, while the ILP watched the promise of 1919 fade away.

The existence of the newly formed Communist Party of Canada, and its legal, above-ground manifestation, the Workers' Party, organized in February 1922, provided the CLP with a revolutionary edge that promised internecine struggles in the future. While the CLP remained a reformist organization in the British Labour Party tradition, Workers' Party members such as Jack MacDonald and Henderson's old associate Harriet Prenter injected a strain of revolutionary fervour into the otherwise cautious organization.[91] By the mid-1920s non-communists in the Canadian Labor Party were concerned about, if not adamantly opposed to, the influence of the communists, which they considered out of proportion to the number of workers represented by communist delegates to the CLP. Indeed, communist influence in the CLP was strong enough to be considered communist domination by some trade union delegates.

By 1927 a number of anti-communist trade unions were pulling out of
the CLP, ironically leaving Communist Party members with even more
influence than before. The 1927 annual convention of the CLP produced
a full-blown split in the organization. Led by labour leader Arthur Mould,
some forty delegates met in a separate caucus and decided to create an
organization on a socialist rather than labourist basis instead of attempting to regain control of the CLP from the communists. At the organizational meeting on 11 November 1927, Mould was elected president
of the new organization, with James MacArthur Conner as vice-president
and an executive committee including James Simpson. Known as the
Ontario Labor Party (OLP), this is the organization Martin Robin refers to
as the Independent Labor Party of Ontario.[92]

The confusion that surrounds the redefining of the Ontario and Toronto
left in this period stems from the existence of both the Ontario Labor
Party, at times referred to as the Independent Labor Party, and the Toronto
Labor Party. On 20 November 1927 the Toronto Labor Party, was formed,
"intended to embrace non-communist groups formerly with the Toronto
Central Council of the C.L.P."[93] Meetings on 11 and 20 of November
were both attended by delegates of what Martin Robin calls the "Central
Toronto Labor Party" in the former case, and the "Toronto Central Branch
of the Labor Party" in the latter. Presumably the "Central" Toronto Labor
Party ceased to exist with the formation of the Ontario Labor Party and
the Toronto Labor Party, but the relationship between the Ontario and
Toronto labour parties remains amorphous. The question is an important
one, because Rose Henderson was involved with the Ontario Labor Party,
the Toronto Labor Party, and the Independent Labor Party, which continued its existence into the 1930s.

The First Annual Convention of the OLP held in Toronto on 6–7 April
1928 elected Arthur Mould as president. No convention was held in
1929, but in 1930 the Second Annual Convention was held in Toronto on
18–19 April 1930; the seventy-three delegates returned Mould to the
presidency. The OLP met in convention in London, Ontario, on 3 April
1931 with Henderson present. A common belief in mainstream trade
union circles at the time that the OLP was a "Red" organization is belied
by the defeat, by a vote of thirty-eight to twenty-five, of an amendment
stating: "The Labor party recognizes Russia is endeavoring to establish a
Socialist republic, and is at this time making a valuable contribution to

Socialist thought and ideology." An amended motion, stating "that trade with Russia was in the best interests of workers generally and the Canadian worker in particular," was in accord with many Ontario trade unionists who had no love for the Communist Party or the Bolsheviks. There is no indication of how Henderson stood on the amendment, but given her past opinions on the Soviet Union, it is not unreasonable to believe that she was among the twenty-five voting for the original amendment.

Henderson was on the new executive of the OLP, and we can see her influence in the convention's concern with peace.[94] The 6 April 1931 issue of the *Globe* reports that the convention "spent a busy time with half a dozen resolutions on the theme of peace. One reaffirmed uncompromising opposition to war and preparations for war ... Another resolution pressed for action in favour of peace education in the schools." In addition, a "resolution voted down after a long discussion was one which advocated the establishment of a neutral 'Garden of Peace' somewhere along the boundary line between Canada and the United States. The scheme was regarded as having merit but was opposed because of some practical obstacles to working out the plan." The Peace Garden proposal has clear echoes of the focus put on the international boundary by the Women's Peace Union, in recent years one of Henderson's main involvements.[95]

The 1932 OLP convention was held in Windsor. The delegates called on Prime Minister R.B. Bennett to appoint a royal commission to look into the Beauharnois scandal. The convention "endorsed the proposal of Toronto Socialist members for a $25 weekly dole for a man and his wife and $2.50 weekly for each dependent child." The convention also called for repeal or amendment of Section 98 of the Criminal Code. A resolution calling for a six-hour day and a five-day week was adopted. Deportation of radicals and the unemployed was opposed because it caused dissension between foreign-born and Canadian workers. Henderson was again elected to the executive.[96]

An article entitled "The Labour Party of Ontario" in May 1932 in the *Border City Labour News*, published in Walkerville, reveals why Henderson was a supporter but also why she would not have felt entirely at ease with all members of the organization. The author writes of the communists: "They stand for bloody revolution; we stand for sane and peaceful re-organization by the power of the ballot. They appeal by their insidious suggestions to the barbaric element of vengeance; we appeal by a clean-cut, constitutional method of procedure to your intelligence. The motivating force behind the Communists is hate. The motivating force behind the Labour movement is Justice. They stand for a proletarian dictatorship; we stand for the institution of our Christian Ideals in a great Human Brotherhood. Need we say more?"[97]

Henderson was not an advocate of "bloody revolution," and she believed in "constitutional" methods, Christian ideals, and human brotherhood. On the other hand, her close association with leading communists was based in a belief that Communist Party members were motivated by a genuine desire to help the poor and oppressed, not by hate. As in the case of virtually every organization she was ever involved in, membership in the OLP came with the compromise of at least some of her beliefs.

We can see what made it possible for Henderson to stay in the OLP, however, in the author's further comments in the *Border City Labour News*: "No one can view the crumbling homes of our country today with their lowered vitality, their susceptibility to disease, their possibilities for crime, without realizing that rot has set in. This fair Canada of ours is diseased, and this is the work of our capitalistic system."[98] Here, in the language of a male-dominated labour movement, we see the impact of the generation of maternal feminists of which Henderson was an integral part. It was the "crumbling homes" of the country that signalled the decay and degeneration brought on by the evils of the capitalist system. This was the language of the Rose Henderson of the Montreal juvenile court, now being used in English Canada with the same unmistakable message. Her differences with the OLP notwithstanding, it was a moral universe she knew well.

On balance, it is fair to say that the OLP spearheaded by Mould was a more left-leaning party than the ILP of the early 1920s. Yet it is important, given what we have just observed about the OLP's anti-communism and adherence to Christian socialism, not to discount the impact of the ILP on Henderson's activism in Toronto in the early 1930s. As we have seen in her campaign in the 1919 by-election in St Catherines, and in Nova Scotia in the summer of 1920, there is a legacy to be explored in the Independent Labor Party. Women were a key part of that legacy; we have only to look to James Naylor's identification of Henderson, Flora MacDonald Denison, Laura Hughes, Harriet Prenter, Rose Hodgson, and Minnie Singer as playing a role in building the ILP in Ontario to appreciate their impact on Ontario's political culture.[99]

No direct evidence suggests that Henderson was active in either of the ILP's allied organizations, the Labor Educational Association of Ontario (LEAO) or the United Women's Educational Federation of Ontario (UWEFO), but their trajectories in the 1920s into the 1930s are important in understanding her involvement with the education system in Toronto. The LEAO was organized in Woodstock, Ontario, in 1902. Its name is rather misleading; as Naylor points out, it was actually "a loosely organized provincial federation of labour" that "spearheaded the campaign for the Workmen's Compensation Act."[100] At the Fifteenth Annual Convention of the LEAO held on 24 April 1917, delegates unanimously threw their support behind the creation of branches of an independent labour party. On 1 July 1917 the founding convention of the ILP was held.[101]

According to Naylor, the LEAO aimed for "more thorough organization of women workers of the province."[102] In that cause, the 1919 LEAO convention decided to establish the United Women's Educational Federation, officially founded in Brantford in 1920, as a vehicle for organizing women.[103] Minnie Singer, one of the first persons appointed to the province of Ontario's Mother's Allowance Commission, was elected president. Singer was one of a number of female activists Henderson worked with in Toronto in the 1930s, and one she must have felt a strong connection to, given that Henderson was widely acknowledged to be the leading advocate of mothers' pensions in the Canadian labour movement.

Naylor's claim that "working-class women were at odds with the mainstream of the women's movement" needs to be modified in light of the history of the women's labour movement in Ontario after 1925. At the 1921 provincial convention of the UWEFO, a motion was passed calling for capitalism to "pass peacefully into oblivion."[104] After 1921, "the UWEFO lost the anti-capitalist edge notable at the 1921 convention and followed the LEAO's conservative drift."[105] Over time the attention of the UWEFO "turned inexorably from the workplace to the household."[106] Yet as Naylor points out, the fact that the Women's Labor League, organized by Communist Party member Florence Custance, was interested "in nominating women as movie censors and juvenile-court judges places it within the maternal feminist current that viewed women as moral guardians of society."[107] Missing from Naylor's analysis, because it ends in the mid-1920s, is that the concerns of the LEAO and UWEFO took a left turn

in the late 1920s and early 1930s, in the sense that they lost some of their
focus on the home and shifted their attention to the schools, where opposition to war and militarism became prime concerns. We have already
observed a similar shift in emphasis from the home to the school in the
thinking of Henderson, all the while insisting that, although middle
class herself, her cause remained the working class.

She was now part of a broad-based coalition of left organizations in
which the causes of educational reformers and the causes of labour activists intertwined. These linkages emerge in a consideration of the Twenty-
Ninth Annual Convention of the LEAO held in the Hamilton Labor
Temple on 24 May 1931. At the convention, three of the issues Henderson
was later deeply involved in as a trustee on the Toronto Board of Education
– cadet training, corporal punishment in public schools, and the anti-war
movement – were front and centre in discussions. Speakers charged that
"certain boards of education were making money out of the cadet training
system." The Women's Federation "registered vigorous opposition against
lashes given to youthful offenders. The incoming executive was asked to
communicate a protest to the provincial secretary, Mrs. Rose Henderson,
regarding the lashing of youths as barbarous." The convention also endorsed a resolution "in support of disarmament on land, sea and air."[108]
Many of the issues Henderson later campaigned on, and which she was
sometimes credited with raising, had been part of the left political culture of Ontario for almost a generation by the time she became active on
the Toronto left. It is true, however, that she brought a new vitality to the
pursuit of these issues, and as a prominent Toronto leftist in the 1930s
kept them in the public consciousness.

Having set out Henderson's involvement in the non-communist left,
labour education, and working-class women's political activism, it is necessary to include an understanding of her relationship with the
Communist Party, which in turn involves an understanding of the politics of international Stalinism. Following the death of Lenin in January
1924, Joseph Stalin emerged victorious in the ensuing struggle for control of the Bolshevik Party and the Soviet Union itself. As this struggle
unfolded, Canadian communists were forced to make gut-wrenching,
often life-changing decisions about whether or not to accept Stalin's victory or to side with his opponents. Leon Trotsky was by far the most influential, and therefore most threatening, of Stalin's opponents, and his

lead was the one dissidents in Canada were mostly likely to follow. Canadian communists, notably Maurice Spector, played a crucial role in returning from the Soviet Union with news of Stalin's ascendancy and Trotsky's exile.[109] Spector and Jack MacDonald became leading Canadian Trotskyists, while William Moriarty became the leading exponent of the ideas of the American Communist Party leader Jay Lovestone, who was in turn influenced by Nicolai Bukharin. As the Canadian Labor Party was in the process of breaking up, communists such as MacDonald and Moriarty were under increasing pressure to accept Stalin's control. Among others, they were expelled from the Communist Party of Canada in 1929–30, leaving them looking for a home in a left political culture undergoing the profound changes detailed above.

In 1928–29 the Communist Party shifted out of its united front phase into the Third Period. This shift involved pulling communist-led unions out of the Trades and Labor Congress and the All-Canadian Congress of Labor to form an independent trade union organization called the Workers' Unity League. At the same time, the switch in strategy involved condemning all opponents of Soviet Communism – anarchists, Trotskyists, syndicalists, and social democrats – as social fascists, de facto allies of the German Nazis and Italian fascists. The organizational strategy and ideological framework underpinning the Workers' Unity League has been the subject of much debate among labour historians, with powerful arguments being put forward by both opponents and supporters.[110] That debate serves as the backdrop of a discussion of Henderson's relationship with the Communist Party in this period.

The unemployment issue that became of such importance to the left in the early 1930s is a way of bringing Henderson's relationship with the Third Period Communist Party more clearly into focus. As Andrée Lévesque points out in her biography of Jeanne Corbin, in 1931 the Communist Party, through the aegis of the Workers' Unity League, launched a major campaign in support of non-contributory unemployment insurance.[111] Unemployment was an issue around which usually fractious left tendencies could unite, at least temporarily, a form of "united front" that Third Period Communists – in theory, at least – were compelled to attack. The 25 July 1931 edition of *The Worker* carried an article entitled "The Council for Progressive Labor Action a New Attempt to Mislead the Working Class." According to the article, two or three weeks before a call had been sent out to "all progressive labor bodies" to attend a conference on unemployment. The National Unemployed Workers' Association, the Communist Party's unemployed organization, and the Workers' Unity League were not on the list of progressive labour bodies. The invitation to the conference "was over the signatures of a number of tired and despectable [sic] radicals, including Wm. Moriarty, D. Valin, R. Shoesmith, Rose Henderson, W. Lyons, etc. Everything from fabianism to social chauvinism was well represented in the deluge of balderdash on the subject of unemployment, and like other conferences of a similar character the main item was lacking – the Unemployed themselves."[112]

This kind of invective, typical of the Communist Party's Third Period, has led Canadian labour historians to pay too much attention to the rhetoric and not enough attention to the practice. The party's actions toward Henderson revealed that in practice, it continued to forge alliances with social democrats and independent leftists at this time. Even though *The Worker* attacked both Moriarty and Henderson, a clear distinction must be made. Moriarty, having been expelled from the Communist Party as a "right deviationist," was beyond redemption, while Henderson remained a possible candidate for party membership. She had no skeletons in the party closet and had burned no party bridges.

Henderson has left no record of precisely how she reacted to being wooed by the Communist Party, but the circumstantial evidence suggests that she was circumspect. On 29 December 1931 a "special meeting" of the Toronto Unemployed Association was held; "special invitations" were sent to Tim Buck, Harry Guralnick, and J. Boychuk of the Workers' United Front Committee, and to Henderson, Jimmy Simpson, A.M. Barnetson, J. Romer, and G. Watson of the Toronto Labor Party. Simpson, an Orangeman, demonstrated his true colours to the communists by choosing to speak to a meeting of the Orange Order instead.[113] Barnetson was the only Labor Party candidate who showed up.

Henderson was being wooed by the Communist Party as one of a number of non-communist leftists who could be convinced to at least support communist initiatives, if not join the party. Historians of the Third Period have tended to make the mistake of believing that the party cut itself off from non-communist leftists in the period, mindlessly condemning them all as social fascists. Rhetoric is not reality. In reality, behind the rhetorical excess that one finds in *The Worker*, for example, is the same ongoing effort to strengthen the party by enlisting sympathetic non-communists. The point is that there was no dramatic watershed separating the Third Period from the Second before it or from the Popular Front that followed it. Henderson was picking and choosing her ways of working with the Communist Party in the Third Period, and she continued to do so during the Popular Front. In both periods, she was a cautious ally.

Her caution in working with the Communist Party must not be understood as a failure to have a significant impact on the Toronto left in the early 1930s. Appreciating her full impact requires a fuller exploration of heretofore neglected organizations and relationships on the Toronto left in the late 1920s and early 1930s. More attention needs to be paid to the All-Canadian Congress of Labor (ACCL), organized at a convention in Montreal in March 1927. The convention brought together its most important unit, the Canadian Brotherhood of Railway Employees, with the One Big Union, and a number of communist-led unions in opposition to the international unionism of the Trades and Labor Congress. Two key developments happened in 1929: the Communist unions left the ACCL to join the newly created Workers' Unity League, and at the union's convention Aaron Mosher, president of the Canadian Brotherhood of Railway Employees and leader of the ACCL, called for the creation of a labour party.[114] That party was created, but not until 1931. The ACCL was the "sponsor" of the National Labor Party (NLP), its aim "to organize the workers politically for the purpose of establishing, by constitutional means, an equitable economy and social order."[115]

In spite of its small size, the NLP is an important piece of the puzzle of the Toronto left in the early 1930s, in large part because Elizabeth Morton, Henderson's associate in a number of left organizations, was its secretary.[116] There is a natural tendency to believe, because the ACCL itself was anti-revolutionary, if not anti-socialist, that the NLP shared its politics. That idea would be profoundly misleading, as evidenced by Morton's statement in September 1931 that the party was "to endeavor by political action to capture the machinery of government so as to permit of a complete transformation from the present system of Capitalism to a Socialist Commonwealth, where the physical and mental requirements necessary to sustain the highest and fullest standard of human well-being will be assured." In addition to the revolutionary goal, the party had "immediate objects," the first being to "unite the working class into one political party independent of all political parties with the view of securing working-class legislation."[117]

It is necessary to take a moment to assess what Morton was saying, as the backdrop to Henderson's involvement with the NLP. First, the use of the term "Commonwealth" presaged the creation of the Cooperative Commonwealth Federation the following year, and helps explain why Morton or Henderson might be drawn to it. Second, the desire to create a party of the working class was drawn directly from *The Communist Manifesto* and confirmed the fears of social democrats such as Agnes Macphail and J.S. Woodsworth that they were dealing with people who wanted to create a "foreign" rather than domestic brand of socialism. Third, in spite of the focus on working-class legislation, the revolutionary language embodied the seeds of dissent that would cause rifts between Morton and Henderson and the leadership of the CCF.

The main organ of the National Labor Party was the *Canadian Trade Unionist*. The paper began in December 1925 as the organ of the Canadian Federation of Labor, then of the ACCL. On 29 September 1931, edited by Alex Lyon, it became the "Official Bulletin" of the Amalgamated Carpenters of Canada.[118] At this point it is difficult to decipher the actual relationship of the ACCL and the Amalgamated Carpenters, but one gets the distinct impression that the ACCL has distanced itself from the paper and its radical – by ACCL standards – editor. A Marxist like Elizabeth Morton, Lyon provided a radical edge to the National Labor Party and the *Canadian Trade Unionist* that is not possible to decipher from the names of the party and the paper.[119]

A perusal of the pages of the *Canadian Trade Unionist* in the early 1930s reveals the problem with separating out class, gender, and ethnic histories of the period, a problem already identified in looking at the relationship between Henderson and Ida Siegel. For example, in October 1930 both Siegel and Morton addressed a meeting on unemployment organized by the Local Council of Women.[120] We see here the coming together of the "working class," "middle class," and "Jewish" aspects of women's activism in Toronto. All politically active women in Toronto in this period, Henderson included, could support the NLP's call for the abolition of cadet training in all schools.[121]

Henderson, like the NLP, was swept up in the debate concerning affiliation with the Cooperative Commonwealth Federation.[122] By late fall

1932 the National Labor Party was advocating affiliation.[123] The absence of the NLP from existing histories of the Ontario left in this period is regrettable, in part because Morton and Henderson were the two female members on the NLP's executive committee of twelve members.[124] As a closer look at the history of the formation of the CCF in Ontario reveals, the two women played critical roles in challenging the terms of affiliation of existing organizations to the CCF set out by the CCF leadership. Theirs is an untold but historically meaningful story.

In May 1932 eleven Progressive and Labour members of parliament, led by J.S. Woodsworth and including Agnes Macphail, leader of the United Farmers of Ontario, met in Ottawa to organize the Canadian Commonwealth Party. At a convention in Calgary two months later, in response to the "strongly socialist opinion expressed on the floor," the name was changed to the Cooperative Commonwealth Federation (Farmer Labour Socialist) to reflect the affiliation of existing organizations such as the Independent Labor Party of Manitoba and the Saskatchewan Farmer-Labour Party.[125] The new party dedicated itself to "supplying human needs instead of the making of profits." Following the Calgary conference, Macphail and William Irvine spearheaded the Ontario campaign, enlisting support for a mass rally to be held in Toronto in November, at the same time as the convention of the United Farmers of Ontario.[126]

Histories of this period written by members and supporters of the New Democratic Party have failed, intentionally or not, to convey the dynamics of how the CCF came into being in Ontario. Correspondence that Bert Robinson of the Socialist Party of Canada (Ontario Section) exchanged with Woodsworth and Macphail reveals relationships in which Robinson was clearly taking the initiative, with Woodsworth and Macphail deferring to his opinions.[127] In February 1932, three months before the Progressive and Labour members met in Ottawa, Woodsworth acknowledged in a letter to Robinson that the latter was already attempting to create "a new organization" in Toronto.[128] Late in the summer of 1932 Robinson wrote to Macphail, telling her that the Socialist Party was organizing an Eastern Canada Conference, which involved his writing to J.J. Morrison of the United Farmers of Ontario.[129] On the same day, 7 August 1932, Robinson wrote to Woodsworth, telling him about plans to call an Eastern Canada Conference and noting that he was writing to a number of labour and socialist organizations, including the

Ontario Labor Party, the Quebec section of the Canadian Labor Party, and the National Labor Party.[130]

As Desmond Morton points out, the CCF's claim to labour support was "tenuous" from the outset.[131] Jimmy Simpson went to the September 1932 annual convention of the Trades and Labor Congress in order to win support for the new movement, but the issue was not even put to a vote. Morton also points out that the CCF did not have the support of the All-Canadian Congress of Labor, leaving Woodsworth "to build the CCF on its cantankerous farmer and socialist foundations."[132] Morton's assessment needs qualification. Robinson's August letter to Woodsworth reveals that efforts were made. For the November 1932 meeting in Toronto, according to Terry Crowley, the Socialist Party of Canada (Ontario Section) and the League for Social Reconstruction brought the Toronto Labor Party, representing the AFL-TLC unions, and the National Labor Party, representing the ACCL unions, together.[133] The Toronto and National Labor parties did not represent a majority of members in TLC and ACCL unions, but the political wings of the two union umbrella organizations were there.

In 1933 James MacArthur Conner penned the "Toronto Labor Party Statement." It is a key document in understanding why Henderson, who was vice-president of the Toronto Labor Party, initially opposed affiliation with the CCF. Conner wrote about the "mass meeting" held in Toronto in November 1932, financed by labour and socialist groups. In Conner's version, the names of several hundred men and women were sent to Woodsworth, with the understanding that they wanted to join the existing farmer, labour, and socialist organizations. Two days later, according to Conner, Woodsworth claimed that "an unexpected situation had arisen in Toronto and that people would not join Labour and Socialist parties and he was going to provide for them by the organization of Clubs."[134] Rather than turning the names over to the existing socialist and labour parties, Woodsworth used them to create a third organization, the CCF Clubs. To form the clubs, he appointed a committee that included E.A. Havelock, Frank Underhill, C.B. Sissons, Agnes Macphail, and "three manufacturers," but not a single labour representative. Conner noted that a member of the executive committee of the Ontario Labor Party – possibly Henderson – wrote to Woodsworth to protest "this autocratic action."[135]

Conner's version of events does not coincide with that provided by Robinson as general secretary of the Socialist Party of Canada (OS). Robinson, in a letter to Andrew Glen, pointed out that the hundreds of new people referred to by Conner wanted to join the CCF : "It was no use asking them to align themselves with one or other of the existing groups." Robinson's version of events sanctioned Woodsworth's decision to create the CCF Clubs. This was a decision, according to Robinson, that "we" took – clearly indicating that he did not believe that Woodsworth had acted autocratically.[136] Robinson's version of events is adopted by historian Terry Crowley, who states that more than a thousand people "signed cards indicating they would join the CCF."[137] Which version is the more accurate cannot be determined on the basis of the existing evidence.

The key to understanding the ensuing events is that the main opposition to the actions of Woodsworth and Macphail was coming from the Toronto Labor Party, not the Socialist Party of Canada (OS). That is, it was the "Marxists" who were most supportive of the actions of the CCF leadership, and the members of the TLC-affiliated Toronto Labor Party who were most opposed. The Socialist Party was not, as Crowley argues, one of the "ineffectual groups" involved in the creation of the CCF in Ontario.[138] In his 3 February 1933 letter to Andrew Glen, Robinson noted that D.M. LeBourdais, secretary of the CCF Clubs, was "a signed applicant for membership in the Socialist Party. Phillips, Miller, Cummings, Guyot and others gained their contacts through membership in the Socialist Party, and are now serving in Secretarial and Executive positions in the Clubs." We see here the link between one of the most radical of the non-communist left groups in Toronto in the early 1930s and the most reformist section of the emerging CCF. Robinson, appearances to the contrary, was not capitulating to the leadership of the CCF but genuinely believed that the Socialist Party members would enter the CCF Clubs and radicalize members, who were "far from being socialists."[139]

In his 3 February 1933 letter to Glen, Robinson said that the "Committee of 12 from the Conference" had met about ten days before. The meeting once again demonstrated the opposition of Toronto Labor Party members to Robinson's plans, as Henderson, J.M. Conner, George Watson, and Alderman John Mitchell of Hamilton all abstained on Robinson's motion to call the Labor Conference together to vote for affiliation to the CCF.[140] In a letter Robinson wrote to delegates before the

Labor Conference meeting held in Cumberland Hall, Toronto, on
26 February 1933, he observed, "I want to confide in you about the situation here. Conner and Henderson are opposing the Labour Conference and
the C.C.F. It seems that they are organizing a campaign against it."[141]

It was not true that Henderson was opposed to the Labor Conference,
or indeed to the CCF; she abstained on the vote to affiliate the Labor
Conference to the CCF rather than voting against it. We know by now,
having followed her life on the left, that she could never be opposed to a
broad-based working-class party truly dedicated to the cause of ending
capitalist exploitation and the oppression of women, children, and the
working class. Her instincts told her, and her instincts were right, that the
motives of the leaders of the CCF were not to be accepted at face value.

Her ongoing participation in the Labor Conference is indication
enough that she was not campaigning against it. On Sunday, 5 February
1933, the sub-committees representing the United Farmers of Ontario,
the Labor Conference, and the CCF Clubs met at the office of the CCF
Clubs, 3 Charles Street West, Toronto. Henderson represented the Labor
Conference, along with Arthur Mould, Bert Robinson, Elizabeth Morton,
and Alderman Mitchell. Agnes Macphail and Graham Spry were also in
attendance.[142] It was decided that the fifteen representatives present
would form a provincial council until the three sections met to elect official delegates to it.[143] If we accept Robinson's account of Henderson's
opposition, we are forced to accept that she was campaigning against the
very organization she chose to be a representative of. In fact, there is no
evidence to suggest that she was part of an organized "campaign" against
the Labor Conference or the CCF.

On 20 February 1933 the *Star* reported on the Toronto Labor Party
conference held the day before in the Labor Temple. The party spent five
hours debating its relationship with the recently formed CCF . By a vote
of twenty-five to five, the following motion was adopted: "The Toronto
Labor party makes it a condition of affiliation with the C.C.F. that the
C.C.F. clubs should have no voting power when C.C.F. principles are being discussed unless they are affiliated with farmer, Labor or Socialist organizations." Henderson commented: "I have nothing against the C.C.F.
clubs as long as they don't masquerade under the name of Labor. We are
cursed by white-collared slaves ashamed of the working classes, to whom
they owe their existence. What guarantee have we of these C.C.F. clubs

that when the time comes they will not do exactly the same as MacDonald did in Great Britain? The tragedy of the working classes to-day is middle class rule, and we are being asked to sink our own interests for the benefit of a glorified middle class party."

Several speakers, including Thomas Cruden of the Socialist Party, countered Henderson by defending the clubs, arguing that they would spread the socialist message much more broadly than the labour movement was able to do, thus preparing the ground for it.[144] The crucial point, and also the tragedy from a socialist perspective, is that both Henderson and Cruden were pursuing a socialist future but allowed themselves to be divided by contrasting visions of how to get there.

It cannot be said too many times that the opposition to affiliating with the CCF was coming from the Toronto Labor Party, not from the Socialist Party of Canada (OS). Opposition was not coming from people who were "Marxist sectarians." Gerald Caplan, who claims that John Mitchell was "infinitely more representative of Ontario workers" than Elizabeth Morton, is apparently unaware of Morton's deep involvement with the Amalgamated Carpenters of Canada as a member of the Women's Guild. She was a Marxist, but also a woman with deep roots in the working class and trade union movement. She and Henderson, vice-president of the Toronto Labor Party but not a member of the Socialist Party, emerge as the villains of the piece. Terry Crowley comments on Henderson's "intransigent stance," going so far as to claim that she and Conner "attempted to discredit J.S. Woodsworth."[145] Crowley provides no evidence, and apart from an argument that Henderson was attacking Woodsworth personally by questioning affiliation with the CCF, the claim is invalid. She was as committed to "constitutional" methods as Woodsworth and Macphail, and was as reticent to engage in personal attacks on other members of the left as any individual in this period. Caplan's association of her with "paranoid hostilities" is equally unwarranted; she was questioning affiliation more than she was opposing it, as her later involvement with the CCF demonstrates.[146] As we shall see, most of the paranoia was on the part of the leadership of the CCF and the historians who have defended it.

On 26 February 1933 the Labor Conference met at Cumberland Hall in Toronto, with Mould presiding in the morning, Cruden in the afternoon. The minutes of the first conference were read and adopted. The conference was attended by delegates from thirteen labour party units, including the Ontario Labor Party and the Toronto Labor Party. In addition, there were delegates from the Toronto and Ottawa locals of the National Labor Party, ACCL president Aaron Mosher being the Ottawa delegate. The thirteen Independent Labor Party units included the Ward Five ILP, led by delegate Henderson. There were five branches of the Socialist Party of Canada (OS), seven socialist groups, four workers' associations, five "miscellaneous groups," and thirteen trade union organizations.

It is important at this point to assess the state of labour organization in Toronto and Henderson's place in it. At this time she represented the Ward Five ILP, was on the executive of the Ontario Labor Party, was vice-president of the Toronto Labor Party, and was on the executive of the Labor Conference.[147] Was there another person on the left in the province of Ontario at the time who had this kind of influence? Yet the existing histories have nothing to say about her contribution, preferring to cast her in a negative light as an opponent of the "natural" growth of the CCF out of a sea of faction and Marxist doctrinaires.

The main topic of the 26 February 1933 conference was the recommendation submitted by the Labor Conference Committee of 12: "That all labor and socialist organizations affiliate with the Co-operative Commonwealth Federation, through the Labor Conference." The Toronto Labor Party presented an amendment: "That this Convention go on record making it a condition of affiliation with the C.C.F. that the C.C.F. Clubs should have no voting power when C.C.F. principles are being discussed unless they are affiliated with farmer, labor or socialist organizations." This amendment confirmed the fact that the opposition of the dissidents was directed specifically at the clubs, not at the labor conference or the CCF itself. After a long discussion, the amendment was defeated by a vote of seventy-six to fifty-seven, and the motion carried.[148] How individual delegates voted is not recorded, but we can safely assume that Henderson voted against the motion and for the amendment.

The resolution put forward at this conference by the Socialist Party, and the response to it, is revealing. The resolution read:

The Labor Conference of Ontario representing sixty labor and socialist organizations in this province demand that every working man and woman denounce the existing Federal Government on its avowed intention to persecute and intimidate the working class movement by retaining as a part of the law of this land the infamous Section 98 of the Criminal code, and Sections 41 and 42 of the Immigration act, under which mass deportations are taking place, and furthermore, the workers here represented demand the immediate release of Tim Buck and his seven associates now in Kingston Penitentiary, and the release of all other men and women incarcerated for working class activities; and they furthermore demand discontinuance of the prosecution now under way against Tim Buck on the ground that the attitude of the Bennett government and the venomous propaganda of the Capitalist press toward class war prisoners makes a fair trial unattainable at this time.

It is interesting that such a resolution could pass unanimously, given its defence of Communist Party members and its Marxist language, yet the delegates were not willing to entrust CCF principles to farmer, labour, and socialist organizations within the conference. Even delegates from the League for Social Reconstruction and the Christian Social Order supported the SPC's resolution.[149]

The unanimous vote in favour of this resolution reveals the problem with laying the blame for the ongoing conflict at the doorstep of Marxists, radicals, and sectarians. With its unmistakable Communist Party phrases such as "class war prisoners," the resolution shows that there was a shared language and world view on the Ontario left in the early 1930s that transcended the myriad organizations and political tendencies. Henderson, Conner, and their fellow oppositionists, if only in the most nebulous way, understood that the reorganization of the CCF being advocated by the leadership of the party marked a point of no return in the history of the Canadian left. They understood that the shift from a federation of farmer, socialist, and labour groups to a centralized party based on individual membership represented a concession to liberal capitalist democracy that a class-based, revolutionary politics could not withstand.

The annual convention of the Ontario Labor Party was held in Brantford on Easter weekend 1933. Of the ninety-two delegates who voted on affiliation with the CCF, eighty-five voted in favour and seven abstained. Henderson maintained the position she took at the 19 February 1933 meeting of the Toronto Labor Party, favouring "safeguards for labor." She

supported affiliation "on the principles laid down – farmer, labor and socialist," continuing to evince her concern with the middle-class nature of
the CCF Clubs. Bert Robinson, reporting on the convention to Woodsworth,
wrote that Conner and Henderson, supported by the "Jewish groups and
the Windsor Branches," wanted amendments to the main resolution on
affiliation to the CCF that would change the name of the clubs and compel them to come in through the existing labour groups. Mould ruled
both amendments out of order. During the debate Henderson "made
sentimental appeal against the middle class." Conner ended up voting for
the resolution, while Henderson voted with six others against it.[150]

Of the prominent labour and socialist activists in Ontario in the early
1930s, it was Henderson who held out the longest against labour's affiliation to the CCF on the basis set out by the party leadership. The events of
this Ontario Labor Party convention reveal the problem with lumping
her with Marxian socialists such as Morton, because Morton was one of
the Socialist Party members at the convention who campaigned for "unconditional affiliation" to the CCF.[151] Given that Mould, president of the
Ontario Labor Party, and Robinson, secretary of the Socialist Party of
Canada (OS), had swung the great majority of their memberships in opposition to Henderson and Conner, it is invidious to say the least to suggest that the CCF leadership was in any danger of not getting its way.

Robinson's comments on the role of the Socialist Party quite power-
fully disprove the claim that it was a marginal player in these events. At
the spring 1933 convention of the Ontario Labor Party, six of the sixteen
delegates elected to its provincial executive were members of the Socialist
Party. Robinson wrote to Woodsworth on 16 April: "It is conceded that
the Socialist Party's influence in favor of C.C.F. Affiliation from the com-
mencement has been the largest factor in effecting this last triumph for
Labor in Ontario. I mention this, J.S., in no boastful manner, but as a
reply to those who are impatient with these continued meetings, conferences and conventions; who consider we are wasting time. Frankly, I am
convinced that had the Socialist Party used as much effort in joining with
those opposing affiliation, there would be a different story to tell in Ontario
to-day. By winning Mould, and then Mitchell, victory was ensured."[152]

Throughout this period the Socialist Party was not, as the Caplan-
Crowley paradigm would have it, sabotaging the CCF – it was, in fact, its
strongest advocate in the Ontario labour movement. The Socialist Party

played a pivotal role in beating back the challenge of Henderson, Conner, and their supporters in the Toronto Labor Party. Lost in all of this is Henderson's genuine commitment to the idea that the new party should be a labour party. She was right to be concerned that middle-class elements in the clubs did not have a genuine commitment to the working class and its problems.

By the spring of 1933, however, the stage was set for confrontation between the CCF leadership and the Socialist Party. Robinson ended his 16 April 1933 letter to Woodsworth advocating a united front with the Communist Party, which did not in Robinson's opinion mean agreeing with the Communists on "tactics or philosophy." He noted approvingly that the Ontario Labor Party convention unanimously passed a call to all units of the party to organize "United May Day Conferences." He ended his letter to Woodsworth asking for a speaker for May Day. The die was cast.

The extraordinary growth of the CCF Clubs made Henderson a lone voice crying in the wilderness. By July 1933 some fifty clubs had been organized in Ontario, with a membership of some six thousand.[153] The battle to have club members affiliate through existing labour and socialist organizations now lost, Henderson turned her attention to furthering the cause of the Labor Conference. At the Labor Conference meeting held in Toronto on 23 April 1933 she was named to the seven-member Resolutions Committee that included Elizabeth Morton. Henderson was also elected to a permanent committee of twelve to act as the executive of the conference, a committee that included Mould and Morton.[154] Within days of the Ontario Labor Party convention, where Mould had ruled against the amendments of the Toronto Labor Party and Morton had campaigned for unconditional affiliation to the CCF, Henderson found herself working elbow to elbow with them in the common cause of promoting the interests of labour in politics.

On 7 May 1933 the provisional provincial council of the CCF met at the office of the CCF Clubs. Woodsworth and William Irvine were in attendance, with Woodsworth serving as chair. It was decided that the provincial council should consist of twelve representatives of each of the three sections: the clubs, the United Farmers of Ontario, and the Labor Conference. The work of the council of thirty-six was to be carried out by a nine-person executive committee, with three members from each section. Agnes Macphail was elected president, and Bert Robinson secretary, subject to ratification by the full council. During the meeting a "Platform Committee" was appointed to "draft the provincial political platform of the C.C.F." D.M. LeBourdais was the convenor, the other members being Elmore Philpott, R.J. Scott, president of the UFO, H.H. Hannam, Morton, and Henderson.[155]

Henderson now found herself in a rather paradoxical position. On the one hand, her position on the Platform Committee gave her an important role in defining the policies of the CCF. She was a significant figure in the emerging Ontario CCF, and her public role reflected that importance. On Saturday, 27 May 1933, for example, she spoke at a CCF mass meeting held in Massey Hall, her fellow speakers being Philpott, Cruden, and Woodsworth.[156] The paradox emerges from the first full meeting of the provincial council of the CCF on 5 June 1933. Mould, Morton, and Robinson, all members of the Socialist Party of Canada (OS), were named to the council's executive. Henderson was not.[157] While it is possible that she was named and declined, it does not change the fact that the so-called "sectarians" were now in a much more advantageous position within the CCF than was Henderson, who was less ideologically driven than Mould, Morton, and Robinson.[158]

The Regina convention of the CCF is now upon us. That convention is legendary, and as it has been dealt with in some detail by other authors, it will not be discussed in detail here.[159] The key issue in relation to Henderson's protest against the CCF Clubs is the composition of the Ontario delegates who went to Regina. Ontario was allowed eighty-two delegates, four from the provincial council and twenty-six from each of the sections.[160] In the event, the clubs were represented in Regina by the full twenty-six members, while the UFO sent fourteen members and the Labor Conference only five.[161] Financial and ideological/organizational concerns likely explain the low level of representation by the Labor Conference. We see here further confirmation of Henderson's fears of middle-class influence in the CCF. The Regina Manifesto itself was largely the creation of University of Toronto professor Frank Underhill and McGill University professor Frank Scott. Underhill and Scott were members of the League for Social Reconstruction, organized in the winter of 1931–32. Eugene Forsey recalled receiving the first draft of the Regina Manifesto from Underhill and Scott and that he and King Gordon made only "very minor" changes to it.[162]

Henderson did not attend the Regina convention, and no account of her opinion of its proceedings or of the Regina Manifesto itself has come to light. It is revealing, therefore, that in August 1933 she sought to be the CCF candidate in the Temiskaming provincial riding. She had connections in the region, having campaigned there for ILP candidate Angus McDonald in 1920. She was identified among those who "contested the convention." It appears, therefore, that she was at the convention held in New Liskeard.[163] Her connections with the region notwithstanding, it seems a curious choice to make the month after not going to the Regina convention. Are we seeing evidence here of her need to be in the public spotlight, a greater possibility in a northern Ontario riding than at the CCF convention where she would have been a relatively minor figure, if not perceived as an impediment to the rise of the CCF? It is, of course, possible that she had other commitments in late July 1933, but it seems odd that a woman who for so much of her life was in the middle of the action was missing in action on this occasion.

Little evidence exists concerning Henderson's activities in the fall of 1933, but what evidence there is suggests that she continued to advocate labour unity and was focusing on labour's role in the CCF. The 30 September 1933 edition of the *Star* reported on a meeting held the previous night at the Royal York Hotel by the international trade unions. The meeting discussed labour's attitude to the CCF and the best way to strengthen the Toronto Labor Party. Controller Jimmy Simpson stated that decisions on these issues would be arrived at the following Friday night. Henderson was on the committee set up to prepare an agenda for the meeting and to do the necessary organizational work. Revealingly, she was the only woman on a twelve-person committee that included Toronto Labor Party president George Watson, Jimmy Simpson, and John W. Bruce.

Once again, Henderson proves to be a key figure in advancing our understanding of labour and the left in Canada in the 1930s. It is easy to forget that the Toronto Labor Party, which spearheaded the position that members of the clubs should not sign up in the CCF as individuals but rather through existing labour and socialist organizations, was the political arm of the TLC unions. Henderson's insistence on a labour base for the CCF did not emerge from her short association with the One Big Union or out of ideological Marxism – it emerged out of her long association, since 1912, with the Trades and Labor Congress. Her position has

been misrepresented in a historiography that focuses on the fact that
at the Calgary meeting in 1932, the only labour representative from east
of Manitoba was Aaron Mosher, leader of the Canadian Brotherhood
of Railway Employees and the All-Canadian Congress of Labor. His
subsequent membership on the CCF national executive "aroused strong
anti-CCF feeling among Mosher's TLC enemies," according to Gad
Horowitz.[164] Henderson may not have shared John Bruce's antipathy to
the CBRE and the ACCL, but she did share his opinion in 1933 that the
CCF was not a true labour party.[165] In effect, she was an advocate of the
kind of vision of the CCF that is now almost universally attributed to
David Lewis, who was studying at Oxford when she was working toward
better TLC-CCF cooperation.

In the fall of 1933, our focus shifts from labour to education, as
Henderson's first successful campaign for a position on the Toronto
District School Board is now in view. There seems little doubt, her conflicts with the CCF notwithstanding, that association with the new party
proved beneficial to her campaign. Her ideas on education in this period
are not well known, but in the spring of 1933 she appeared to believe that
the existing schools were places "where people are taught to think for
themselves." There was in her ideas the suggestion that the CCF would
gain control of the education system and educate students away from the
capitalist system and toward an acceptance of socialism.[166]

The position Henderson took on the education system did not go unnoticed in the Communist Party. At this time Stanley Ryerson was publishing a two-part series entitled "Education and the Proletariat" in
Masses.[167] Ryerson wrote: "Reformist leaders have again and again put forward ideas of 'revolution through education', of transforming capitalism
into socialism in the schools. The ludicrousness of such proposals, in a society where education is as much a part of the state machinery, controlled
by the financial oligarchy, as the army or the police force, is only equalled
by their insidiousness as means of deceiving the masses. The CCF, from
Mrs. Rose Henderson, 'PH.D.' down, is vociferous in such assertions."[168]

There is no question that Ryerson, a young man of middle-class background in a largely proletarian party, was establishing his credentials by attacking Henderson's middle-class naiveté. In addition, the quotation marks
around "PH.D." indicate either that he did not believe Henderson actually
had one, or else reflected the dismissive attitude of someone who could not

believe that a person with a doctorate could be so misguided. The attack was also spurred by the context of the Third Period, which compelled Ryerson to go after Henderson as a "social fascist." These personal and political motives notwithstanding, there was more than a little truth to the critique. Given Henderson's attacks on class privilege, corruption, and the overweening power of capitalism in Canadian society, it is rather astonishing that she actually believed that young people were being taught to think for themselves in schools. It is equally surprising that she appeared to believe that young people educated in the existing school system would come to understand the need to support the CCF and replace the capitalist system.

In her defence, it is easy to forget in our own jaded world the immense optimism instilled in many Canadian socialists by the seemingly meteoric rise to prominence of the CCF. She was riding that wave, and as 1933 came to a close, she was not the only socialist in the land making these kinds of hyperbolic statements. Neither her ideas about the education system nor her earlier opposition to the basis on which the Ontario CCF was being organized now impeded her standing in the party. On 7 December 1933, at a special meeting of the Toronto and District Council of the CCF, the "municipal platform" was read clause by clause and agreed to. The proposed platform for the Board of Education was read clause by clause and agreed to. All concurred in the choice of Rose Henderson as the Ward Five candidate for the board.[169]

On 2 January 1934 the *Star* assessed the changed political landscape of the city as a result of the municipal elections. Newly elected controller Jimmy Simpson stated that his association with the CCF had helped rather than hindered his campaign. He observed that his supporters knew that he would not lend his support "to any kind of confiscation or unconstitutional action." He praised the *Star* "for its splendid campaign on my behalf," and also commented that organized labour was "a great factor in my success." The report described him as "the first man ever to be elected to the Toronto board of control as a C.C.F.-Labor candidate." Outgoing Ward Five trustee Harold Menzies attributed his defeat to Henderson to the CCF, Simpson's organization, and the swing in the women's vote caused by the fact that Dr Caroline Brown did not run. He also acknowledged that Henderson had run a good campaign.

There was a new party in town, and it had made a splash, but the fact remained that sixteen of the twenty trustees on the new Board of

Education were Conservatives. The Conservative Party supporters were joined by a lone Liberal, Reginald Shaw, two independents, and Rose Henderson, the first ever CCF representative on the board. Protestant dominance also remained; eight trustees were United Church, seven were Anglican, and one was Presbyterian. There was one "Hebrew" – Siegel – and two Catholics. Henderson was not identified with a religion.[170] Although a Quaker, in later years she would be identified as Anglican. The *Star* may not have known her religion, but it did know that she had "a long record of adherence to labour and social service policies." Her career as a school trustee, according to the editor, would be "followed with interest."[171]

As Henderson launched herself into the last hectic and fruitful years of her life, her election to the Board of Education seemed to rekindle her old concern with children, peace, and the impact of war. She participated in the celebration of the fourteenth anniversary of the League of Nations at the Humewood School on Wednesday, 10 January 1934. Addressing the young people of the League of Nations Pioneers, she emphasized "the horror and futility of war. She recounted some of her experiences in a post-war trip through Germany, impressing upon her audience the sorrowful conditions prevailing among innocent children denied the happiness which is their right."[172] On Monday, 15 January 1934, she sat at the head table with Alice Chown, Siegel, and other prominent women at a banquet attended by more than one hundred people organized by the Women's International League for Peace and Freedom. The speaker was Nora Frances Henderson, a Hamilton "alderman." Nora Henderson, who would be a candidate for the Reconstruction Party in the 1935 federal election, touched on a number of themes that Rose Henderson had been espousing for many years. She "emphasized the importance of a new attitude of mind toward others" and "wondered if the people were alarmed that democracy was giving way to nationalism." Like Rose Henderson, she called on women "to clean up the mess" and "decried military balls and adulation of the military."[173]

So much had changed in Rose Henderson's life, but in the mid-1930s the home continued to be a metaphor for the world. Now, the home would begin to give way to the school.

8

Home, School, and Labour Hall

Having won election to the Toronto and District School Board, Henderson was launched on a career that saw her solidification as a member of the CCF and a respected, if controversial, figure in the public life of Toronto. If we look ahead a year, we see how quickly she established herself in this period of her life. In her first year on the board, she forged a reputation that made her a difficult opponent, as the *Toronto Daily Star* noted heading into the campaign for 1935: "S.H. Menzies is to run for council in Ward Five instead of staging an attempt to return to the board where he lost his seat a year ago to Mrs. Rose Henderson."[1] The CCF paper, the *New Commonwealth*, announced: "TORONTO VOTES C.C.F. ... Dr. Rose Henderson Re-elected at Head of Poll." Her victory, the paper claimed, "was a tribute to the work she has done on the board."[2] The Quaker paper reported, not entirely accurately, given the support Henderson received from the *Star*, that she "led the poll, and without newspaper support."[3]

As 1933 turned to 1934, Henderson's life of public activism increasingly centred on the Toronto public school system and the lives of disadvantaged children in it. Early in her days as one of a small number of female trustees on the male-dominated board, she signalled the kind of positions she would take in the remaining three years of her life. It is fair to say that she had changed, that the fiery supporter of the One Big Union of 1919 was now a woman who moved more freely, and perhaps more comfortably, in middle-class circles, less likely to denounce the evils of the capitalist system in the no-holds-barred style that characterized her rhetoric in the 1920s. Yet she had always been maternalist in her politics, always willing to assess the ideas and actions of her compatriots on their own terms, not as part of a class-based identity politics that dismissed middle-class men and women out of hand. She had never been quite as radical as her rhetoric and reputation would suggest, so the decline in her radicalism can appear more pronounced that it was. As she aged, the flames of the old fire did not leap quite so high, but the embers burned with the same fierce intensity. She left an indelible mark on the political culture of her adopted city, as she continued to expose the hypocrisy of the better offs and shone as bright a light as she could on the dark corners of Toronto the Good.

Even more so than in earlier periods, Henderson's theory and practice in Toronto in the mid-1930s are difficult to outline, in large part because she has left no personal correspondence and no body of published articles. The historian is left to piece together an amazingly full life without the materials to make that life as full as it actually was. Choices must be made; there is the constant danger of at times making too much of the evidence and at others too little. The story of Henderson's life as a public activist in Toronto of the mid-1930s must at this point be characterized by caution and circumspection, by the discipline necessary to resist the temptation to go beyond the evidence in search of the "real" Rose Henderson. But this is, after all, Rose Henderson, and she was audacious. In her spirit I will be audacious when I believe her own ideas and opinions, or those of her colleagues, call for the biographer to be audacious. Anything less would fail to do her justice.

Henderson gave her maiden speech to the TDSB on 18 January 1934. Right away she established a pattern that would repeat itself over the course of the next three years, of voting with the minority on controversial issues. Many of these issues now seem dated, inconsequential, and mundane. We do well to remind ourselves of the character of the maternal feminists of Henderson's generation; no ideal was beyond realization, no simple act of kindness without meaning, no small reform that did not contribute to major change. There is truth in a critique that she was no longer the fiery radical of 1919, but that fiery radical was part myth, and we can still find the Rose Henderson of 1919 in the Rose Henderson of 1934.

In Canadian literary memory, Toronto emerges as a place of childhood innocence, a world before drugs, gangs, and terrorism. Author Robert Thomas Allen writes of growing up in the Toronto of the inter-war period: "I think the old Toronto was a better city for kids ... The city didn't

sprawl into the country then; the country came right into the city ...
There were horses and carts in the streets and stables behind some of the
houses. The automobile age had arrived but hadn't taken over."[4]

It was still possible for young boys especially to get away from the city
in the many ravines that wound through the city, and to look forward to
the sights, sounds, and thrills of the annual Canadian National Exhibition.
By the mid-1930s, however, Henderson knew a very different Toronto,
one in which seven children were killed by automobiles in May 1934, up
from one in May 1933.[5] Henderson's Toronto was a world in which children played in the streets, not on Toronto Island, the world of local officials defending the status quo, not the childhoods later idealized by
authors. Henderson observed: "It should be possible to lessen street dangers for little children ... Parents must realize their own responsibility
and should know the streets are primarly [sic] for traffic and not play."[6]
Magistrate R.J. Browne had a different perspective, commenting that the
"motorist, being in charge of the death-dealing machine, has a great responsibility, but I wouldn't condemn him. He has to put up with a lot
from the children. When a car comes along to disturb their game in the
middle of the road, they often will pass insulting remarks or make insulting gestures." Magistrate Browne's placing the blame on young children
for being killed in the streets by automobiles places in stark relief the
kind of attitudes Henderson and like-minded Torontonians were fighting
in the midst of the Great Depression.

Early in her career on the TDSB, Henderson made it be known that she
would be a champion of needy children in the public school system. On
7 February 1934, at a meeting of the Management Committee of the
Board of Education, she spoke out in support of poor, disadvantaged children, as the main topic of discussion at the meeting was the curtailment
of public health services in the schools. In her comments she "suggested
that physical defects might be on the increase among the pupils because
of undernourishment. From her observation of schools which she had visited she had noted pupils who were evidently suffering from malnutri-
tion."[7] Her concern with the under-nourishment of schoolchildren was
linked to her concern with the lack of health services. The 21 February
1934 Management Committee meeting of the board dealt with the "alleged inadequacy of medical and nursing services in Toronto public
schools." Reports were coming in that every Monday morning "there

were long lines of children returning from absence due to illness and waiting for examination before being readmitted to their rooms." Some children had to wait an hour and a half or more before returning to their classrooms. Trustee Bigelow moved that "in view of the obvious lack of adequate medical service in some schools, the matter should be brought to the attention of the health authorities." Insight into the political culture of Toronto at the time is revealed by the fact that the vote on the motion was tied four to four, meaning that half the trustees voting were opposed to bringing the plight of these children to the attention of the health authorities. A tie meant the motion was lost. Ida Siegel and Henderson voted for Trustee Bigelow's motion.[8]

Almost exactly a year later, following her re-election to the board, Henderson began her second term by focusing on the health and hygiene needs of pupils. At the 31 January 1935 meeting of the School Property Committee, Henderson and Mrs Norman (Margaret) Mackenzie made a plea that public school students be provided with hot water, towels, and soap in order to wash their hands and faces. Henderson observed that in some areas of the city "there are several families, numbering as many as 30 persons, living in one house. Children have not the facilities for washing in many homes and cannot help going dirty to school." The article added that Henderson "previously had moved for a survey of schools particularly in the congested districts with a view to making a start at putting hot water connections where they were most needed. The committee asked for a report as to the cost."[9] By now a familiar pattern had been established of Henderson demanding changes that would benefit schoolchildren regardless of cost, and conservative members of the board responding with a call to assess the financial impact.

Henderson was not the only progressive thinker on the board, and the causes she fought for were not her creation, but it is fair to say that she spent more time actually visiting schools and maintaining contact with teachers and children than any other board member. On 22 December 1934 the *Star* reported that a list of comments by trustees was found on a seat in the visitors' gallery following the board's final meeting of 1934. The anonymous visitor had quoted Henderson to the effect that "I am in the homes of the people day by day and I know what the needs are."[10] Her dedication was a double-edged sword, because the cost of using the board's fleet of passenger cars was an ongoing subject of debate at board meetings and in the press. By the end of her first year on the board, she was logging more time in the board's cars than any other trustee. She was unrepentant, stating at the 6 December 1934 meeting of the TDSB, "I have used the cars and I do not apologize. I question whether the members who do not visit the schools are competent to deal with the matter."[11]

On 20 June 1935 she won a partial victory in her fight for greater use of the board's cars in a meeting of the Property Committee. As it stood, the cars could only be used for functions to which all members were invited. Trustee Isadore Markus moved that trustees be allowed to the use the cars for any school function in any part of the city. Henderson supported Markus, protesting "that she had been humiliated by press reports of how she had used the cars, and affirmed that she had used them only on school business." Following Markus's argument that trustees should know about all the schools, she "insisted she could not intelligently vote on questions affecting schools without first hand knowledge of the job or the situation." She pointed out that "there were invitations to the women trustees, and it was difficult for them to go unless they had a car."

In the end, she and Markus did not get use of the cars in all wards, but the committee did decide "to relax restrictions to allow trustees to use cars to attend school functions in their own wards."[12] At the 26 June 1935 regular meeting of the board it was made official, as ten of seventeen trustees voted to allow individual members to use the cars to attend school functions in their own wards.[13] Revealingly, all three female members – Rose Henderson, Dr Minerva Reid, and Margaret Mackenzie – voted in favour of the change.[14]

There is more meaning in this debate than meets the eye. At the 11 April 1935 meeting of the board, the car log for the previous three months revealed that of the top five users, three were women – Henderson, Reid, and Mackenzie.[15] At the 26 June 1935 meeting these same three female trustees supported relaxing the regulations governing the use of board cars in their own wards. In Toronto in the mid-1930s men were much more likely to own cars than women. In addition, middle-class women travelling alone, especially at night, as school functions required female board members to do, was a relatively recent phenomenon. Trustee W.H. Butt understood that Henderson was helping to transform the role of women in Canadian public life, asking her at the 20 June 1935 meeting of the Property Committee if she was trying to put the issue "on a sex basis."[16] Butt's accusation notwithstanding, Henderson's concerns were justified, and apparently shared by Reid and Mackenzie. Once again we see that Henderson, working-class hero, was also a spokesperson for middle-class women, a dual role she played until the end of her life.

Of even more importance than Henderson's legacy as a defender of the right of middle-class women to travel without fear is her legacy as an opponent of corporal punishment. In March 1934 the release of statistics on corporal punishment in Toronto schools in 1933 revealed that 11,000 strappings had taken place, with some schools averaging two strappings a day. The numbers compelled Dr C.C. Goldring, superintendent of schools, to send out a circular suggesting more caution in punishing pupils, and there was a decline of nearly five hundred strappings a month. The decline notwithstanding, 2,465 strappings were administered in March, April, May, and June 1934.[17] Dr Spaulding drew attention to the fact that the 11,000 strappings included seventeen kindergarten pupils.[18]

Corporal punishment in Toronto schools was not Rose Henderson's issue; a broad range of Torontonians of all social classes, men and women, Catholics, Jews, and Protestants wanted it banned or at least more tightly regulated. However, in the fall of 1934 Henderson was able to impress the issue more forcefully into the public conscience. In the first week of September 1934 she initiated the school year's concern with corporal punishment by asking: "To what extent has corporal punishment been used in the public schools since the last report was made on this subject? … In what schools were the greatest number of punishments? … In what classes and by what teachers?"[19] At the Board of Education meeting held on 4 October 1934 she made "an attempt to get a special committee named to study the question of strappings in the schools, its cause and its effect on pupils." She urged the creation of a "pupils' and teachers' council" that would establish in each school a "modern form of discipline." Noting the more than six hundred strappings a month still being administered in Toronto schools, she argued that "if it is an offence for a man to beat his wife I think it should be an offence for a teacher to beat a child." In response, Trustee Shepherd moved that "the Henderson motion" be sent to the Management Committee, and the board duly voted to do so.[20]

On 6 October 1934 the *Star* ran a story under the byline "Two Thrashings Per Day Average in Some Schools," sensationalizing a story the paper had reported on 24 March 1934 in much more subdued tones.

It commented on the "decided drop" that had occurred in strappings since the publication in March 1934 of the figures for 1933 and repeated the finding that since Dr Goldring had sent out his circular, the number of incidents had declined by about five hundred a month. The reporter observed this was "not enough to satisfy Trustee Dr. Rose Henderson, who wants to see the experiment of pupils' and teachers' councils tried in the schools, a measure of self-government in discipline." The article then quoted a number of prominent Torontonians opposed to corporal punishment, including Charles Ring, past president of the Lions' Club, the Honourable Paul Leduc, provincial minister of mines, and E.E. Woollon, vice-president of the Toronto and District Labor Council.[21]

While it is true that Henderson's campaign against corporal punishment was part of a widespread campaign already in existence, there can be no doubt that she, through the aegis of the *Star*, gave it a prominence it would not otherwise have had. Henderson had a way of making issues compelling; she was the champion of what one might call the politics of immediacy. She had a talent for getting the citizens of Toronto to take notice of issues they might have passed by in the course of their busy lives. Crucial to her influence was the *Star*, which adopted her as the voice of progressive Toronto, for reasons that can only be surmised.

On 10 October 1934 the Management Committee of the board voted six to two recommending the creation of a special committee to investigate corporal punishment in the schools. Henderson stated that "621 strappings in a month were too many." She wondered "if the strap is so necessary," pointing out that in Sweden, Norway, and Denmark the strap had been virtually abolished. "She feared that a teacher lost the respect of a child when she raised her hand." Ida Siegel noted that the "tendency of the thrashed boy was to resent the thrashing and to resolve that he would get even." Henderson picked up on the point, commenting that "she had six newspaper clippings which told of teachers beaten up by pupils who had nursed grievances."[22]

At the board meeting on Thursday, 18 October 1934, a deputation identified as the Ward Five Unemployed Association and Toronto Children's Council protested against the strapping of students at the Niagara Street School. The delegation was introduced by Rose Henderson. Their spokesperson, Minnie Shelley, enunciated a position that had clearly been developed under Henderson's influence: "We ask that the strapping be cut out altogether." Many children, she stated, "have grown up during the depression and are undernourished and nervous, which makes it more difficult for them to study. The answer to this condition is not the strap."[23] In response to Shelley's request that corporal punishment be ended, the board chair "invited the representatives to meet with him and other members of the Board and discuss these matters, at a date to be arranged."[24]

There was tremendous resistance to ending corporal punishment in Toronto schools, and early in 1935 Henderson abandoned her call for an outright ban. At the TDSB meeting on 21 February 1935 she "gave notice of motion that corporal punishment be administered hereafter only by principals and in the principals' offices, preferably after school hours and not within sight or hearing of other pupils."[25] A "careful record" was to be kept by the principal administering the punishment.[26] On Wednesday, 6 March 1935, the *Star* reported that the following evening Henderson would bring another motion before the board that no corporal punishment be administered before the child had been examined by a medical attendant.[27] Just how much she had already conceded in her initial goal of ending corporal punishment in the schools is evidenced by the provision in her motion of 21 February giving the principal the right to suspend any student opposing the punishment.[28]

At the 7 March 1935 meeting of the TDSB she failed to convince the board to "tighten up" on corporal punishment. Having already conceded so much, she was clearly frustrated, if not angry. In her speech she evinced the self-righteousness that lurked beneath the surface of her social activism, commenting: "I cannot hope to educate all the members in so short a time." She turned to one of her tried and true strategies, using the example of more "progressive" nations to shame her fellow board members, saying: "We should follow the lead of five nations that have practically wiped out corporal punishment. Where this has been done it has been found that crime has decreased." Then, returning to the argument she had made about the crucial role played by environment in explaining the actions of children, she noted: "Many children have not enough food or rest. I am not criticizing teachers but I feel great care should be given in cases where the child has been under strain of abnormal living conditions." In the end her motion was saved, Mrs. Margaret Mackenzie moving that the motion go back to the Management Committee to be re-drafted. Following the debate "the Henderson motion" was sent to the

Management Committee.[29] It was now five months since the first "Henderson motion" had been sent to the Management Committee, and the second was on its way to the same committee. The fighter was bloodied but not yet beaten.

Henderson cast her net widely in her search for allies. As we have seen in the case of the Ward Five Unemployed Association, she organized delegations to board meetings on a regular basis to swing support in her favour. She had other allies as well, as revealed at the 20 March 1935 Toronto Monthly Meeting of the Society of Friends. At the meeting John Copithorne submitted a minute to be sent to the board on behalf of the Social Service Committee expressing its concern about corporal punishment. Henderson "spoke to the question and cited the great number of such punishments of children between the ages of five and ten years. Suggestions were made that copies of the minute ... be sent to the Department of Education and to our Quarterly and Yearly Meetings."[30] In the process, Henderson let her opponents know she could not be ignored because she had too many allies in too many places in the public life of Toronto.

Her support base notwithstanding, she was fighting an uphill battle, even against the mothers she spent so much time and effort in defending. She was far from speaking for all mothers, including a "mother of two boys" who wrote a scathing letter to the editor of the *Star*. In the letter signed "VERITAS," the mother scorned Henderson's position on discipline in the schools. She wondered "what sort of education will be maintained in a school where children know that they would have to be medically examined before being punished. I think it high time that all this sickly sentimentality be stopped and our boys and girls punished by the teachers should they deserve it." The writer expressed concern about the "terrible lack of discipline around," and the fact that the coming generation would be a "spineless one."[31] Six days later, at the 27 March 1935 meeting of the Management Committee, the question of corporal punishment was "laid over" for two weeks at Henderson's request.[32] At the meeting she was heard to say that it was an unpopular subject, perhaps a reflection of the fact that she had read the previous week's letter to the editor in the *Star*. As in the case of children being struck and killed by automobiles while playing in the street, she was battling long-held attitudes toward children and discipline that could not be overcome in a day, a week, a month, a year, or even a decade. She had to be bold, but at times that boldness had a price.

On 3 April 1935 she spoke to the Rowntree CCF Club in York Township. She justified the call for better medical care in Toronto schools by exposing the case of a pregnant fourteen-year old girl who had been strapped three times in the space of five months. Children who were "continually irritable in class should be given a special medical inspection and not the strap, which is used far too much." She continued: "The health and welfare of our children should come first and instead of cutting down we should be adding to our expenditure because the children need more protection than ever before. A great many wooden-headed people are running and administering the schools." She went out of her way to assure her audience that she was not attacking the teachers, but insisted that "we have people administering the schools who know nothing about education and less about children." Consulted by the *Star* for a reaction, board chairman C.M. Carrie stated that what Henderson had to say was not new, and that the situation of the pregnant fourteen-year old was an "isolated case."[33]

While the issue was not revolutionary change, as it was during the labour revolt of 1919, Henderson still had the ability to outrage her opposition to the point of harming her own cause. It is surely no coincidence that within a week of her attack on Toronto school administrators, an attack that became public, action was taken on "the Henderson motion." In an April 1935 meeting of the Management Committee, Chairman Bigelow "ruled that the motion of TDSB Chairman Henderson for further restrictions on the use of the strap should be discussed in private session." When asked by TDSB Chairman Carrie for the reason, Bigelow replied: "One of the members made statements which got into the papers about a girl of 14 who got into trouble." The Management Committee then agreed that the discussions should be private.[34] The TDSB was in special session on 13 December 1935 to complete revision of its by-laws, and Henderson made an effort to amend the by-law on corporal punishment. She wanted some restrictions, including "the requirement that medical certificates should be secured if there were a question as to a pupil's health." She withdrew her motion when she got little support.[35]

Henderson fought long and hard to end corporal punishment in Toronto schools, then to change the conditions under which strappings took place. Just one of many opponents of the practice, she forced the issue upon the public conscience with a determination and effectiveness unmatched by her fellow critics. She publicized, again in a way few other social activists did, the relationship between the physical and mental health of Toronto students and the behaviour that resulted in corporal punishment. On the other hand, there is no doubt that her attacks on school administrators closed doors that she herself had opened; she alienated potential supporters and strengthened an already powerful opposition to reforming the practice of corporal punishment. She lost her fight, and there was to be no significant change in her lifetime. More than thirty-four years after her death, in July 1971, the TDSB voted to ban the use of the strap in Toronto schools. Henderson did not cause that ban, but its history only makes sense if her contribution is part of the story.

Her campaign against strapping in Toronto schools was part of a much larger critique of violence, militarism, and war, and its impact on the youth of Canada. One of her allies was the *Star*, which in its 17 April 1935 issue carried comments by prominent Torontonians on the paper's "new series of war exposure pictures." The article led off with comments by Henderson: "Some people may object to the shockingness of some of the pictures, but until people realize that war is a shocking business we will never have peace. Last Sunday I talked to 150 young men, who all said they would not volunteer for war now that they have seen the photographs in The Star. I thoroughly endorse the enterprise and public service The Star has displayed in going to such lengths to obtain these pictures."

Raymond Booth, pastor of the Friends Church, observed that the photographs "are more effective peace propaganda than all the sermons and all the leaflets in the world." Rabbi Maurice Eisendrath of Holy Blossom Synagogue concurred, stating these pictures "do more than any sermon" to convey the "hellishness of war." There was a war of a kind going on in the public life of Toronto as war clouds gathered in Europe, placing Henderson in familiar company among Jews, Quakers, Communists, social democrats, Christian pacifists, and others. Their challenge would not go uncontested.

On 18 April 1935 the *Star* reported that Henderson had brought to the board's attention the fact that J.R. Moore, principal of Parkdale Collegiate, had allowed three military officers to speak to the students and appeal for recruits. Henderson opposed the schools being "turned into recruiting grounds ... We do not want to cultivate war-mindedness among our youth at this stage in the world's affairs. There is enough of that." The incident was to be reported on by Superintendent Goldring and reviewed by the board. The *Star* noted that the "attitude of Dr. Goldring has been consistently to oppose anything in the nature of propaganda being allowed in the schools. He recently reported against a peace-promotion plan which involved the writing of letters by pupils to be sent to schools in other countries, and the use of a so-called 'world peace flag,' holding that even peace propaganda should not be conducted in schools."

Both of these peace initiatives, which bore the imprint of Rose Henderson, were considered "political" initiatives by Goldring and like-minded members of the Toronto board, which was increasingly becoming a battleground between pro- and anti-militarist factions. The mind of youth was the target, and this was a war that Henderson knew well. She was not able to control events in Europe, but she could fight the good fight at home.

At the board meeting on 2 May 1935 there was a "brief but brisk debate on the visit of three militia officers to Parkdale Collegiate seeking recruits." Trustee Markus "gave notice of motion that hereafter no recruiting for military units should be allowed in the schools." Henderson "asked what steps were being taken by Dr. C. C. Goldring, superintendent, to see that such an incident did not occur again."[36] On 6 June 1935 the board voted eleven to eight to defeat the motion of Trustee Isadore Markus "that recruiting for military purposes be prohibited in the Secondary Schools." The motion was seconded by Henderson.[37] All three female trustees voted for the motion. Henderson was quoted as saying, "Patriotism is not necessarily militarism. We can teach the boys discipline and give them high ideals without putting guns in their hands and training them to kill their fellow men."[38] As she did in the First World War period, she chose to retain the discourse of the society in which she lived rather than replacing it with an alternative. Instead of attacking "patriotism" and "discipline" in and of themselves, she chose to retain the words while changing the meanings.

If Henderson was forthright in her critique of the militarism of the British Empire, her attitude on moral issues was more equivocal, evincing the powerful legacy of her Victorian upbringing, yet at times characterized by a tolerance and understanding of young people that belied that same upbringing. The edges of her critique had softened since her

halcyon days, but she retained the same marvellous capacity to understand the actions and ideals of working-class youth in terms of the social
and economic conditions in which they found themselves through no
choice of their own. Whether the issue was smoking, drinking, movies, or
bathing suits, her position on the TDSB meant that she was front and centre
in debates concerning issues affecting Toronto youth, and the *Star* continually looked to her as a spokesperson for progressive opinion in the city.

She was an advocate of many of the changes in the Ontario education
system widely championed by the educational reformers of the period. She
shared the period's concern with "the continued high dropout rate, truancy,
and the general unruliness of the adolescent student body, as well as about
the irrelevance of a classical academic curriculum" to the burgeoning school
population of the 1930s.[39] She was one of many advocates in the Toronto
of the 1930s of vocational training for boys, and "business" or "commercial" training for girls. Cynthia Comacchio asserts that "organized labour
objected to this kind of education," because it sought to train young people
"in the attitudes appropriate to modern industry."[40] Directly countering
Comacchio's assertion, Henderson argued that the movement for technical
education was led by "labour bodies" and brought about by the demands of
"the people."[41] We must remember that the labour movement had a long
history of advocating the creation of technical schools, and that Henderson
had lived most of her life in Quebec, where technical schools were a desired
alternative to the classical curriculum that trained doctors, lawyers, and
priests. The R.B. Russell Vocational High School in Winnipeg stands as
testament to the fact that Russell, a Marxist and leader of the Winnipeg
General Strike, was, like his fellow radical Richard Johns, a long-time advocate of technical and vocational education.

This is not to deny the validity of Comacchio's point about the role that
vocational education played in disciplining a youth workforce for capitalist production, a role Henderson failed to adequately critique. It would be
a mistake, however, to then assume that she was a typical product of the
Victorian era who sought to discipline youth on moral and ethical issues
as well. We can find in her the Victorian moralist, but in pushing the
point too far we would be guilty of misrepresenting her.

The nuance and richness of Henderson's attitudes toward the behaviour
of young people in Toronto is revealed in the positions she took on smoking and drinking. In English Canada, the work of female historians of

youth evinces a puzzling neglect of these two key elements of changing
youth habits in mid-twentieth century Canada. Joan Sangster, in her
study of female juvenile delinquency, deals briefly with Aboriginal girls
and drinking, but not non-Aboriginal girls and drinking, unintention-
ally leaving the impression that drinking was considered a problem for
the former but not the latter.[42] There is no discussion of cigarette smoking. Comacchio's *The Dominion of Youth* mentions smoking in passing,
noting that the Ontario Minors' Protection Act of 1927 banned the sale
of tobacco to young people under the age of eighteen.[43] There is virtually
no discussion of alcohol consumption, a seemingly significant omission in
a work that identifies its focus as "the salient concerns of ordinary adolescent lives."[44] If we are to understand the political culture's "interpretation of leisure as modern evil," Henderson is in some ways a more reliable
guide to the lives of ordinary young English Canadians in the 1930s than
either Sangster or Comacchio.[45] She takes us into the schools, homes, and
beverage rooms of Toronto, introduces us to young people making their
way in a changing moral and ethical universe, and gives us insights to
think about that change our perceptions of who we are and where we
came from.

Henderson was at the forefront of concerns with youth smoking cigarettes and consuming alcohol because the schools were in the front lines of
the battle against "immorality." On 20 June 1934, at a meeting of the
Management Committee of the TDSB, cigarette smoking by high school
students "keyed the members of the school management committee up to
some tension" when they received a request from the Toronto district
Women's Christian Temperance Union "to have the teaching of the
dangers of narcotics stressed."[46] Chair Dr E.T. Guest requested that
Superintendent Goldring provide information as to the teaching done in
the schools. Henderson, who may have been behind the WCTU request,
"wanted data on cigarette smoking" and "how much trade the tuck shops
near schools did with the students." She suggested that Goldring "might
tell us if smoking has increased not only among the boys but among the
girls, too." She added: "I had a girl brought to me by her parents recently
...and she was quite a bad nervous case, due to smoking."[47] Although
twenty years had passed, Henderson was still making the link between
smoking and nervous debility she made when she appeared before the
government commission in April 1914.

In September 1934 she once again placed her imprint on the public conscience of Toronto. The smoking habits of high school boys and girls were discussed at the Management Committee meeting on 12 September 1934. Henderson "said she had interviewed people who kept restaurants near schools in her ward and nine out of twelve had told her there was an increase in smoking by students. She feared what would happen the younger generation with beer and wine flowing so freely." Her concern had been heightened when she "saw two young girls, not more than sixteen, taken out of a beverage room on Yonge St. the other night."[48] Here Henderson appears to be the Victorian social crusader, riding to the rescue of young damsels in distress, exaggerating the threat and self-righteously providing the solution.

Before making this judgment, however, we must pause to examine our impressions of Toronto of the 1930s. How could two teenage girls drink in a beverage room in Toronto the Good, when many of us believe that women were not even allowed in beverage rooms of the times? This imagined Toronto, where the sidewalks were rolled up at night, is just that – imagined. A "drink" meant hard liquor, not beer, which at the time was barely considered to be alcohol. We recall that in the mid-1920s the provincial Conservatives under premier G. Howard Ferguson had introduced 4.4 per cent beer, claiming that it was not intoxicating.[49] In 1934, the first year Henderson served on the Board of Education, Ontario licensed "beverage rooms" with an area set aside for "Ladies and Escorts." These areas were found in almost all licensed hotels, and according to Craig Heron, "were heavily patronized from the beginning."[50] While Henderson may have been guilty of her usual hyperbole, and may have exaggerated the beer and wine "flowing so freely," her perception was more accurate than the prevailing mythology. She introduces us to a rather different Toronto from the traditional one of Anglo-Celtic prudery.

In September 1934 the *Star* made young people's drinking and smoking a public issue in a way it had not been the previous June, as attention focused on students returning to school. On 13 September an article entitled "High School Girls Smoke 'And Why Not?' They Ask" came to the conclusion smoking was widespread among high school girls. The article observed: "In the West Toronto district in which Mrs. Rose Henderson of the board of education lives, nine out of 12 shops visited reported the sale of cigarettes to high school pupils to be on the increase. They have no explanation." In a second story in the same issue, liquor commissioner E.G. Odette responded to Henderson's claim of two girls being taken out of a Yonge Street hotel intoxicated: "I wish Mrs. Henderson and other citizens would come to me with the facts when they see such cases ... It's not much use for people to talk about these things if they do not report them to us ... we will be glad of any information of cases like that. We will be glad to hear from Mrs. Henderson." Queried by the *Star*, Henderson said: "I am writing to Mr. Odette and I will be glad to give him all the particulars I can ... I am concerned about the girls and boys ... The two girls wanted to go down Yonge St. in the direction of the bright lights, but the policeman on duty there turned them on to a side street." She "asserted that the policeman should certainly have made a report against the hotel where the girls got their liquor," adding, "I am not criticizing the law or the administration of it, and I do not condemn Premier Hepburn for putting the act into force ... Mr. Henry would have done so and have boasted of it if he had come back into power. But I am concerned about the protection of the young people from drinking habits."[51]

On 26 October the *Star* quoted a number of "educationists" to the effect that beverage rooms were worse than "the old open bar." Henderson commented: "A young girl living in a poor and squalid home told me that the beverage room is the only place where I can take my boy friend. I cannot take him home to our two rooms. But in the beverage room it is warm and bright." Rather than condemning behaviour she clearly did not agree with, she put the emphasis on environment, not the moral failings of young people. As she would have with a young offender in the Montreal Juvenile Court, she contextualized the behaviour of this young girl in her home life. The beer parlour had electric lights and running water – toilet facilities – that many young people did not have in their own homes. Rather than condemning youth, Henderson condemned the society that allowed such a contradictory state of affairs to exist.

On 29 October the *Star* published an editorial based on Henderson's observations about the girl in the beverage room with her boyfriend. Of all the dozens of comments on beverage rooms by prominent Torontonians the paper published, the editor referred to Henderson's observations as "particularly provocative of thought," confirming her powerful influence on social reform thought in the city. He continued:

This is more than a comment on beer parlors; it is an indictment of society. It is an indictment of churches whose doors are closed and of the social system which makes no adequate provision for young people who wish to be together and who find their warmest welcome in a beverage room … It is one of the worst features of the beer parlor, this attracting of young couples and encouraging them to drink together there. But it carries a moral for others besides the government which permits these places to exist. It is a reproach to society which provides no better place …the beer parlor is waiting to receive them – to receive them, and to extend to them that very questionable hospitality which appears to be the best that society is prepared to offer.

Determined to give young people in Toronto a fighting chance, Henderson threw herself into the campaign against beer parlours located near schools. On 4 December 1934 she attended a meeting of the Toronto Temperance Federation to organize the anti-beer parlour forces in Ward Five. The meeting opposed the establishment of a beer parlour at the corner of Ossington Avenue and College Street. Henderson noted that the proposed parlour would be just up the street from the Commercial High School: "It would offer too much temptation to these pupils, to say nothing of other students who would pass it daily … It is the duty of all parents to protect children from this traffic which has been, in a sense, forced upon us. I have gone to these beer parlors to see what is going on. I want to tell you if they are allowed to go on as they have been doing we will have to answer to our young people for the destruction of their lives. We have forced this thing on them without their consent or choice."[52]

On 18 December Henderson attended a meeting at Trinity United Church, where Raymond Booth of the Society of Friends condemned beverage rooms as "evil institutions" before a hundred invited temperance workers. During the meeting Henderson "wanted to know if people would stand up in municipal election meetings and demand that the candidates commit themselves on the beverage room question."[53]

On 7 February 1935 the Board of Education carried a motion by a vote of seventeen to two against the establishment of a beverage room between the Regal Road School and the Earlscourt School. Henderson "declared the board should represent the people and protest against beer parlors so close to schools." On 21 February 1935 the board unanimously passed a motion protesting the establishment of a beverage room being proposed for a hotel at the corner of Dundas Street East and Broadview Avenue. The motion included a general board policy opposing beverage rooms "in close proximity to schools or on main roads leading to schools."[54]

Henderson's reference to "the people" echoes the language of the Progressive Era when she lived in Montreal before the First World War; here she was in Toronto, fighting for the "people" against the "liquor interests," for all the world like an American muckraker in the tradition of Ida Tarbell and Upton Sinclair. Even in her most Marxist days, she always had much of the Progressive in her, much of that social reformer whose conception of the people she represented was a moral as much as a class majority.

Yet another danger to the morals of young people was the movies. Comacchio argues that movies "stood unchallenged as the most potent of the new cultural forces affecting youth."[55] The movies increased in popularity among young people as church attendance declined, leading church leaders, concerned parents, and middle-class moral reformers to blame them for juvenile delinquency in boys and "sexual immorality" in girls. The fact that many young people were attending the movies without parental permission, or even knowledge, created a moral panic. In part the concern could be traced to a tragic Montreal fire that took place in January 1927. In a fire in the Laurier Palace Cinema, seventy-eight children died, the inquest following the fire supposedly revealing that three-quarters of those in the theatre were there without their parents' permission.[56] In Ontario the fire prompted the Canadian Council on Child and Family Welfare to publish a "White List" of approved films for youth later in 1927. The list did little to slow the flood of young Canadians into the nation's movie theatres.

Henderson, who was living in Montreal at the time of the Laurier Palace fire, showed as much concern about the impact of movies on young people as the effect of beverage rooms. On 2 May 1934 she attended the annual luncheon of the St Clair United Church Women's Association, where she pointed out to the three hundred guests that "the cinema was a problem that needed the attention of the womanhood of Canada."[57] In July 1934 civic leaders, members of the Toronto Board of Control, the Toronto Board of Education, and service club leaders met to discuss solutions to the "salacious movie problem." Henderson said that "some years ago with a group of interested women she made survey of some 300 pictures and found that in 50 of them there were murders, in 11 there were rape or attempted rape scenes, in over 50 there were drunkenness, in half a dozen there were raids on houses of ill fame, and in others scenes of free love, of carousing, and various forms of sensuality. 'Only about half a dozen were really fit for children,' she said. 'And I don't think the movies have improved much since then.'"[58]

Her campaign against the nefarious effects of motion pictures was part of a wider campaign that included drama productions in Toronto schools. At the board meeting on 21 February 1935 one of the issues concerned a production of the play *Bird in Hand* at the Western-Tech Commerce School, which featured a drinking scene. Henderson commented: "We should not allow something to be presented of the sort that is complained of in the films ... What they see impresses children most."[59] On 27 March the Management Committee decided to make the principals the censors of plays presented in their schools, and to send the proposal to the upcoming meeting of the board. In one of her more memorable explanations, Henderson asserted that "undesirable stage shows helped to fill penitentiaries." A twenty-first century sensibility has great difficulty drawing a direct cause and effect relationship between high school plays and crowded prisons, but for Henderson it was an integral part of her world view.

This world view, however, did not necessarily make her part of the morality police. She was concerned about the morals of Toronto's young people, but she was also on their side. The issue at times took on a humorous edge. The 22 August 1935 edition of the *Star* included an article under the headline "Swimmers in Trunks Held Too Anthropoid." The article reported that so far that season 202 summonses had been issued under a Harbour Commission by-law prohibiting swimming in trunks only. Edward W. Beaton, secretary of the Boulevard Canoe Club, indignantly denied a *Star* reporter's suggestion that male members of the club were using hair remover to appear "a little less anthropoid" in their trunks. An official with the Toronto Canoe Club was equally appalled by the suggestion. Questioned about the by-law, Henderson replied:

There are ... things to be said for and against it. The young people of to-day are allowed more latitude than ever before, but there doesn't seem to be anything indecent about the swimming costumes of to-day. We should give the young people a certain amount of latitude, but I don't believe in nakedness ... I've seen a great deal of bathing this year, and on very few occasions did I see anything objectionable. We in the city get so little sunshine there is much to be said for leaving off as much of the old-fashioned attire as possible, and still observe the rules of decency. I approve of observing those rules. But I do think the young people of to-day can be trusted to use common sense.[60]

Henderson shows more compassion here, more genuine ability to identify with young people than many maternal feminists of her day. She continues, "If society denies our young men and women a normal life, it must expect them to live what we call an abnormal life. The older generation must accept the responsibility. We can't put up a big wall keeping boys and girls apart. We can't keep them from falling in love. If we have made it impossible for them to marry, they will make the most out of their friendship and love as best they can."[61] Henderson's compassion for young people, especially girls, does not mean that she abandoned her belief that motherhood remained the calling of woman. The "progressive" and the "reactionary" emerged starkly in comments she made in September 1934 in reference to the increase in the number of divorces in the 1930s. Not surprisingly, she attributed the rise to economic conditions but also to the fact that young people were rejecting "a great deal of the unmoral hypocrisy of the days of their mothers and grandmothers ... It is impossible for young people to live a normal, healthy life under present economic conditions ... It is impossible for a family to live happily in two or three rooms. They are often crowded up against several other families in the same house ... Marriage is not a romance; it is a business. There may be romance in the beginning, but a discussion of the family budget, when there is no budget, soon banishes romance. I think if we give our young people a chance to live, we won't need to be worried about divorce. The average girl, under proper conditions, will not renege her motherhood. She will stay on the job."[62] Henderson's position that to be a mother is to "stay on the job" is striking, one that embodied the dialectic that production is reproduction, reproduction is production.

For her the plight of youth in Depression-era Canada was alarming and demanded drastic action. Addressing a CCF forum entitled "The Changing Social Order" in Oshawa on 3 March 1935, she stated: "If I had a son living to-day I would sooner see him thrown into the lake than to see him decay as thousands of our young men are doing to-day." She claimed "it was the duty of the older generation of to-day to fight continually, and lay down their lives if necessary in order that the younger generation might be given the opportunity of living their own lives to the fullest." Referring to the many young people in prison, she "charged that the criminal social order that is in vogue to-day was driving young men to their destruction."[63] Her reference to criminality being "in vogue" was almost certainly an allusion to the popularity of American gangster films in Toronto theatres; as Comacchio points out, these films "idealized the modern urban outlaw, all too often cultivated from the ranks of male juvenile delinquents."[64] Henderson believed that young males, given a choice, would choose healthier pursuits, but the society in which they lived was not providing those choices. The contemporary echoes of Henderson's position, especially in relation to the situation of young black males in Toronto, continue to reverberate.

In part, Henderson's concern with unemployed youth derived from her travels in Europe, where she was exposed to the rise of youth groups and their connections to the military and the rise of fascism. In the *Star* of 13 December 1934, several prominent Torontonians were quoted on the topic of providing for unemployed youth. Henderson was the only woman quoted:

I'm strongly in accord with the idea of some large-scale effort to provide our young people with activities until we can find careers for them … I am in favor of doing everything we can to throw our schools and churches open to them for recreational and other purposes. If we give them a chance, they won't go wrong. The best substitute in Canada for the national youth activities such as they have in Italy and Germany along military lines, is to find jobs so they can exercise their normal functions and their right to work, to legitimate recreation and to marry and found homes. Failing that we ought all to work together to see that they are not left to have natural ambitions and ideals warped. There should be something else besides walking the streets, cheap movies and beer parlors for our jobless younger generation.[65]

Once again we see the idea that young people had "natural" or normal inclinations; when they went wrong, it was not because of "human nature" or the personalities of young people themselves but rather the influences they were exposed to in the society at large.

There is no denying, with the advantage of hindsight, the existence of a Victorian, middle-class, moralistic Henderson who advocated temperance and decried the deleterious effects of the cinema on young people. Yet we must also recognize another Henderson, one who more than most Canadian citizens of her generation active in public life had a sympathy for and insight into young people, an empathy that was uncommon, especially in a woman in her mid-sixties. Indeed, we might remind ourselves that the young people of Toronto still walk the streets, still succumb to cheap thrills, and still go wrong. But they also, as Henderson reminds us, still go right more often than wrong when treated with respect and given a fighting chance.

As we turn our attention to Henderson's activism in the CCF, we must remember that it was impelled not just by her commitment to women and the working class but also to her ongoing passion to make the world a better place for children and youth. In her Oshawa talk on 3 March 1935 she noted that "the present generation was in the midst of one of the greatest social changes the world had ever known." The "older generation" needed to "lay down their lives," if necessary, to ensure that the younger generation could live life to the fullest. Following this appeal, she compared Canada in the 1930s to the Roman Empire, in which "98 per cent. of the Romans were propertyless and the other two per cent. controlled all the money of Rome. Does that not closely parallel conditions in this present day world."

She then proposed the solution: "Until people learn to use the ballot properly, you will always have strikes, in which men fight for their just rights, broken up by the police baton ... Capitalists claim that we must have great changes in the system but they claim we must not touch the present capitalist system ... This is impossible, as we have now reached a stage where it is absolutely necessary that the people control the machinery that produces."[66] We see here the necessary bridge between Henderson's anti-capitalism and advocacy of youth and her decision to join the CCF. She believed in the eradication of capitalism – really believed in it – but that change had to be brought about by an awakened populace in an intelligent, "constitutional" manner. In 1933 the CCF was, or at least appeared to be, the closest thing to her vision.

Understanding her involvement with the CCF in the last months of 1933 and the early months of 1934 requires a fresh look at the anti-communist campaign launched in the wake of the Regina Conference in July 1933. In August 1933 Elmore Philpott "warned Communists alleged to be in the Labour Conference that they would be tolerated no longer."[67] Gerald Caplan observes that "there is considerable reason to doubt that Communists in the Labour section ever gained any major positions of influence. Philpott's main antagonists were in reality a handful of uncontrollable doctrinaire radicals who insisted on their right to cooperate with anyone sharing similar ideals in order to achieve common aims."[68] The language is crucial: Caplan distinguishes between communists and "uncontrollable doctrinaire radicals," in positions of influence advocating cooperation. The sin, according to Caplan, was cooperating with communists, not *being* a communist. Henderson was one of Caplan's "uncontrollable doctrinaire radicals" because her advocacy of a united front made her a greater threat to the CCF than members of the Communist Party.[69] In a sense Caplan is right, but this characterization of Henderson has led to serious misrepresentation of who she was and what she was trying to accomplish.

In early September 1933 Philpott proposed a full-scale reorganization of the CCF, replacing the tripartite structure of United Farmers, Labor Conference, and CCF Clubs with a single provincial unit. A provincial council would be given the power to suspend or expel any member and the right of refusal of any application for membership. Apparently in reaction to the attendance of former Communist Party member William Moriarty at the Regina Conference, Philpott proposed to ban any former member of the Communist Party from CCF membership, a plan Caplan calls a "disgraceful resolution."[70] In response Arthur Mould, president of the Labor Conference, called an emergency meeting in Toronto for 29 October 1933. The meeting decided, quite rightly, that Philpott's plan was intended to eliminate the Labor Conference. Voicing its opposition to the ban on former Communist Party members, the meeting called for the resignations of Philpott and D.M. Lebourdais.[71]

On 17 November 1933 a mass meeting of the CCF was held at Massey Hall, where Agnes Macphail and Philpott called on the radical element in the party to leave and join the Communist Party. Philpott denounced not the "uncontrollable doctrinaire radicals" but rather the advocates of bloody revolution, clearly suggesting that Communist Party members, not the Rose Hendersons and Elizabeth Mortons, were the real problem for the CCF. Terry Crowley, following Caplan's lead, lumps Henderson into a group of radicals he refers to as the "noxious lesion" attached to the Ontario CCF.[72] However, the evidence suggests that the portrayal of her as a cancer in the party is more the work of Caplan and Crowley than a reflection of the attitudes of party leaders such as Philpott.

A week later, on 23 November 1933, the CCF and representatives of the international unions met at the Labor Temple on Church Street. Alluding to rumours that the Labor Conference was being "squeezed out" of the CCF, Philpott denied them.[73] John Bruce of the Plumbers' and Steamfitters' Union "made a severe attack" on the National Labor Union and the Workers' Unity League. He was emphatic that "labour" meant unions affiliated with the American Federation of Labor, and that there was no room in the CCF for the National Labor Union.[74] The National Labor Union was small, and it has been neglected by historians, but it was a significant factor in disputes rending the Labor Conference. In the spring of 1933, at least, Morton and Henderson were both on the executive committee of the National Labor Union, further implicating them as "doctrinaire radicals" in the minds of CCF leaders. The two women were the *bêtes noires* of Bruce and CCF leaders, their sin being that they wanted all labour forces to belong to the Labor Conference, including the National Labor Union.

A CCF meeting held the next night, 24 November 1933, at Cumberland Hall, featured the kind of Marxist opposition to CCF leaders like Philpott that Henderson has been tarred with. At this meeting Roger Guyot, identified as a Frenchman who had come to Canada twelve years earlier, and a member of the Socialist Party of Canada (OS), took Philpott to task for misrepresenting what he considered majority opinion in the CCF. Guyot, who identified himself as a Marxian Socialist, opposed excluding Communist Party members and former officials of the party from CCF membership.[75]

While Guyot has virtually disappeared from the historical record, Henderson has been attacked in his place. In reality, there is little direct evidence on which to form an opinion of her attitude to the CCF leadership at this time. On 8 December 1933 she chaired a CCF meeting in the Labor Temple, filling in for the absent Jimmy Simpson. The role she played here, combined with her regret that the hall was only partially filled, hardly supports a charge that she was impeding the growth of the CCF, let alone sabotaging it.[76]

The issue that brought it all to a head was cooperation with the Canadian Labor Defense League (CLDL), a Communist Party "front organization" created in 1922 to defend communists incarcerated in "capitalist" prisons. In this instance the CLDL sought to defend Communist Party member A.E. Smith, who had claimed at a public meeting on 17 January 1934 that a recent assassination attempt on the life of Communist Party leader Tim Buck in the Kingston Penitentiary was orchestrated by the federal government. As a result of this statement, Smith was indicted for sedition by a grand jury. When Woodsworth, Macphail, and Angus MacInnis began using cooperation with the CLDL as a pretext for attacking the Labor Conference, and especially the Socialist Party members of it, Mould pointed out to Woodsworth that it was the CCF Clubs, not the Labor Conference, that had initiated cooperation with the CLDL in defence of Smith. Members of the Labor Conference were being blamed for an initiative that came from the clubs, suggesting that the real issue was not Marxist influence or cooperation with the Communists but rather middle-class concern about the power of labour in the CCF. Henderson had made the same point a year earlier.

On 17 February 1934 the Ontario Provincial Council of the CCF met in the Labor Temple in London, Ontario. Two resolutions adopted at this meeting throw into relief the problems with existing interpretation of events and with the image of Rose Henderson, one of nine representatives of the Labor Conference at the meeting. At this time a resolution was circulated by the Friends of Soviet Russia, a Communist Party organization, "in favor of full diplomatic and trade relations between Canada and the Union of Soviet Socialist Republics." The meeting carried a motion to this effect by Morton, seconded by Philpott. The second resolution was moved by Henderson, the only other one in the minutes to deal with an international issue: "Moved by Henderson, seconded by Morton, 'that this Council express its abhorrence of the ruthless actions of the Dolfuss government of Austria in suppressing the justifiable fight of the workers to preserve their political rights ... we express our sympathy with the Socialists of Austria who are fighting to save their country from the terror of Fascism, which destroys all the democratic rights of the people.'"[77] The motion was carried.

The problems with the existing interpretation of events emerge quite starkly from Caplan's account of this convention, which is entirely based on a letter Philpott wrote to Macphail on 19 February 1934. Caplan presents Philpott's version of events rather than the version that emerges from convention minutes. What those minutes reveal, symbolized by Philpott seconding a motion put forward by Socialist Party member Morton, is that Caplan, Crowley, and other historians of this period have in many instances created a false dichotomy between the "champions" of the CCF and the "doctrinaire radicals" who threatened the party with their support for the Soviet Union and advocacy of a united front with the communists and other left-wing organizations. Historians of the CCF have condemned the Rose Hendersons and Elizabeth Mortons for taking positions for which the Elmore Philpotts have been exonerated. In addition, it is more than a little embarrassing that two women who were "doctrinaire radicals" were leading the campaign against fascism at a time when much of the male leadership of the CCF seemed more concerned that this was a "communist" initiative than they were with the threat of fascism itself.

Events quickly heated up following the 17 February 1934 meeting. At a mass protest rally in Massey Hall the next day, Smith charged Woodsworth and his colleagues in the House of Commons with being responsible for the sedition charge brought against him. An understandably outraged Woodsworth declared that any CCF member continuing to work with the CLDL would be expelled, while Philpott declared that a similar fate awaited anyone in the clubs who did the same thing.[78] In response Morton, as secretary of the Labor Conference, declared that the conference would defy the provincial council's decision. On 23 February 1934 UFO leaders Hannam and Scott informed Macphail that the UFO was withdrawing from the CCF. On 26 February 1934 the UFO and club sections acting, as Caplan points out, "separately but likely in collusion," sent a petition to the CCF national executive demanding that the Labor Conference be expelled from the Ontario CCF.[79] The real target, Caplan points out, was the Socialist Party, whose forty-eight members managed to place eight of the twelve Labor Conference delegates sitting on the provincial council.[80] The CCF leadership was caught in a difficult situation, trying to rid itself of the "doctrinaire radicals" without alienating the great majority of labour supporters the party needed to expand in Ontario.

On 1 March 1934 the UFO formally withdrew from the CCF. The reso-lution came at a meeting on 10 March, which the UFO did not attend. Given that the UFO had formally withdrawn from the CCF on 1 March, it is invidious for Caplan to claim that Macphail and Philpott were sur-prised when the UFO did not attend. Once again, Caplan's version of the 10 March meeting comes from Philpott, the man who quit the CCF two days later. The absence of the UFO led to deadlock between the CCF Clubs and the Labor Conference. Woodsworth and MacInnis made a good show of wanting the Provincial Council to solve the deadlock; then Woodsworth "produced a detailed statement prepared in advance by the national exec-utive outlining the problem and its proposed solution," replete with a claim that the Labor Conference had been victimized by "well-known Communist tactics."[81] Caplan argues that the "charges of Communist infiltration were untrue" and that the real problem was "inflexible, un-compromising, utterly dogmatic" radical socialists.[82] He exonerates Mould, who later did join the Communist Party. Thomas Cruden, president of the Socialist Party, is exempted from Caplan's attack, as is Bert Robinson. So whom is Caplan attacking? Standing back from the analysis of Caplan and Crowley, the two individuals who emerge as lead-ing "doctrinaire radicals" are Morton and Henderson. Morton went on to join the Communist Party, Henderson to sit on the CCF Provincial Council. Truly, we need to revisit what is going on here, because the existing characterizations are as misleading as they are revealing.

On 18 March 1934, according to Caplan, "members" of the Labor and Club sections met informally with Woodsworth and approved a plan based on individual membership in the provincial CCF. Caplan does not explain who these "members" were and why, given the vociferous opposition to in-dividual membership in the Labor Conference, they agreed to the plan. The Labor Conference, according to Caplan, "was in opposition to whatever was put forth by any leaders other than its own." The clear implication is that the Labor "members" who met with Woodsworth on 18 March 1934 were not from the Labor Conference. In effect the leaders of the CCF, constantly decry-ing labour and socialist leaders who did not represent their working-class constituents, were willing to enlist leaders who did not represent their con-stituency when it was in their political interests to do so.[83]

There is virtually no evidence to suggest that Henderson was deliber-ately attempting to disrupt the progress of the CCF. If she was guilty of anything, it was attempting to avoid conflict, to keep the party's attention focused on labour ideals and the task at hand. On 29 March 1934 she addressed the Weston CCF Club, where she stated that a policy "of reducing the political freedom of the people, a policy of oppression and fascism, such as is being gradually pursued in Canada and elsewhere is not going to bring peace ... More money is being spent on war now than ever before in history while people suffer untold torture from lack of the necessities of life. The leaders of the nation are following the very same policy that almost led to complete disaster after 1914. Our doom is certain unless we do something to replace this policy with sanity."[84] As much as possible, she avoided placing herself in direct conflict with other Toronto leftists; if she was guilty of anything, it was shying away from full engagement in the conflict, preferring to focus on the big issues in both national and international contexts.

At a 31 March 1934 meeting held at Cumberland Hall, the Labor Conference "refused to join the new set-up of the C.C.F. merely as individuals." In defending federation, the delegates "repeatedly insisted that they would never resign their 'right' to join a united front outside the C.C.F. with left wing labor movements such as the Canadian Labor Defence League and the National Unemployed Council." At a meeting of the Ontario Labor Party the day before, a special committee had been quickly struck to respond to the proposed new constitution of the CCF's Ontario section. The committee was emphatic in declaring that affiliation to the Labor Conference must be through working-class bodies – trade unions, labour parties, socialist groups, and working-class educational parties.[85] While no direct evidence exists, it seems certain that Henderson agreed with this position.

A key Labor Conference convention was held on 30 March 1934, with MacInnis as delegate for Woodsworth. Labor Conference leaders "were frank in their opinions that the National C.C.F. Council would not dare oppose the conference in its demand for the retention of its identity as a federated labor body."[86] Speakers at the conference insisted that the CCF had to be organized on the principle of federation set down at the Regina Conference, a position forcefully championed by Jack MacDonald.[87] Morton charged that the new constitution proposed by the national council, which called for convention representation to be based on party membership rather than the strength of affiliated groups, was an attempt "to

rule out of the C.C.F. all those who would make it a working class movement." MacInnis argued that the problem was "the divided ranks of Labor
in Ontario."[88]

From the beginning, the Ontario CCF convention that opened on 14 April
1934 did not go well for the Labor Conference. Morton was defeated in
the vote for secretary by national council candidate Herbert Orloff. Then
Woodsworth named MacInnis chair of the convention. Twenty-first century critics of the depoliticization of Canadian social democracy need look
no further than Woodsworth's declaration at this convention "that discussion of general resolutions and even of proposed policies must be elimin-
ated."[89] In his analysis Caplan abandons all pretence of being an objective
historian; the Labor delegates, he claims, were "impotent except in creating confusion and wasting time ... the more their impotence was revealed,
the more vociferous and objectionable they became." The Labor Conference,
according to Caplan, had now become "tiny."[90] The new officers elected
following rancorous debate produced the kind of provincial council that
Henderson had seen coming, an amalgam of mainstream labour, middle-
class professionals, and Christian socialists.

Whatever her concerns about the new CCF in Ontario, she had made
her peace with it by the spring of 1934. Her motives for deciding to contest the 19 June 1934 provincial election in Bracondale, a riding in west
central Toronto bracketed by Christie and Oakwood, are not known. The
timing was not propitious; Conservative premier George Henry, like his
federal counterpart R.B. Bennett, was reeling from the impact of the
Depression and facing the ebullient and dynamic Mitchell Hepburn of
the Liberals. The CCF was an unknown entity in Ontario politics, lacking
both money and support to launch a serious campaign in all but a handful
of ridings. Henderson was one of thirty-seven CCF candidates in a province with a total of ninety seats. As Caplan points out, the CCF did not
even have official policies on key issues such as prohibition and funding
for Catholic schools, leaving it in the position of running a largely negative campaign attacking the waste and parasitism of the capitalist system
and the two old-line parties.[91]

Henderson's candidacy, coming so soon after the internecine struggle
in the CCF over the Labor Conference, is a dagger in the heart of the claim
that she was one of the dangerous radicals attempting to wreck the party.
In addition to the problematic histories of Caplan and Crowley, Henderson

must be rescued from J.T. Morley's sweeping and mistaken claim that by the spring of 1934 "the CCF clubs had been thoroughly infiltrated with Communists and Marxists of more exotic persuasions."[92] Morley is wrong on two counts; neither the clubs nor the Labor Conference was thoroughly infiltrated, and the clubs, if they were infiltrated by anyone, were infiltrated by Liberals. As Caplan points out, it is a stretch to claim that even the Labor Conference was "infiltrated" by Marxists. Henderson has been swept up in the house cleaning, her genuine concerns about middle-class hypocrisy thrown in the garbage, her lifelong struggle for the working class, women, and children whom the CCF claimed to champion relegated to the dustbin of history.

In reality, it was her credibility and respectability as a recently elected trustee on the Toronto Board of Education that characterized her role in the party, not her supposed threat. She did not stand out in a party whose leading members regularly called for the end of the capitalist system, used words such as "dictatorship" to describe the Bennett government, and called for the nationalization of everything from banks to mines. She was not alone in speaking out about the effect of the capitalist system on children, but it was a particular focus for her, and she had an inimitable way of getting her point across. In Islington on 13 June 1934 she stated: "There are 42,000 children in the province neglected and sick, but if your cow gets sick the department of agriculture rushes out a specialist as soon as possible – because a cow means property and a profit."[93] She believed in the Regina Manifesto's call for the eradication of capitalism, because only then would the people of Canada and the world, especially the children, realize their full human potential.

Given the party's recent founding, lack of money, and internal problems, it is an overstatement to claim that the 1934 Ontario campaign was "a disaster" for the CCF.[94] Sam Lawrence was elected in Hamilton East. Henderson was one of the CCF candidates to make a respectable showing in Toronto. In Bracondale, Conservative candidate A.R. Nesbitt won with 6,200 votes. He was followed by Liberal candidate E.C. Bogart with 5,803, CCF candidate Henderson with 2,412, Communist Party candidate Thomas Sims with 262, and Socialist-Labor candidate William White with 32.[95] Henderson received a higher percentage of the vote than she had in Montreal in 1921, or in New Westminster in 1925, and more than double the 7 percent of the vote the CCF received in the province as a whole.

In spite of her defeat as a CCF candidate, Henderson increasingly framed her public activism in terms of her membership in the party. In the summer of 1934 she was a part of a labour dispute – one of the few she engaged in following the demise of the Labor Conference and her election to the Toronto Board of Education. The dispute began when a group of female workers, members of Dressmakers' Local 72 of the International Ladies Garment Workers Union, stopped work when management refused to increase extremely low piece rates. The workers left the factory on 11 July, were locked out by the company the next day, and then declared they were on strike.[96] The union was taking advantage of the fact that the hearings of the Price Spreads Commission had focused attention on the conditions in department stores and on the T. Eaton Company in particular. As a response to Depression conditions, in 1934 the Bennett government set up a Select Committee on Price Spreads and Mass Buying, headed by the minister of trade and commerce, H.H. Stevens. Public outcry followed revelations of corruption in the garment industry and the low wages and poor working conditions of the non-union women workers employed in the industry. The outcry provided the impetus for the government to turn the select committee into a royal commission. As Mercedes Steedman points out, "garment unions were quick to see the possible advantages of such public exposure."[97]

The dressmakers' strike at Eaton's created, as Ruth Frager points out, an unusual degree of support for the striking workers. Frager suggests that while the CCF executive "tried to help the women strikers, the role of key CCF women was particularly important in mobilizing strike support."[98] Early in August the CCF provincial executive met at least twice with Arthur Roebuck, minister of labour and attorney-general. The delegation asked Roebuck to mediate, recognize the union, and investigate and prosecute violations under the Minimum Wage Act.[99] Dr Lorna Cotton was one of the delegation's spokespersons, along with Arthur Williams.[100] As Frager notes, CCFers Jean Laing and Henderson "helped lead the strike-support campaign" and "played prominent roles."[101] On 8 August 1934 both women spoke at a mass meeting held on behalf of Dressmakers' Union, Local 72, ILGWU, at Queen's Park.[102] In addition, they were instrumental in convincing the Local Council of Women to support the strikers.[103] This was no mean accomplishment, given the historic hesitancy of the National Council of Women to be identified with striking workers, if not the labour movement itself.

In spite of the unusually widespread support the strikers received, the strike was lost. Henderson's support for the strikers, who were members of an AFL-TLCC union affiliate, won her no kudos among the leadership of Canada's mainstream labour movement. On 10 September 1934 the Jubilee Conference of the Trades and Labor Congress was held at the Royal York Hotel. As the delegates assembled, it was quickly revealed that tolerance for "political" speeches had dramatically declined in the TLCC since the First World War: "Without mincing words, President Moore sternly reminded the conference that there would be no outside speeches or 'qualifying addresses' given in connection with any resolution. He asserted that, in his opinion, the delegates present were fully capable of dealing with any and all the resolutions before them from the floor of the convention. His candid disqualification came when it was suggested that Dr. Rose Henderson should speak to the first resolution, one of five dealing with matters of education and educational reforms."[104]

The woman who addressed the 1912, 1916, 1917, and 1918 conventions of the TLCC was no longer to be heard, a reflection of the changed nature of the Canadian left since the formation of the Communist Party. Yet it seems unlikely that Moore's opinion of Henderson had changed dramatically since the days when he praised her as one of Canada's leading female activists. She was not identifiably more radical in 1934 than she was in 1912; indeed, it can be argued that she had lost some of her edge. It was not so much she who had changed as the world in which she lived and worked. She politicized issues, and that in itself was enough to raise the cry of "communist."

Mistrust of Henderson in this period was in part tied to her activism on behalf of youth, an activism that put her in constant contact with Communist Party members. There is no simple way to write about this activism, because it involves unpacking the intersection of the Cooperative Commonwealth Youth Movement, the League against War and Fascism, and the Canadian Youth Congress. The existing treatments of the battle for the minds of socialist youth that took place in 1930s Canada barely scratch the surface of the complexities and meanings of this struggle. Henderson was front and centre in it, and with her as our guide, we can begin to unpack its significance.

On 20 July 1934 the Toronto Conference of the Canadian Youth Congress against War and Fascism held an open meeting at the Cumberland Hall.

Over one hundred young people attended, including delegates from the YWCA and "the Young Trotskyites." Henderson was the principal speaker. She made a "stirring appeal to the Youth of Canada to join wholeheartedly in the struggle against the twin evils of Fascism and War, and to work for a new social order which will make possible a lasting peace." Young people, she stated, "are by nature inclined toward peace ... but their minds are poisoned by the insidious propaganda of the War-Makers and those who would derive profit from a new international slaughter."[105] The report of this meeting in the CCF press suggests that this was a non-communist initiative involving the CCF, the YWCA, the League of Nations Society, the League for Social Reconstruction, and "the Toronto Regiment."[106] Norman Penner's claim that the League against War and Fascism "brought into being the Canadian Youth Congress" is problematic, because the League held its first congress in October 1934, *after* the meeting of the Canadian Youth Congress against War and Fascism.[107]

We can safely conclude that Henderson was one of the organizers of the congress being pursued by the Communist Party. By the fall of 1934 she was appearing in front page headlines in *The Worker*, highlighting her involvement in organizing the congress, to be held in October 1934.[108] The Party's praise of Henderson, described as "actively engaged in furthering the fight against war," did little to reassure concerned CCF leaders; nor did the singling out of the contribution being made by Morton.[109] In addition, Henderson was taking advantage of her position on the Board of Education to "secure one of the school auditoriums for the sessions of the Congress."[110] This was one of a number of instances in which she acted as facilitator of left political meetings and conferences in Toronto in the 1930s by arranging the booking of rooms in school buildings.[111]

The first Canadian Congress against War and Fascism was held 5–7 October 1934 at the Hygeia Hall at the corner of Elm and Yonge.[112] Although the Communist Party was nominally still in its Third Period, condemning all non-communists as "social fascists," the welcome to the delegates reveals that the Popular Front had already arrived. The National Committee "greets your attendance at the first congress called to unite the workers, farmers, professional people and intellectuals into a solid front against threatening war and growing fascism!"[113] In the Fourth Session, held on Sunday afternoon, there was a discussion on "Women, Fascism and War" led by Morton, Siegel, Henderson, and Laing.[114]

Henderson "urged that the force of women's organizations and intelligence be thrown behind the movement against war and fascism." Drawing
on her travels in Europe, she spoke of women under fascism in Italy and
Germany, declaring that under Hitler "there is no iniquity that man has
not practiced upon women."[115] The slave woman, Henderson stated,
could only produce a slave man. It is difficult to distinguish her analysis
of women under fascism from the position being advanced by the
Communist Party in this period. It is instructive, however, that the evidence of the Communist Party's condemnation of "fascism's misogyny"
cited by Joan Sangster is taken from the February and March 1935 issues
of the *Daily Clarion*, indicating the possibility that the CPC took its position from Henderson, not the other way round.[116]

Henderson was now committed to the CCF, but she remained suspect
not just because of her association with Communist Party members but
also because of her work with youth in the CCF. She was a speaker when
the Ontario section of the national CCF Cooperative Commonwealth
Youth Movement (CCYM) was organized at its first annual convention on
13–14 October 1934 at the Cumberland Hall. Featured speaker E.A.
Havelock described the real work of the CCYM as fighting capitalism in
Canada; forthright resolutions were passed on educating young people in
the principles of international socialism, organizing youth to confront the
"joint terrors of war and fascism," and promoting and supporting industrial unions.[117] These were all positions that could be supported by the
Communist Party and the small group of Trotskyists in Toronto at this
time, making the CCYM an object of "infiltration" by Marxist-Leninists.
Woodsworth, MacInnis, and David Lewis were all concerned about CCF
youth and the danger that they would be "seduced" by communists and
Trotskyists.

At the CCYM conference Henderson stated "that she was devoting all
her time to the welfare of youth in the schools."[118] As the most important
bridge between social democratic youth and the school system in Toronto,
she was suspect both in the CCF and on the Board of Education. On
Thursday, 1 November 1934, the board received a deputation from the
CCYM led by Spencer Cheshire and Murray Cotterill, introduced by
Henderson. [119] The delegation "asked for the use of certain secondary
schools for the holding of co-operative classes, self-governed, to study
sociological and economic problems, and also for recreation purposes,

athletics and open forums." In response, the board ordered Dr Goldring to "report to the management committee on the request."[120] The meeting of the management committee held on 7 November 1934 agreed with the recommendation of the superintendent of schools and denied the CCYM the use of schools for holding classes.[121]

By the fall and early winter of 1935 the city of Toronto featured a left political culture that continued to cause problems for a CCF leadership that sought to clearly distinguish itself not just from the Communist Party but from a wide array of socially progressive organizations and philosophies. What the CCF leadership was up against is revealed at a mass rally on 11 November 1934 against war and fascism at Massey Hall, which was "filled to capacity."[122] Speakers included Rabbi Eisendrath, Henderson, Dorothy Detzer, the national secretary of the US Section of the Women's International League for Peace and Freedom, Communist Party leader Leslie Morris, Marxist CCFer and League against War and Fascism activist E.A. Beder, and WILPF stalwart Anna Sissons.[123] The CCF leadership had to deal with more than its members speaking and organizing alongside communists and Marxists; they had to grapple with the catholic nature of the CCF itself, as revealed on a single evening in December 1934. On Sunday, 16 December 1934, Henderson spoke to the Parkdale CCF Forum at the Arcade Assembly Hall, 107 Roncesvalles Avenue. Four other CCF forums were held the same evening, including J.F. White, on behalf of the League against War and Fascism, speaking on "Fascism Prepares for War," and Maurice Spector speaking on "Do Armament Firms Cause War?" Needless to say, a "Stalinist" and a Trotskyist speaking at CCF open forums was not likely to result in a good night's sleep for Woodsworth and Macphail.

For all Henderson's genuine efforts to bring labour unity to the Canadian working class, the political reality of mid-1930s Toronto was that now she had to make choices. She could no longer maintain membership in labour organizations that were taking different positions on joining the CCF and were in any event in the process of ceasing to exist. In order to understand her choices, it is necessary to realize that the disbanding of the Labor Conference in March 1934 had not ended the conflicts among the CCF, the Ontario Labor Party, and the Independent Labor Party. Mould, who disappears from Caplan's treatment as of March 1934, was not quite done. On Good Friday, 19 April 1935, delegates attended an intended unity convention of the Ontario Labor Party and the Independent Labor Party at the Labor Lyceum. According to the *Star*, the purpose of the convention was to "accept the manifesto of the C.C.F., adopted at its Regina convention, together with the C.C.F. immediate program, and recognize the Dominion-wide C.C.F. organization as the political instrument for the conducting of municipal, provincial and federal election campaigns."[124] According to the *Globe*, delegates from the international unions "declined vehemently to sit in meetings with alleged Communists."[125] The "alleged Communists" appear to have been delegates from the Workers' Unity League invited to the convention by Mould.[126] The convention split, holding separate conventions in separate rooms. At the ILP convention the delegates voted unanimously to accept the "entire program" of the CCF.[127]

Henderson attended the ILP meeting, thus breaking with Mould. She thereby cast her lot with the AFL-TLCC unions, in the process severing her past involvement with the National Labor Union. She was elected to the executive, along with president George Watson, honorary president James Simpson, and secretary James MacArthur Conner. Simpson, speaking at the breakaway convention, made no secret of where he stood by calling Mould a communist.[128] Conner, it is worth recalling, was part of the "conspiracy" with Henderson to prevent the Labor Conference from affiliating with the CCF. Continued advocacy of a broad left coalition notwithstanding, Henderson had now thrown in her lot with CCFers who were adamant opponents of cooperation with the Communist Party.

On Saturday, 20 April 1935, the day after the split in the ranks of the Independent Labor Party and the Ontario Labor Party, the annual conference of the Ontario Section of the CCF was held at the Royal York Hotel. Two hundred delegates and two hundred visitors attended. Mould, William Douglas, and E.A. Beder came to the convention as a delegation representing the Ontario Labor Party. But the convention, "with an overwhelming vote, enthusiastically rejected the request of the defunct Ontario Labor Party to be represented by fraternal delegates."[129] A similar request from the Socialist Party of Canada (OS) had been turned down by the provincial council prior to the convention. The die was cast.

Henderson's election to the executive of the Independent Labor Party marks a meaningful transition in her political life. Her support for the

One Big Union in 1919–20 notwithstanding, her main allegiance, going back to her first speech to the Trades and Labour Congress convention in 1912, had been to the international unions. Although a former executive member of the Ontario Labor Party, she was clearly moving away from the influence of Mould and making her peace with CCF leaders including Simpson, past disagreements with him notwithstanding. At the convention John Mitchell was re-elected president, and Graham Spry was re-elected vice-president, confirming the CCF's moderate trajectory. Henderson's choice also meant accepting a tacit alliance with social democrats in England and the United States. Sir Stafford Cripps spoke on behalf of the British Labour Party and read a telegram from party leader George Lansbury. Norman Thomas brought greetings from the Socialist Party of America. It was heady company for CCF delegates, but a bridge had been burned and there was no going back.

It is not possible to tell the extent to which Henderson consciously tailored her political involvements, especially her activities in association with Communist Party members, to avoid clashing with the CCF leadership. We do know that she did not stop cooperating with Communist Party members on her own terms, and she continued to promote unity within the ranks of labour and the left. In these last years of her life, however, it is possible to detect a more restrained Henderson, who made contributions behind the scenes as well as in the public eye. One way to do that was to take on the role of facilitator of meetings and conferences of peace, women's, youth, and left-wing organizations, a role that emerged quite clearly in her work with the Canadian Youth Congress (CYC).

The origins of the CYC are a matter of some dispute. According to Norman Penner, it was inspired by the American Youth Congress and began in Canada in August 1934 as the youth wing of the League against War and Fascism.[130] As we have observed, however, the Canadian Youth Congress against War and Fascism meeting took place on 20 July 1934, attended by an eclectic group of social activists. The records of the CYC challenge Penner's interpretation, claiming that in 1934 "a small group of university students and young social workers and business people, most of them church members, saw that the innumerable small groups of young people who realized and wished to do something about the problems of their world, were too small and isolated to make much impression: they needed a means of acting together for common aims."[131]

Whatever the role of the Communist Party in creating the CYC, it undoubtedly played a major role in shaping attitudes toward this type of "united front." The need for Henderson to tread carefully is revealed in a letter that James Simpson wrote from the mayor's office to CYC secretary John Stewart in February 1935 in response to a conference invitation: "I am always a little skeptical as to those conferences which include the Communist Party's representatives. It seems to me that if your organization is admitting the C.C.F. Youth delegates and at the same time intending to invite delegates from the Communist Party, it is placing the C.C.F. Youth in a rather compromising position, inasmuch as the C.C.F. policy is non-collaboration with the Communists. If I am astray on this matter kindly keep me informed. Otherwise your efforts are to be commended, but I must offer the one reservation which I always do to protect myself from being a conscious tool of the Communist Party."[132]

Any historian of the CCF in this period immediately recognizes that Simpson's salutation "Dear Comrade Stewart" notwithstanding, the statement could easily have been made by Woodsworth. This strategy, the hard-line position enunciated by the voice of reason, had now become standard on the part of leading members of the CCF. Simpson's concerns notwithstanding, the Young Communist League was invited to participate in CYC discussions prior to the organizational conference in May 1935, an invitation that was accepted.[133]

Henderson did not belong to any of the youth groups affiliated with the Canadian Youth Council, but she assisted in the work of organizing the May 1935 congress.[134] In spite of concerns about the involvement of the Young Communist League and the Cooperative Commonwealth Youth Movement, the Board of Education agreed to the use of the Central Technical Auditorium on 24–25 May 1935, a request no doubt put forward by Henderson on behalf of the congress.[135] In May 1935 delegates and observers from more than two hundred organizations met in Toronto and discussed and passed resolutions on peace, employment, and education.[136] It is not difficult to see why Henderson supported the CYC's education policies, and she may have had a hand in drafting them. The CYC opposed "all efforts to utilize the schools for the militarization of young people, or for anti-democratic indoctrination." Like Henderson, the congress called for changes to the curriculum to give students a better understanding of the society they lived in, and the improvement of individual and group hygiene.[137]

We do well to pause for a moment to remember that the Communist Party at this point was still in its Third Period, still officially denouncing people like Henderson as "social fascists." The official beginning of the Popular Front occurred at the Seventh Congress of the Communist International held in July and August 1935. In key speeches on 2 and 13 August, the general secretary of the Comintern, Georgi Dimitrov, advocated a "people's front" against fascism. In reality communist parties and communist leaders around the world had been drifting away from the Third Period for at least a year before it officially came to an end. In September 1934 the Soviet Union had joined the League of Nations, which it had denounced since its formation in 1919, signalling its search for collective security against possible Nazi aggression. Penner argues that in Canada the convention of the League against War and Fascism held in October 1934 "launched the Canadian Communists into the anti-fascist popular front period."[138] The Canadian Youth Congress was, for all intents and purposes, a Popular Front organization, and the nature of its cause made it difficult even for Simpson to dissuade party members such as Henderson from participating in it. At this point the communists were taking more of a Popular Front than a Third Period approach to respected non-communist leftists such as Henderson.

As John Manley points out, in the Canadian context the Communist Party had been attempting to legitimize itself by "exploring Canadian radicalism's pre-bolshevik roots" since 1933.[139] Looking to the heritage of William Lyon Mackenzie and the patriots of the rebellions of 1837–38 enabled Canadian communists to construct a Popular Front that included Prime Minister Mackenzie King, who also saw himself as an inheritor of his famous grandfather. As Manley reveals, the Popular Front involved "a turn away from the language of class" and the embracing of "the people," a language that even leading Liberals like King could embrace.[140] It also meant that leading communists, including Tim Buck, had to learn to use a language Henderson had been using for almost three decades.

There were limits, of course; even the most popular of fronts could not include the hated Trotskyists. By inference it included anarchists and syndicalists, but in reality it did not, as the undeclared war on anarchists and syndicalists in Spain attested. Ironically, as Penner points out, the communists were willing "to accept a form of unity with groups that did not oppose fascism."[141] Indeed, by June 1936 the executive of the Toronto Youth Council comprised delegates of the Young Communist League,

Canadian Union of Fascists, and British Union of Fascists, among others.[142] Whether or not Henderson was aware of the executive's composition is unknown, but it may explain why she did not become involved in the CYC in any official capacity.

However we define the Popular Front, it did signal a major change in the dynamic of the Canadian left. Sangster puts it well: the change in Communist Party tactics meant that "the pink tea pacifists they had earlier opposed now became sought-after allies in the fight against fascism."[143] In the process, communists "helped to shape a rising tide of protest against social and economic inequality." For women, the Popular Front "generated new opportunities for activism and inspired innovative organizing techniques." Yet, as Sangster quite correctly points out, "the CPC's primary goal was to draw women into the fight against fascism, not to understand why they were oppressed and how that might be changed."[144] Debates about the relative degree of autonomy the Canadian Party had vis-à-vis directives from the Communist International notwithstanding, the Comintern's main concern was pushing back the rising tide of international fascism.

While valid, Sangster's position on women and the Popular Front does not quite do justice to the change that came about at the Seventh Party Congress of the Communist International. In his 2 August 1935 speech Georgi Dimitrov spoke directly about the threat of fascism to women, stating that it "enslaves women with particular ruthlessness and cynicism," adding that "there cannot be a successful fight against fascism and war unless the wide masses of women are drawn into the struggle." He went further, supporting the organization of separate women's groups and frankly acknowledging that abolishing them in the past "has often done great harm."[145] It would be a mistake not to understand the notable increase in left-wing women's groups in the Popular Front period as inspired, if not caused, by the Communist Party of Canada.

Sangster's careful, yet apt, observation that the Communist Party "helped to shape" events during the Popular Front is reflected in Henderson's relationship with the party as a CCF candidate in the 1935 federal election. By the fall of 1935 her campaign had been in progress for some months. On 21 May 1935 she "was unanimously selected as the official federal candidate for the Parkdale and North Parkdale C.C.F. clubs."[146] On 31 May 1935 the North and South CCF Clubs welcomed her to their new committee rooms on Roncesvalles. During her speech she commented, "There are times in one's life ... when no matter how hard you try, you cannot express yourself in the way you wish to. I have been in the Labor movement in Canada, in Great Britain and quite a bit in the U.S.A and I have this to say that wherever I have been and whatever I have done, I have never failed the labor movement. In this election I feel more keenly than ever my duty and responsibility to you and I can assure you from next Monday on until the last shot is fired, I shall be giving the major part of my days and my evenings to winning this election."[147]

It is instructive that Henderson professed her loyalty to the labour movement as a whole, not to the CCF. Launching her election campaign, she cautions us against pushing her adherence to the CCF too far, and warns us against believing that her commitment to labour and the left was collapsed into her party loyalty. It was this perspective that led her to continue to work with Communist Party members and made her a believer in the Popular Front.

While the sources are silent on the campaign in June and July 1935, the 17 August 1935 edition of *The Worker* announced that the first of a series of weekly meetings organized by the Women's Labor Election Committee was to be held at the Labor Temple, 167 Church Street, on Tuesday, 20 August 1935. The committee, "made up of active Communists and C.C.F. women, is out to organize a solid vote against capitalist candidates on the part of all working women." The chair was to be Jean Laing. Henderson, "the only labor woman nominated in this city," was to speak. It is instructive that Laing was identified as a member of the committee but not Henderson; it seems unlikely that the editor of *The Worker* would have failed to identify Henderson as a member if she was one. While it is not true, as Sangster points out, that both women "were simply naïve pawns of the CPC," it appears that Henderson maintained a more arm's-length relationship than Laing did. Later in the campaign *The Worker* noted that CCF and Communist Party candidates from Trinity, Parkdale, Davenport, and High Park had been invited to speak in the Spadina Concert Hall on 1 October 1935, but no evidence has surfaced affirming that Henderson did so.[148]

Despite her support for a united front with the Communist Party, she was aided in her campaign by high profile CCFers. On 28 August 1935 Hamilton East CCF MLA Sam Lawrence spoke at two street-corner meetings on Henderson's behalf.[149] On Sunday, 22 September, Frank Underhill, a professor at the University of Toronto, was scheduled to give a talk in the committee room at 405 Roncesvalles.[150] On 15 September 1935 Henderson attended the meeting of the Ontario CCF Provincial Council at the provincial office, 225 Richmond Street West, as one of thirty-five federal election candidates. If she was entertaining doubts about the CCF's commitment to socialism, they were likely assuaged by the debate on the peace resolution, which stated that the CCF "stands resolutely against all imperialist wars" and "refuses to allow Canada to be involved in a war fought to make the world safe for capitalism." She had no trouble supporting a CCF that "looks forward to the establishment of world economic planning between nations at peace" and whose policy "is definitely international as against narrow nationalism."[151] She made some sacrifices in joining the CCF, and she wanted to get elected, but she was not willing to abandon her long-held antagonism to the capitalist system. At a 14 September 1935 meeting that "drew a capacity crowd," she "attacked capitalism in all its forms for its failure to provide even the essentials of life and challenged its ability to maintain even the present standard of living."[152]

Even after she became committed to the CCF, Henderson retained much of the world view of First World War era Canadian socialists. Responding to critics who charged that people's forums were "political" meetings, she defended then by claiming that they were in reality educational forums and "necessary to acquaint the people with the need for a new social order."[153] For her, the creation of a "new social order" – for all intents and purposes the overthrow of the capitalist system – was something to embrace, not fear. It was not a matter of politics but a matter of education. It was, in effect, to recognize the truth. While we will likely never know for certain, the existing evidence suggests that she never fully understood why her message was threatening to the voters of the city of Toronto in general and her riding in particular. Given her rhetoric, however, there can be little doubt that Liberal and Conservative voters in Parkdale in the fall of 1935 got the message loud and clear: Henderson was a threat to the world they lived in and wanted to retain.

In attempting to get elected, Henderson was dealing with the impact of her own politics in addition to her association with the Communist Party. On 10 October 1935, four days before the federal election, the

Communist Party declared that it was supporting at least twenty-two CCF candidates. The party claimed there was a "joint committee" of the Communist Party and the CCF in West York, where the CCF candidate was Fred Fish. In Toronto Greenwood, Bert Leavens was being "supported by a labor conference in which the local Communist Party plays a leading role. The campaign here is an example to all C.C.F. candidates." The article continued, "Many other C.C.F. candidates have been interviewed by committees of Communists and their replies have satisfied the Communists of their sincerity. These are therefore receiving support in their campaign to a greater and lesser degree, depending on the strength of Communists in their ridings, etc." Henderson was included in the list of candidates the Communist Party was supporting.[154]

While it is not clear if the interviews referred to actually happened, it is clear that the Communist Party was attempting to direct relations between itself and the CCF. Non-communists on the Toronto left were expected to meet expectations and standards set by the Communist Party, the rhetoric of the Popular Front notwithstanding. While the evidence is episodic and circumstantial, it does suggest that Henderson was circumspect in her dealings with the party, participating in Popular Front activities while maintaining, as Sangster points out, her own conception of socialism. The problem, of course, is that Henderson was campaigning for a revolutionary transformation of capitalist society, albeit by peaceful means, a politics not likely to be understood, let alone accepted, by the majority of voters in Parkdale. She was attempting to defend a principled left politics, but in the end the contradictions in her own politics, and her association with the Communist Party, overwhelmed her dedicated efforts, hard work, and genuine commitment to the women, workers, and poor of her riding.

In the course of her campaign, Henderson continued to be one of the most recognizable female social activists in the city of Toronto. Her status is revealed by the fact that at a CCF mass meeting held at the Parkdale Assembly Hall on 11 October 1935, the main speakers were her and Mayor Simpson. Other speakers included Fred Fish, the CCF candidate in York West, and E.B. "Ted" Jolliffe, the CCF candidate for St Paul's.[155] In party histories of the CCF/NDP, Jolliffe is a much more prominent figure than Henderson because he became the first Ontario provincial leader of the party in 1942, but in 1935 in Toronto, Henderson was much better known. The day after the CCF mass meeting, the *Globe* carried a group photo of Agnes Macphail, Lorna Cotton Thomas, Mrs George Black of the Yukon, Nora Frances Henderson, Rose Henderson, and Minerva Reid. These five women comprised one-third of the female candidates in the 1935 federal election. Henderson was lauded as "one of the first women interested in labor organization in Canada."[156]

We have now entered a high point of women's left political activism, a high point that characterized the CCF as well as the Communist Party. On Sunday, 13 October 1935, when Henderson spoke to the Parkdale CCF forum at the Parkdale Assembly Hall at 10 Lansdowne Avenue, also on the program was Dr Cotton, described as "one of the C.C.F.'s most dynamic women speakers." On the same evening, Eileen Tallman of the Cooperative Commonwealth Youth Movement spoke at the Davenport open forum, and Mary McNab spoke at the High Park CCF open forum.[157] Henderson's candidacy in Parkdale enlisted the support of the best and brightest of the non-communist left in Toronto. It was a great leap forward for women in Canadian public life, but the hurdles remained in place, and many of them were too high for even the most determined women.

Henderson was as idealistic and optimistic a female campaigner as there was to be found, but even she must have been terribly disappointed on election night. When the votes were counted in Toronto Parkdale, she had finished fourth behind Conservative candidate David Spence with 9,604 votes, Liberal candidate J.L. Prentice with 7,704 votes, and Reconstruction candidate C.A. Hurlbut with 3, 576 votes. Henderson was not far behind Hurlbut with 3,243 votes, almost 13.5 per cent of the total.[158] Asked for her reaction to the poor results for the CCF in the election, she put the best face possible on them, stating that the CCF "should not take its defeat to heart."[159]

Whatever the reasons for her defeat, she did not attribute it to the united front and being associated with the Communist Party. Her ongoing association with party members continued, as evidenced at the Second National Congress of the League against War and Fascism held on 6–8 December 1935 in Toronto. At noon on Saturday, December 7, a luncheon and round table discussion was held at the YMCA, organized by the Women's Committee. In her "brilliant address" Communist Annie Buller stated that the trade union movement had not given enough attention to the organization of women in industry. She used the example of

Quebec, pointing out the "deplorable" results of only 2 per cent of Quebec women in industry being unionized. Henderson "described many cases of legislative discrimination against women, ranging from sixth century England to the present day Quebec old laws still on the statute books of Canada. The church has always combined with the state through the ages regarding the subjection of women, and the dogma that woman owes man unqualified obedience has been handed down with the blessing of the church. Dr. Henderson agreed with Miss Buller that there can be no true freedom, equality and success until men and women work together co-operatively."[160]

CCF leaders and the general public might be excused for thinking that there was no identifiable difference between Henderson and leading Communist Party women. As we have discovered, however, she also had an active political life in the company of Liberal and Conservative middle-class women, creating problems for any attempt to characterize her as a communist. We are now nearing the end of her life, and she continues to float just beyond our grasp.

Henderson's continuing involvement with the CCF and association with Communist Party members took place in conjunction with her on-going work with middle-class women's organizations in the mid-1930s. As a trustee on the Toronto Board of Education, she moved in circles that included prominent middle-class – indeed, upper-class – women in Toronto society. In addition to her work on the board, she was quite active in the Toronto Home and School Council. The West Branch of the Home and School Council included Ward Five, Henderson's ward, and Dewson, Essex, and Palmerston schools. While Henderson spoke on numerous occasions to Home and School Associations, she does not appear to have had a position on the council itself or in any of its individual school associations.[161]

There is no denying that she was now engaging in activities that do not accord with the radical image she developed in the 1919 period. No detailed or in-depth record of her involvement with the Home and School Council exists, but there are enough scattered sources to create a portrait of her activities. On 15 February 1934 the *Star* reported that she attended the celebration of founders' day of the Home and School movement at the Palmerston Home and School Club and spoke briefly on "Goodwill."[162] In March 1934 she was one of the speakers at a meeting of the Dovercourt Home and School Club.[163] On 23 April 1934 the *Star* reported that the

Palmerston Avenue Home and School Club had held a centennial tea on Saturday afternoon, at which Henderson poured. On 10 May 1934 she gave an address on "Art in Relation to Education" at the annual meeting of the Hodgson Home and School Club. On 5 June 1934, at the "finale" of the Dovercourt Home and School Club, she spoke on the Board of Education's work.[164] On 6 June 1934 she was one of the guests at the banquet given by the Edith L. Groves Home and School Club in honour of the school's 1934 graduating class.[165]

Her activities in the summer and fall of 1934 reveal quite clearly the falsity of distinguishing activist women on the basis of class, ethnicity, and religion. On 10 August 1934 Henderson, Beryl Plumptre, Minerva Reid, and Ida Siegel were guests at a luncheon in honour of the women delegates attending the Canadian Teachers' Federation.[166] Henderson often found herself in their company; Siegel, of course, was one of the progenitors of the Home and School Council and a crucial link between Jewish social activism and Anglo-Celtic maternal feminists. We see Henderson's links to Siegel and Reid again in October 1934, on the occasion of the second annual Home and School Council festival held in the Jarvis Street Collegiate. Patronesses of the festival included Mrs William Stewart, wife of the mayor, Mrs R.S. McLaughlin, president of the provincial Home and School Council, Siegel, Reid, and Henderson.[167]

Typically in her speeches to Home and School Clubs, Henderson outlined her work on the Board of Education and the Home and School Council. In the mid-1930s, women in prominent positions in public life were the exception, and these women simply talking about what they did was in and of itself a new phenomenon and a subject of some wonder and curiosity for other women. Most other talks were about women, the peace movement, or both, and tended to have titles such as "World Friendship," the title of a talk Henderson gave to the Dovercourt Home and School Club at its regular monthly meeting on 6 November 1934. In her talk she stressed "the responsibility of the mothers of the world in the moulding of their children's ideals for peace or war."[168]

Her involvement with the Home and School Council suggests the stronger influence of maternal feminism among middle-class, Anglo-Celtic feminists in Canada than in the United States, where the equal rights tradition of feminism was stronger.[169] In tandem with this argument, Frager states that because Jews in Toronto had less political influence than Jews in New York, female Jews in Toronto were less amenable to forming alliances with Anglo-Celtic middle-class feminists.[170] Henderson may have been an exception; in January 1934 she was the guest speaker at the regular meeting of the Hebrew Maternity Aid Society, an organization she spoke to on a number of occasions. Her subject was the "Importance of Women in Politics," and a vote of thanks was moved by Ida Siegel.[171] Henderson, the middle-class Anglo-Celtic feminist, was speaking to an organization dedicated to improving the lives of Jewish mothers on a topic emphasizing an equal rights agenda.[172] In the minds of both Jewish and Anglo-Celtic feminists, maternal feminism and equal rights were complementary, not antagonistic. It is not necessary to denigrate the salience of class or ethnic hierarchies of power in order to make the crucially important point that these women, as women, were together helping to transform a political culture in which the great majority of women remained on the margins of public life.[173]

Fighting for a heightened role for women in public life came much more easily to Henderson than overcoming opposition to separate schools. Catholics and the education system had become a hot button issue in Toronto politics since the election of the Hepburn Liberals. Catholics had been agitating for decades for more public support of separate schools, and the Conservative administration of G. Howard Ferguson had taken tentative steps in that direction. The Depression accelerated the campaign, given that discrimination against Catholics resulted in a lower socio-economic standing and subsequent weakness of the tax base for separate schools. As a result, the Catholic Taxpayers' Association (CTA) was created in 1932.[174] Led by Chairman Martin J. Quinn, the CTA organized a province-wide campaign to gain a share of corporation and utility taxes.

Ontario Orangemen feared that Quinn and the CTA "had elicited some kind of secret pledge from Hepburn to help the Catholic schools."[175] Following the election of the Hepburn Liberals, it did not take long for the issue to make its presence felt at meetings of the Toronto Board of Education. As the backdrop for Trustee Guest's motion at the 20 September 1934 meeting, a resolution was circulated declaring that "this Board of Education, on behalf of the Public School supporters of Toronto, protests against any legislation or regulation which will impair their revenues, or which will in any way divert government grants or local taxes for school purposes, to which they are now legally entitled, towards the maintenance of Roman Catholic Separate Schools, or of any system of sectarian or denominational schools." Copies of the resolution were sent to the premier, the minister of education, and members of the legislature representing the City of Toronto. The resolution was carried by a vote of sixteen to two, Henderson voting with the majority.[176]

Henderson was a fervent supporter of the public education system, but there are reasons to believe that she was not among the more bigoted anti-Catholics of her day. Given that she was of Irish Protestant descent, there is the obvious temptation to associate her with Orange tendencies, especially if we recall her friendship with the rabidly anti-Catholic James L. Hughes. She was a lifelong critic of the established church, and what has been recorded of her speeches to the League against War and Fascism reveal that she considered the province of Quebec, with its Catholic domination of women, to be notably culpable. She was as forthright a champion of the public education system as one could find, and there is every reason to believe that she would fervently oppose the extension of public funding to the separate school system.

There is also reason to be cautious. At the 24 January 1935 meeting of the board of trustees, Chairman C.M. Carrie, also chairman of the legislation committee of the Grand Orange Lodge of Ontario West, "secured the board's approval to a motion protesting against the Separate School's claim for a share of corporation taxes in Ontario, but in the face of opposition dropped a clause of it which reproved Premier Hepburn for alleged bias toward the Roman Catholic case." Henderson commented, "This board has always been anxious to avoid politics. I do not see why we should reprove the premier even though he might deserve it." Carrie agreed to drop the clause referring to the premier, and Henderson voted for the motion as amended.[177] The vote was fifteen to two, Minerva Reid and Margaret Mackenzie voting against.[178]

Henderson was no champion of Roman Catholic rights, but she was opposed to taking unfair political advantage of the conflict. On 30 November 1935 the *Star* reported on a dispute concerning Mayor Simpson and the separate school board concerning the fact that in 1934 the provincial government had made textbooks "an essential part of relief." The separate school board had spent $1,500 on books for indigent children, and went to the welfare department in Toronto and requested the provincial rebate of $1,000 to which it felt it was entitled. The Toronto Board of Control voted against it. Henderson, again distancing herself from Simpson, commented that needy children "have nothing to do with religion or politics ... Neither has the board of education an interest in the application of the separate school board. Whatever it is entitled to, let it have. I am opposed to making a political football of the subject."[179] On 27 December 1935, at a CCF rally for municipal candidates at Massey Hall, she stated in reference to the textbook controversy, "There are those who care little for religion who would create a 'North and South Ireland' situation between two provinces in Canada."[180] Echoing her response to the anti-Quebec bigotry she faced in St Catharines in 1919, she sought to head off turning opposition for increased funding to Catholic schools into an attack on Quebec and French Canadians.

While the evidence does not exist for definitive statements, the few, scattered comments by Henderson suggest that, by the standards of a later day, she was anti-Catholic; on principle she opposed giving Catholics a share of corporation and utility taxes. What is also clear, however, is that she opposed Protestants taking sectarian positions and using anti-Catholicism as a tool for gaining political advantage. Her comment at the 27 December 1935 rally also suggests that she saw anti-Catholicism in Ontario as anti-Quebec sentiment, and deplored the kind of sectarianism in Canadian politics she was familiar with from the Irish context. It was her classic dilemma: how to remain principled in a world in which remaining principled of necessity involved conflict.

Her success in the elections to the Toronto Board of Education indicate that her defence of the public education system, and her opposition to giving Catholics a share of corporation and utility taxes, won the support of voters in Ward Five. The 21 December 1935 issue of the *New Commonwealth* carried her picture on the front page, the caption stating that she had won "wide commendation" for her work on the Board of Education in the past year. The *Canadian Friend*, which a year earlier claimed that no Toronto newspapers supported her, commented that although she "was first elected against great odds, [she] has become so well and favorably known for her work that this year all four newspapers supported her."[181]

As she began her third term on the board, her star had definitely risen in the city's constellation of public figures. It was now possible to find, even in the fervently Tory *Toronto Evening Telegram*, a newfound respect for

her, a willingness to look beyond her radical reputation to assess what she
was actually doing in her role as trustee, peace activist, advocate of women
and youth, and champion of the labour movement. She was respected
across the political spectrum, in middle-class as well as working-class
circles, and she was as likely to be found in the company of Jewish activists in Toronto as in the company of Anglo-Celtic ones. Yet the diversity
of her activities and associates meant that she was never fully a member of
any one organization or political tendency. Even as she came to accept the
changed organizational structure of the CCF, she continued to advocate a
united front with the Communist Party, of which she was not a member.
As a result, she was always in some sense an outsider in whatever organization she was a part of. She was in but not of the CCF, of but not in the
Communist Party. She was an active participant in the activities of Jewish
left and Anglo-Celtic middle-class women's organizations, but was not
actually a member of any Jewish organization or organizations such as the
Local Council of Women and the Home and School Council. As we enter
the last year of her life, we do well to recall the silence in the sources concerning who she was and how the people she worked with thought about
her. Even as she became one of the most recognizable figures in the public
life of Toronto, she remained in many ways an enigmatic figure.

9

War and Peace – Again

On 2 January 1936 the *Globe* ran pictures of the four women elected to the Toronto Board of Education – Ida Siegel, Margaret Mackenzie, Rose Henderson, and Minerva Reid. The accompanying headline read "Women Cast Votes in Record Numbers."[1] The CCF paper pointed out not only the big vote polled for Jimmy Simpson in his failed attempt to be re-elected mayor but also the fact that Henderson polled more votes than any other Board of Education candidate. While Simpson polled "the highest vote ever accorded a mayoralty candidate in Toronto running without daily newspaper support," Henderson "was supported by daily newspapers though running on a straight C.C.F. ticket."[2] The *New Commonwealth* noted the historic nature of her victory, finishing nearly one thousand votes ahead of the chairman of the Board of Education, C.M. Carrie, a leader of Toronto's Orange Order, in Ward Five.[3]

By 1936 Henderson was part of a women's movement beginning to batter down male dominance of Toronto politics, challenging the Anglo establishment in general and the Orange Order in particular. This was no longer as male-dominated a political culture as it once was, no longer the bailiwick of the Orange Order, no longer a two-party political landscape. As we move into the last year of Henderson's life, we pause to take a look at this world, still an Anglo-Celtic, Tory world, but also the world of Sunday evening socialism. We choose 19 January 1936; if we want, we can go to the Labor Temple at 167 Church Street, where former Communist Party member and leader of the Workers' Party Jack MacDonald is speaking on "Workers Unity against War," a meeting held under the auspices of the "Provisional Conference against Capitalist Wars." We have a choice of five CCF open forums: Kenneth Woodsworth speaking at Parkdale Assembly Hall on "Japanese Imperialism in the Far East"; Frank Underhill speaking at 346 Parliament Street on "Canada's Foreign Policy and the League of Nations"; Robert Rowat speaking at 863 Queen Street West on "Youth and Politics;" Rose Henderson speaking at 936 Gerrard Street East on "War and Fascism"; or Communist Party union organizer Harvey Murphy (his topic not known) speaking at Woodbine Auditorium, 1383 Queen Street East.[4] Before going to one of these talks, perhaps some of us might have attended the morning service at Holy Blossom Synagogue – the public cordially invited – to hear Rabbi Maurice Eisendrath speak on "Building a Co-operative Commonwealth in Zion." Lenin once said that no Chinese wall separates the working class from the ruling class, and the title of Eisendrath's talk reveals that no wall of identity separated Jewish and Gentile dreams of creating a socialist society in the Toronto of the mid-1930s.

Whether or not this world of Sunday evening socialism was now an accepted part of the political culture of Toronto the Good very much depends on whom you ask. We might say much the same about Henderson. By 1936 she had become in some sense part of the "establishment" of Toronto, an integral part of the city's political culture, grudgingly accepted even by her ideological opponents. She moved as freely in middle-class circles as she did in the homes of the poor.

Henderson was one of a number of prominent women on the Toronto left who were by now a public presence, if not an accepted part of the city's middle-class circles. On Friday, 17 January 1936 the *Star* reported: "Members and friends of Dewson school ex-pupils association are anticipating a pleasant evening of dancing and cards the latter part of this month at their first annual 'at-home' in the Boulevard club, under the patronage of Mayor and Mrs. McBride, Dr. Rose Henderson, Mr. and Mrs. C.S. Bottomley, Mr. and Mrs. A. J. Roden, Mr. and Mrs. George Stevenson and Mr. and Mrs. Ralph Langdon."[5] On Monday, 3 February 1936, Mrs Plumptre – who was on the city council – Rose Henderson; Margaret Mackenzie, Minerva Reid, and Ida Siegel were guests of honour at a tea held by the University Women's Club.[6] On Saturday, 15 February 1936, Henderson was one of the "prominent guests" invited to a reception in honour of Mayor McBride given by the Local Council of Women at Sherbourne House. The other guests included Mr and Mrs Arthur Lismer.[7]

On Thursday, 27 February 1936, Founders' Day was celebrated by the Dewson Home and School Association. A minute of silence was observed in memory of the late principal J.W.O. Rogers, and Henderson introduced the new principal, R.W. Coulson. Mrs A.B. Silcox, in outlining the work of the Home and School Associations, stated: "We cannot separate the home from the school any more than we can separate the heart from the body."[8] This sentiment, reinforcing as it did the shift in focus that took place in maternal feminism following the First World War, helps explain Henderson's involvement with middle-class women and their organizations. She did not see a contradiction between her activism as a champion of the cause of labour and her involvement in education, because it was the children from poor and working-class homes who stood to benefit the most from integrating the home and the school.

Once again it is important to reiterate that there was no stark dichotomy between Anglo-Celtic Toronto and Jewish activists such as Ida Siegel. On 9 March 1936 a "Staff Night" was observed at Hillcrest School, as teachers received parents in their classrooms. Henderson, Dr N.S. McDonald, Dr Hugh Ross, and Siegel spoke to some four hundred Home and School members.[9] Siegel's participation speaks to her crucial role in founding the Home and School Association in Toronto, and also to the fact that she continued to be involved after the association became identified with middle-class women of the Anglo-Celtic establishment. The lines are blurred, and the historian cannot understand what is happening on the ground by drawing clear lines of distinction on the basis of class and ethnicity. Middle-class women were women after all, and Henderson and Siegel maintained ties with them when they shared a common cause.[10]

The ease with which Henderson moved between middle-class and communist circles is exemplified by her attendance at two meetings that took place on the same day. On Thursday, 19 March 1936, the *Star* announced a women's mass meeting to be held on Sunday, 22 March 1936, at 182 Main Street. Under the auspices of Fellowship House, the topic under discussion was "Women and Their Power to Preserve the Peace of the World." Speakers included "Dr. Rose Henderson," Miss Jim Watts of the New Theatre League, Elizabeth Morton of the League against War and Fascism, and Alice Cooke of the Women's Progressive Association.[11] "Miss Jim Watts" (who was actually Jean Watts) and Alice Cooke were both members of the Communist Party. The fact that this meeting was held at Fellowship House also reveals the extent to which the religious motivations of the Quakers in opposing war were compatible with the socialist motivations of Communist Party women in the era of the Popular Front. Later on this same day, the West Toronto Women's Progressive League held a meeting at Grace Church. Henderson addressed the women on the civic budget and the relief situation, along with Aldermen Fred Conboy and Donald MacGregor of Ward Six.[12]

The complexity – and for some observers, no doubt, the hypocrisy – of Henderson's political trajectory comes more sharply into focus in the last year of her life. On the one hand, 1936 was the year in which she settled more comfortably into her role as a leading member of the CCF in Ontario, while at the same time insisting on maintaining her relationship with Communist Party members and participating in Popular Front activities. It was a difficult juggling act, and few leftists of her day kept the balls in the air longer and with greater aplomb. There was in her politics that ongoing tension between her desire to be part of a mass-based opposition to the capitalist system and her need to maintain the freedom to follow her conscience. The former meant supporting the CCF, while the latter meant retaining the right to be critical of its leadership and supporting communist initiatives when she felt that the CCF was dragging its feet. One lens will not do; we need two or more to see the Rose Henderson who sat on the provincial council of the CCF and conformed to majority opinion, and the Rose Henderson who still needed to follow her social- ist conscience.

By 1936, Henderson was part of a world-wide socialist critique of fas- cism that saw the rise of Mussolini and Hitler as a manifestation of a new stage of capitalism. On Sunday, 2 February 1936, she spoke at the Labor Temple Open Forum in Hamilton. In her speech she described fascism as "the instrument which capitalism is forced to use ... on a world-wide scale." Making the standard CCF argument, she emphasized the link be- tween war and fascism and pointed out that the use of force was "inevit- able" under capitalism. Capitalism would become "industrial feudalism" if the working class did not unite against it. She concluded: "A working class divided is a working class easily conquered, easily cowed ... Where a mass mind exists, that is, a slave mind, war is possible, but where the workers are united against the war plans, and national unity is broken, war is impossible."[13] Critics seeking to portray her as having shifted to the right would do well to note that her advocacy of working-class inter-nationalism was now linked to a more explicit assertion of the need to break down nationalism than was to be found in her thought in the First World War period.

Being anti-fascist meant opposing militarism, and opposing militar-ism meant fighting the influence of militarism on youth, necessitating a continued campaign against cadet training and militarism in Toronto schools. In the fall of 1935, at a meeting of the Toronto and District School Board, Henderson had "filed an inquiry as to cadet training in certain high schools – what time is taken for it and how the cost is borne."[14] The report of the superintendent of schools presented to the Board of Education on 7 November 1935 indicated that cadet training was still being carried on in some high schools. On 6 February 1936 Henderson presented a notice of motion pointing out that a board resolu-tion had called for the end of cadet training in June 1934, and reminded the board of the findings of the November 1935 report. Her notice of motion "resolved that the principals of all secondary schools be informed of the necessity of adhering to the decision of the Board that such training shall be discontinued."[15]

The 19 February 1936 edition of the *Evening Telegram* carried an editor-ial entitled "Dr. Henderson Again Rides Her Hobby Horse." The writer regretted the fact that the Board of Education "felt compelled, as a meas-ure of economy, to discontinue cadet training in the schools when the government grant was cut off." It noted that cadet training continued at several Toronto schools "after school hours, and at no expense to the Board." That Henderson was criticizing this voluntary effort was "scarce-ly believable." Public opinion, the article stated, was with the "fourteen hundred boys" enjoying the drilling and marching. Apparently at some point Henderson had charged that cadet training made boys "blood-thirsty," an "absurd idea" in the opinion of the *Evening Telegram*. Dr Henderson, the article concluded, was "the unfortunate victim of an under-developed theory."[16]

Henderson's opposition to cadet training was part of a campaign by peace activists and anti-militarists that was by now three decades old. Cadet training in Canadian schools dated to 1907, when Lord Strathcona set up a special trust fund for military training. Peace activists were espe-cially alarmed that the number of students involved in cadet training, and the budget for it, dramatically increased during the First World War and continued to do so in the 1920s. As Thomas Socknat points out, pacifistic groups were concerned about "the trend towards a militaristic society."[17] In 1927 the Toronto branch of the Women's International League for Peace and Freedom published a pamphlet entitled "Military Training in Canadian Schools and Colleges." The WILPF pamphlet received "a hearty endorsement" from the Society of Friends.[18] In the House of Commons, the annual grant for cadet training was vociferously opposed by Agnes Macphail and by J.S. Woodsworth, a lifelong pacifist. By the 1930s, therefore, Henderson was inspired and influenced by three major areas of involvement in her life – the WILPF, the Quakers, and the CCF – to be a forceful campaigner against cadet training.

Henderson was one cog in a much bigger wheel, but a much more important cog than the existing literature suggests. Socknat, based on an interview in 1976 with Ida Siegel, argues that it was she who brought the cadet training issue "to a head" by publicizing "the practice of financially rewarding teachers according to the number of cadets in their classes, which resulted in favouritism being shown to cadets over other students." Her actions led to the ending of cadet training in 1931.[19] As we have seen, Siegel's version of events is misleading. Government-sponsored cadet training ended in 1934, not 1931, and a number of Toronto schools continued it without government funding after 1934. By 1936 all four women on the TDSB – Mackenzie, Reid, Siegel, and Henderson – were publicly identified with the campaign against cadet training, but in the public mind it was Henderson who was the moving spirit.

On 20 February 1936 Henderson brought a resolution before the board, "pointing out that the 1933 board had passed a resolution discontinuing cadet training from June, 1934." Her resolution moved that all secondary school principals be required to abide by the decision taken by the 1933 Board of Education. She charged that there were "more than a 1,000 pupils in Toronto public and secondary schools undergoing military training in violation of the 1933 resolution" and said she could see "no benefit in the board passing resolutions if they were not enforced." Trustee Tidy mocked her resolution, remarking that the members who voted for the resolution in 1933 were "Bolshevists, pacifists and Communists."

Trustee Walker compared Henderson's resolution to the days of pro-hibition. Henderson asked: "So long as we stand for war, what sense is there in offering up a prayer to open this meeting?" Trustee Carrie "vigor-ously objected" to Henderson's statement and declared that board mem-bers were not in favour of war.[20] An amendment to Henderson's motion, moved by Guest and seconded by Tidy, asked that "permission be granted to carry on Cadet training in the secondary schools as a voluntary extra-curricular activity and without expense to the Board."[21] Although all four women trustees voted against it, the amended resolution passed.

If Henderson's pacifism and campaign against militarist influence in Toronto schools placed her on the radical fringe, her position on funding for separate schools brought her much closer to the Protestant establishment. In February 1936 the separate school question once again reared its much-contested head. Rumours appeared in the Toronto newspapers that new legislation was being prepared by the Hepburn Liberals, as the Orange Lodge and Catholic Taxpayers' Association (CTA) rushed to the barricades. The controversy spilled over onto the Board of Education, which on 6 February 1936 carried a motion by C.M. Carrie "protesting against any 'further concessions to the separate schools' by the Hepburn government in the matter of division of taxes." Siegel was the only member to vote against it.[22]

Then, in a speech in Oshawa on 9 February 1936, Martin J. Quinn, president of the CTA, made a veiled threat that if Catholics did not get their fair share of taxes, the CTA would defeat the Liberals at the next election. Hepburn stayed the course, rising in the Ontario legislature on 3 April 1936 to introduce the divisive bill. Catholics were not to get a share of public utility taxes, but the bill did oblige corporations "to div-ide their taxes for school support in proportion to the creed of their share-holders; if the corporations were so complex or widespread that the beliefs of their shareholders could not be determined, the taxes would be appor-tioned in each municipality according to the ratio of Protestants and Catholics in the community (not, as the Catholics had requested, on the basis of school population)."[23]

Predictably, the issue was not long in finding its way into Board of Education debates. On 7 April 1936 the *Star* reported that the night be-fore "two votes of condemnation were thrown at the Hepburn govern-ment ... concerning its school legislation." The first vote opposed the

intermediate school bill and the second opposed the corporation tax bill. The
discussion went on for three and a half hours; Henderson voted with the majority but, based on the newspaper report, she was not a significant presence
in the debate. A third motion "asking the government to take a referendum
of Ontario electors on the question of putting the separate schools back to the
status they held before Confederation carried by 14 to 1." The motion, by
Trustee Orr, "urged that the separate schools should be deprived of all the
extensions or concessions they had obtained since 1863." Again there was a
lone opponent, this time Dr H.H. Spaulding, not Rose Henderson.[24]

It is only possible to sketch in the broadest outlines, while exercising
great caution, Henderson's position on funding for Catholic schools. She
was not, by all accounts, a rabid anti-Catholic, of which there were many
in the Ontario of the 1930s, but she did vote in favour of Trustee Orr's
referendum motion. She was opposed to the extension of Catholic rights,
but her apparent silence at this meeting suggests that she may have been
uncomfortable with the vitriol the issue produced. We recall her desire in
the debate on Catholic rights the year before not to turn the issue into a
political football. The legislation passed in the early hours of 9 April 1936
in the face of threats from the Orange Order, and not before three Liberal
members had joined the Conservatives in voting against the measure.[25]

Henderson's stance on Catholic rights was part and parcel of her opposition to any proposal with the potential to decrease funds to the public
education system in the middle of the Depression. Her opposition to spending cuts by the board won her the criticism of the *Evening Telegram*, which
described her as being "rather conspicuous among the fads-and-frills, free-
and-easy spending fraternity on the board."[26] On 23 March 1936 the
Evening Telegram's letters to the editor section published her response:

Allow me to thank you for your editorial criticizing my stand in opposing cuts in our school budget. I have learned much from honest
criticism during my years of public service. I wish at the same time to
correct a few errors, and state facts that should be known to the parents and taxpayers of the city ... in dealing as we are with the future
well-being of our children, I consider any cuts on education that will
curtail the school services at a time of such social need a false and dangerous economy ... It costs $92 per annum to send a boy to public
school, but to keep a youth in penitentiary for the same length of

time costs $560 ... We need not, and cannot, afford to lessen the capacity of our educational system to produce educated and useful Canadian citizens. We must put the burden of taxation where it can best be borne ... and not on the shoulders of poor parents and children nor yet on our teachers, who during this depression have given an example of devotion and self-sacrifice that many of our political leaders would do well to follow ... Grants for military expenditures have risen by millions, while school grants, wages and salaries of teachers have fallen by millions. I fear that our national balance is on the wrong side.

While it can be argued that Henderson was unnecessarily alarmist concerning the proposed extension of funding to Catholic schools, her motives must be understood in relation to her overall vision of the relationship between the education of youth and the health of the society. In no discernable way had her ability to defend the most vulnerable members of society diminished, and she retained her great insight into the linkages of home, school, and nation. She was "sentimental," yes, but at the same time she had the facts and figures, and on occasion even won the grudging respect of her fiercest political opponents.

By early 1936 she had made her peace with the CCF, and she occupied a position on its provincial council. In the process she had lost some freedom of action, but as an "educationist" she was able to bring the cause of poor parents and the teachers who were teaching their children directly into the political policy-making of the CCF. Such a development occurred at the meeting of the CCF Provincial Executive held on Friday, 3 April 1936, at the provincial office. At the meeting Henderson presented a resolution on cadet training and another on cuts to teachers' salaries, with the request that they be placed before the "Convention." It was moved and seconded that they be "re-drafted by Walter" and presented to the convention as emergency resolutions.[27]

On 24 April 1936 a meeting of the Provincial Executive was held at the provincial office, with William Dennison and Henderson representing the provincial council.[28] By the spring of 1936, therefore, she had become part of a male-dominated CCF provincial council that was leery of, if not openly hostile to cooperation with the Communist Party, and was struggling mightily to avoid any associations that might damage the party's electoral prospects. We do not know exactly how John Walter "re-drafted" Henderson's resolutions on cadet training and cuts to teachers' salaries, but we can be reasonably certain that the re-drafting removed any rough edges to make the resolutions more palatable to the leadership of the party. Henderson paid a price for party loyalty, and we are reminded of the letter she wrote to Charles Lanctot in October 1919, in which she stated that she could not belong to any political party because of the compromises it entailed. Some of those compromises had now been made.

Yet Henderson saw no contradiction between acting in the best interests of the party and remaining true to working-class unity. Early in 1936 she signalled her continuing desire to participate in united front activities. On 11 February 1936 she attended a meeting of the East York Worker's Association (EYWA) in R.H. McGregor School in support of Arthur H. Williams, who had been elected reeve of East York Township in December 1935.[29] Williams had become EYWA president in June 1933, and had run unsuccessfully for the CCF in the riding of York East in the 1935 federal election held on 14 October.[30] His election as reeve was contested on the basis of provincial government legislation passed in April 1935 prohibiting anyone whose rent was three months in arrears from holding public office. Township residents – some 45 per cent of whom were on relief – considered the cost of a second election outrageous. A successful protest was organized involving members of both the CCF and the Communist Party, and when no opponent emerged to contest a second election, Williams retained his reeveship.[31] Henderson was thus part of a united front strategy that raised the hackles of the CCF leadership.

Much of Henderson's reputation as a CCF maverick rests on her involvement with the May Day parade of 1936. She was much more prominent in 1936 than she had been in 1935, perhaps a reflection of her past and ongoing association with the Communist Party, an association that must have made her at least leery of working with Trotskyists such as Jack MacDonald. As Ian Angus points out, MacDonald was a major figure in the 1935 May Day celebrations, when the CCF and the Trotskyists worked together on the Workers' May Day Committee, distinct from the Communist Party's United May Day Committee.[32] That Henderson was a featured speaker in 1936, but not in 1935, may suggest she had distanced herself from a May Day celebration boycotted by the Communist Party because of the prominence of the Spartacus Youth League and the Workers' Party of Canada.[33]

For Canadian socialists, 1936 was a meaningful year, as it was the fiftieth anniversary of Haymarket. As a result, it was a meeting of the "Golden Jubilee May Day Conference" that took place on 24 April 1936 at the Labor Temple on Church Street. More than one hundred organizations were represented. Planned events included a city-wide parade, a mass meeting in the afternoon at Queen's Park, and an evening meeting in the Arena Gardens. The afternoon speakers were to be Henderson, Arthur Williams, and Tim Buck, and the evening speakers were to be Tom Mann, already a legendary British trade union leader, Reverend R.J. Irwin, and George Watson. Jack MacDonald protested that the Workers' Party had been refused permission by the executive "to display avowedly Communistic banners" reading "Forward to the New Fourth International" and "To Victory under the Banner of Lenin and Trotzky." His protest was voted down. The delegates did approve a May Day Manifesto to be "distributed throughout the city in pamphlet form." It called for protest by labor against 'capitalist enslavement and exploitation' and claimed that the capitalist class 'now begins to throw aside all pretense of democratic government and prepares to maintain its rule by open, brutal fascist, methods,' which seek to 'regiment the whole nation in the interests of finance.'"[34]

Three days later, on 27 April 1936, Henderson attended a meeting of Mount Dennis property owners that strongly protested against the York Township Council curbing the water supply of relief recipients. In the course of her speech, she called the Canadian Bankers' Association "a menace to the social welfare of the Dominion" and stated that "the day is not far distant when the government will control the banks instead of the financial interests." Here she was echoing the Regina Manifesto, which called for the socialization of chartered banks, control of finance being "the first step in the control of the whole economy." Referring to the banks, Henderson declared that the Toronto Board of Education was "already under the iron heel of these leeches."[35] It is difficult, if not impossible, to disentangle the CCF influence from the Communist Party influence in this statement, although it is not difficult to understand why her conservative colleagues on the Board of Education thought of her as a communist.

In its report on the 1936 May Day parade, the *Star* stated that for "the first time here, the pageantry of color, music, floats, costumes and form enlivened the scene, and added excitement to it." The parade of thousands of men, women, and children included labour bands, floats of slum houses, and youths in physical culture uniform.[36] In the evening, the "lightest moment" came when "Tom Mann seized Dr. Henderson in his arms and led her in a dance demonstration on the platform." On that platform the dominant figure was British Communist Mann, "fiery and vigorous at 80."[37]

The meeting of the CCF Provincial Council held on Saturday, 9 May 1936 took a much dimmer view of the May Day proceedings. A motion was carried to the effect that "Spence, Conner and Mrs. Laing, all of whom participated in the May Day Demonstration by acting as Executive officers of the May Day Conference, be expelled through the regular routine of expulsion, that is by instructing their clubs to expel them and if the club fails to do so by expelling the club itself." A second motion stated that clubs failing to expel the offending members by 1 June would themselves be automatically expelled. A third motion called for the expulsion of the Lakeview CCF, Earlscourt CCF, New Dawn CCYM, and the East York Workers' Association for carrying banners bearing the CCF name in the May Day parade "contrary to the resolution of the Provincial Executive of which they were notified on April 25th., 1936." A motion was carried to the effect that "Dr. Rose Henderson be reprimanded at the next Council meeting for having spoken while a member of the Provincial Council, at the May Day meeting in the Arena Gardens; and that hereafter all members of the Provincial Council be forbidden to take any part in demonstrations which tend in any way to implicate the CCF with other political organizations."[38]

The 11 May 1936 issue of the *Star* identified Ben Spence as chair of the United May Day Conference, James M. Conner as treasurer, and Jean Laing, a member of the Toronto District Labor Council, as financial secretary.[39] Their individual clubs had been ordered to expel all three. The CCF provincial council was also investigating the CCF signs that were used in the parade. Herbert Orloff, secretary of the CCF provincial council, said the expulsions were the result "of these members of the C.C.F.

breaking the specific order of the C.C.F. convention that no C.C.F. member was to assume office in the May Day conference, although individual members were given permission to march." Orloff explained that the clubs had the authority to expel individual members, but if they failed to do so, the provincial council could expel the clubs. He stated that the Lakeview, Earlscourt, and New Dawn C.C.Y.M. clubs had been expelled for carrying banners (it is not clear if they were not supposed to carry banners or if the issue was what was on the banners). Henderson was not expelled, Orloff explained, because she did not hold an executive position on the May Day Conference, but she was reprimanded for speaking: "She didn't break any definite ruling of the C.C.F. convention ... but we held that being a member of the provincial council of the C.C.F., she should have known better than to run the chance of involving the organization."[40]

Henderson declared that she was "astounded" at being reprimanded for speaking on the same platform as communists at the Arena Gardens. Although indignant at being told what to do by "callow youths and inexperienced people," she said she had no intention of resigning from the CCF. Her language is instructive, indicating as it does the fact that she was older than many of the CCF officials involved in her censure, and also that she saw herself more as belonging to her long history on the Canadian left than as a member of the CCF per se. In her view, the CCF action "in pronouncing sentence upon her without giving her an opportunity to be present or make any explanation, made those responsible 'worse than the Communists.'"[41] Her critique of the CCF would be made again, and reveals a pattern of treatment of dissidents – and perceived dissidents – that would characterize the CCF-NDP in the coming decades.

A meeting of all the Hamilton CCF units held on 12 June 1936 indicated that CCFers outside Toronto were not happy about the disciplinary measures. The "whole time of the conference was spent in discussing the action of the Provincial Council in suspending a number of individuals and units in Toronto for a breach or misunderstanding of the articles of the constitution as drafted at the national convention in Regina." Henderson and Alice Loeb "were visitors at the conference and were given the privilege by the chairman to present all angles of difficulties experienced in Toronto regarding the disciplinary action taken."[42] It is significant that both CCF visitors from Toronto were women, as this was a crucial moment for women on the non-communist left.

It was in the spring of 1936 that the leadership of the CCF moved decisively to complete the process of extracting the CCF from association with the Communist Party, a process that had its first decisive moment with the dissolution of the Labor Conference. The ideological concerns of the CCF leadership had a powerful gender component as well, as leading party figures such as David Lewis and Angus MacInnis had serious reservations about independent women's organizations, especially ones in which CCF and communist women were both involved. Understanding events requires taking a wider perspective than has been the case in the past, a perspective that needs to include the CCF Women's Joint Committee, the role of women in the Conference to Defend Arrested Regina Trekkers, and the Progressive Women's Association.[43] In this endeavour the light shines brightly on Henderson, but the key figure is Jean Laing.[44]

The presence of Alice Loeb at the conference of Hamilton CCF Clubs in June 1936 suggests the involvement of the CCF Women's Joint Committee (WJC) in defending Henderson. It appears that the committee's first meeting was held in Toronto on Wednesday, 5 February 1936, at 3336 Yonge Street. Delegates from "many clubs" were in attendance, although only nine women were identified by name, including Laing, Loeb, and Berta Hamilton.[45] Henderson did not attend. She did attend the next meeting of the WJC held on Wednesday, 19 February 1936, at 4 Alexander Street. She spoke, expressing "the feeling that C.C.F. women should cooperate for the good of all." Laing spoke on the trial of the Regina trekkers to be held on 11 March 1936.[46]

The committee next met at Alexander Street on 6 March 1936. Henderson "spoke on women's inequality in salary with men as borne out in the recent school teachers cut in salary. She pointed out that women have been for years trained by law and tradition to consider themselves inferior to men both in ability and training." Apparently the group was already running into opposition within the CCF, because Elizabeth Morton "spoke on the misunderstanding as to what this group wants to do, and suggested we publish a statement in the Commonwealth as to what this group is trying to do."[47] One likely source of conflict emerged from a 27 April 1936 letter from Laing addressed to "Dear Friend" under the letterhead of the "Conference to Defend Arrested Regina Trekkers."[48] Laing noted that the trials of the Regina trekkers were taking place and that the conference had received an appeal for funds. Sponsors listed on the letterhead include Henderson, Siegel, Ben Spence, and J.L. Cohen.[49] Although Cohen was not a member of the Communist Party, he had laid claim to the title of Canada's leading labour lawyer by defending communists, including Harvey Murphy in a 1929 trial.[50] No doubt the CCF leadership felt vindicated when by October 1936 the list of sponsors of the conference included Communist Party members Norman Freed, Leslie Morris, and Harvey Murphy. By October 1936 the conference's composition confirmed the suspicions of the CCF leadership that women of the WJC such as Laing and Henderson were involved in causes being targeted for takeover by the Communist Party.

On 16 May 1936, M. Tilton, secretary of the WJC, sent letters to Herbert Orloff, secretary of the CCF Provincial Council and J.S. Woodsworth, national chairman of the CCF. The letters stated that at a WJC meeting held in Toronto on 12 May 1936, "a resolution of confidence was passed unanimously in Dr Rose Henderson, Mrs Jean Laing, Mr Ben Spence and Mr J. McArthur Conner."[51] A week later the provincial council made it quite clear that it wanted nothing to do with the WJC. At the 9 May 1936 meeting of the provincial council, Orloff "read a letter from the CCF Women's Joint Committee dated April 17/36 requesting the names of all women members of the CCF in Toronto. Moved and seconded, that since this group is not affiliated to the CCF and has no official status in the CCF, that this information be not given to them."[52] Presumably this letter had been tabled but was now being brought out and dealt with openly and decisively, the May Day activities of Laing and Henderson having demonstrated that they were not to be trusted with influence over women in the CCF.

Even more worrisome for the CCF leadership than the Conference to Defend Arrested Regina Trekkers was the Progressive Women's Association (PWA). A Communist Party initiative, the PWA sought to draw more women into active political involvement through lobbying on women's issues such as childcare, child welfare, and consumer issues.[53] Organized on a ward basis, the PWA was an attractive organization for Henderson, who had been the Ward Five representative of the Independent Labor Party and was now the trustee for Ward Five on the Board of Education. Her involvement with the PWA did not sit well with all members of the WJC. At the group's 26 May meeting a "further letter from the Women's Progressive Assoc. was read asking for delegates to the conference on May 27. Mrs. Reade moved the letter be filed as the appointed representatives had another important meeting to attend." [54] Given that Reade and Tilton had been appointed delegates to the PWA conference at the meeting on 12 May 1936, there seems little doubt that they had been spooked about associating with the Communist Party women in the organization.

On 27 May 1936 the Women's Conference of the Ward Eight PWA was held at the Prince George Hotel. In her opening remarks, Alice Cooke, a Communist Party member and Ward Eight PWA's honorary president, called for the organization of a "progressive women's council." [55] It can only be surmised, given the existence of a Progressive Women's Association, why Cooke saw the need for a "progressive women's council." One possible reason came into view after the speeches had been given and Henderson arrived after the floor had been thrown open for discussion. Coming from another engagement, she "was greeted by applause" and "immediately given the floor." Her address was described as "an inspiration to all present":

[She] gave a picture of the pitiful conditions under which some of the unemployed were forced to live, cases she herself had come in contact with, in her district. She related that, according to history, no less than 3 million women in Europe and about 100,000 on this continent at one time were burned as witches at the stake. They were the women who challenged the social order and the conditions then, she pointed out. 'The Fascists realize that they can rule a country more effectively if women are held in ignorance, and that is why Mussolini and Hitler have pushed the women back out of public life, out of the schools, out of the universities, and back into the kitchens'. Dr. Henderson spoke of the power that united, the women could be to abolish the wrongs and give the coming generation a better life. [56]

As Joan Sangster points out, communist women in the PWA were attempting to overcome the apathy of women, housewives in particular, and there were few women in Canada with a longer history of attempting to motivate women to become politically active than Henderson. [57] As was the case in the early 1930s, she was still much sought after in Communist Party circles.

Following her talk, elections were held for officers for the "permanent council." Eleven officers were elected, including Henderson as president, Alice Cooke as corresponding secretary, Anne Smith as recording secretary, Elizabeth Morton as treasurer, Annie Buller as organizational committee convener, and Bella Gordon as educational committee convener. Henderson "closed the conference by pointing out the tremendous force that a progressive women's council could be in improving conditions. She foresaw this new organisation developing into a powerful force in the struggle for a better life, and in the fight for peace."[58] Neither the association nor the new council fulfilled her dreams. If the council's aim was to make it more appealing to CCF women, the PWA had gone about it the wrong way, because Cooke, Smith, and Buller were all communists, Gordon may have been a communist, and in the CCF Morton was perceived to be a communist. An even greater problem was that separate women's organizations were no more welcome among many male communists than they were among many male CCFers. Making Henderson the president, and changing the name, did not solve the essential problem.

It is not possible to prove that Henderson becoming president of the Progressive Women's Council hurt the WJC, but it cannot have helped. Two weeks after the PWA conference the last minutes of the CCF Women's Joint Committee were recorded on 9 June 1936. Those minutes reveal that Henderson and other members of the committee knew that the WJC was in trouble, with Henderson urging those in attendance to keep up the meetings.[59] They were not kept up, and Henderson, one of the WJC's guiding spirits, paradoxically played a role in its demise.

Her full impact can only be appreciated by understanding the relationship between the death of the WJC and the reinstatement of the CCF units expelled for participating in the May Day celebrations. At the 13 June 1936 meeting of the CCF Provincial Council, which Henderson attended, secretary Orloff read a letter from the WJC, dated 9 June 1936, requesting that two delegates be allowed to attend the next meeting, "to explain the functions and the work of this organization." A motion to that effect, moved by Henderson and seconded by Orloff, was carried. However, the council did not receive a delegation from the WJC, but it did receive one from the expelled CCF units. The council decided to readmit the members of the expelled units on condition that they "reaffirm their loyalty to the CCF and agree to abide by the policy and decisions of the CCF."[60]

Henderson's Popular Front activism reveals a complex and at times contradictory legacy. There was clearly a conflict of interest between her involvement with the wjc, the Conference to Defend Arrested Regina Trekkers, and the Progressive Women's Association on the one hand, and her position on the ccf Provincial Council on the other. As a member of that council, she was part of the process of demanding that ccfers not associate with Communist Party members, while she had just been made president of the pwa, which was heavily influenced, if not controlled, by Communist Party members. She was too experienced and too intelligent a woman not to be aware of the contradiction. Her own admonition against sacrificing principle to party had come back to haunt her.

The ccf leadership did not support the wjc, and there were individuals on the provincial council who saw to its demise. It is too easy, and historically misleading, however, to self-righteously condemn them. The ccf was as much entitled to maintain adherence to what it considered its fundamental principles and policies as were feminists, pacifists, anarchists, and communists. The case of the Conference to Defend Arrested Regina Trekkers, if the increasing involvement of Communist Party members such as Norman Freed, Leslie Morris, and Harvey Murphy is any indication, demonstrates that it was a Popular Front organization that increasingly came under the direction, if not control, of the Communist Party. The concerns of the ccf leadership were too valid to be dismissed as paranoia and overreaction. If the leadership is to be held accountable for the dismantling of the wjc, Henderson must be held accountable as being at least complicit in that dismantling. In this case, party and gender can only explain so much.

Henderson was a person of loyalty to the causes she fought for and individuals she worked with. The dilemma was that as a ccfer in the Popular Front, she was juggling a number of loyalties, and it was not possible to keep them all in the air. She managed better than most, but in the spring of 1936 she made the choice to remain loyal to the ccf. While there is no smoking gun to establish a direct cause and effect relationship between that decision and the demise of the wjc, there is enough circumstantial evidence to suggest that one of the wjc's creators was also one of its destroyers. Henderson continued to work with Communist Party members, and Communist Party members continued to perceive her as an ally on the left wing of the ccf, but her choice had been made.

On the eve of the CCF National Convention in August 1936 it appears that Henderson had already conformed to the orthodoxy developing under Woodsworth and Lewis, her reputation as a "radical" notwithstanding. At the meeting of the provincial council on 2 August 1936, Graham Spry reported that he had not been successful in negotiating a reconciliation with the CCF units expelled for participating in the May Day rally, and that new negotiations had been carried out by Orloff and Cohen. At a conference held on 30 July 1936 it had been proposed that all CCF units and members covered by the 9 May 1936 expulsion order "be declared reinstated and that all members affirm their mutual determination effectively to co-operate in advancing the cause and policies of the C.C.F. and upholding its Constitution." Walter moved, with Henderson seconding the motion, "that subject to the acceptance of the said declaration by the Continuing Committee," all expelled units and members who declared their allegiance to the CCF and its policies be declared reinstated. The motion was carried. It was then moved by Henderson, seconded by Spry, that the provincial council "request of the Continuing Committee and Conference that no resolution on such controversial questions as the united front be brought in at the meeting of the Continuing Committee tonight."[61] While Henderson's intent in putting forward this motion can only be surmised, it certainly appears that she was attempting to close off debate on the issue.

She was not the only feminist in the party who had fallen in line with the male leadership. When she moved that "one member of the Provincial Council be appointed to confer with one member of the Continuing Committee in order to draw up an official statement for the press and that both groups agree that no other statement be given to the press by any other individual," Lorna Cotton seconded her motion.[62] With the approach of the CCF National Convention, this official statement was clearly intended to convey to the public that the CCF was united and had put its internal problems behind it. By the summer of 1936 Henderson had made her decision to abide by the program and policies of the CCF, although there is an important caveat. Her role at the upcoming national convention quite clearly demonstrated that, while she was now critiquing the party from within as a dedicated member, she had not abandoned her feminist socialist conscience or become a blind follower of the party hierarchy. She had not abandoned cooperation with the Communist Party, and was still more than willing to push the leadership of the CCF to put the interests of working-class unity ahead of the partisan interests of the party.

In his address opening the CCF National Convention at the King Edward Hotel on Monday, 3 August 1936, Woodsworth launched a frontal assault on the "vacillating and contradictory policies of the Communist party." His attack, for example, on the CPC's trade union policy was entirely credible: "At first the Communists attempted to bore from within; then began setting up dual unions; now they urge everyone to get back into the A.F. of L." Having attacked the CCF as "social Fascist" in the early 1930s, the CPC was now "embarrassingly conciliatory."[63] We do not know how Henderson reacted to Woodsworth's speech, but we can be fairly certain that she was not offended by it, because she had been circumspect herself in dealing with the Communist Party since arriving in Toronto. She was also alive to any kind of hypocrisy (albeit seemingly less critical of her own), and cannot have failed to acknowledge the elements of truth in Woodsworth's critique.

Later generations accustomed to the rhetoric and policies of the New Democratic Party tend to forget that even social democrats in the 1930s called for revolutionary change. Woodsworth's speech revealed why it was possible for socialists such as Henderson to get beyond their mistrust of the CCF leadership and to accept party discipline. Woodsworth called the CCF a "revolutionary party," a party that wanted "complete economic change." After all, the Regina Manifesto ended with the clarion call: "No C.C.F. Government will rest content until it has eradicated capitalism and put into operation the full programme of socialized planning which will lead to the establishment in Canada of the Cooperative Commonwealth." Unlike the communists, however, CCFers believed this revolutionary change could be brought about "by peaceable means." Commenting on impending war in Europe, Woodsworth stated: "Only the abolition of capitalism with its social injustice, its imperialism, its militarism, will end the age-long curse of war."[64] These were sentiments that Henderson had been expressing for twenty years, and as she sat listening to Woodsworth, she must have been convinced that she had made the right decision. As we shall see, she had not been entirely won over to the position of the CCF leadership, but Woodsworth's words ensured that she would stay in the fold.

In the course of the convention, Henderson demonstrated the breadth of her knowledge and vision, her understanding of and appreciation for the country and its peoples, as her long life of public activism drew to a close. During the second session, after E.J. Garland, the national organizer, gave his report, she asked what contacts he had made with labour organizations. She referred to the "splendid struggle" put on by labour men in Nova Scotia – "about eight years ago we were able to put back into the House there four labour men and one former labor member ... You have some of the best speakers in the Dominion in Nova Scotia, amongst the steel workers, the fishermen, the mine workers, and I think this recent cave-in shows the type of individual that Nova Scotia has developed."[65] The party would need to carefully consider the speakers it sent to Nova Scotia, she said: they "would have to have a great deal of knowledge of the labor movement in Canada."[66] Garland responded by saying that not much could be done by the CCF in Nova Scotia, in part because workers were "devoting all their time" to the cooperative movement, in part because of the "bitter civil strife" between the Amalgamated Mine Workers and the United Mine Workers.[67]

Garland's positing of the problem as caused by workers devoting time to the cooperative movement quite starkly revealed the contradictions in the policies of the CCF leadership. Later in the convention, during the fifth session, Henderson participated in the debate on the resolution about cooperatives. "I would like to mention the people in Wales," she said: " – Small stores put out of business, only stores left in existence were the cooperative stores. I am in favour of cooperation. When we really learn the cooperative system, we are moving in the right direction. I endorse the resolution."[68] In his opening address, Woodsworth had spoken in favour of "co-operative efforts of all kinds," adding that the "socialist point of view is sufficiently developed that we can now safely advocate consumers' and producers' co-operative societies."[69] Garland's claim that worker involvement in cooperatives in Nova Scotia was a reason not to be putting money and resources into CCF organizing there speaks to the shortsightedness found among prominent members of the party. Henderson had first-hand knowledge of the Maritimes; she knew of and appreciated the long history of struggle of the Maritime working class. She had a broader and deeper vision of the country and its working class than many of her better known and more celebrated male counterparts in the CCF.

That broader, deeper vision was also revealed when Henderson entered the debate about appointing a French organizer for Quebec. Quebec delegate Michael Rubinstein proposed appointing two organizers, one of them French.[70] Henderson supported Rubinstein's proposal and rejected Angus MacInnis's suggestion that only funds raised in Quebec be made available for a French organizer: "The Dominion of Canada in the House of Commons is even to-day largely dominated by French Canada and that is to be taken into consideration, and in the Province of Quebec, there is a tremendous social ferment and a tremendous movement for united front and instead of waiting, we should organize this tremendous movement in French Canada. It is not enough to say we should collect funds from French Canada to do the job. I should say we should economise on the other provinces to capture to some extent the movement in French Canada."

The minutes contain a handwritten comment following several more interjections, stating that Rubinstein had "accepted the suggestion that the matter of the appointment of a French organizer be left to the National Council to appoint as soon as funds are available."[71] That organizer, Jacques Casgrain, would not be hired until the fall of 1943.[72] The leadership of the CCF failed for many years to take Henderson's sage advice, and the New Democratic Party inherited the legacy of the party's neglect of Quebec in these early years.[73]

In the second session of the convention, a Mr Gardiner moved that "the National Council immediately take steps to obtain the release of the convicted Regina Trekkers, Corbin Mine strikers and other such political prisoners wrongfully imprisoned. And further that all Provincial Executive Committees throughout this Dominion be requested to demonstrate their whole-hearted and active support of this resolution." The motion, seconded by Luke Teskey, led to comments by Woodsworth and M.J. Coldwell indicating that they interpreted "whole-hearted and active support" as meaning "mass pressure." Coldwell argued that "mass pressure" would make the release of the prisoners "more doubtful," because "a Government hesitates to be placed in the position of yielding to mass pressure." He concluded by saying that "the delegates are in a position to judge what is behind these remarks," and no doubt most delegates understood the allusion to Communist Party tactics. Woodsworth followed Coldwell, saying that clemency could be asked for, not demanded. He concurred that "it would be ill-advised to urge mass pressure." The *Star* reported Coldwell saying that mass pressure "can have political repercussions ... The government doesn't like to act in any particular case, especially when any outside pressure is being used."[74]

The efforts of Woodsworth and Coldwell were to no avail and failed even to persuade some moderates in the party. E.A. Beder disagreed with Coldwell, saying that governments "are susceptible to mass pressure." Jean Laing observed, "I have every belief in mass pressure being brought to bear. If it were not for protests during the days gone by we would not be sitting here to-day. We would not have even the measure of the freedom which we now enjoy." Even King Gordon argued that there was "nothing unconstitutional about mass pressure."[75] Henderson joined the chorus of support for Gardiner's motion: "I believe in mass pressure. I have never found mass pressure failing ... If I know anything of the struggle of the masses of the people, you cannot name to me one measure of social justice put on the statute books that we have not had to suffer for. Therefore I support, heartily, this resolution." Following several more comments, David Lewis moved the original question. The amendment to refer it to the committee to be redrafted was defeated, and the original resolution was carried.[76]

The debate on mass pressure was followed on the third day of the convention, 5 August 1936, by a debate on the united front that lasted more than three hours. The focal point of the discussion was a national council report acknowledging the need to cooperate with "other groups" in carrying out the "socialist activity of the C.C.F."[77] Debate revolved around an amendment proposed by Murray Cotterill that would have replaced "other groups" with "other than political groups."[78] The *Star* commented that "more than 50 speeches were made mentioning the Communist party," in spite of the fact that chair E.J. Garland continually reminded the delegates "that communism was not mentioned in the report of the national council on the subject."[79] Cotterill's amendment had the unintended consequence of making the Communist Party the issue, because it was no mystery to the delegates that "political" meant communist.

In order to rescue Henderson from the condescension of later generations, it is necessary to situate her in relation to other party stalwarts. In the context of the economic devastation on the prairies, Louise Lucas argued that "we must co-operate with anyone who can co-operate to bring food and shelter and we cannot stop to ask what political leanings they have, what the political relation is or anything else." Alice Loeb commented: "It is impossible absolutely to work out any sort of peace demonstration and exclude any political party or any other movement. Peace meetings or any sort of activity for peace must necessarily be wide open to every man, woman or child who will come into it. It would be crazy to exclude anyone." Of even greater significance was the position of Tommy Douglas, now raised to virtual sainthood in the New Democratic Party, in part because he embodied social democratic values in Canada – and by inference anti-communism. Douglas described as "ridiculous and unsound" the suggestion that CCFers stay away from involvement in organizations such as the Canadian Youth Congress because of the presence of Communist Party members.[80]

The defeat of Cotterill's amendment notwithstanding, Woodsworth, Coldwell, and their supporters won a major victory when by a "unanimous" vote the convention adopted a section of the national council's report stating that "this convention declares that decisions regarding such co-operation shall rest with the provincial council concerned, subject to review by the national council if in its opinion such co-operation conflicts with the platform and constitution of the CCF."[81] The vote may have been unanimous, but it seems almost certain that there were abstentions, including Rose Henderson. Henderson, who was on the Ontario Provincial Council, responded to the declaration by asking: "Does that mean that when a strike breaks out or when we have to immediately associate ourselves, that we have to wait before we dare to move? – before we get the decision of the provincial council?" Delegate Robinson supported her position: "It seems to me that is another way of saying the CCF will take no part in the activities."[82] Cotterill was outraged by Robinson's accusation, but future actions of the national and provincial councils would reveal that it contained more than a little truth.[83]

History is written by the winners, and the winners get to determine the historical legacy of the losers. One of the winners who has determined our understanding of the 1936 CCF national convention is David Lewis, who became part-time national secretary of the CCF in 1936, then full-time secretary in 1938. In his account of the 1936 convention, he associates himself with Woodsworth's emphasis on "the dangers of the communist-inspired united front."[84] Missing from Lewis's account is the fact that at the convention he talked about his involvement in an unemployment association in Ottawa, observing: "I know that behind it there are Communists but I would not refuse to participate in that club and it would be a betrayal to Socialist principles and Socialist actions if I had refused to participate in these activities which I did."[85] This was no one-time mistake on Lewis's part; in 1937 he was taken to task by Woodsworth for advising the CCF not to run a candidate against Communist Party candidate Joe Salsberg in the Toronto riding of St Andrew in the Ontario provincial election.[86]

Not only has Lewis been remembered as a party champion who fended off the threat of the Rose Hendersons, but in the process Henderson has been personally attacked in an unwarranted manner. Lewis's only reference to Henderson occurs in the section of his book in which he discusses the "unintended comedy" that took place at the 1936 convention. Although he does describe Henderson as a "dynamic activist in all progressive causes," that accolade follows a description of her as "a small, rather emaciated-looking woman." Referring to her defence of the united front, he characterizes a heckler mocking her physical appearance as an "innocent" action.[87] Joan Sangster comments that Lewis's observation "seems in bad taste."[88] Given that Henderson was now quite likely in ill health, Sangster's criticism is understated. Lewis was in no position to be mocking Henderson, for there was little to distinguish her principled united front work from his attempt to legitimate his "Socialist principles" by defending his own united front activities.

As important as the 1936 CCF National Convention was to the future of the Canadian left, it was but a small piece of a puzzle made up of more momentous events of the time, from the Spanish Civil War to Jesse Owens confronting Adolf Hitler's Nazi Germany at the Berlin Olympics. For Henderson and other Canadian peace activists who now realized but could scarcely make themselves believe that the world was once again rushing headlong into war, 1936 was a year of peace activism. The July issue of the *Canadian Friend* reported:

One of the most effective bits of peace work which Toronto has experienced for a long while was brought about through the vision and hard work of Rose Henderson, Quaker member of the Board of Education. Under her leadership, and in co-operation with the Art Gallery, Society of Friends, Superintendent of Public Instruction, and others, a Peace Poster Contest was arranged, the participants being art students of the four technical schools of the city. Nearly 100 posters were judged as worthy to be exhibited in the art gallery. Three prizes were awarded exhibitors from each school. The posters have been in great demand and will be formed into a travelling exhibit. The best half dozen will be printed by a prominent publishing firm. The exhibit has been secured for the yearly meetings at Pickering College. The whole project has served to awaken peace idealism among the youth of the city in a really remarkable way.[89]

The WILPF's newsletter of July 1936 confirmed these observations, noting that Henderson had a peace poster competition in the four Toronto technical schools and that more than 150 posters were submitted.[90] An exhibit of the posters in the Art Gallery of Ontario was opened by Arthur Lismer, who "spoke very highly of the exhibit both from the artistic and the educational angle." The posters were subsequently shown at "several large conferences" in Ottawa, Toronto, and other locations, and the idea had spread to other districts.[91]

Henderson's peace activism on the local level was matched by her involvement in the international movement. In August 1936 she travelled with eight other delegates to the World Peace Conference in Brussels, in a delegation led by Communist Party leader A.A. MacLeod. Thomas Socknat describes it as a "fourteen-man Canadian delegation," when in reality it was only nine delegates, and four of them – Henderson, Margaret Crang, Mrs John Grieve and Mrs C.D. Farquharson – were women.[92] The women's role has been further marginalized by the fact that a delegation to the youth conference in Geneva was leaving Toronto at the same time and included future Liberal cabinet minister Paul Martin Sr. and CCF leader Tommy Douglas.[93] At the time, however, women's organizations fully appreciated the significant role the women were playing. The Women's Conference for Peace organized a tea and reception for the Toronto women delegates to the Brussels conference, the guests of honour being Rose Henderson and Mrs Grieve.[94]

On 20 August 1936 a farewell party organized by the Toronto and District Council of the League against War and Fascism was held at Union Station, with many friends and sympathizers there to send the delegation off. Friends of the delegates to the youth conference in Geneva were in attendance as well. In a world grown tired and cynical in a post-Stalinist, post-Nazi age, it is almost beyond our imaginations to picture that delegates and friends "danced until shortly before train time."[95] It is a premonition of Ed McCurdy's song "Last Night I Had the Strangest Dream," in which McCurdy, in a world in the clutches of the Cold War, envisioned the end of war:

And the people in the streets below
Were dancing 'round and 'round
While swords and guns and uniforms
Were scattered on the ground.

The dancing at an end, the train pulled out of the station. It was perhaps one of the happiest moments of Henderson's life: everything we know about her tells us that she believed, really believed, that it was still possible to stop the gathering storm of war.

It was to be her last journey overseas. When she returned, as was the case when she came back from the Soviet Union in 1924, she was much in demand as a speaker. At the Board of Education meeting on 1 October 1936, the chair welcomed her back.[96] On 3 October 1936 the *Star* ran a report on her trip to the World Peace Congress. In her account of the trip, she gave witness to the terrible paradox tearing at the souls of Canadian peace activists. The trip was inspiring, in that delegates attended from fifty-one countries; fifteen hundred delegates were anticipated, and five thousand arrived. "There were trade unionists from every nation," she noted, "and they pledged themselves to peace and to use their particular craft to stop war."[97] The *Canadian Friend* would comment in its November edition: "One cannot listen to Dr. Rose Henderson without feeling that an overwhelming majority of the people of the world desire to live in peace with their neighbours."[98] But while Henderson was hopeful and inspiring, she was not naïve. She knew that the question in Europe was "not whether there is going to be another war, but how soon will it start." Always a keen observer, she saw the reality, "for what a nation prepares for they usually get and there is military activity in all the countries."[99]

In the ensuing months her talks about her trip exemplified the depth and breadth of her influence on Toronto's political culture. On Thursday, 8 October 1936, she spoke on "The World Peace Congress" at a luncheon organized by the WILPF.[100] On Sunday, 1 November 1936, she spoke to the Broadview Central Forum at 819 Gerrard Street East on "The Significance of the World Peace Congress at Brussels."[101] In the last week of November she was the guest speaker at an "open meeting" of the Hebrew Maternity Aid Society at the Primrose Club, where her topic was the "Significance of the Brussels World Peace Congress." In these last months of her life she maintained the links with Jewish Canada that she had cultivated a generation earlier in Montreal; Ida Siegel gave the vote of thanks.[102] On Sunday, 24 January 1937, Henderson gave the same talk under the auspices of the Theosophical Society.

The eclectic nature of her associations notwithstanding, she continued in her peace work to be identified with the Communist Party. On 15 October 1936 the Board of Education voted nine to seven to allow the Canadian Youth Congress to hold a meeting in Jarvis Collegiate auditorium on Sunday, 18 October 1936.[103] In all probability the request for the use of the school had come from Henderson. Trustee Carrie opposed granting permission to the CYC and attempted to generate his own mini–Red Scare. He read the names of individuals who were to attend the meeting and declared, "I have been told that these are internationally known Communists. I went to the proper quarter and got that information. Are we going to allow these Communists to use our schools to spread their doctrines?" Carrie's attack may or may not have been directed at Henderson personally; in any event she was quick to expose the hypocrisy in his charge, one already discredited by the fact that he would not reveal the source of his information. She made Carrie appear more than a little foolish, pointing out that one of his "Communists" was a well-known Liberal and son of a prominent Toronto businessman. Another young man, she added, was the son of a Toronto missionary.[104] She may have been utopian about the united front and the peace movement, but as always, her critics had damn well better have their facts straight before taking her on.

In 1936 Toronto's municipal election was held early in December, a change from the traditional New Year's Day, and a stage on the road to elections being held in the first week of November. It was an unusually low-key affair, shunted aside from prominence by a number of dramatic international events and an early winter cold snap. The Spanish Civil War was raging, the pages of the Toronto press full of pictures of bombed-out buildings in Madrid. But even the brutal reality of civil war could not outdo the "real" story of the day, the impending abdication of Edward VIII and his marriage to American divorcee Wallis Warfield Simpson.

Pictures of the couple, individually and together, and pictures of other members of the royal family flooded the pages of major Toronto dailies, as speculation reached fever pitch. How were slum housing conditions in Cabbage Town and the relentless growth of the Nazi war machine to compete, let alone a municipal election?

On Monday, 7 December 1936, 112 candidates were in the running for forty-one seats. Henderson, running again in Ward Five, was one of forty-one candidates seeking election to eighteen places on the Toronto Board of Education. The leading mayoral candidate, W.D. Robbins, who had been on City Council for eighteen years, was running against J.B. Laidlaw and Robert Harding. The left was well represented; Communist Party leader Tim Buck was one of eight candidates seeking four positions on the Board of Control. In the aldermanic races, social democrats were pitted against communists; in Ward Four, CCFer Herbert Orloff squared off against Communist Party member J.B. Salsberg, while in Ward Five, labour stalwart James M. Conner opposed CPCer Stewart Smith in a contest with thirteen candidates. In Ward Five, one of Henderson's three opponents was communist Annie Buller. No doubt the two women found time during the campaign to reminisce about the old days in Montreal.[105]

The presence of communist candidates was not indicative of a sharp class divide in political loyalties. On 3 December 1936, the Toronto Trades and Labor Council voted to endorse Robbins for mayor – also the choice of the conservative *Evening Telegram*. For some Trades and Labor Council members, the choice had less to do with support for Robbins and more to do with opposition to J.B. Laidlaw, president John Noble describing him as "an enemy of organized labor."[106] Henderson had won even the grudging respect of Toronto's conservative press; in its recommendations for trustees for the Board of Education, the *Telegram* noted that she "has gained an increasing vote in the past two or three years. Voters in Ward Five should be sure and return the present members for next year."[107] It was a qualified endorsement, however, as respect for Henderson's accomplishments existed alongside the message that it was better to vote for her than for communist Annie Buller.

On election day Robbins soundly defeated J.B. Laidlaw for the mayoralty. In Ward Five, Communist Party leader Stewart Smith bested the field of thirteen. For the *Star* the biggest surprise was the election to the Board of Education of Communist Party member John Weir in Ward

Four.[108] The *Telegram* was more alarmed than surprised, running an editorial entitled "Communist Danger Grows Greater." In its attempt to rationalize communist strength, the paper attributed the victories of Smith and Weir to the "large foreign and non-Anglo-Saxon populations" in Wards Four and Five. It described the light vote and lack of public interest as "an aid to organized minorities such as the Communist group."[109] The *Telegram* got its wish in the Board of Education elections in Ward Five, where Henderson headed the poll, more than three thousand votes ahead of Annie Buller.

Henderson was now entering her fourth term as a board trustee. In addition to attending regular meetings of the board, she was on the Management Committee, where she sat with John Weir, as well as on the Advisory Vocational Committee, where she sat with labour representative Jean Laing. It was no doubt heartening for her to have left-wing allies in Weir and Laing, the latter a compatriot from the days of the CCF Women's Joint Committee. Their presence, however, did not change the fact that the Depression had scarcely eased its grip, and austerity remained the rallying cry of conservatives on the board. Even small victories were only to be won at the cost of great effort.

At the meeting of the Advisory Vocational Committee on 12 January 1937, Henderson moved, and Laing seconded, "consideration of a report of the Superintendent with reference to the reasons for the decrease of 2159 in the night school enrolment, bearing in mind such matters as the effect of the increased fees, the unsettled economic conditions, reduced advertising and the reduction in the night school appropriations."[110] The motion, deferred until the next regular meeting of the committee, reflected the concern with providing evening classes for disadvantaged youth that Henderson had demonstrated since first joining the board. At the 26 January meeting, she moved that "in view of the great contribution made to the social, economic and educational life" of Toronto in past years by evening classes, and "the great need for protecting our unemployed youth," the board should address the hardships created by increased fees, reductions in grants, and a decline in the number of classes. Labour representatives, backed by several trustees, advocated a return to a $2 fee for students in Toronto vocational night classes, replacing the existing $5 and $3 fees. Laing, in words that could as easily have been Henderson's, "argued that juvenile delinquency might cost more than night classes, and it would be better to spend tax money on the classes." Following a lengthy discussion, Henderson moved that the committee defer consideration of her motion until the special meeting to be held on 2 February for the purpose of considering estimates.[111] She would not live to fight that other day.

In the last month of her life Henderson continued to upset the Board of Education's sense of decorum by being "political" on issues such as peace. On 13 January 1937 the Management Committee voted six to three to refuse the request of the Toronto Youth Council "to allow posters advertising a peace play contest to be put up in the schools." The *Star*'s admittedly vague account of the debate is nonetheless instructive, because it spoke to one of the paradoxes of the advances for women that Henderson fought for so long and hard. Dr Goldring's response to the request was to argue that contests "interfere with the regular work of the schools." He added that while such contests might be appropriate in countries such as Italy and Germany, they were not appropriate for Canada, which fought only defensive wars. As always, Henderson had no difficulty spotting the hypocrisy in Goldring's argument, noting that she hoped Canada would not become involved in a war, "yet we must realize that in the last year the Canadian government voted $27,000,000 for war purposes."

In response to Henderson's observation, chair Margaret Mackenzie commented: "We are not concerned with the matter of peace itself but rather with the point as to whether we will allow the routine of our schools to be interrupted."[112] Mackenzie's ruling revealed the depoliticization of the women's movement that accompanied its increasingly important role in Canadian public life.

The full paradox was revealed eight days later, at the board's 21 January 1937 meeting, when Mackenzie introduced a delegation from the Toronto Youth Council. Miss Clysdale of the council stated that on 30 and 31 January 1937 the first Toronto Student Congress would be held in the Economics Building at the University of Toronto. She asked "that the Council be permitted to place a notice in each secondary school advertising the congress; and also that principals be authorized to make an announcement regarding the congress, if they so desire." Henderson supported Mackenzie's effort by introducing Dorothy Marks and Anna Sissons, also on the Youth Council. Marks and Sissons "requested that the Children's Committee of the Toronto Youth Council be permitted to display, in the high and public schools of the Board, posters announcing a 'Peace Play Competition' sponsored by the said Committee and open to all pupils." Henderson's hand was also much in evidence when correspondence from the Toronto Monthly Meeting of Friends requested "favourable consideration of the request of the Toronto Youth Council for permission to advertise a 'Peace Play Competition' in the schools under the direction of the Board."[113] Following a motion of support by Henderson, the superintendent stated that he was "opposed to advertising of any description in the schools, particularly as such contests tend to interfere with school work." On vote the board decided not to consider the request.[114]

There is a temptation to see anticlimax in Henderson's last days, the fiery radical of 1919 reduced to conceding ground on putting posters in Toronto schools in a world plunging headlong into another war. We would do well, however, to remember that for the feminists of her generation, the international was always intertwined with the local, the most mundane daily task always envisioned as the stairway to a much higher purpose.

On 30 January 1937 Rose Henderson died unexpectedly, or so it seemed, of a cerebral hemorrhage – the same condition that had killed her husband, Charles, in January 1904. In the *Globe and Mail* report on her death, we find the assertion that "she had not been in good health for some time."[115] She collapsed while attending a meeting of a committee on penal reform on Sherbourne Street. At the meeting "she had outlined her talk on juvenile delinquency which she expected to bring before the penal reform commission which meets this week in Toronto."[116] James MacArthur Conner, who would himself pass away the next year, stated that she "died the death she desired … She always said she would like to die in harness advocating a better and fuller social order.'[117] It was fitting also that she died in the arms of Jean Laing, who observed that her compatriot was "radical in a day when it was not popular to be so."[118]

Given how little knowledge there is of Henderson in our own generation, it is revealing that in her own day even Toronto's conservative establishment recognized her impact and contribution. The *Telegram*, echoing the opinion of Henderson expressed in *Le Monde Ouvrier/The Labor World* in Montreal in the First World War period, observed that she "was a notable speaker with a continent-wide reputation and an earnest student of all questions ethical and philosophical, which touched the welfare of the people."[119] Minerva Reid, Henderson's colleague on the Board of Education, captured the meaning of her life in noting that the children of the city had suffered a greater loss than had the board.[120] Not surprisingly, the *Star* was unstinting in its praise, calling her an "exceptional, almost unique" woman. She was "blessed with brains, an original and independent mind and a love for humanity that made her a pioneer in progressive movements." She "gave of her personality unstintedly for the public good." "The world," the editorial writer concluded, "does not produce many Rose Hendersons."[121]

On the left, Henderson's death was lamented by social democrat and communist alike. The *New Commonwealth* observed that she had made "a great contribution, not only to the labor movement, but to many social welfare movements." Her life was devoted to advancing the welfare of the people, and particularly the women and children. Lorna Cotton commented, "Every Canadian, regardless of political views, owes Rose Henderson a debt of gratitude." Herbert Orloff, secretary of the CCF Provincial Council, said she was "a champion of many vital causes, and never failed any of them."[122] A *New Commonwealth* editorial began: "Few women in Canada commanded more respect from a wider group of people than Dr. Rose Henderson." She "had many qualities, and those qualities won the admiration of even those who were opposed to her views ... she was unsparing in her efforts and loyal in her views, and always made friends and won respect." She was "a champion of just causes," and the paper offered "a sincere tribute to her service to the cause of the common people."[123]

Revealingly, it is in the Communist Party's *Daily Clarion* that one finds the most extensive tributes. Stanley Ryerson's mocking of Henderson's claims to a PhD belonged to the sectarianism of the Third Period's condemnation of CCFers like her as social fascists; in the heady days of the Popular Front, she could be remembered as an ally in the class struggle. At the 31 January 1937 meeting of the Party's central committee, John Weir introduced a resolution expressing condolences by stating that Henderson "was one of those in the C.C.F. who fought for labor unity." His resolution was unanimously adopted: "The central committee of the Communist party expresses its deep regret at the sudden passing of Dr. Rose Henderson of Toronto. She was a veteran in the labor movement of Winnipeg, Toronto and Montreal and a staunch fighter for working-class unity. We extend condolences to her bereaved relatives and to her party, the C.C.F."[124]

The Popular Front context notwithstanding, there was something genuine about the response of Communist Party members that stood in marked contrast to the fulsome yet strangely distant appreciations of her companions in the CCF. John Weir, recently elected to the Board of Education for the first time, said that Henderson had showed him "the ropes": "She went with me to the schools in my ward, introducing me to the principals, pointing out needs in the schools that would otherwise have escaped my inexperienced eye, discussing with me problems affecting our work." Echoing the observations of many non-communists, he observed that she had fought for "every progressive measure." The news "that Dr. Henderson is no more came as a tremendous shock and has filled me with a sense of grievous loss."[125]

Communist Party leader Tim Buck's dedication to Henderson is worth quoting at length:

> Every active worker in the progressive political movement will experience a sense of deep loss at the tragic news of the death of Dr. Rose Henderson. The labor movement has sustained a loss, the women's movement and the Women's Temperance League have sustained a loss as has the anti-war movement … To emphasize, at this time, the fact that many differences existed between ourselves and her would be wrong. Differing from us as she did, she was a consistent supporter of the struggle for unity, one of the group of progressive C.C.F.ers who carried through the united May Day celebrations last year, one of the diminishing group of old timers who, in their varied way, have left their mark upon the movement. Her memory will remain green in the minds of the working people.[126]

There was, revealingly, no similar acknowledgment of Henderson's contribution by Woodsworth, Lewis, and other leading members of the CCF.

Other prominent Communist Party members echoed Buck's sentiments. William Kashtan, secretary of the Young Communist League, observed: "Her passing is a severe blow to the labor movement and to the young people of Toronto. She displayed great interest in the youth movement, particularly the students and their problems. She was always ready to do her share in bringing the needs of the youth to the attention of the public." Annie Buller, described as Henderson's "running mate" in the recent school board elections, said that people in Ward Five "found in her a woman who desired to improve the educational and welfare facilities in schools in the working-class districts. She was active in the cause of peace and worked to have cadet training abolished in all schools." Said alderman Stewart Smith, "The progressive movement in Toronto has lost one of its foremost fighters in the person of Dr. Rose Henderson. Her long record of service to the labor movement and, in particular, to the cause of peace, has won her a place in the hearts of the people." Harvey Murphy said her death had "taken from our midst a courageous woman who has distinguished herself in the battle against injustice. The unemployed people have lost a real champion. Along with other sections of the progressive movement the Ontario Federation on Unemployment mourns her death."[127]

On 2 February 1937 the *Daily Clarion* ran a "Buck Tribute on Henderson" that repeated some of the statements made by the Communist Party leader in the previous day's paper. In this story Buck tied Henderson more closely to the Communist Party, noting that she was "secretary of the Society for Cultural Relations with the U.S.S.R. for two years, and her speeches on the Soviet Union are still remembered everywhere where workers who were in the movement 13 years ago gather." Given Buck's penchant for falsifying the historical record, it should be noted that in this case he was right on both counts – Henderson did give a series of talks on the Soviet Union in 1924, and she was indeed secretary of the Society for Cultural Relations. Nor is there any reason to doubt Buck's claim that shortly before her death she was giving her "time and energy in the cause of Spanish democracy. A member of the executive committee of the Friends of Spanish Democracy, as well as of the League Against War and Fascism, she was active in its work right until our last meeting only a few days before her death."

Henderson's funeral took place on Wednesday, 3 February 1937, at 3 PM, in the Central Technical School at Lippincott and Harbord Streets. In an article entitled "Throngs Mourn Dr. Henderson," the *Daily Clarion* reported that citizens "in all walks of life" attended in large numbers. Teaching staff had been allowed to leave school at the afternoon recess. The class, gender, religious, and ideological persuasions of the mourners in attendance spoke to Henderson's impact on the political culture of Toronto. G. Raymond Booth of the Society of Friends, in a deeply felt and genuinely honorific eulogy, captured her essence when he said that she was "ever impatient in the presence of injustice." Pallbearers were C.M. Carrie, James M. Conner, Tim Buck, John Mitchell, George Watson, and Dr A.G. Hall, again a reflection of Henderson's ability to bring together individuals who would not ordinarily be united in a common purpose.

This remarkable ability was reflected in a poem in the 5 February 1937 edition of the *Daily Clarion*. It was by Laura Romney Davis, one of the earliest and most influential members of the Bahá'i community in Toronto.[128] How the poem, simply entitled "Rose Henderson," made its way into the Communist Party paper remains a mystery, but it provides striking evidence that there were Communist Party members who shared Davis's feelings about Henderson:

THE world has lost a friend,
For Death has passed this way,
And leaving, took your hand
To lead you far away.

AND we who loved you best
Think back upon your life,
Its joys, its loves, its tears,
Its harmony and strife.

YOU gave us all you had,
Your life, your mind, your will,
Dynamic spirit that you were,
And now you lie so still.

YOUR vision was so wide,
Your understanding, broad,
You saw each soul upon its path
Struggling to its God.

AND yours the helping hand
In many a time of need,
To love, to give, to lift,
That was your creed.

A SOUL of flame you were
Impatient to advance,
You demanded for each child of earth
To have an equal chance.

AS Comrade, Worker, Friend,
In each you were so true!
I count my greatest wealth
To know the soul of you.

Davis was decades younger than Henderson, but the poem exemplifies the impact a woman in her sixties had on the youth of Toronto. On 5 February 1937 the *Star* carried a letter to the editor from the East York Workers' Youth group entitled "A Noble Woman." The letter described the meeting of the group four days earlier, which "heard with deep sorrow of the passing of a fearless fighter in the interests of youth." The "fine points of Dr. Rose Henderson's life in the labor movement ... showed how young people have respected and admired the courage of this upright, courageous, kind and loving person, in the struggle for peace, democracy and freedom of speech and assembly." The letter goes on to say that Henderson was "known in almost every part of the world for her speeches and appeals against existing conditions, in peace conferences, in large mass meetings and demonstrations, sponsored by all organizations for progressive action ... Who will take her place in the struggle for the betterment of society, for higher ideals?" The next day essentially the same letter appeared in the *Daily Clarion* under the title "Her Memory Is Ever Dear."[129]

It is perhaps fitting to give the last words of praise for Rose Henderson to an anonymous writer who spoke for the untold thousands of men, women, and children in Canada and around the world who benefited from her life and work. The 10 February 1937 edition of the *Globe and Mail*, under the headline "Noble Woman Crusader," carried a letter by "Fabian." In part, it read:

Those of us who knew her intimately and shared her aspirations for a nobler Canada are fully aware how difficult it will be to fill the breach her death has created.

I met her first in 1914, during her campaign against conscription. Having just previously arrived from the Old Country with the expectation of finding a land flowing with milk and honey, with opportunities for all, I was amazed to discover an army of unemployed and bread-lines from Halifax to Vancouver. I listened for a storm of protests against the stupidity of such an intolerable state of affairs, but in vain; until Dr. Rose Henderson crossed my path speaking against conscription and championing the cause of the oppressed.

For more than twenty years no woman in Canadian life so fearlessly fought in the interests of unpopular causes, or so painstakingly exposed the weaknesses in our national life. I can recall no other woman who has so undauntedly beaten trails toward social legislation that has now become the law of the land, or so gallantly sacrificed herself in the interests of women and children.[130]

Perhaps the writer, in stating that Henderson "painstakingly exposed the weaknesses in our national life," revealed why she has so long been a neglected figure in Canadian history.

The weeks and months following her death saw a number of attempts to ensure that her life and work would be remembered. Three days after her funeral, on 6 February 1937, secretary Orliffe informed a meeting of the CCF Provincial Executive that a memorial fund was being raised to honour Henderson's memory.[131] Within days of her death, the Women's International League for Peace and Freedom initiated a Rose Henderson Peace Memorial Fund "as an expression of our deep gratitude to Dr. Henderson for the work that she had done for the cause of peace." The fund was intended to "make it possible for a small part of her work to be continued."[132] At the 1 April 1937 meeting of the Board of Education, a suggestion was made that the Clinton Street School be named the Rose Henderson School.[133]

More than a year after her death the *Star* was still revealing her legacy, when it identified the sponsors of the Rose Henderson Memorial Camp. Located in Pleasant Valley in Pickering, the camp was in its fifth year of operation, and more than thirty organizations were "co-operating in the work of building a camp controlled by the parent organizations, for boys and girls from eight to 14." Such cooperation had been made possible by Henderson, who "founded the joint committee of all parent organizations interested in camp work" in 1936.[134]

Time marches on, and the human endeavour of another day fades from our memory. Little is left of the efforts made following Henderson's death to keep her memory alive. The Clinton Street School was not renamed in her honour. There is no trace of the Rose Henderson Peace Memorial Fund set up by the WILPF. After 1938 there was no news in the *Star* concerning the Rose Henderson Memorial Camp in Pickering. A walk along Montrose Avenue where she lived in the 1930s reveals that her properties are gone, the existing dwellings beginning at the number where her units ended. In 1969 the dwellings she owned were torn down to build an extension on the Montrose Avenue Public School.

Standing on the sidewalk, it seems all too familiar, one more piece of Henderson's life gone forever. But the school is there, a legacy to her unceasing efforts on behalf of the children of Toronto, and to the education and advancement of the people of the world. If she were alive today, I think she would say that the most important part of her life still stands. Indeed there is no injustice, because her many contributions to the city of Toronto, the citizens of Canada, and the people of the world, are with us still. When we look back at the long sweep of her life, to that insatiable desire of hers to fight the cause of the marginalized and exploited wherever they were to be found, we can appreciate the full contribution of Rose Henderson. No person anywhere, during the course of her life, was able to see all of it or appreciate its full import. We are more fortunate, because we can look back and appreciate a life that was truly well lived.

Conclusion

When Rose Henderson died, she was claimed by social democrat and communist alike. Each political tendency wanted to see her as its own, to claim that she espoused its politics, its way of looking at the world, its solution to ending the oppression of the capitalist system. Yet as time passed and the histories of the Cooperative Commonwealth Federation and the Communist Party were written, Henderson largely disappeared from the historical memory of both. She was never "pure" enough, never dependable enough as an exemplar of either left tendency to be enshrined in the pantheon of great social democrats or great communists.

She has met a similar fate in the history of the women's and peace movements. She has never found a place in the history of the suffrage movement, in histories of the Local Council of Women, or in accounts of the Women's International League for Peace and Freedom. She has been an episodic presence; for all that was right about Rose Henderson, there was always enough that was wrong to make her someone to forget rather than to remember.

Yet her biography reveals that she had a significant, if not profound, impact on all of these organizations and more. She has become a marginal figure in Canadian history because she was not organizationally significant to the trade union movement, the Jewish community, French Canadian society, or the middle-class women's movement. She affected the lives of hundreds, if not thousands, in each of these groups, but when the histories of these groups were written, her memory was lost and forgotten, because she was not "one of them." In a sense she was always on the outside, never quite integrated into any of the myriad organizations she helped found, support, and champion. She was a movable conscience, and her impact was everywhere, but only a retelling of her life is able to put most of the pieces of the puzzle back together. The puzzle remains unfinished, but what we have brings her and the political culture of which she was so much a part more clearly into view.

In part Henderson's historical obscurity is a product of the decline of the left and the influence of the labour movement in Canadian society. Henderson was a middle-class female reformer, but she was also one of Canada's foremost champions of the labour movement; much of the labour press of Canada considered her a leader in labour's cause. Editors, reporters, letter writers, and labour men and women who knew her testified to her courage, intelligence, passion, dedication, and devotion. No woman, perhaps no person, in the years between the First and Second World Wars so deeply impressed the working men and women of this country. To organized labour she was no ordinary woman, but the collective Canadian memory does not rank highly the heroes of the left and organized labour.

As this life of Rose Henderson so amply demonstrates, however, her impact on Canada's political culture reached beyond the left and the women's movement. She spent nearly forty years in French Canada, and her life is a window through which we can view the two solitudes, both the myths and the realities of Hugh MacLennan's now legendary metaphor. Indeed, Henderson's close association with Montreal's Jewish community brings together the histories of the three largest communities in Montreal in a way that we have not seen before. Yes, there were marked linguistic, religious, and cultural differences, but her life compels us to see that those distances were not as great as we once thought. The three solitudes may not agree about the nature of that relationship, but Henderson brings us to a place where they are at least sharing the same space.

Much has been written about the relationship between religion and socialist thought in early twentieth century Canada, and Henderson adds a significant element to our understanding. We have known for a long time that Canadian socialists, even ones who became Marxists, often came out of the major Protestant denominations, and continued to speak and write in a religious idiom even as they condemned organized religion. Henderson's involvement with the Bahá'í's, the Quakers, and the Theosophists expands our understanding beyond the Protestant denominations to much smaller, less well-known spiritual tendencies that have been too easily dismissed as utopian. "Utopian" is not a bad word when talking about Henderson, as it is not a bad word when speaking of the women activists of her day, who were virtually all utopians in the best sense of that word. Anyone who is unwilling to walk the line between utopian idealism and the naïve and delusional cannot know, understand, or respect Henderson and the women activists of her generation.

Henderson also forces us to reassess the utopianism of the women's peace movement. How we think about an attempt to institute an amendment to the American Constitution outlawing war tells us a great deal about how we view our own world and the future of the human race. We can dismiss the Rose Hendersons as being hopelessly naïve, and attack – as have critics of pacifism for generations – the whole idea of putting an end to war. Our other choice is take these women seriously, to honour their commitment and their dedication, to come to grips with the fact that the planet on which we live can no longer afford an international arms trade or the profit-mongering that drives it. We may not agree with the tactics of these women, we may continue to find reasons to criticize, but we can no longer afford to dismiss them, because it is the fate of our world that we are dismissing.

Henderson's life stands as testament to the fact that the scientific socialism of Marx and Engels replaced, but did not destroy, the utopian socialism upon which it was partly founded. Her politics of class notwithstanding, Henderson was in the tradition of the utopian socialists in her desire to liberate all humanity at once. Working-class men and women were her driving force, but there was a place in the struggle for anyone, regardless of race, gender, or class, who was genuinely committed to the main goal. Even as a member of the CCF, she never evinced the fear of the power of organized workers that compelled the CCF's political leadership and intellectual brain trust to recoil from placing the future in the hands of the men and women it claimed to represent. Henderson lashed out in frustration at working-class men and women only when they failed to grasp the reins of power, not when they did.

Between the first wave feminism of the suffrage era and the second wave feminism of the 1960s and 1970s was home and school feminism. Henderson, Ida Siegel, and their female compatriots were part of a distinct wave of feminism that took the maternal feminism of the first wave into direct opposition to male-dominated institutions such as the Toronto Board of Education. In this unceasing struggle they asserted the identity of women as mothers *and as persons*, refusing the stereotypes of their own day and the categories of later generations of feminist historians. Henderson embodied home and school feminism as fully as any woman activist of her day, and she was a beacon for Canadian women who looked forward to a brighter future in the public life of Canadian society.

In the end it does not matter who Henderson "really" was, or what we might choose to call her politics: ethical socialist, no doubt; maternal feminist, without question; champion of labour, beyond dispute. It is difficult, if not impossible, however, to call her one of these things without in some sense diminishing the others. Turning to the categories of class and gender, it is dangerous, indeed perhaps folly, to say that one more fully embodies her life and work than the other. Henderson forces us to think about women and workers in a way that makes the shared oppression and the shared resistance all that really matter. She takes us wherever we need to go; it is a revealing journey, full of sight and sound, replete with the daily struggles and millennial yearnings of men, women, and children struggling to be free.

Rose Henderson was at home every day of her activist life in the only "party" that really mattered to her – humanity itself. She was the champion of a republican tradition stretching back to ancient Greece, a tradition founded in the proposition that individuals create themselves and their society in the process of active participation in public life. She was a woman for the people; for her, the struggle was not to destroy class or gender or religious or ethnic hierarchies of power, but rather to end oppression in all its forms. Her life stands as compelling testimony to both the difficulty and the necessity of realizing her vision.

Notes

INTRODUCTION

1 Toronto, City Council Minutes, 1 February 1937, 31, no. 154.
2 *Toronto Globe and Mail*, 1 February 1937.
3 *Toronto Daily Star*, 5 February 1937.
4 Pennington, *Agnes Macphail: Reformer*; Crowley, *Agnes Macphail and the Politics of Equality*; French and Stewart, *Ask No Quarter*; Faith Johnston, *A Great Restlessness*; Lewis, *Grace: The Life of Grace MacInnis*.
5 Caine, "Feminist Biography and Feminist History," 249.
6 Sangster, "The Making of a Socialist-Feminist," 14–28.
7 Mann Trofimenkoff, "Feminist Biography," 2.
8 Bradbury, "Women's History and Working-Class History," 23–43.
9 Taylor, *Eve and the New Jerusalem*, 263–4.
10 Ibid., 6.
11 Brown, "'Savagely Fathered and Un-Mothered World,'" 539.
12 Caine, "Feminist Biography and Feminist History," 252.
13 Manley, "Women and the Left in the 1930s," 107.
14 Bacchi, *Liberation Deferred*, 148.
15 Sangster, *Dreams of Equality*, 96–7.

CHAPTER ONE

1 *Toronto Daily Star*, 17 February 1922.
2 *Daily Clarion*, 1 February 1937.
3 Census of Canada 1891, "Montreal," District #172, St Lawrence Ward, Division #4, Family #246.

4 Census of Canada 1901, "Montreal," St Lawrence Division, Sub-District A, Polling Sub-Division #27.

5 Census of Canada 1891, "Montreal," District #172, St Lawrence Ward, Division #4, Family #246.

6 Census of Canada 1901, "Montreal," St Lawrence Division, Sub-District A, Polling Sub-Division #27.

7 *Toronto Daily Star*, 1 February 1937.

8 Census of Canada 1901, "Montreal," St Lawrence Division, Sub-District A, Polling Sub-Division #27. Although *Lovell's Directory* confirms that Charles A. Henderson, bookkeeper, was residing at 137 St George Street, Montreal, in 1890–91, a birth record for Ida Henderson has not been found in the City of Montreal.

9 Archives Nationales du Québec (ANQ), Fonds du Ministère de la Justice (FMQ), E17, 5007/1919, Lomer Gouin to Mon cher ami, 13 July 1919. In all probability "Mon cher ami" is Attorney-General Louis-Alexandre Taschereau, later Liberal premier of Quebec.

10 McGill University Archives, *Royal Victoria Hospital Medical Register*, "Charles Henderson," Case #8547.

11 La Bibliothèque Centrale de Montréal, Fonds Drouin, bobine #1124D, Sepultures: St James Methodist; *Montreal Daily Star*, 15 January 1904.

12 The Society of Friends was founded in seventeenth century England by George Fox (1624–91). Commonly known as Quakers, the Friends emerged out of a critique of the established church and its emphasis on hierarchy, ritual, and theological "hair-splitting." The Friends believe in a direct experience of God that allows women and children, as well as men, to minister. In the nineteenth century Quakers distinguished themselves as campaigners against slavery and in the twentieth century as tireless advocates of international peace.

13 Archives de la Ville de Montréal (AVM), bobine 804, Evaluations: Feuilles de route, St Laurent, vol. 5 (1900), 51.

14 In the 1911 Census of Canada, in the column for "Profession, Occupation, Trade or Means of Living," the census-taker wrote "Income" for Rose Henderson.

15 Lavigne and Stoddart in "Women's Work in Montreal at the Beginning of the Century" reveal that in 1900 some 44 per cent of workers in the textile industry were women, and by 1915 still 42 per cent were; see also Myers, *Caught*, 153–6.

16 Ames, *The City below the Hill*, 9.

17 Copp, *An Anatomy of Poverty*, 70.

18 Ames, *The City below the Hill*, 112.

19 Copp, *The Anatomy of Poverty*, 81.

20 Ames, *The City below the Hill*, 114.

21 Copp, *The Anatomy of Poverty*, 22.

22 Ibid., 21.

23 Ibid., 32.

24 Province of Quebec, *Annual Report of the Quebec Department of Labour* (1922), 87–8, quoted in Copp, *The Anatomy of Poverty*, 49.

25 Copp, *The Anatomy of Poverty*, 25–6.

26 Ibid., 51.

27 Quoted in ibid., 52.

28 Ibid., 60.

29 Ibid., 63.

30 Ibid., 67.

31 "Montreal Women's Club," *Woman's Century*, February 1916.

32 *Toronto Daily Star*, 17 February 1922.

33 Ibid.

34 *Montreal Daily Herald*, 27 January 1912.

35 Caroline Béïque, née Dessaulles (1852–1946), born in St-Hyacinthe, Quebec, co-founder with Marie Gérin Lajoie in 1907 of the Fédération Nationale Saint-Jean-Baptiste, married lawyer and senator Frédéric Béïque, president of the FNSJB from 1907 to 1913, feminist activist in the temperance movement, reform of the Code Civil, and access of women to higher education. In 1939 she published *Quatre-vingts ans de souvenirs: Histoire d'une famille*. See Université de Sherbrooke, Bilan du siècle, "Caroline Béïque (1852–1946), activiste, féministe," http://bilan.usherbrooke.ca/bilan/pages/biographies/322.html.

36 Library and Archives Canada (LAC), Sir Wilfrid Laurier Papers (WLP), reel C-855, frames 132953-132956, Caroline Béïque to Sir Wilfrid Laurier, 29 November 1907.

37 LAC, WLP, reel C-855, frame 132957, Sir Wilfrid Laurier to Caroline Béïque, 2 December 1907. Colorado was the model because Benjamin Barr Lindsey (1869–1943) had been appointed judge of the juvenile court in Denver in 1901. Judge Lindsey's court became famous around the world. The "father" of the juvenile court was also a leader in the campaign against child labour.

38 Béïque, *Quatre-vingts ans de souvenirs*, 265.

39 AVM, bobine 730, *Evaluations: Estimations*, St Laurent, vol. 5, 72.

40 Jones and Rutman, *In the Children's Aid*; Rooke and Schnell, *Discarding the Asylum*.

41 Myers, *Caught*, 29.

42 Ibid., 29–30.

43 According to Caroline Béïque, it was Choquet's wife who was instrumental in convincing him to take up the cause of troubled youth, (Béïque, *Quatre-vingts ans de souvenirs*, 265).

44 For Clément, see Myers, *Caught*, 105.

45 Thomas Fisher Rare Book Library (TFRBL), Canadian Pamphlets and Broadsheets Collection, *Second Annual Report of the Children's Aid Society* (Montreal: Commercial Stationery Co., 1909).

46 Lavigne and Pinard, *Les Femmes dans la société québécoise*; Dumont, Jean, Lavigne, and Stoddart, *Quebec Women: A History*, originally published in French as *L'Histoire des femmes au Québec depuis quatre siècles*; Dumont and Toupin, *La pensée féministe au Québec*. It is especially striking that the latter collection includes fourteen articles by Eva Circé-Côté and none by Rose Henderson, in spite of the fact that the two women were writing for *The Labour World/Le Monde Ouvrier*, the paper of the Montreal Trades and Labor Council, in the same period. At one point Henderson had her own column. For Eva Circé-Côté, see *Andrée Lévesque, Eva Circé-Côté: Libre penseuse, 1871–1949* (Montreal: Les éditions du remue-ménage 2010).

47 Mackenzie King Diaries, 12 January 1911–13 January 1911.

48 Ibid., 17 January 1911–18 January 1911.

49 LAC, Mackenzie King Papers (WLMK), reel C1970, MG26, J4, vol. 30, file 170 "Opium Traffic," Memo re Letters Endorsing Cocaine Bill, C22896-C22899.

50 For Bruchési, see Linteau, *Histoire de Montréal depuis la Confédération*, 182.

51 Vigod, *Quebec before Duplessis*, 16.

52 Census of Canada 1891, Montreal, St Lawrence Ward, Sub-District F, District #172, Division #4, Family #246, 54.

53 Census of Canada 1901, Montreal, St Lawrence Ward, Sub-District A, Polling Sub-Division #27.

54 Christie and Gauvreau, *A Full-Orbed Christianity*, 21.

55 Robert Wiebe, *The Search for Order, 1877–1920*, xiii.

56 Bacchi, *Liberation Deferred*, 9.

57 Christie and Gauvreau, *A Full-Orbed Christianity*, 77.

58 Harrison, *State and Society in Twentieth-Century America*, 121.

59 Ibid.

60 Copp, *The Anatomy of Poverty*, 85.

61 Ibid., 86.

62 The classic formulation of this argument is in Kolko, *The Triumph of Conservatism*.

63 Henderson, *Kids What I Knows*.

64 May, *The End of American Innocence*, 21.

65 Hofstadter, *The Age of Reform*, 261.

66 May, *The End of American Innocence*, 23.

CHAPTER TWO

1 English, *Borden: His Life and World*; English, *The Decline of Politics*; Brown, *Robert Laird Borden*, vols. 1 and 2.

2 The Women's Social and Political Union (WSPU) was organized in Manchester in 1903 by Emmeline Pankhurst, aided by her daughter Christabel. The WSPU "was soon to embrace militancy, intimidation and violence" (Phillips, *The Ascent of Woman*, 165).

3 *Montreal Daily Star*, 28 August 1912. In his memoirs Borden comments that after the meeting the British suffragettes "sent out to Canadian suffragettes a most amusing misinterpretation of my remarks" (MacQuarrie, *Robert Laird Borden,* vol. 1, 170).

4 For women and suffrage see Cleverdon, *The Woman Suffrage Movement in Canada*; Bacchi, *Liberation Deferred?*

5 Bacchi, *Liberation Deferred?*, 133.

6 *Montreal Daily Star*, 30 August 1912.

7 Ibid.

8 Schreiner, *Woman and Labor*. Olive Schreiner (1855–1920) was the author of the classic novel *The Story of an African Farm*. Her critique of the bourgeois woman was in turn inspired by Mary Wollstonecraft's critique of "indolent" women who abandoned their duties as wives and mothers and took up lives of "vanity and dissipation" (Wollstonecraft, *A Vindication of the Rights of Woman*, 247).

9 Lipton, *The Trade Union Movement of Canada, 1827–1959*; Horowitz, *Canadian Labour in Politics*; Robin, *Radical Politics and Canadian Labour, 1880–1930*; Palmer, *Working-Class Experience*; Morton, *Working People*.

10 Trades and Labor Congress of Canada (TLCC), *Report of Proceedings, 1912*, 43.

11 Ibid.

12 Henderson added that institutions were doing good work, but the home was preferable.

13 TLCC, *Report of Proceedings, 1912*, 43.

14 Ibid., 43–4.

15 Ibid.

16 *Montreal Daily Star*, 11 September 1912.

17 Ibid. For the origins and activities of the Baron de Hirsch Institute, see Tulchinsky, *Taking Root*, 119–26, 137–47.

18 Allen, *The Social Passion*, 18–19.

19 Ibid., 20.

20 Henderson, "Pensions for Mothers," *Social Service Congress – 1914 Report of Addresses and Proceedings* (Toronto: Social Service Council of Canada, 1914, 112–13).

21 J.J. Kelso, "A Pension for Widowed Mothers," *Social Service* (November 1904).

22 Christie, *Engendering the State*, 98.

23 Ibid., 22.

24 Ibid., 98–9.

25 Henderson, "Pensions for Mothers," 109.

26 *Montreal Herald and Daily Telegraph*, 3 March 1914.

27 Christie and Gauvreau, *A Full-Orbed Christianity*, 77.

28 McLaren, *Our Own Master Race*, 54. Dr Peter H. Bryce (1853–1922) was the first secretary of the Ontario Board of Health (1882–1904) and chief medical officer of the federal Department of Immigration (1904–21).

29 McLaren, *Our Own Master Race*, 27. Helen MacMurchy (1862–1953) attended the Women's Medical College and the University of Toronto, where she earned her MD in 1901. She worked for the Ontario government from 1906 to 1919 and was the first head of the Division of Maternal and Child Welfare in the federal Department of Health, 1920–1934 (*Toronto Daily Star*, 13 October 1953).

30 McLaren, *Our Own Master Race*, 46.

31 Ibid., 14.

32 Henderson, "Pensions for Mothers," 111.

33 Ibid., 110.

34 Ibid., 112.

35 Ibid., 114.

36 Christie, *Engendering the State*, 6.

37 Ibid., 9.

38 Henderson, "Pensions for Mothers," 109.

39 Christie, *Engendering the State*, 29.

40 TLCC, *Report of Proceedings*, 44.

41 *Toronto Daily Star*, 5 February 1915.

42 Valverde, *The Age of Light, Soap, and Water*, 164.

43 Christie, *Engendering the State*, 148.

44 Henderson, "Pensions for Mothers," 114.

45 Christie, *Engendering the State*, 115.

46 LAC, Records of Federal Royal Commissions, RG33/95, *Royal Commission on Industrial Relations at Montreal, Thursday, May 29th, 1919*, 156.

47 Christie, *Engendering the* State, 312.

48 Henderson, "Pensions for Mothers," 112.

49 Christie, *Engendering the State*, 129.

50 Ibid., 130.

51 Kealey, *Enlisting Women for the Cause*, 234.

52 "Proceedings and Evidence of the Select Committee Appointed to Inquire and Report as to the Expediency of Making Any Amendments to the Existing Laws for the Purpose of Remedying or Preventing Any Evils Arising from the Use of Cigarettes," *Journals of the House of Commons of the Dominion of Canada* (Ottawa: J. de L. Taché, 1914), 34.

53 "Proceedings and Evidence," 35.

54 Ibid., 36.

55 Biologist Jean-Baptiste Lamarck (1744–1829) was the author of the theory of the inheritability of acquired traits, also known as directed evolution. Lamarckians such as Henderson believed that acquired characteristics passed on to offspring were mental and moral as well as physical. By the First World War, Lamarck's critics believed that his theory had been refuted by the German evolutionary biologist August Wiesmann (1834–1914).

56 "Proceedings and Evidence", 40.

57 *Canadian Cigar and Tobacco Journal* 20, no. 5 (May 1914).

58 Myers, *Caught*, 115.

59 Ibid., 119.

60 Henderson, "The Need for a Woman's Court," *Woman's Century*, April 1915.

61 Henderson, "Juvenile Court," *Woman's Century*, August 1915.

62 Myers, *Caught*, 115.

63 Ibid., 207.

64 *Canadian Jewish Chronicle*, 10, 17, and 24 March 1916.

65 Valverde, *The Age of Light, Soap, and Water*, 56.

66 Ibid., 106.

67 Ibid., 111–12. I am not in a position to argue that Henderson never linked opium with Chinese men seducing white women, but the existing evidence clearly suggests that her major concern was the impact of opium on young people in Montreal.

68 Tulchinsky, *Taking Root*, 149–51, 269; Myers, "On Probation," 182–3.

69 *Canadian Jewish Times*, 13 February 1914.

70 *Canadian Jewish Chronicle*, 5 February 1915.

71 Maeterlinck, *The Blue Bird*.

72 Ibid., 269.

73 Ibid., 279–80.

74 Heller, *Prophets of Dissent*, 11.

75 Ibid., 24–5.

76 Ibid., 49.

77 Ibid.

78 The Bahá'i faith was founded by Mizra Husayn-Ali (1817–1892), known to his followers as Baha'u'llah, in 1863, when he announced a revelation he had received in 1852. In that year he was imprisoned following an attempt by followers of the Bab to assassinate the Shah of Persia. The Bab was Sayyid Ali'Muhammad, who in 1844 had declared himself the Bab, or "door" in Arabic, a title in the Shi'a Muslim faith indicating a special relationship with the Twelfth or "Hidden" Imam. The Bab was executed in 1850, and Baha'u'llah was imprisoned in the wave of repressions that followed the assassination attempt in 1852. Released from prison, he fled Persia with his family, arriving in Baghdad in 1853. In 1863 he left Baghdad for Istanbul. In 1868 Turkish authorities exiled him to Acre, a port city in the Holy Land. In spite of nearly constant persecution, the faith continued to grow, and when Baha'u'llah died in 1892, he was succeeded by his son Abbas Effendi, known to his followers as Abdu'l-Baha. In 1894, the Bahá'i faith was established in the United States by Ibrahim George Keirallah. See Will van den Hoonaard, *The Origins of the Bahai Community of Canada, 1898–1948* (Waterloo: Wilfrid Laurier University Press, 1996), 10, 16.

79 van den Hoonaard, *The Origins of the Bahá'i Community of Canada, 1898–1948*, 18–20. For Jackson's work with the Knights of Labor and defence of the Haymarket martyrs in the United States, see Kealey and Palmer, *Dreaming of What Might Be*, 19–20.

80 For Abdu'l-Baha's stay in Montreal, see van den Hoonaard, *The Origins of the Bahá'i Community of Canada,* 43–60.

81 *Star of the West*, 3, no. 1 (21 March 1912): 8.

82 Tulchinsky, *Taking Root*, 107.

83 On Sunday, 7 March 1915 Henderson spoke to the Young People's Literary Society of Temple Emanu-El, an event chaired by Rabbi Nathan Gordon; her "many views and points were enthusiastically received" (*Canadian Jewish Chronicle,* 12 March 1915). On 7 June 1915 she was to speak at the YMHA Hall on "How to Keep the Boys away from the Juvenile Court" (*Canadian Jewish Chronicle*, 4 June 1915).

84 Ibid., 30 July 1915.

85 Ibid., 15 October 1915.

86 Ibid., 29 October 1915.

87 Myers, *Caught*, 123–4. For concern with the delinquency of Jewish boys in both Montreal and Toronto at this time, see Tulchinsky, *Taking Root*, 175–6.

88 *Canadian Jewish Chronicle*, 29 October 1915. The 10 December 1915 issue observed that Henderson's lectures "are attracting large crowds."

89 *Kindling* was adapted for the stage by newsman Charles Kenyon (1880–1961), based on a novel co-written with playwright and critic Arthur Hornblow (1865–1942). Kenyon went on to become a Hollywood screenwriter, his credits including *Show Boat* (1929) and *A Midsummer Night's Dream* (1935). See Higashi, *Cecil B. De Mille and American Culture*, 71.

90 Margaret Illington (1879–1934) was born Maude Ellen Light in Bloomington, Illinois, and was appearing in *Kindling* in a Hamilton production in September 1912, at the same time that Henderson was attending the annual convention of the Trades and Labor Congress in Guelph. According to the *Hamilton Spectator*, 13 September 1912, Illington was "classed among the greatest of the American emotional actresses."

91 Higashi, *Cecil B. De Mille and American Culture*, 80.

92 Henrik Ibsen (1828–1906), Norwegian playwright, theatre director, and poet, is widely known as the father of modern drama. Other famous plays by Ibsen include *An Enemy of the People* and *The Wild Duck*, published in

1882 and 1884, respectively. Henderson lectured on *A Doll's House* on a number of occasions, and at least once on Ibsen's 1894 play *Little Eyolf*. See *British Columbia Federationist*, 28 January 1921.

93 Phillips, The *Ascent of Woman*, 212.

94 *Canadian Municipal Journal* 12, no. 3 (March 1916).

95 McKay, *Reasoning Otherwise*, 34.

96 Valverde, *The Age of Light, Soap*, and Water, 109.

97 Watters, a former member of the Socialist Party of Canada, was a supporter in this period of a British-style labour party. See Robin, *Radical Politics and Canadian Labour*, 147–8.

98 TLCC, *Report of Proceedings*, 1916, 127.

99 Engels, *Socialism: Utopian and Scientific*, 33. It is a myth that Engels dismissed out of hand the ideas of the utopian socialists. Engels called Charles Fourier "assuredly one the greatest satirists of all time," and characterized his critique of the situation of women in bourgeois society as "masterly" (39).

100 *The Labor World/Le Monde Ouvrier*, 4 November 1916.

101 Ibid. In all probability Henderson was one of the organizers of the people's forum, if not its guiding spirit.

102 Henderson, "The High Cost of Living," *The Labor World/Le Monde Ouvrier*, 28 October 1916.

103 Christie, *Engendering the State*, 95.

104 In her speech to the Social Service Congress, Henderson noted that the TLCC "have at their last two conventions passed resolutions in favor of mothers' pensions, and urged its adoption," a development in which she played a major role (Henderson, "Pensions for Mothers," 115).

105 Christie, "Engendering the State," 9.

CHAPTER THREE

1 For both the unity and division created in the labour movement by registration and conscription, see McCormack, *Reformers, Rebels, and Revolutionaries*, 124–35.

2 The War Measures Act was passed in the immediate aftermath of the declaration of war on Germany in August 1914. The act gave the government virtually unlimited powers to censor, search, seize, and prosecute dissidents, real and perceived (Kealey, "State Repression of Labour and the Left in Canada, 1914–20," 285).

3 Copp, *The Anatomy of Poverty*, 139.

4 Henderson, "The Cradle and the Nation," *Woman's Century*, January 1917.

5 For organized labour's opposition to women's wage labour and organizing women workers, see Linda Kealey, *Enlisting Women for the Cause*, 18; Newton, *The Feminist Challenge to the Canadian Left, 1900–1918*, 80–1; and Sangster, "The 1907 Bell Telephone Strike: Organizing Women Workers."

6 Henderson, "The Cradle and the Nation."

7 *Montreal Daily Star*, 3 March 1917.

8 *Montreal Gazette*, 3 March 1917.

9 TLCC, *Report of Proceedings, 1917*, 136–7.

10 *Le Monde Ouvrier*, 18 May 1918. For Bella Hall (Gauld), who later became a member of the Communist Party, see Kealey, *Enlisting Women for the Cause*, 250.

11 Naylor, *The New Democracy*, 79.

12 Ibid., 112.

13 Robin, *Radical Politics and Canadian Labour*, 125. According to Naylor in *The New Democracy*, 95, it was held on 1 July 1917.

14 Naylor, *The New Democracy*, 79.

15 *Labour Gazette* (June 1918), 461–2.

16 For Joseph Marks, see Kealey and Palmer, *Dreaming of What Might Be*, 308–10; Naylor, *The New Democracy*, 78–9. For the leading role Minnie Singer took in the women's auxiliary of the International Association of Machinists see Linda Kealey, *Enlisting Women for the Cause*, 83–5. For Singer's work as one of two female members of the Ontario Mothers' Allowance Commission, see Christie, *Engendering the State*, 125; Naylor, *The New Democracy*, 89, 148–9, 227.

17 Mother Bloor (1862–1951) was born Ella Reeve on Staten Island, New York, on 8 July 1862. Her early involvements included the Women's Christian Temperance Union and the suffrage movement. In 1897 she joined Eugene Debs and Victor Berger to form the Social Democratic Party. In 1898 she moved to the more radical Socialist Labor Party led by Daniel De Leon. In 1902 she became a member of the Socialist Party of America. In 1905 she helped author and fellow Socialist Party member Upton Sinclair gather information on the Chicago stockyards that made its way into his classic work *The Jungle*. In the ensuing years she gained fame as a trade union organizer and indefatigable supporter of labour in industrial disputes. In 1919 she was expelled from the Socialist Party of America,

then joined with others to organize the American Communist Party. She served on the Central Committee of the party from 1932 until 1948. In 1940 she published her autobiography entitled *We Are Many*. Mother Bloor died in Richlandtown, Pennsylvania, on 10 August 1951 at the age of 89. See Brown, "The 'Savagely Fathered and Un-Mothered World' of the Communist Party, U.S.A."

18 *Labor News*, 31 May 1918.

19 *Industrial Banner*, 31 May 1918.

20 Ibid., 31 May 1918.

21 Ibid., 7 June 1918.

22 TLCC, *Report of Proceedings, 1918*, 108.

23 Ibid., 109. For the persecution of immigrant workers deemed "enemy aliens," see Avery, *"Dangerous Foreigners."*

24 Kealey, "State Repression of Labour and the Left in Canada, 1914–20," 293–304.

25 *Labor World*, 23 November 1918.

26 For the National Council of Women, see Shaw, *Proud Heritage*; Strong-Boag, *The Parliament of Women*; Griffiths, *The Splendid Vision*.

27 My reading of *Woman's Century* leads me to agree with Veronica Strong-Boag's observation that "the Council maintained strict limits on its sympathies for labour, particularly organized labour." For example, in 1917 the council vetoed a resolution in favour of placing a union label on NCWC publications by a vote of 137 to 111. Such a relatively close vote, however, does not justify a blanket characterization of NCWC members as "anti-labour." See Strong-Boag, *Parliament of Women*, 302–3.

28 van den Hoonaard, "Rose Henderson: Biographical Zoning and the Bahá'í Context of Her Social Activism," 21.

29 Manley, "Women and the Left in the 1930s," 105.

30 *Woman's Century*, Special Number, September 1918.

31 Struthers, *No Fault of Their Own*, 17.

32 Ibid., 19.

33 Ibid., 17.

34 Ibid., 18–19.

35 LAC, Department of Labour, RG 27, vol. 183, file 614.05. I have not found any information pertaining to Henderson's attendance at meetings of the Employment Service Council or committee work.

36 Struthers, *No Fault of Their Own*, 18.

37 Ibid.

38 Ibid., 19.

39 LAC, Privy Council Records, vol. 3787, file 1919, nos. 2266–2270, 14–20 February 1919. Henderson is not specifically named as having attended these meetings.

40 *Toronto Daily Star*, 11 February 1919.

41 Ibid.

42 Ibid.

43 *Industrial Banner*, 14 February 1919.

44 *Toronto Daily Star*, 11 February 1919.

45 Ibid.

46 Ibid.

47 Ibid.

48 Ibid.

49 Ibid.

50 Ibid., 14 February 1919.

51 The federal legislation had just gone into effect on 1 January 1919 (Cleverdon, *The Woman Suffrage Movement in Canada*, 43, 136).

52 Naylor, *The New Democracy*, 115. On Sunday, 16 February 1919, the day after the by-election in St Catharines, Henderson spoke at St George's Hall on Elm Street in Toronto on the "The Causes of Industrial Unrest" (*Toronto Daily Star*, 15 February 1919).

53 Ibid., 13 February 1919.

54 Ibid., 11 February 1919.

55 Ibid., 14 February 1919.

56 Gregory Kealey, "1919," 90.

57 LAC, Records of Federal Royal Commissions (FRC), RG33/95, *Royal Commission on Industrial Relations at Montreal, Thursday, May 29th, 1919*, 166.

58 LAC, FRC, RG 33/95, *Royal Commission on Industrial Relations at Montreal, Thursday, May 29th, 1919*, 164. Henderson's words have become synonymous with the spirit of revolt that characterized the Canadian left in 1919. See Gregory Kealey, "1919," 93; Linda Kealey, *Enlisting Women for the Cause*, 234.

59 Bercuson, "Labour Radicalism and the Western Industrial Frontier, 1897–1919."

60 Gregory Kealey, "Labour and Working-Class History in Canada: Prospects in the 1980s."

61 Bercuson, *Confrontation at Winnipeg: Labour, Industrial Relations, and the General Strike*, 201–2.

62 Bercuson, "Through the Looking Glass of Culture," 107.

63 Ewen, "Quebec: Class and Ethnicity," 131.

64 Ibid., 107.

65 *Le Monde Ouvrier*, 7 June 1919. For Ulrike Binette, see Ewen, "Quebec: Class and Ethnicity," 128.

66 Ibid.

67 *Montreal Gazette*, 1 July 1919; *Labor News*, 11 July 1919; *Labor World*, 5 July 1919. For the national context of state repression of radical dissent in the First World War period, see Gregory Kealey, "State Repression of Labour and the Left in Canada, 1914–20."

68 *Montreal Gazette*, 1 July 1919.

69 ANQ, FMJ, E17, dossier 5007/1919, Chef de Police P. Bélanger à M.E.R. Décary, 2 July 1919.

70 Ibid., Ernest Décary à Sir Lomer Gouin, 8 July 1919.

71 Ibid., Premier Ministre à Ernest Décary, 11 July 1919.

72 Ibid., Charles Lanctot (?) à Sir Lomer Gouin, 11 July 1919. It is possible, but less likely, that this letter was written by Attorney General Taschereau himself.

73 Ibid., Lomer Gouin à Mon cher ami, 13 July 1919.

74 Ibid., Charles Lanctot to the Hon. Minister of Justice, 15 July 1919.

75 Ibid., W. Stuart Edwards to Charles Lanctot, 22 July 1919.

76 Robert Boyd Russell (1889–1964) was born in Scotland and emigrated to Winnipeg in 1911. He quickly became a powerful presence in the International Association of Machinists, joined the Socialist Party of Canada, and championed industrial unionism. Charged with seditious conspiracy for his leading role in the Winnipeg General Strike, he served a year of a two-year prison sentence. Upon his release he became the heart and soul of the One Big Union (OBU), which he helped found but which was already in serious decline. In 1956 he presided over the dissolution of the OBU into the Canadian Labour Congress. His decades-long advocacy of technical and vocational education is evidenced by the R.B. Russell Vocational High School in Winnipeg (Campbell, *Canadian Marxists and the Search for a Third Way*, 168–219).

77 ANQ, FMJ, E17, dossier 5007/1919, John Allen to Charles Lanctot, 8 August 1919.

78 Ibid., Charles Lanctot to A.T. Andrews, 21 August 1919.

79 Ibid., A.T. Andrews to Charles Lanctot, 8 September 1919.

80 Ibid., Charles Lanctot to Rose Henderson, 13 September 1919.

81 Ibid., Charles Lanctot to Rose Henderson, 18 September 1919.

82 Although the typescript is dated 12 January 1912, internal evidence reveals that it should actually have been dated 12 January 1913. The typescript quotes from Fabian Tract #164, and says that it was published "in June last." The tract, entitled "Gold and State Banking: A Study in the Economics of Money," was written by Edward R. Pease and published in June 1912. The paper also quotes from the American Socialist Party writer William English Walling's *Socialism As It Is: A Survey of the World-Wide Revolutionary Movement*, published in 1912.

83 Presumably, the non-workers are mostly women and children, who in true maternal feminist fashion are safely ensconced in nurturing, loving homes.

84 Mitchell, "'Legal Gentlemen Appointed by the Federal Government,'" 20.

85 Provincial Archives of Manitoba, Robert Boyd Russell Collection, MG10, A14–2, Winnipeg Strike Trials – Court of King's Bench, *King vs Russell* – Summation of the Prosecution.

86 ANQ, FMJ, E17, dossier 5007/1919, Charles Lanctot à F-X. Choquet, 30 September 1919.

87 Ibid., J.H. Edgar to Sir Lomer Gouin, 3 October 1919.

88 Ibid., Lomer Gouin à L.-A. Taschereau, 4 October 1919.

89 Ibid., Charles Lanctot to Rose Henderson, 6 October 1919.

90 Ibid., Charles Lanctot to J.H. Edgar, 6 October 1919.

91 Ibid., Charles Lanctot à M. Le Greffier de la Couronne and de la Paix, 6 October 1919.

92 *Le Monde Ouvrier*, 12 July 1919.

93 ANQ, FMJ, E17, 5007/1919, Rose Henderson to Charles Lanctot, 6 October 1919.

94 Heron, "Labourism and the Canadian Working Class," 51.

95 ANQ, FMJ, E17, dossier 5007/19, F.-X. Choquet au Procureur Général, 12 November 1919.

96 Ibid., Louis-Alexandre Taschereau à F.-X. Choquet, 13 November 1919.

97 Samuel William Jacobs, born Lancaster, Ontario, 6 May 1871, graduate of McGill and Laval universities, called to the Quebec Bar 1894, K.C. 1906, married Amy Stein 23 April 1917, life governor of the Montreal General Hospital, member of the committee that successfully opposed the efforts of

Queen's University, Kingston, to be declared a national university by the federal parliament while remaining "distinctively Christian." He was federal Liberal member for Montreal's Cartier riding from 1917 until his death in 1938. See Rabbi Wilfred Suchat, *The Gate of Heaven: The Story of Congregation Shaar Hashomayim of Montreal, 1846–1996* (Montreal & Kingston: McGill-Queen's University Press, 2000), 112–15; LAC, MG 27 III C3, Samuel W. Jacobs Papers, "Biography."

98 LAC, MG27, Series III C 3, vols. 1/2, Samuel W. Jacobs Papers, file May 1918 – June 1919, Rose Henderson to Samuel Jacobs, mid- to late November 1919(?).

99 ANQ, FMJ, E17, dossier 5007/1919, Rose Henderson to Louis-Alexandre Taschereau, 13 December 1919.

100 Mitchell, "'Legal Gentlemen,'" 23.

101 Ibid., 29.

102 *Labor World*, 5 July 1919.

CHAPTER FOUR

1 *Toronto Globe*, 13 January 1920.

2 Ibid. The headline reads: "Woman Judge Addresses Club." For the "girl problem" in Quebec, see Myers, *Caught*, especially chapter 3. For the "girl problem" in Ontario, see Comacchio, *The Dominion of Youth*, especially chapter 1; and Sangster, *Girl Trouble*.

3 For Dorothy Glen, see Linda Kealey, *Enlisting Women for the Cause*, 248.

4 Griffiths, *The Splendid Vision*, 148.

5 *Toronto Evening Telegram*, 14 January 1920.

6 Ibid.

7 Ibid.

8 *Toronto Globe*, 14 January 1920.

9 Claeys, *The French Revolution Debate in Britain*, 64.

10 See, for example, Elizabeth Robins Pennell, *Mary Wollstonecraft Godwin* (1885); Emma Rauschenbusch-Clough, *A Study of Mary Wollstonecraft and the Rights of Woman* (1898); Brougham Villiers, *The Case for Women's Suffrage* (T. Fisher Unwin, 1907); W. Lyon Blease, *The Emancipation of English Women* (Constable & Co., 1910); Ethel Snowden, *The Feminist Movement* (Nation's Library, 1913).

11 Penfold, "'Have You No Manhood in You?'" 272.

12 Ibid., 288.

13 *Industrial Banner*, 5 March 1920. The identity of the author is revealed by the pamphlet put out at this time by the Ontario Independent Labor Party, authored by Rose Henderson, and entitled "Mr. Workingman."

14 "Mr. Workingman, Listen!," *Industrial Banner*, 5 March 1920.

15 Ibid. "Mr. Workingman, Listen!" was published as "Some Cogent Reasons Why Working Men Should Join Fighting Labor Party" by the *Workers' Weekly* in Stellarton, Nova Scotia, on 21 May 1920.

16 *Industrial Banner*, 9 April 1920.

17 Ibid., 16 April 1920.

18 Ibid., 9 April 1920. For the Farmer-Labour government elected in Ontario in 1919, see Tennyson, "The Ontario General Election of 1919: The Beginnings of Agrarian Revolt."

19 LAC, Meighen Papers Series I, MG26, I, vol. 2.

20 *Hansard*, 27 May 1920. For the Progressive Party, see W.L. Morton, *The Progressive Party in Canada*.

21 *Hansard*, 31 May 1920.

22 Ibid., 1 June 1920. While Henderson may have spoken on behalf of the OBU in northern Ontario at some point in 1919, I have not found any evidence that she did so while campaigning for Angus McDonald. See Linda Kealey, *Enlisting Women for the Cause*, 234–5.

23 *The Citizen*, 4 June 1920.

24 Ibid., 11 June 1920.

25 *Workers' Weekly*, 4 June 1920.

26 Quoted in *The Citizen*, 18 June 1920.

27 *The Citizen*, 25 June 1920.

28 *Workers' Weekly*, 11 June 1920.

29 Ibid., 25 June 1920.

30 Quotation from *The Citizen*, cited in the *Labor World*, 3 July 1920.

31 *Workers' Weekly*, 2 July 1920.

32 Ostensibly, Martens was negotiating trade deals with Canadian companies, and in June 1920 he reported that the Canadian government had agreed to open up a trade bureau provided it was strictly economic in character. See Black, *Canada in the Soviet Mirror*, 36.

33 LAC, DL, RG27, vol. 168, file 613.04:1, Gideon Robertson to Arthur Meighen, 23 July 1920; Arthur Meighen to Gideon Robertson, 29 July 1920; Gideon Robertson to Colonel Cortlandt Starnes, 29 July 1920;

Colonel Cortlandt Starnes to Gideon Robertson, 30 July 1920. For Starnes, see Gregory Kealey, "Spymasters, Spies, and Their Subjects," 20, 22, 27.

34 LAC, DL, "Information Respecting the Russian Soviet System and Its Propaganda in North America," August 1920, 15.

35 *Canadian Labor Press*, 28 August 1920.

36 *The Citizen*, 10 September 1920.

37 Ibid.

38 The attack on the OBU was repudiated by OBU secretary Victor Midgley, who exchanged telegrams on the issue with Gideon Robertson in early September 1920. See *BC Federationist*, 10 September 1920.

39 *Industrial Banner*, 14, 21 February 1919; Naylor, *The New Democracy*, 114–15.

40 Naylor, "Ontario Workers and the Decline of Labourism," 286.

41 *Toronto Globe*, 6 September 1920.

42 *The Citizen*, 17 September 1920. The same quotations had been given in the *Industrial Banner*, 10 September 1920.

43 One gets the sense at this point of a woman who was somewhat uneasy with conflict, who tended to move on rather than be the focal point of disputes. As her many associations, both religious and secular, attest, she spent much of her life looking for an organizational form to match the idealism and passion of her vision.

44 *BC Federationist*, 10 September 1920. See as well the RCMP report in Kealey and Whitaker, *R.C.M.P. Security Bulletins*, 128.

45 Kealey and Whitaker, *R.C.M.P. Security Bulletins*, 226.

46 *BC Federationist*, 26 November 1920.

47 Kealey and Whitaker, *R.C.M.P. Security Bulletins*, 192.

48 *Manitoba Free Press*, 30 April 1921.

49 Ibid., 12 May 1921.

50 The official return for St Lawrence and St George indicates that Liberal candidate Herbert Marler spent $42,743.34, and Conservative candidate C.C. Ballantyne spent $26,082.30, while Labour candidate Rose Henderson spent $544.75. Ballantyne claimed that Marler actually spent "at least three times" the amount reported (LAC, Meighen Papers, Series 3, MG 26 I, vol. 60, reel C-3438, C.C. Ballantyne to the Right Hon. Arthur Meighen, 27 February 1922.

51 *Canadian Jewish Chronicle*, 18 November 1921.

52 Mann Trofimenkoff, in *The Dream of Nation*, 198, pulls no punches in her assault on Bourassa, arguing that he "lashed feminism with a vehemence

that indicated more the febrile state of his imagination than the reality of
Canadian feminism."

53 Socknat, *Witness against War*, 58.

54 *Toronto Star*, 3 February 1922.

55 Queen's University Archives (QUA), Andrew Glen Papers (AGP), box 2,
file 7, Central Executive Report, Annual Convention of the Independent
Labor Party, Toronto, 21 October 1922.

56 Ibid., file 6, J.W. Buckley to Mr. and Mrs. Glen, 21 February 1922.

57 Ibid. file 7, Central Executive Report, Annual Convention of the
Independent Labour Party, Toronto, 21 October 1922.

58 Note the continued influence of Lamarckianism.

59 *Toronto Globe*, 9 March 1922. It is a measure of Henderson's influence that she
was the main speaker; she was followed by Professor Dale, head of the Social
Service Department at the University of Toronto, who gave a "short talk."

60 *BC Federationist*, 10 September 1920.

61 McClung, *In Times Like These*, 41.

CHAPTER FIVE

1 Kissane, *The Politics of the Irish Civil War*; Cottrell, *The Anglo-Irish War*.

2 For Katherine Hughes, see O Siadhail, "Hughes, Katherine (Catherine)
Angelina," *Dictionary of Canadian Biography*, vol. 15, *1921–1930*, 494–7.

3 Boyle, "A Fenian Protestant in Canada," 165–6.

4 *Canadian Annual Review* (1921), 306.

5 Armand Lavergne (1880–1935) was a Quebec lawyer and politician.
Elected to the House of Commons as the Liberal member for Montmagny
in 1904, he was expelled from the party by Wilfrid Laurier in 1907. He
then sat as a Nationalist member from Montmagny from 1908 to 1916. In
1925 he became a Conservative and served as the federal Conservative
member for Montmagny from 1930 until his death in 1935 (Réal Bélanger,
"La Vergne, Armand," *Canadian Encyclopedia Online*).

6 *Canadian Annual Review* (1921), 307.

7 Ibid.

8 *BC Federationist*, 15 October 1920.

9 Ibid., 1 April 1921.

10 Ibid., 11 February 1921.

11 *Montreal Gazette*, 8 November 1921.

12 Ibid. Revealingly, the *Canadian Annual Review* (1921), 309, claims that Bourassa made the exact opposite argument.

13 Kealey and Whitaker, "Notes of the Work of the C.I.B. Division for the Week Ending 7th October," *R.C.M.P. Security Bulletins,* 192.

14 *Toronto Globe,* 13 March 1922.

15 Boyle, "A Fenian Protestant in Canada: Robert Lindsay Crawford, 1910–22," 173.

16 *Maritime Labor Herald,* 5 August 1922. The "black and tan" reference is to the soldiers, mostly unemployed veterans of the First World War, who were enlisted to supplement the dwindling ranks of the Royal Irish Constabulary, England's police force in Ireland, during the Irish Civil War. The Black and Tans, acting more like an army of occupation than a police force, took especial pleasure in terrorizing Irish civilians and committed a series of atrocities against them.

17 *Maritime Labor Herald,* 16 September 1922. This reference may indicate that Henderson was in Cork at the time of writing this article.

18 Ibid.

19 *OBU Bulletin,* 28 September 1922.

20 Ibid.

21 Robin, *Radical Politics and Canadian Labour,* 220–21. Robin's source is the *Labor News,* 25 April 1919.

22 Manley, "Women and the Left in the 1930s," 104. For more recent misinformation traceable to Martin Robin's original error, see Little, "'No Car, No Radio, No Liquor Permit,'" 21, 40.

23 Henderson, "Labor, Capital and the War," *Woman's Century* – Special Number (September 1918).

24 Sapurji Saklatvala (1874–1936) was born into a Parsi merchant family in Bombay (Mumbai). He moved to England in 1905 and joined the Independent Labour Party in 1909. In 1921 he left the ILP to join the Communist Party of Great Britain. As a Communist Party member he won the London riding of Battersea North in the 1922 general election for Labour. Saklatvala was defeated in the election of 1923, then re-elected in 1924 without Labour Party support. He was defeated in the 1929 general election. He died of a heart attack at his London home on 16 January 1936. See H.C.G. Matthew and Brian Harrison, eds., *Oxford Dictionary of National Biography* (Oxford: Oxford University Press, 2004), vol. 48, 675–77.

25 Henderson, "Native of India Elected to the Mother of Parliaments," *OBU Bulletin*, 4 January 1923.

26 Cline, *E.D. Morel*, 1–3; Hochschild, *King Leopold's Ghost*, 177.

27 Hochschild, *King Leopold's Ghost*, 181.

28 Ibid., 206–7.

29 Cline, *E.D. Morel*, 65.

30 Reinders, "Racialism on the Left," 1.

31 Ibid., 5. The number of copies of the third edition was increased to 15,000. See Morel, *The Horror on the Rhine*.

32 Reinders, "Racialism on the Left," 21.

33 *Maritime Labor Herald*, 25 October 1924.

34 Thomas Fisher Rare Book Library (TFRBL), Robert Kenny Collection (RKC), Pam 0213, Rose Henderson, *Woman and War*, 15.

35 Henderson, "Character Sketch of the Life of E.D. Morel," *BC Federationist*, 26 December 1924.

36 Ibid.

37 Morel, *The Horror on the Rhine*, 11.

38 Ibid., 8.

39 Ibid., 10.

40 Ibid., 13.

41 Ibid., 19.

42 Reinders, "Racialism on the Left," 26.

43 Ibid., 27.

44 Ibid., 7.

45 Ibid., 18.

46 Henderson, "England Is Merry England No More," *Maritime Labor Herald*, 10 March 1923.

47 In her 19 July 1923 article in the *OBU Bulletin*, Henderson praised Smillie's wife as well as Smillie: "Some day I shall endeavor to write a book on Heroes in the Labor Movement. In that book a special chapter will be devoted to Mrs. Smillie, one of the finest products of the Labor movement which [it] has been my privilege to meet."

48 Henderson, "Bob Smillie, M.P.," *OBU Bulletin*, 19 July 1923.

49 Smillie, it needs be noted, supported Morel's campaign (Reinders, "Racialism on the Left," 8).

50 Henderson, "Bob Smillie, M.P."

51 For the SPC's critique of leadership, see Campbell, "Making Socialists," 54–5.

52 A single article entitled "The British Labor Party a Mass Party Lead [sic] by Weaklings and Traitors" appeared in the *Maritime Labor Herald* on 29 September, two days after the third article of the series appeared in the *OBU*.

53 *OBU Bulletin*, 20 September 1923.

54 Ibid., 20 September 1923.

55 Ibid., 27 September 1923.

56 Ibid., 4 October 1923.

57 Ibid.

58 *Labor Statesman*, 19 September 1924.

59 *BC Federationist*, 26 September 1924.

60 Henderson gave a talk with the same title at St George's Hall in New Westminster on Tuesday, 7 October 1924 (*BC Federationist*, 3 October 1924).

61 Ibid.

62 Ibid., 10 October 1924.

63 Fitzpatrick, *The Russian Revolution, 1917–1932*, 87.

64 Goldman, *Women, the State and the Revolution*, 72–6. In one sense Henderson was correct. Bolshevik policy in the 1920s on juvenile crime was "child centred" and bore a striking resemblance to Henderson's approach. Like Henderson, Soviet criminologists saw juvenile crime as a function of environment. Yet by the time Henderson got to the Soviet Union, this attitude to homeless children and juvenile delinquents had begun to harden (ibid., 79, 90).

65 *BC Federationist*, 10 October 1924.

66 Henderson's popularity at this time in British Columbia is evidenced by the fact that she spoke at Duncan on Saturday evening, 18 October 1924; at Northfield on Sunday afternoon, 19 October; at Nanaimo on Sunday evening, 19 October; and at Ladysmith on Monday evening, 20 October (*BC Federationist*, 17 October 1924).

67 Ibid.

68 Ibid.

69 Figes, *A People's Tragedy*, 528.

70 Ibid., 745.

71 Gabel, *And God Created Lenin*, 89–90.

72 Ibid., 115.

73 Ibid., 152–3.

74 Ibid., 337; Figes, *A People's Tragedy*, 750.

75 Czech writer Karel Capek (1890–1938) published the play in 1921. While the play introduced the word "robot" into the English language, and Capek

is often credited with coining the term, he gave the credit for the idea to his brother Josef. The word *robota* in Czech is variously translated as "serf labour," "drudgery," and "hard work." In the 1930s Capek's work focused on the Nazi threat. His brother died in the Bergen-Belsen concentration camp.

76 BC *Federationist*, 31 October 1924.

77 Ibid., 12 December 1924. On 9 January 1925 Henderson addressed the first meeting of the Junior Labor League in South Vancouver (*Labor Statesman*, 9 January 1925).

78 *Labor World/Le Monde Ouvrier*, 25 April 1925.

79 OBU *Bulletin*, 4 June 1925.

80 For Weaver, see Sangster, *Dreams of Equality*, 97, 198–9.

81 *Labor Statesman*, 15 August 1924.

82 Henderson gave three lectures: "The Religion of the New Democracy" on Sunday, 16 August; "The Art of the Future" on Thursday, 20 August; and "Postwar Conditions of Capital and Labor" on Thursday, 27 August (OBU *Bulletin*, 13 August 1925).

83 *Canadian Farmer-Labor Advocate*, 3 July 1925. For Jack Logie and Summerland, see Wagar, "Theosophical Socialists in the 1920s Okanagan."

84 *Canadian Farmer-Labor Advocate*, 12 June 1925.

85 W.J. Curry, "The Summerland Summer School," *Canadian Labor Advocate*, 28 August 1925.

86 In 1875 Madame Helena Petrovna Blavatsky (1831–1891), in association with Henry Steel Olcott, founded the Theosophical Society in New York City. By the 1920s one of the best known theosophists was Annie Besant (1847–1933), an English socialist, women's rights activist, writer, and orator who moved to India in 1893, where she campaigned for Indian self-government. In the last decade of her life she visited branches of the Theosophical Society around the world. See H.C.G. Matthew and Brian Harrison, *Oxford Dictionary of National Biography* (Oxford: Oxford University Press, 2004), vol. 5, 504–07; vol. 6, 188–90.

87 *Canadian Theosophist* 17, no. 12 (15 February 1937).

88 For the Canadian Federation of Women's Labour Leagues and its publication, *The Woman Worker*, see Hobbs and Sangster, *The Woman Worker, 1926–1929*.

89 *Canadian Farmer-Labor Advocate*, 10 July 1925. The article is reprinted in the 22 August 1925 issue of *Labor World/ Le Monde Ouvrier*.

90 This is not to deny that Henderson was concerned with the lot of farm women. At the War Conference in Ottawa in February-March 1918, she

was a member of the Agricultural Production Committee with Nellie McClung, Dr Margaret Gordon, L.A. (Constance) Hamilton, Cora Hind, Irene Parlby, and Violet McNaughton (*Manitoba Free Press*, 2 March 1918).

91 Henderson's position conforms to Carol Bacchi's observation that eastern suffragists "attributed the farm women's hardships to their husbands" (*Liberation Deferred?*, 127).

92 *Canadian Farmer-Labor Advocate*, 17 July 1925.

93 Charles Fourier, *Théorie des quatre mouvements et des destinées générales* (1808); Karl Marx to Ludwig Kugelmann, 12 December 1868, MECW, vol. 43, 184. The possibility of Marxist influence is heightened by Henderson's use of the term "inherent contradictions."

94 Henderson, "Awakened Woman," *Canadian Farmer-Labor Advocate*, 24 July 1925.

95 *Canadian Labor Advocate*, 31 July 1925. This article is reprinted in the 6 August 1925 issue of the OBU *Bulletin*.

96 Strong-Boag, The *New Day Recalled*, 1.

97 Ibid., 2.

98 *Canadian Labor Advocate*, 7 August 1925. This article is reprinted in the 12 September 1925 issue of *Labor World/Le Monde Ouvrier*.

99 *Canadian Labor Advocate*, 21 August 1925.

100 Ibid., 23 October 1925.

101 TFRBL, RKC, box 22, file: Rose Henderson, "Farmer-Labor Candidate Mrs. Rose Henderson New Westminster Constituency."

102 *Labor Statesman*, 6 November 1925.

103 *Canadian Jewish Chronicle*, 5 March 1926.

104 Ibid., 26 March 1926. In the first half of April, Henderson addressed a "large gathering" of the Mizpah Deborah chapter of Hadassah on the symbolism of Maeterlinck's drama *The Blue Bird* (*Canadian Jewish Chronicle*, 16 April 1926). Gerald Tulchinsky helps us understand why Jewish women in Hadassah would be attracted to Henderson's message and why she would respect the organization's activism and "moral influence" in *Taking Root*, 202.

105 *Labor World/Le Monde Ouvrier*, 27 March 1926.

106 Black, *Canada in the Soviet Mirror*, 69. Black misleadingly refers to Henderson as a "teacher."

107 The RSVP form for the general meeting can be found in VOKS, series 6, section 1, file 3/1926.

108 VOKS, series 6, section 1, file 3/1926, Rose Henderson to Madame Kameneva, 3 May 1926. Madame Kameneva replied on 22 June 1926, thanking Henderson for her "kind letter and greetings." She was happy to learn that the general meeting was an "unqualified success," given that the Canadian SCR "is the only cultural and scientific connecting link between the North American countries and the Soviet Union." See ibid.

109 Ibid., Rose Henderson to Madame Kameneva, 2 June 1926.

110 Ibid.

111 Ibid., Thomas R. Parsons to Madame Kameneva, 29 April 1926.

112 Ibid., Thomas R. Parsons to Mrs O.D. Kameneva, 9 October 1926. There is a second letter of introduction of the same date for Dr Campbell Hargraves of Western Canada.

113 Ibid., Rose Henderson to Mrs O.D. Kameneva, November (?) 1926.

114 VOKS, series 6, section 1, file 3/1926.

115 Ibid., A. B(R?)ushukoff and I. Korinetz to Madame Rose Henderson, 14 December 1926.

116 VOKS, series 6, section 1, file 6/1929–30, Report of Anglo-American Section July-August-September 1930.

117 Ibid., Report British Empire Section 1st–30th December, *1930*.

118 As of the fall of 1921 the One Big Union had raised much-needed funds through a series of pools. The most lucrative one involved predicting the results of overseas soccer matches. The soccer pool caused subscriptions to soar but also drew the attention of the authorities. The *OBU Bulletin* attempted to avoid prosecution by changing the type of pool; one of the least successful efforts involved predicting temperatures in North American cities (Morton, *At Odds*, 55–7).

119 Henderson, "Woman, The Backbone of Capitalism," *OBU Bulletin*, 9 December 1926.

120 Henderson, "What's the Matter With Us?," *OBU Bulletin*, 2 June 1927.

121 Henderson, "Youth in Rebellion," *OBU Bulletin*, 20 January 1927.

122 Henderson, "The Modern Girl," *OBU Bulletin*, 3 February 1927.

123 Ibid.

124 Henderson, "A Message to Working Women," *OBU Bulletin*, 27 January 1927.

125 Violet McNaughton (née Jackson) was born in England in 1879. She immigrated to Canada in 1909. She organized the Women's Grain Growers in Saskatchewan, and was first president of the Saskatchewan Equal

Franchise League, later the Political Equality League. She was editor of the column "Mainly for Women" from 1925 to 1950. In 1934 she was awarded the Order of the British Empire by King George V. She died in 1968. See Georgina M. Taylor, "McNaughton, Violet Clara (1879–1968)," *Encyclopedia of Saskatchewan Online*; *Montreal Gazette*, 6 February 1968.

126 Saskatchewan Archives Board, Violet McNaughton Fonds, A1 E52, subject files: Peace Movements, 1916–1939, Rose Henderson to Violet McNaughton, 18 May 1927.

127 Henderson, "The British Labour Party," *Canadian Unionist* 2, no. 3 (September 1928).

128 Henderson, "An English Summer School," *Canadian Unionist* 2, no. 2 (August 1928).

129 Henderson, "The Tragedy in Wales," *Canadian Unionist* 2, no. 7 (January 1929).

130 Henderson, "The Plight of the Women in the South Wales Coalfield," *Canadian Unionist*, 2, no. 8 (February 1929).

131 Mann Trofimenkoff, "Feminist Biography," 1, 7.

132 Ibid., 7.

CHAPTER SIX

1 Bacchi, *Liberation Deferred?*, 114.

2 *Toronto Daily Star*, 31 October 1914.

3 Bacchi, *Liberation Deferred?*, 31.

4 Henderson, "Woman and the War," BC *Federationist*, 27 September 1918.

5 Ibid.

6 Early, *A World without War*, 186.

7 Alonzo, *The Women's Peace Union and the Outlawry of War*, xix.

8 Fowler, *Carrie Catt*, 40.

9 BC *Federationist*, 27 September 1918.

10 Alonzo, *The Women's Peace Union*, 49.

11 For the history of the WILPF, see Bussey and Tims, *Pioneers for Peace*; Carrie Foster, *Women for All Seasons*; Catherine Foster, *The Women and the Warriors*; and Schott, *Reconstructing Women's Thoughts*.

12 Schott, *Reconstructing Women's Thoughts*, 9, argues that the Women's Peace Party was "on the far left of the spectrum of peace advocates." As with the case of the Women's Peace Union, I have some difficulty in advancing an

argument that non-resistance is a more "left wing" position than supporting "virtuous wars."

13 Ibid., 72.

14 Laura Hughes, the daughter of prominent Toronto educators and reformers
James L. Hughes and Ada M. Hughes, was the niece of Colonel Sam
Hughes, Prime Minister Borden's minister of militia until sacked late in
1916. She moved to Chicago following her marriage in December 1917 to
conscientious objector Erling Lunde. See Roberts, "Women against War,"
55, 58.

15 Chown, *The Stairway*, 236.

16 Fowler, *Carrie Catt*, 9.

17 Byrns was born in Lafayette, Indiana, in 1876. In 1917 she resigned from
the National American Woman Suffrage Association when president
Chapman Catt supported the American entry into the war. In 1920 she was
a Socialist Party candidate for state representative. Like Henderson, she
placed greater emphasis on the economic causes of war than many of her
fellow pacifists (Alonzo, *The Women's Peace Union*, 12, 14–15). Caroline
Lexow Babcock was born in New York City in 1882. Educated at Barnard
College, she was the daughter of New York State Senator Clarence Lexow
and his wife, Katharine Morton Ferris (ibid., 25).

18 Schott, *Renconstructing Women's Thoughts*, 81, 83.

19 Alonzo, *The Women's Peace Union*, 15.

20 Ibid., 18.

21 Roberts, "Women against War," 58. For Prenter's anti-militarism during
the First World War, see Naylor, *The New Democracy*, 20. A major figure in
the Political Equality League, in 1920 Prenter established a women's page
in the *Industrial Banner*. In the federal election of 1921 she ran as a Labour
candidate in Toronto West. She was also active in the Independent Labor
Party, the Workers' Party of Canada, the Women's Labour League, and the
Canadian Labour Party, as well as the WILPF (Naylor, *The New Democracy*,
110, 143–4, 146, 237).

22 Swarthmore College Peace Collection (SCPC), Women's International
League for Peace and Freedom Papers (WILPF), 1915–1978, reel 57, frames
1739–1742, Laura Lunde to Miss Balch, 7 November [1919]. Note that
Henderson was a probation officer, not a judge, of the Montreal Juvenile
Court, and that she was at this time on the verge of losing her position as
a result of the raid on her residence on 1 July 1919.

23 Ibid., Laura Lunde to Miss Balch, 7 November [1919].

24 Roberts, "Women against War," 58.

25 Kealey, *Enlisting Women for the Cause*, 202.

26 Balch, co-founder and at this time secretary of the WILPF, was co-recipient of the Nobel Peace Prize in 1946.

27 SCPC, WILPF Papers, 1915–1978, reel 57, frames 1748–1750, Harriet Dunlop Prenter to Miss Balch, 13 January 1920.

28 Ibid., frame 1755, Emily Green Balch to Laura Hughes Lunde, 4 February (?) 1920.

29 Socknat, *Witness against War*, 58.

30 QUA, AGP, box 1, file 5, Literature Report, 15 October 1921.

31 Communist Party of Canada, *Canada's Party of Socialism*, 20. Penner, in *Canadian Communism*, 62, argues that the Workers' Party convention "was much more important to the history of Canadian communism than the secret Guelph meeting of May 1921" that created the Communist Party.

32 SCPC, WILPF Papers, 1915–1978, reel 57, frame 1817–18, Harriet Prenter to Emily Greene Balch, 24 March 1922.

33 *BC Federationist*, 20 February 1925.

34 Ibid., 13 February 1925.

35 Ibid., 27 February 1925.

36 Ibid., 3.

37 Ibid., 11, 12.

38 *Canadian Labor Advocate*, 18 September 1925.

39 Ibid.

40 Alonzo, *The Women's Peace Union*, 15.

41 Schott, *Reconstructing Women's Thoughts*, 109.

42 Born in 1881, Frazier was a farmer who graduated from the University of North Dakota in 1901 (Alonzo, *The Women's Peace Union*, 35).

43 Ibid., 41.

44 In a letter of 20 July 1926, Babcock explained to Christine Ross Barker that Henderson had been suggested to the WPU by Wilfred Wellock, a war resister who had toured the United States and possibly Canada in the fall of 1925 (SCPC, WPU, DG-44, reel 88.8, Christine Ross Barker Correspondence).

45 Ibid., reel 88.12, Correspondence H, Rose Henderson to Elinor Byrns, 12 April 1926.

46 Ibid. The word I have rendered as "base" could be "bare."

47 Ibid., Caroline Babcock to Rose Henderson, 20 May 1926.

48 Ibid., Rose Henderson to Caroline Babcock, 9 June 1926.

49 Ibid., Caroline Babcock to Rose Henderson, 17 June 1926.

50 Ibid., Rose Henderson to Caroline Babcock, 6 July 1926.

51 LAC, MG 26, J.1, vol. 154, WLMK, Correspondence, Primary Series 1926 (Grange-Hutchison), Rose Henderson to Mackenzie King, 8 July 1926.

52 The position caused great debate and dissension within the Communist Party of Canada. Buck held on tenaciously to the theory until 1930, when he was finally forced to acknowledge his error and accept the Communist International's definition of Canada as an imperialist country, not a colony (Penner, *The Canadian Left*, 86–96).

53 Buck, *Lenin and Canada*, 72.

54 Penner, *The Canadian Left*, 97.

55 LAC, MG 26, J.1, vol. 154, WLMK, Correspondence, Primary Series 1926 (Grange-Hutchison), Mackenzie King to Rose Henderson, 9 July 1926.

56 SCPC, WPU, DG-44, reel 88.12, Correspondence H, Rose Henderson to Caroline Babcock, 17 November 1926.

57 Ibid., Rose Henderson to Caroline Babcock, 23 December 1926.

58 Ibid., Caroline Babcock to Rose Henderson, 13 January 1927.

59 Ibid., reel 88.13, Correspondence H, Caroline Babcock to Rose Henderson, 28 March 1927.

60 Ibid., Caroline Babcock to Rose Henderson, 31 May 1927.

61 Ibid., Rose Henderson to Caroline Babcock, 21 March 1930. The word rendered as "diferent" appears as such in the typed copy. Equally plausible is "definite," and I cannot rule out a third possibility.

62 Ibid., Rose Henderson to Caroline Babcock, 1 April 1930.

63 Ibid., Caroline Babcock to Rose Henderson, 5 August 1930. This is the last letter in the Henderson-Babcock correspondence.

64 Alonzo, *The Women's Peace Union*, 128.

65 Ibid., 129. More credit on this issue should go to Christine Ross Barker, who appears to have been the longest serving and most involved of the Canadian supporters of the Women's Peace Union.

66 *Toronto Daily Star*, 11 January 1934.

CHAPTER SEVEN

1 On 15 March 1912 Henderson purchased the lot from a John L. Mitchell for the sum of $4,000. Two days earlier, on 13 March 1912, she had sold an

adjoining lot to Mitchell for $4,600. She also had a mortgage with Mitchell, discharged on 14 June 1921 (Toronto Land Registry Office, Plan 1191, Lot 28, 3–4).

2 Speisman, *Jews of Toronto*, 255. The riding is now Trinity-Spadina.

3 Toronto Land Registry Office, Plan 1191, Lot 28, 5.

4 Moritz and Moritz, in *The World's Most Dangerous Woman*, 141, quote Emma Goldman in the early 1930s to the effect that at the time the "poorest furnished apartment" in Montreal was $45 or $50 a month, rents in Toronto being cheaper. I have estimated rent in Henderson's apartments at $35 to $40 a month. If anything, the figure was likely lower in the early 1930s.

5 On 12 September 1932 Henderson turned ownership of the property over to her daughter, Ida. The amount remaining on the 1926 mortgage suggests that Henderson had been paying it off at an average rate of $750 a year. Whether she retained all, part, or none of the rental income following the transfer is unknown.

6 White, *Too Good to Be True*, 65.

7 Heron, *Booze*, 180.

8 Ibid., 275.

9 White, *Too Good to Be True*, 126.

10 Heron, *Booze*, 276.

11 White, *Too Good to Be True*, 69.

12 Ibid., 71.

13 Ibid., 159–60.

14 Ibid., 23.

15 Ibid., 194.

16 Ibid., 206–7.

17 Ibid., 103.

18 Ibid., 106.

19 Speisman, *Jews of Toronto*, 252.

20 White, *Too Good to Be True*, 111.

21 Speisman, *Jews of Toronto*, 319.

22 White, *Too Good to Be True*, 238.

23 Speisman, *Jews of Toronto*, 332.

24 Tulchinsky, *Branching Out*, 19.

25 Pierce, *Fifty Years of Public Service*, 16–17.

26 Bacchi, *Liberation Deferred?*, 29.

27 Cleverdon, *The Woman Suffrage Movement*, 8.

28 Bacchi, *Liberation Deferred?*, 32.

29 Pierce, *Fifty Years of Public Service*, 70.

30 Henderson, "The Departure of the Harvesters," *Canadian Unionist*, vol. 2, no. 5 (November 1928).

31 Archives of Ontario (AO), Quaker Archives (QA), MS303, B-2-49, reel 21, Toronto Monthly Meeting of Friends (TMMF), 19 October 1930.

32 *Canadian Friend*, November 1930, vol. 27, no. 5, reports that Henderson "was named and welcomed" as a member of the Toronto Monthly Meeting.

33 AO, QA, MS303, B-2-49, reel 21, TMMF, 19 November 1930.

34 Ibid., 17 December 1930.

35 Ibid., 20 January 1931.

36 Ibid., 18 March 1931.

37 Ibid., 15 April 1931.

38 Ibid., Newmarket Monthly Meeting, 7 May 1931.

39 *Toronto Daily Star*, 4 November 1929.

40 Ibid., 5 November 1929.

41 Moritz and Moritz, *The World's Most Dangerous Woman*, 96.

42 *Toronto Daily Star*, 13 November 1929.

43 Ann Augusta Stowe-Gullen, née Stowe, was born in Mount Pleasant, Canada West, on 27 July 1857. The daughter of Emily Stowe, she was the first woman to receive a medical degree in Canada in 1883. A founder of the National Council of Women of Canada, in 1903 she succeeded her mother as president of the Dominion Women's Enfranchisement Association. Stowe-Gullen taught at the Ontario Medical College for Women and sat on the University of Toronto Senate from 1910 to 1922. A leading figure in the suffrage and temperance movements, she was awarded the Order of the British Empire in 1935. She died in Toronto on 25 September 1943. See Carlotta Hacker, "Stowe-Gullen, Ann Augusta," *Canadian Encyclopedia Online*; Carlotta Hacker, *Indomitable Lady Doctors* (Toronto/Vancouver: Clark, Irwin, 1974), 29; Cleverdon, *The Woman Suffrage Movement in Canada*, 27.

44 *Toronto Daily Star*, 27 January 1930. Henderson was to preside at a talk at the Labour Forum on 167 Church Street on Sunday, 2 February 1930. The talk, given by Harry Sifton, was entitled "The Future of Democratic Government in Canada" (*Toronto Daily Star*, 1 February 1930).

45 *Toronto Daily Star*, 6 November 1930.

46 Speisman, *Jews of Toronto*, 216.

47 Rabbi Maurice Eisendrath (1902–73), born in Chicago, Illinois, was assist-
    ant contributing editor of the *Canadian Jewish Review*, co-founder of the
    Canadian Conference of Christians and Jews, and president of the Union of
    American Hebrew Congregations.

48 Speisman, *Jews of Toronto*, 216–17.

49 van den Hoonaard, "Biographical Zoning and Bahá'í Biographical
    Writing," 12.

50 Samuel Lewis, Ida's father, was of Lithuanian origin. The family came to
    Toronto from Pittsburgh in 1893.

51 Speisman, *Jews of Toronto*, 145–8.

52 Ibid., 181. Both Ida's father and her brother Abraham were Zionists.

53 Ibid., 170.

54 Ibid., 261.

55 Ibid., 150.

56 Ibid., 161n11.

57 Ibid., 152.

58 Dehli, "Love and Knowledge," 207.

59 Moritz and Moritz, *The World's Most Dangerous Woman*, 95.

60 *Toronto Daily Star*, 5 November 1930.

61 Ibid., 12 November 1930.

62 Ibid., 15 November 1930.

63 Moritz and Moritz, *The World's Most Dangerous Woman*, 100.

64 *Toronto Daily Star*, 1 June 1931.

65 Ibid., 11 December 1931. On the same evening candidates for the board of
    trustees also addressed the Oakwood Home and School Club.

66 Henderson was running for the Board of Education as a candidate of
    the Toronto Labour Party (*Labor Advocate*, vol. 2, no. 2 [December
    1931]).

67 AO, QA, MS303, B-2-49, reel 21, TMMF, 20 April 1932.

68 *Toronto Daily Star*, 28 October 1932.

69 Ibid., 29 October 1932.

70 Crowley, *Agnes Macphail and the Politics of Equality*, 67.

71 *Toronto Daily Star*, 17 December 1932.

72 Ibid., 29 December 1932.

73 Ibid., 31 December 1932.

74 Ibid., 30 December 1932.

75 Ibid., 17 December 1932.

76 Ibid., 3 January 1933. The minutes of the Toronto Monthly Meeting for January 1933 reveal that Henderson was then on the Friends Service Committee, which had Peace, Social Service, and Temperance sections (AO, QA, MS303, B-2-49, reel 21, TMMF, 18 January 1933).

77 *Toronto Daily Star*, 9 February 1933.

78 Ibid., 4 April 1933.

79 Ibid., 19 May 1933.

80 Ibid., 26 May 1933.

81 Ibid., 1 June 1933.

82 Mrs Harris McPhedran was the wife of John Harris McPhedran, a Toronto physician. Dr McPhedran, who knew Frederick Banting and Charles Best, was president of the Canadian Medical Association in 1944–45 and a life member of the Ontario Medical Association. Baroness de Hueck was born Ekaterina Fyodorovna Kolyschkine in Russia in 1896. In 1912 she married her first cousin Boris de Hueck. A Red Cross nurse during the First World War, she fled the Soviet Union with her husband following the revolution. In 1943, her first marriage annulled, she married the American reporter Eddie Doherty. In 1947 she and Doherty established Madonna House in Combermere, Ontario. She died there in 1985.

83 Maurutto, "Private Policing and Surveillance of Catholics," 121.

84 Ibid., 121–2.

85 Ibid., 124–5.

86 *Toronto Daily Star*, 7 November 1933.

87 It is entirely possible, of course, that de Hueck and McPhedran were interested in Henderson *because* she was in close contact with Communist Party members.

88 Naylor, *The New Democracy*, 106–7.

89 Ibid., 235.

90 Ibid., 236.

91 As Naylor points out, MacDonald had declared the ILP "moribund" as early as January 1921, before the Communist Party was even formally organized (*The New Democracy*, 238).

92 Robin, *Radical Politics and Canadian Labor*, 265.

93 Ibid.

94 *Labor News*, 24 April 1931.

95 On 21 April 1931 Henderson spoke in Mount Dennis on "Child Welfare." According to the *Star* (22 April 1931), there were "more than 500 members"

of the Ontario Labor Party in attendance to hear Henderson on child welfare, Jimmy Simpson on "Health Insurance," and J.W. Buckley on "Unemployment and Unemployment Insurance." There may have been five hundred people in attendance, but they were certainly not all members of the Ontario Labor Party The next night Henderson spoke to the York Township Labor Party (*Toronto Daily Star*, 23 April 1931).

96 Ibid., 28 March 1932; *Labor Leader*, 1 April 1932.

97 *Border City Labour News*, 24 May 1932

98 Ibid.

99 Naylor, *The New Democracy*, 146, 148.

100 Ibid., 79.

101 Ibid., 125.

102 Ibid., 137.

103 Ibid., 140–1.

104 *Industrial Banner*, 27 May, 3 June 1921.

105 Naylor, *The New Democracy*, 141.

106 Ibid., 140.

107 Ibid., 143.

108 *Labor Leader*, 29 May 1931; *Labor News*, 24 June 1931. Presumably Henderson was secretary of the Ontario Labor Party; Alderman Rod Plant of Ottawa was secretary-treasurer of the Labour Educational Association of Ontario, and Jean Laing was secretary of the UWEFO. See *Labour Gazette*, June 1931, 667.

109 Maurice Spector (1898–1968) was editor of *The Worker* and chair of the Communist Party of Canada in the 1920s. Expelled from the CPC in 1928 for Trotskyism, he organized a Canadian branch of the American-based Communist Labor Association in 1929. In 1932, with Jack MacDonald, he organized the International Left Opposition (Trotskyist) in Toronto. Spector later moved to New York and became a significant figure in the American Troskyist movement. See Palmer, "Maurice Spector, James P. Cannon, and the Origins of Canadian Trotskyism."

110 For the debate, see Angus, *Canadian Bolsheviks*, 277–88; Manley, "Canadian Communists, Revolutionary Unionism," 167–91; Desmond Morton, *Working People*, 142–5; Palmer, *Working-Class Experience*, 253–4.

111 Lévesque, *Red Travellers*, 61–8.

112 In August 1931 Henderson was a Yonge Street delegate to the Canada Yearly Meeting of Friends at Coldstream, Ontario (AO, QA, MS303, B-1-3, reel 13, Canada Yearly Meeting of Friends, 20 August 1931).

113 *The Worker*, 2 January 1932.

114 Horowitz, *Canadian Labour in Politics*, 64.

115 *Labour Gazette* 32 (May 1932): 549.

116 Elizabeth Morton was a member of the Women's Guild of the
Amalgamated Carpenters of Canada, a member of the Women's Labour
League, active in the Socialist Party of Ontario, secretary of the Labour
Conference, an activist in the East York Workers' Association, internation-
al delegate for the League against War and Fascism, and a member of the
Women's Joint Committee of the CCF. She was one of a small minority of
women who attended the founding convention of the CCF in Regina in
July 1933 (Sangster, *Dreams of Equality*, 112).

117 *Canadian Trade Unionist*, 29 September 1931.

118 For Lyon speaking out against anti-Asian racism in the labour movement
in the First World War period, see Campbell, *Canadian Marxists and the
Search for a Third Way*, 175. Naylor has revealed that Lyon was a member
of the OBU, then a member of the Workers' Party, in the early 1920s
(Naylor, *The New Democracy*, 242, 246).

119 Morton introduced her new column, "The Canadian Labor Woman," in
the 31 January 1930 issue of the *Canadian Trade Unionist*.

120 *Canadian Trade Unionist*, 13 October 1930.

121 Ibid., 29 September 1931.

122 Henderson's involvement with the National Labor Party was not extensive, but she did speak under its auspices. In January 1932, she gave a talk
in defence of free speech to the NLP's National Labor Forum (*Canadian
Trade Unionist*, 29 February 1932).

123 Ibid., 30 November 1932.

124 *Canadian Unionist*, vol. 6, no. 12 (May 1933).

125 Thompson with Seager, *Canada 1922–1939*, 231.

126 William Irvine (19 April 1885–26 October 1962), Scottish-born author of
The Farmers in Politics (1920), was first elected to the House of Commons
for the Dominion Labour Party in Calgary East in 1921, defeated in 1925,
and elected in the Alberta riding of Wetaskiwin in 1926 as a United
Farmers of Alberta candidate. He formed, along with his good friend J.S.
Woodsworth, the famous Ginger Group in the House of Commons.
Defeated by a Social Credit candidate in the 1935 federal election, Irvine
was re-elected in the Cariboo riding of British Columbia in 1945 but
was defeated in the 1949 election. He was unsuccessful in three election

attempts in the 1950s. He is remembered for his advocacy of group government and opposition to capital punishment in the 1920s and his unfailing support of the CCF throughout its existence. See McKay, *Reasoning Otherwise*, 205–6.

127 The Socialist Party of Canada (Ontario Section) was organized in Toronto on 7 February 1932. With a membership that likely never exceeded fifty, the SPC (OS) was nevertheless a key player in the formation of the CCF in Ontario. Too revolutionary for the leadership of the CCF and not revolutionary enough for the communists, leading figures in the SPC (OS), including Robinson, Morton, and Mould, have been forgotten, marginalized, or vilified by historians of both the CCF-NDP and the Communist Party because they did not accept the "line" of either party.

128 TFRBL, Woodsworth Memorial Collection (WMC) 35, box 10A, folder 61, J.S. Woodsworth to Bert Robinson, 3 February 1932.

129 Ibid., folder 50, Agnes Macphail, Bert Robinson to Agnes Macphail, 7 August 1932.

130 Ibid., folder 56, Bert Robinson, Bert Robinson to J.S. Woodsworth, 7 August 1932.

131 Morton, *Working People*, 148.

132 Ibid.

133 The League for Social Reconstruction, the "brain trust" of the CCF, emerged out of an August 1931 meeting of University of Toronto history professor Frank Underhill and McGill University law professor Frank Scott. Largely middle class in membership, the LSR's emphasis on social democracy and a planned economy is revealed in the titles of two books it published in the 1930s, *Social Planning for Canada* in 1935 and *Democracy Needs Socialism* in 1938 (Horn, *The League for Social Reconstruction*).

134 LAC, CCF Papers, MG 28, IV, I, vol. 41, Provinces, 1932–1958, Ontario – General Correspondence, 1932–February 1940, Toronto Labor Party Statement – per J.M. Conner.

135 Ibid.

136 QUA, AGP, box 3, file 11, Bert Robinson to Andrew Glen, 3 February 1933.

137 The number in attendance is given in Thompson and Seager, *Canada 1922–1939*, 231, and the quotation is from Crowley, *Agnes Macphail and the Politics of Equality*, 117.

138 Ibid., 120.

139 QUA, AGP, box 3, file 11, Bert Robinson to Andrew Glen, 3 February 1933.

140 Ibid.

141 LAC, CCF Papers, Provinces, 1932–1958, MG 28, IV, I, vol. 41, Ontario – General Correspondence, 1932–February 1940, Toronto Labor Party Statement – per J.M. Conner.

142 Graham Spry (1900–83), Canadian broadcaster, journalist and diplomat, was born in St Thomas, Ontario. He studied history at Oxford as a Rhodes Scholar. He was instrumental in convincing Prime Minister R.B. Bennett to create the Canadian Radio Broadcasting Commission, later the Canadian Broadcasting Corporation. A co-founder of the League for Social Reconstruction, Spry contributed to the writing of the Regina Manifesto. Chair of the Ontario CCF, 1934–36, he helped organize the Mackenzie-Papineau Battalion. In 1938 he married Irene Biss (1907–98), a leading Canadian economic historian and social democrat in her own right. From 1946 to 1968, Spry was agent general for Saskatchewan in the United Kingdom, Europe, and the Near East, for most of that period under the CCF government of Tommy Douglas. In 1962 he was at the forefront of the defence of medicare during the Saskatchewan doctors' strike. A Companion of the Order of Canada, he died in Ottawa (Robert E. Babe, "Spry, Graham," *Canadian Encyclopedia Online*).

143 TFRBL, WMC 35, CCF, Minutes of Provincial Council and Executive Meetings, box 1, file 1933.

144 *Toronto Daily Star*, 20 February 1933.

145 Crowley, *Agnes Macphail and the Politics of Equality*, 121.

146 Caplan, *The Dilemma of Canadian Socialism*, 25.

147 As previously noted, Henderson may also at this point have been on the executive committee of the National Labor Party with Elizabeth Morton.

148 TFRBL, WMC 35, box 12, file LSR, Minutes of Labor Conference Held in Cumberland Hall, Toronto, 26 February 1933.

149 Ibid. On Sunday, 26 March 1933, Henderson was to speak to the Theosophists at 52 Isabella Street, on the topic "Bernard Shaw: The Man and His Message" (*Toronto Daily Star*, 25 March 1933).

150 LAC, CCF Papers, MG28, IV, I, vol. 41, Provinces, 1932–1958, Ontario – General Correspondence, 1932– February 1940, Bert Robinson to Comrade Woodsworth, 16 April 1933.

151 Ibid.

152 Ibid.

153 Caplan, *The Dilemma of Canadian Socialism*, 25.

154 TFRBL, WMC 35, box 12, file LSR, April 1933, Minutes of Labor
Conference in Cumberland Hall, Toronto, April 23rd.

155 TFRBL, WMC 35, CCF, Minutes of Provincial Council and Executive
Meetings, box 1, file 1933. Elmore Philpott (2 May 1896–9 December
1964) was defeated when he ran for the leadership of the Ontario Liberal
Party against Mitchell Hepburn in 1930. In 1933 Philpott resigned his
position as an editorial writer with the *Globe* to join the CCF. He succeeded Lebourdais as president of the Ontario Association of CCF Clubs.
He resigned from the CCF in March 1935, then announced that he was re-
joining the Liberal Party. He moved to British Columbia in the 1940s,
where he served one term as MP for Vancouver South, 1953–57.

156 *Toronto Daily Star*, 26 May 1933.

157 TFRBL, WMC 35, CCF, Minutes of Provincial Council and Executive
Meetings, box 1, file 1933, Provincial Council of Ontario, 5 June 1933.

158 Ibid.

159 Whitehorn, *Canadian Socialism*, 38–45; Forsey, *A Life on the Fringe*, 53–6.

160 TFRBL, WMC 35, CCF, Minutes of Provincial Council and Executive
Meetings, box 1, file 1933, Provincial Council of Ontario, 5 June 1933.

161 Caplan, *The Dilemma of Canadian Socialism*, 36–7.

162 Forsey, *A Life on the Fringe*, 53–4. King Gordon was a professor of
Christian ethics at the United Theological College in Montreal and a
member of the Fellowship for a Christian Social Order.

163 *Labor News*, 31 August 1933.

164 Horowitz, *Canadian Labour in Politics*, 64.

165 Ibid., 65.

166 *Toronto Daily Star*, 27 May 1933.

167 Stanley B. Ryerson (1911–98), born into a middle-class Toronto family,
educated at the Sorbonne in Paris; served on the Central Committee of the
Communist Party of Canada, 1935–69, left the Communist Party in
1971; author of *1837: The Birth of Canadian Democracy*, *French Canada: A
Study in Canadian Democracy*, and *Unequal Union*. See Gregory Kealey,
"Stanley Brehaut Ryerson: Canadian Revolutionary Intellectual," 103–31,
and "Stanley Brehaut Ryerson: Marxist Historian," 133–70.

168 Ryerson, "Education and the Proletariat, Part II," *Masses* (May-June
1933).

169 TFRBL, WMC 35, box 10B, CCF Miscellaneous Material, file CCF Toronto District Council, "Minutes of Special Meeting of T & D Council," 7 December 1933.

170 *Toronto Daily Star*, 2 January 1934.

171 Ibid., 4 January 1934.

172 Ibid., 11 January 1934.

173 Ibid., 16 January 1934.

CHAPTER EIGHT

1 *Toronto Daily Star*, 5 December 1934.

2 *New Commonwealth*, 5 January 1935.

3 *Canadian Friend* 31, no. 8 (February 1935). The *Star* on 2 January 1935 identified Henderson as an Anglican, not a Quaker, a characterization likely based on misinformation, possibly based on a desire to heighten her credibility in the Toronto establishment.

4 Allen, *When Toronto Was for Kids*, quoted in Kilbourn, ed., *The Toronto Book*, 85–6.

5 *Toronto Daily Star*, 2 June 1934.

6 Ibid.

7 *Toronto Globe*, 8 February 1934.

8 *Toronto Daily Star*, 22 February 1934.

9 Ibid., 1 February 1935.

10 Ibid., 22 December 1934.

11 Ibid., 7 December 1934. The November 1934 log of use of school board cars showed that for the first time Henderson "led the list of trustees for regular time" (*Star*, 11 December 1934).

12 Ibid., 21 June 1935.

13 Ibid., 27 June 1935.

14 The TDSB's motor car log for June 1935 indicates that only five trustees used the board's cars. Henderson was by far the heaviest user; her 47¼ hours were followed by M.A. Brillinger's 23 hours, and S.T. Bigelow's and Lorne Trull's 10½ hours each (ibid., 13 July 1935). Ida Siegel was not on the 1935 board, having contested an aldermanic seat in Ward Four. She finished fourth, but was re-elected to the Board of Trustees for 1936, a telling commentary on the hesitancy of voters to elect women to "political" positions not explicitly linked to the care of children.

15 Ibid., 12 April 1935.

16 Ibid., 21 June 1935.

17 Ibid., 6 October 1934.

18 Ibid., 24 March 1934.

19 Toronto and District School Board Archives (TDSB), Minutes of the Board of Education for the City of Toronto (MBECT) 1934, 6 September 1934.

20 *Toronto Daily Star*, 5 October 1934. Earlier in the afternoon on 4 October, Henderson attended the regular monthly meeting of the Women's Association of the Danforth Avenue United Church. She gave an address on "Your Work" that dealt with child welfare and social service.

21 *Canadian Friend* 31, no. 5 (November 1934) reported that "Rose Henderson, Quakeress, ... is engaged in bringing to light much information about corporal punishment in Toronto schools and has succeeded in getting the appointment of a special committee to study student government systems."

22 *Toronto Daily Star*, 11 October 1934.

23 Ibid., 19 October 1934.

24 TDSB, MBECT 1934, 18 October 1934.

25 *Toronto Daily Star*, 22 February 1935.

26 TDSB, MBECT, 21 February 1935.

27 *Toronto Daily Star*, 6 March 1935.

28 TDSB, MBECT, 21 February 1935.

29 *Toronto Daily Star*, 8 March 1935; TDSBA, MBECT 1935, 7 March 1935.

30 *Canadian Friend* 31, no. 10 (April 1935).

31 *Toronto Daily Star*, 21 March 1935.

32 Ibid., 28 March 1935.

33 Ibid., 4 April 1935. On Sunday evening, 31 March 1935, Henderson had spoken to the South York CCF Club in the Orange Hall at Vaughan Road and Lauder. She was to speak on Sunday, 7 April 1935, to the Beaches CCF Club in the Masonic Temple on Balsam Avenue (*New Commonwealth*, 30 March and 6 April 1935).

34 *Toronto Daily Star*, 11 April 1935.

35 Ibid., 14 December 1935.

36 *Toronto Daily Star*, 3 May 1935.

37 Ibid., 6 June 1935.

38 *Toronto Daily Star*, 7 June 1935.

39 Comacchio, *Dominion of Youth*, 107. In July 1934 Henderson called Latin and geometry "time-wasters," part of a curriculum that was turning high school students into "nervous wrecks" (*Toronto Daily Star*, 11 July 1934).

40 Comacchio, *Dominion of Youth*, 108.

41 *Toronto Daily Star*, 11 July 1934.

42 Sangster, *Girl Trouble*, 153, 156.

43 Comacchio, *Dominion of Youth*, 167.

44 Ibid., 2.

45 Quoted in ibid, 165.

46 *Toronto Daily Star*, 21 June 1934.

47 Ibid.

48 Ibid., 13 September 1934.

49 Heron, *Booze*, 275.

50 Ibid., 291.

51 *Toronto Daily Star*, 14 September 1934.

52 Ibid., 5 December 1934. Henderson was on the executive committee of the Ward Five division of the Toronto Temperance Union.

53 *Toronto Daily Star*, 19 December 1934.

54 Ibid., 22 February 1935.

55 Comacchio, *The Dominion of Youth*, 167.

56 Ibid., 168.

57 *Toronto Daily Star*, 3 May 1934.

58 Ibid., 11 July 1934.

59 Ibid., 22 February 1935.

60 Ibid., 22 August 1935.

61 Ibid., 24 September 1934.

62 Ibid., 27 September 1934.

63 Ibid., 4 March 1935.

64 Comacchio, *Dominion of Youth*, 171.

65 Ibid., 13 December 1934.

66 Ibid., 4 March 1935.

67 Caplan, *Dilemma of Canadian Socialism*, 42.

68 Ibid., 42.

69 This is, to say the least, a debatable interpretation of what Philpott actually said.

70 Caplan, *Dilemma of Canadian Socialism*, 43.

71 Ibid., 43–4.

72 Crowley, *Agnes Macphail and the Politics of Equality*, 126.

73 *Toronto Evening Telegram*, 24 November 1933.

74 Ibid.

75 Ibid., 25 November 1933.

76 Ibid., 9 December 1933.

77 TFRBL, WMC 35, Minutes of CCF Ontario Provincial Council, 17 February 1934, box 1, file 1934.

78 Caplan, *The Dilemma of Canadian Socialism*, 52.

79 Ibid., 53.

80 Ibid.

81 Ibid., 55.

82 Ibid., 57.

83 Ibid., 58.

84 *Toronto Daily Star*, 31 March 1934.

85 Ibid.

86 *Toronto Evening Telegram*, 31 March 1934.

87 Ibid.

88 Ibid.

89 Ibid., 14 April 1934. According to a report in the *Telegram* of 16 April 1934, Simpson was knocked to the floor at one point when he tried to break up a fight between two delegates who were "under the influence of liquor."

90 Caplan, *The Dilemma of Canadian Socialism*, 59.

91 Ibid., 64–5.

92 Morley, *Secular Socialists*, 40.

93 *Toronto Daily Star*, 13 June 1934.

94 Caplan, *The Dilemma of Canadian Socialism*, 66.

95 *Toronto Globe*, 21 June 1934.

96 Frager, *Sweatshop Strife*, 142–3.

97 Steedman, *Angels of the Workplace*, 161.

98 Frager, *Sweatshop Strife*, 143.

99 For background on the campaign against abuses of the Minimum Wage Law as they affected women in the needle trades, see Steedman, *Angels of the Workplace*, 164.

100 *New Commonwealth*, 11 August 1934.

101 Frager, *Sweatshop Strife*, 143.

102 *Toronto Daily Star*, 7, 8 August 1934.

103 Frager, *Sweatshop Strife*, 143.

104 *Toronto Globe*, 11 September 1934.

105 *New Commonwealth*, 28 July 1934.

106 Ibid.

107 Penner, *Canadian Communism*, 135.

108 *The Worker*, 22 September 1934.

109 Ibid.

110 Ibid., 26 September 1934.

111 The 20 October 1934 issue of *The Worker* contained a sketch of Henderson that can be interpreted as depicting an aging woman suffering from health problems that would end her life little more than two years later.

112 In all probability Hygeia Hall was a preferred location, but it may also reflect the fact that Henderson was unable to book a school auditorium. Not surprisingly, there was great opposition to holding "political" meetings in school buildings, especially if they were of a left-wing nature.

113 TFRBL, Kenny Collection, Can Bro 0589, Program First Canadian Congress Against War and Fascism October 6th, and 7th, 1934, Toronto, Ontario.

114 Ibid.

115 Ibid., Can Pam 0588, Report First Canadian Congress Against War and Fascism, October 6th and 7th, 1934, Toronto, Ontario. Henderson is listed as being on both the presiding committee and the program committee.

116 Sangster, *Dreams of Equality*, 143, 252n44, 252n45.

117 *New Commonwealth*, 20 October 1934.

118 Ibid.

119 TDSB, MBECT 1934, 1 November 1934.

120 *Toronto Daily Star*, 2 November 1934.

121 TDSB, MBECT 1934, 7 November 1934.

122 *New Commonwealth*, 17 November 1934.

123 Ibid. Dorothy Detzer (1893–1981) campaigned for disarmament and economic justice and against the exploitation of Africa. She served as national executive secretary of the US section of the Women's International League for Peace and Freedom from 1924 to 1946. In 1948 she published *Appointment on the Hill*.

124 *Toronto Daily Star*, 18 April 1935.

125 *Toronto Globe*, 20 April 1935.

126 *New Commonwealth*, 27 April 1935.

127 Ibid.

128 *New Commonwealth*, 27 April 1935. Mould would appear to justify Simpson's attack a few days later by appearing on the platform of the May

Day rally in London, Ontario, with Communist Party member and personal friend Sam Scarlett. See Campbell, *Canadian Marxists and the Search for a Third Way*, 160.

129 *New Commonwealth*, 27 April 1935.

130 Penner, *Canadian Communism*, 138.

131 McMaster University, William Ready Archives (MUWRA), Canadian Youth Congress Fonds (CYCF), series 1, box 1, file 1, "Youth Council: What? Why? How?," no date.

132 MUWRA, CYCF, series 3, subseries 1, box 4, file 2, James Simpson, mayor, to W. John Stewart, secretary of the Canadian Youth Council, 20 February 1935.

133 Ibid., file 3, William Kashtan, national secretary of the Young Communist League of Canada to the Canadian Youth Council, 15 April 1935.

134 Ibid., file 2, W. John Stewart, secretary of the Canadian Youth Council to the Honourable Herbert A. Bruce, Lieutenant Governor of Ontario, 4 March 1935.

135 It appears that the request was initially turned down but then reversed when the board received a cheque for $42 to cover its expenses (*Toronto Evening Telegram*, 4 May 1935).

136 Socknat, *Witness against War*, 165–6; Comacchio, *Dominion of Youth*, 202–3. Norman Penner makes no mention of this conference.

137 MUWRA, CYCF, series 4, box 15, file 1, "Resolutions of the Congress Committee on Education," no date.

138 Penner, *Canadian Communism*, 134.

139 Manley, "'Audacity, Audacity, Still More Audacity,'" 20.

140 Ibid.

141 Penner, *Canadian Communism*, 139.

142 MUWRA, CYCF, series 3, subseries 1, box 4, file 2, *Youth Council Meeting, 3 June 1936*.

143 Sangster, *Dreams of Equality*, 124.

144 Ibid.

145 See www.marxists.org/history/international/comintern/7th-congress/index.htm.

146 *Toronto Daily Star*, 22 May 1935; *New Commonwealth*, 25 May 1935.

147 *New Commonwealth*, 15 June 1935.

148 *The Worker*, 21 September 1935.

149 *New Commonwealth*, 31 August 1935.

150 Ibid., 21 September 1935.

151 TFRBL, WMC 35, CCF Minutes of Provincial Council and Executive Meetings, 1933–1944, Ontario CCF Provincial Council Meeting, 15 September 1935, box 1, file 30, June–December 1935.

152 *New Commonwealth*, 21 September 1935.

153 *Toronto Daily Star*, 23 September 1935.

154 *The Worker*, 10 October 1935.

155 *Toronto Daily Star*, 11 October 1935.

156 The *Toronto Daily Star* had published a group photo of the same five women in its issue of 28 September 1935.

157 *Toronto Daily Star*, 12 October 1935.

158 *Toronto Globe*, 15 October 1935.

159 Ibid.

160 TFRBL, RKC, Can Pam F 0012, Proceedings, Second National Congress against War and Fascism, Toronto, Ontario December 6th, 7th, 8th, 1935.

161 City of Toronto Archives, Guild of All Arts, series 217, file 66, Education, Toronto Home and School Council, *Year Book*, June 1935.

162 *Toronto Daily Star*, 15 February 1934. Henderson attended a Board of Education meeting held that same evening (TDSB, MBECT 1934, 15 February 1934).

163 *Toronto Daily Star*, 23 March 1934.

164 Ibid., 6 June 1934.

165 Ibid., 7 June 1934.

166 Ibid., 10 August 1934.

167 Ibid., 20 and 27 October 1934. Henderson attended a meeting of the management committee on 24 October 1934 (ibid., 25 October 1934).

168 Ibid., 7 November 1934.

169 Frager, *Sweatshop Strife*, 146. Equal rights feminism was strongest in the United States, where the National Woman's Party (NWP) proposed an Equal Rights Amendment in 1923. Equal rights feminists thought of themselves as "true feminists," a slighting of maternal feminists who advocated protective legislation for women. According to Christine Bolt (*Sisterhood Questioned?*, 59), the NWP alienated British and American maternal feminists "by its singleminded advocacy of equal rights legislation," but no evidence has been found to suggest a comparable antagonism in Toronto in the 1930s.

170 Frager, *Sweatshop Strife*, 147.

171 *Toronto Globe*, 31 January 1934; *Toronto Daily Star*, 31 January 1934. In the evening Henderson attended a meeting of the Management Committee of the TDSB. See TDSB, Appendix to the Minutes of the Board of Education for the City of Toronto 1934.

172 Frager, *Sweatshop Strife*, 147. Frager senses the problem with drawing too stark a dichotomy and warns that the differences should not be exaggerated.

173 In January 1935 Henderson took one of the small steps forward for women when she acquired a seat on the Advisory Vocational Committee of the Toronto Board of Education. Dr W.H. Butt of Ward Seven stepped down so that there could be a woman on the committee (*Toronto Daily Star*, 16 January 1935).

174 McKenty, *Mitch Hepburn*, 41.

175 Ibid., 46.

176 TDSB, MBECT 1934, 20 September 1934

177 *Toronto Daily Star*, 25 January 1935.

178 TDSB, MBECT 1935, 24 January 1935.

179 Ibid., 30 November 1935.

180 Ibid., 28 December 1935.

181 *Canadian Friend* 32, no. 8 (February 1936).

CHAPTER NINE

1 *Toronto Globe*, 2 January 1936.

2 *New Commonwealth*, 4 January 1936.

3 Ibid.

4 *Toronto Daily Star*, 18 January 1936.

5 Ibid., 17 January 1936.

6 Ibid., 31 January 1936. On 14 February 1936 Henderson attended a party at Niagara Street Public School for former principal Allan B. Shantz. Henderson and C.M. Carrie, the trustees for Ward Five, "paid tribute to the work of Mr. Shantz and the valuable influence of Niagara Street school" (*Star*, 15 February 1936).

7 Ibid., 14 February 1936.

8 Ibid., 29 February 1936.

9 Ibid., 10 March 1936.

10 On 12 March 1936 the Dufferin Old Girls' Association held its eleventh annual banquet. Henderson was one of the many head table guests, who

included the wife of former mayor Sam McBride, the wife of former
Conservative Ontario premier George S. Henry, Alderman Mrs Plumptre,
Margaret Mackenzie, and Ida Siegel (*Toronto Daily Star*, 14 March 1936).

11 There is a notice of this meeting in the *New Commonwealth*, 21 March 1936.

12 *Toronto Daily Star*, 23 March 1936.

13 *New Commonwealth*, 8 February 1936.

14 *Toronto Daily Star*, 18 October 1935.

15 TDSB, MBECT 1936, 6 February 1936.

16 *Toronto Evening Telegram*, 19 February 1936.

17 Socknat, *Witness against War*, 112.

18 Ibid., 113.

19 Ibid., 132.

20 *Toronto Globe*, 21 February 1936. On Sunday, 1 March 1936, Henderson
spoke at the Friends' Meeting House on Maitland Street on "New Trends
toward World Peace" (*Toronto Daily Star*, 29 February 1936; *Canadian
Friend*, 32, no. 10 April 1936).

21 TDSB, MBECT 1936, 20 February 1936.

22 *Toronto Daily Star*, 7 February 1936.

23 McKenty, *Mitch Hepburn*, 78–9.

24 *Toronto Daily Star*, 7 April 1936.

25 McKenty, *Mitch Hepburn*, 80.

26 *Toronto Evening Telegram*, 7 March 1936.

27 LAC, CCF Papers, MG28 IV I, vol. 49, Ontario Council and Executive
Minutes, 1934–39, Minutes of Provincial Executive, 3 April 1936, reel
C-9284. John Walter, a Kitchener businessman, came out of the
Association of CCF Clubs. A former member of the American Socialist
Party, he once introduced Eugene Debs at a rally in Syracuse, New York.
Also a former member of the Social Democratic Party of Canada, in 1939–
40 Walter assisted Emma Goldman in her campaign against the incarcera-
tion of Attilio Bortolotti, an anarchist and leading Canadian anti-fascist.
See TFRLB, WMC 35, box 10a, folder 62, John Walter; Moritz and Moritz,
World's Most Dangerous Woman, 188, 190.

28 LAC, CCF Papers, MG28 IV I, vol. 49, Ontario Council and Executive
Minutes 1934–39, Minutes of Provincial Executive, 24 April 1936, reel
C-9284. William David Dennison (1905–1981) was a long-time Toronto
alderman and controller and was mayor of Toronto from 1966 to 1972. In
the 1920s he was a member of the United Farmers of Ontario, and became

a CCF supporter in the 1930s. He was an unsuccessful CCF candidate in Toronto's Rosedale riding in the 1935 federal election. Elected in the 1943 Ontario provincial election for the downtown Toronto riding of St David, he was defeated in the 1945 provincial election. Re-elected in the 1948 provincial election, he was defeated in the 1951 election, following which he was elected to Toronto City Council (*Globe and Mail*, 4 May 1981).

29 *Toronto Daily Star*, 12 February 1936.

30 Library of Parliament. Williams was born on 4 December 1894 in Tredegar, Wales.

31 Schulz, *East York Workers' Association*, 33.

32 Ian Angus, *Canadian Bolsheviks*; www.socialisthistory.ca/Docs/TrotOrigin/MayDay35.htm.

33 The Workers' Party of Canada that published *The Vanguard* was a Trotskyist party, the forerunner of the League for Socialist Action. It should not be confused with the Workers' Party of Canada, the above-ground organization of the Communist Party launched in February 1922.

34 *Toronto Daily Star*, 25 April 1936.

35 Ibid., 28 April 1936.

36 Ibid., 1 May 1936.

37 *Toronto Evening Telegram*, 2 May 1936. Tom Mann (15 April 1856–13 March 1941) was born in Foleshill, near Coventry. A leader of the 1889 London Strike, he became president of the General Labourers' Union that emerged from it. He emigrated to New Zealand in 1901, then went to Australia where he became an organizer for the labour and socialist movements. He returned to England in 1910, and helped organize the Communist Party of Great Britain in 1920–21. Following his retirement in 1921 he travelled the world as an advocate of socialism. After a speech made in Belfast in October 1932, he was sent to prison. In 1934 he was put on trial for sedition in Cardiff but was acquitted. In his autobiography (London: Nicolson and Watson, 1934), Philip Snowden describes Mann as "the most volcanic speaker I have known, and a man of marvellous physical vigour." See H.C.G. Matthew and Brian Harrison, eds., *Oxford Dictionary of National Biography* (Oxford: Oxford University Press, 2004), vol. 36, 453–56.

38 LAC, CCF Papers, MG28 IV 1, vol. 49, Ontario Council and Executive Minutes 1934–39, Minutes of Provincial Council, 9 May 1936, reel C-9284.

39 The Reverend Ben Spence was one of Toronto's leading temperance advocates. A member of the CCF provincial council in the mid-1930s, he served

as the first chairman of the Committee to Aid Spanish Democracy. He was also a member of the national council of the League against War and Fascism.

40 The three expelled members did not understand why Daniel Nesbitt, vice-president of the May Day Conference, was not expelled. Nesbitt, representative of the Amalgamated Clothing Workers, was a member of the Jewish Farband, which was affiliated with the CCF. The provincial council had apparently overlooked him, although Orloff claimed that because he had not renewed his membership for 1936, he was technically not a member of the CCF. Orloff (later Orliffe) was born in Newcastle, England, in 1905. He received a BA in history and politics from the University of Toronto in 1926 and graduated from Osgoode Law School in 1929. He served as secretary of the CCF provincial council from 1934 to 1939, as a trustee on the Toronto Board of Education, as an alderman for Ward Four, and as a member of Toronto Board of Control from 1961 to 1967. He died in July 1967.

41 *Toronto Daily Star*, 11 May 1936.

42 *New Commonwealth*, 20 June 1936.

43 For the CCF Women's Joint Committee, see John Manley, "Women and the Left in the 1930s." For the WJC and the PWA, see Sangster, *Dreams of Equality*, 111–13, 137–8, 140–1, 157.

44 Laing was active in the Toronto Women's Auxiliary of the International Association of Machinists in the First World War period. In the early 1930s she was secretary of the United Women's Educational Federation of Ontario, organized at the 1919 convention of the Labour Educational Association of Ontario. In 1934 she was hired as an organizer by the International Ladies' Garment Workers' Union, in which capacity she led the strike of Eaton's dressmakers in the late summer of 1934. In October 1934 she was a discussant at the first Canadian Congress of the League against War and Fascism. In January 1936 she was elected to the executive of the Toronto Trades and Labour Council. In the mid-1930s she was a leader of the Toronto Unemployed Single Women's Association. In the late 1940s she was a member of the Ontario Women's Committee of the CCF, involved, as Sangster observes, in "politicizing the homemaker." See Manley, "Women and the Left," 105; *Labour Gazette*, June 1931, 667; TFRBL, RKC, Can Bro 0589, Program First Canadian Congress against War and Fascism October 6th and 7th, 1934; Sangster, *Dreams of Equality*, 112, 217.

45 Alice Loeb, the wife of Bernard Loeb, was quite active in the WILPF in the 1920s and 1930s, serving at one point as president of the Toronto chapter. In the 1930s she and Anna Sissons organized Armistice Day peace demonstrations. Loeb was on the executive of the Ontario Association of CCF Clubs, and served as head of the CCF Literature Committee. She was also a participant in the First Canadian Congress against War and Fascism, October 1934. See Sangster, *Dreams of Equality*, 111; Caplan, *Dilemma of Canadian Socialism*, 26; Socknat, *Witness against War*, 113, 132.

46 TFRBL, WMC 35, box 10B, CCF Miscellaneous Materials, CCF Women's Joint Committee/Correspondence and Related Papers, Minutes of Meeting, 19 February 1936.

47 Ibid., Minutes of Meeting, 6 March 1936. The minutes identify fourteen women by name.

48 Ibid., Jean Laing to Dear Friend, 27 April 1936.

49 Jacob Lawrence Cohen (1898–1950) was born in Manchester and immigrated to Canada in 1908 with his family. His father died in 1911, and Cohen took on much of the responsibility for supporting his family. He worked his way through law school and graduated in 1918. Over the next two decades he became the most influential labour lawyer in Canada. The lawyer for the union in the legendary Oshawa strike of 1937, he was a member of the National War Labour Board during the Second World War, supporting the right of labour to strike and bargain collectively. He was disbarred in 1947 for assaulting his young secretary, then reinstated in January 1950. Four months later, on 24 May 1950, he committed suicide. See MacDowell, *Renegade Lawyer*.

50 Betcherman, *The Little Band*, 47–9.

51 TFRBL, WMC 35, box 10B, CCF Miscellaneous Material File: CCF Women's Joint Committee Correspondence and Related Papers, M. Tilton to Mr Herbert Orloff, 16 May 1936; M. Tilton to J.S. Woodsworth, 16 May 1936.

52 LAC, CCF Papers, MG28 IV 1, vol. 49, Ontario Council and Executive Minutes 1934–39, Minutes of Provincial Council, 9 May 1936, reel C-9284.

53 Sangster, *Dreams of Equality*, 137–8.

54 TFRBL, WMC 35, box 10B, CCF Miscellaneous Material, CCF Women's Joint Committee Minute Book 1936, Minutes of Meeting, 26 May 1936.

55 TFRBL, WMC 35, Box 10B, CCF Miscellaneous Material, file: CCF Women's Joint Committee Correspondence and Related Papers, Women's Conference

of the Ward 8 Women's Progressive Association Held on Wednesday May 27th, at the Prince George Hotel, Victorian Room, Toronto.

56 Ibid.

57 Sangster, *Dreams of Equality*, 138.

58 TFRBL, WMC 35, box 10B, CCF Miscellaneous Material, file: CCF Women's Joint Committee Correspondence and Related Papers, Women's Conference of the Ward 8 Women's Progressive Association Held on Wednesday May 27th, at the Prince George Hotel, Victorian Room, Toronto.

59 TFRBL, WMC 35, box 10B, CCF Miscellaneous Material, CCF Women's Joint Committee/Minute Book, 1936, Minutes of Meeting, 9 June 1936.

60 QUA, CCF-NDP Papers, series III, box 29, Minutes of the Provincial Executive and Council 18 August 1934 to 2 April 1942, Meeting of Provincial Council, 13 June 1936.

61 LAC, CCF Papers, MG28, IV, I, vol. 49, reel C-9284, Provinces, Ontario Council and Executive Minutes, 1934–39, Minutes of Provincial Council, 2 August 1936.

62 Ibid.

63 *Toronto Daily Star*, 4 August 1936.

64 Ibid.

65 Henderson was referring to the Moose River Mine Disaster. On 12 April 1936 mine timekeeper Alfred Scadding, David Robertson, chief of staff at Toronto's Hospital for Sick Children, and Herman Russell Magill, a Toronto lawyer, were trapped in the Nova Scotia gold mine. After heroic efforts by local miners to free them, Scadding and Robertson were rescued just after midnight on 23 April 1936. Magill had died three days earlier. J. Frank Willis arrived in Moose River on 20 April 1936 and created North America's first ever twenty-four hour news event that reached some 100 million people in Canada, the United States, and Britain (CBC Digital Archives, http://archives.cbc.ca/on_this_day/04/12).

66 LAC, MG 28, IV, I, vol. 10, CCF National Conventions and Inter-Provincial Conferences, 1932–60, 1936 Convention Minutes, 2nd Session, 3 August 1936.

67 For the Amalgamated Mine Workers see Earle, "The Coalminers and Their 'Red' Union," and Frank, *J.B. McLachlan*. For the United Mine Workers see MacEwen, *Miners and Steelworkers*; Mellor, *The Company Store*; and Frank, *J.B McLachlan*.

68 LAC, CCF Papers, MG28, IV I, vol. 10, National Conventions and Inter-Provincial Conferences, 1936 Convention Minutes of 5th Session.

69 *Toronto Daily Star*, 4 August 1936.

70 For Michael Rubinstein, a Montreal lawyer, see Lévesque, *Virage à gauche interdit*, 87, 114.

71 LAC, CCF Papers, MG28 IV I, vol. 10, National Conventions and Inter-Provincial Conferences, 1936 Convention Minutes of 3rd Session.

72 Horn, "Lost Causes," 149–50. In the event, it was an ill-fated appointment; in 1944 Casgrain was fired following reports of "heavy drinking, extravagant expenditures, and failure to honour commitments" (Lewis, *The Good Fight*, 246).

73 For a succinct and revealing explanation of the CCF's weakness in Quebec, see Lévesque, *Virage à gauche interdit*, 94–5.

74 LAC, CCF Papers, MG28, IV I, vol. 10, National Conventions and Inter-Provincial Conferences, 1936 Convention Minutes of 2nd Session, 3 August 1936.

75 Ibid. Delegate Floor stated that as prisoners of a cause the trekkers would not want any bargain made with the government. Woodsworth, who "retorted" to Floor's comment, apparently felt that his integrity was being impugned (*Toronto Daily Star*, 4 August 1936).

76 Ibid.

77 Ibid., 6 August 1936.

78 LAC, CCF Papers, MG28, IV, I, vol. 10, National Conventions and Inter-Provincial Conferences, 1932–1960, 1936 Convention, 7th Session – Minutes.

79 *Toronto Daily Star*, 6 August 1936.

80 LAC, CCF Papers, MG28, IV, I, vol. 10, National Conventions and Inter-Provincial Conferences, 1932–1960, 1936 Convention, 7th Session – Minutes.

81 *Toronto Daily Star*, 6 August 1936.

82 While I do not know for certain, in all probability this is Bert Robinson, former official in the Socialist Party of Canada (Ontario Section).

83 LAC, CCF Papers, MG28, IV, I, vol. 10, National Conventions and Inter-Provincial Conferences, 1932–1960, 1936 Convention, 7th Session – Minutes.

84 Lewis, *The Good Fight*, 101.

85 LAC, CCF Papers, MG28 IV I, vol. 10, National Conventions and Inter-Provincial Conferences, 1932–1960, 1936 Convention, 7th Session – Minutes.

86 Lewis, *The Good Fight*, 107–8; Young, *The Anatomy of a Party*, 267–8. Young goes too far when he claims that Lewis "was himself carried away by

the logic of the popular front idea." Lewis's primary commitment, right or wrong, was always to the CCF and its policies, and his support for Salsberg may have had as much to do with wanting to help a fellow Jew in a still anti-Semitic society as it had to do with any ideological commitment to the Popular Front.

87 Lewis, *The Good Fight*, 102.

88 Sangster, *Dreams of Equality*, 249n36.

89 *Canadian Friend* 33, no. 1 (July 1936).

90 While Henderson did not organize the competition alone, Socknat's observation that she "helped to organize" the competition can be interpreted as suggesting that someone else played a more important role (*Witness against War*, 132).

91 SCPC, WILPF Papers 1915–1978, reel 58, frame 57, Women's International League for Peace and Freedom, Toronto Branch Newsletter, July 1936.

92 Socknat, *Witness against* War, 165; *Toronto Daily Star*, 21 August 1936. Margaret Crang (1910–92) was elected to Edmonton City Council in 1933 as a Canadian Labor Party candidate. A labour lawyer, Crang supported the CCF and worked with Communist Party unemployed organizations. She went to the 1936 World Peace Congress in Brussels as a representative of the Edmonton branch of the League against War and Fascism. After the Congress she went to Spain. For Crang and the controversy that swirled around her actions in Spain see Larry Hannant, "'My God, Are They Sending Women?'" Mrs John Grieve may be the wife of the John Grieve who served as the Liberal member of the Ontario legislature for Middlesex North, 1914–19. Mrs C.D. Farquharson may have a connection with the C.D. Farquharson junior public school in Scarborough, Ontario.

93 Socknat, *Witness against War*, 167.

94 *Toronto Daily Star*, 17 August 1936.

95 Ibid., 21 August 1936.

96 TDSB, MBECT 1936, 1 October 1936.

97 *Toronto Daily Star*, 3 October 1936.

98 *Canadian Friend* 33, no. 5 (November 1936).

99 *Toronto Daily Star*, 3 October 1936.

100 Ibid., 5 October 1936

101 *New Commonwealth*, 31 October 1936.

102 *Toronto Daily Star*, 28 November 1936.

103 The previous evening Henderson had attended a meeting of the Special Committee of the Board of Education (*Toronto Daily Star*, 15 October 1936).

104 *Toronto Daily Star*, 16 October 1936.

105 *Toronto Evening Telegram*, 30 November 1936.

106 Ibid., 4 December 1936.

107 Ibid., 5 December 1936.

108 *Toronto Daily Star*, 8 December 1936.

109 *Toronto Evening Telegram*, 8 December 1936.

110 TDSB, Minutes of Advisory Vocational Committee, 12 January 1937.

111 Ibid., 26 January 1937.

112 *Toronto Daily Star*, 14 January 1937.

113 TDSB, MBCET, 21 January 1937.

114 Ibid.

115 *Toronto Globe and Mail*, 1 February 1937.

116 *Toronto Daily Star*, 1 February 1937.

117 *Daily Clarion*, 1 February 1937.

118 *Toronto Globe and Mail*, 1 February 1937.

119 *Toronto Evening Telegram*, 1 February 1937.

120 *Toronto Daily Star*, 1 February 1937.

121 Ibid., 2 February 1937.

122 *New Commonwealth*, 6 February 1937.

123 Ibid.

124 *Daily Clarion*, 1 February 1937.

125 Ibid.

126 Ibid.

127 Ibid.

128 For Romney Davis, see Macke, *Take My Love to the Friends*.

129 *Daily Clarion*, 6 February 1937.

130 This letter had appeared two days earlier in the *Star*, with the paragraph beginning "I met her first" omitted.

131 LAC, CCF Papers, MG28 IV I, vol. 49, Ontario Council and Executive Minutes 1934–39, Minutes of Provincial Executive, 6 February 1937, reel C-9284.

132 *Daily Clarion*, 10 February 1937. A similar announcement appeared in the 10 February 1937 edition of the *Globe and Mail*.

133 *Toronto Daily Star*, 2 April 1937.

134 Ibid., 26 May 1938.

Bibliography

ARCHIVAL COLLECTIONS

Archives de la Ville de Montréal (AVM).
Archives Nationales du Québec (ANQ):
   Fonds du Ministère de la Justice.
Archives of Ontario: Quaker Archives
City of Toronto: Council Minutes.
City of Toronto Archives:
   Guild of All Arts.
La Bibliothèque Centrale de Montréal.
Library and Archives Canada (LAC):
   Arthur Meighen Papers; Cooperative Commonwealth Federation Papers;
   Department of Labour; Privy Council Records; Mackenzie King Diaries;
   Mackenzie King Papers; Records of Federal Royal Commissions; Sir Wilfrid
   Laurier Papers.
McGill University Archives: Royal Victoria Hospital Medical Register.
McMaster University, William Ready Division of Archives:
   Canadian Youth Congress Fonds.
Queen's University Archives:
   Andrew Glen Papers; CCF/NDP Papers.
Swarthmore College Peace Collection:
Women's International League for Peace and Freedom Papers.
Women's Peace Union Collection.

Thomas Fisher Rare Book Library (TFRBL):

   Canadian Pamphlets and Broadsheets Collection; Robert A. Kenny
   Collection; Woodsworth Memorial Collection.

Toronto and District School Board Archives:

   Violet McNaughton Fonds.

CONTEMPORARY PUBLISHED SOURCES

Canadian Annual Review.

Government of Canada, *Census of 1891, 1901, 1911.*

Hansard.(Canada).

Journals of the House of Commons of the Dominion of Canada.

Labour Gazette.

Lovell's Directory, Montreal.

Social Service Council of Canada.

Toronto City Directory.

Toronto Land Registry Office.

Trades and Labour Congress of Canada, *Report of Proceedings*, 1912, 1916, 1917, 1918.

LABOUR AND SOCIALIST PAPERS

Border City Labour News.

British Columbia Federationist.

Canadian Farmer-Labor Advocate.

Canadian Labor Advocate.

Canadian Friend.

Canadian Labour Press.

Canadian Trade Unionist.

Canadian Unionist.

The Citizen.

Cotton's Weekly.

Daily Clarion.

Industrial Banner.

Labor Advocate.

Labor Leader.

Labor News.

Labor Statesman.

Le Monde Ouvrier/The Labor World.
Maritime Labor Herald.
New Commonwealth.
One Big Union Bulletin.
Socialist Action.
The Worker.
Workers' Weekly.

NEWSPAPERS AND NON-LABOUR PAPERS

Canadian Jewish Chronicle.
Canadian Jewish Times.
Canadian Municipal Journal.
Canadian Theosophist.
Hamilton Spectator.
Manitoba Free Press.
Montreal Daily Star.
Montreal Daily Herald.
Montreal Gazette.
Star of the West.
Toronto Daily Star.
Toronto Globe.
Toronto Evening Telegram.
Toronto Mail and Empire.
Woman's Century.

INTERNET SOURCES

www.marxists.org/history/international/comintern/7th-congress/index.htm.
www.socialisthistory.ca/Docs/TrotOrigin/MayDay35.htm

SECONDARY SOURCES

Allen, Richard. *The Social Passion: Religion and Social Reform in Canada*, 1914–28. Toronto: University of Toronto Press 1971.
Alonzo, Harriet Hyman. *The Women's Peace Union and the Outlawry of War, 1921–1942*. Knoxville: University of Tennessee Press 1989.

Ames, Herbert B. *The City below the Hill*. Introduced by P.F.W. Rutherford.
    Toronto: University of Toronto Press 1972.

Angus, Ian. *Canadian Bolsheviks: The Early Years of the Communist Party of
    Canada*. Montreal: Vanguard 1981.

Avery, Donald. *"Dangerous Foreigners": European Immigrant Workers and Labour
    Radicalism in Canada, 1896–1932*. Toronto: McClelland & Stewart 1979.

Bacchi, Carol Lee. *Liberation Deferred? The Ideas of the English-Canadian
    Suffragists, 1877–1918*. Toronto: University of Toronto Press 1983.

Béïque, Caroline. *Quatre-vingts ans de souvenirs: Histoire d'une famille*. Montreal:
    Éditions Bernard Valiquette 1939.

Bercuson, David. *Confrontation at Winnipeg: Labour, Industrial Relations and the
    General Strike*. Montreal and Kingston: McGill-Queen's University Press
    1990.

– "Labour Radicalism and the Western Industrial Frontier, 1897–1919."
    Canadian Historical Review 58, no. 2 (1977).

– "Through the Looking Glass of Culture: An Essay on the New Labour
    History and Working-Class Culture in Recent Canadian Historical
    Writing." *Labour/Le travailleur* 7 (spring 1981).

Betcherman, Lita-Rose. *The Little Band: The Clashes between the Communists and
    the Canadian Establishment, 1928–1932*. Ottawa: Deneau, n.d.

Black, J.L. *Canada in the Soviet Mirror: Ideology and Perception in Soviet Foreign
    Affairs, 1917–1991*. Ottawa: Carleton University Press 1998.

Bolt, Christine. *Sisterhood Questioned?: Race, Class and Internationalism in the
    American and British Women's Movements, c. 1880s–1970s* (New York and
    London: Routledge 1994).

Boyle, John W. "A Fenian Protestant in Canada: Robert Lindsay Crawford,
    1910–22." *Canadian Historical Review* 52, no. 2 (1971).

Bradbury, Bettina. "Women's History and Working-Class History." *Labour/Le
    Travail* 19 (spring 1987).

Brown, Kathleen A. "The 'Savagely Fathered and Un-Mothered World' of the
    Communist Party, U.S.A.: Feminism, Maternalism, and 'Mother Bloor.'"
    Feminist Studies 25, no. 3 (fall 1999).

Brown, Robert Craig. *Robert Laird Borden: A Biography*. Vols. 1 and 2. Toronto:
    Macmillan 1975.

Buck, Tim. *Lenin and Canada*. Toronto: Progress Books 1970.

Bussey, Gertrude, and Margaret Tims. *Pioneers for Peace: The International League
    for Peace and Freedom, 1915–1965*. London: WILPF British Section 1980.

Caine, Barbara. "Feminist Biography and Feminist History." *Women's History Review* 3, no. 2 (1994).

Campbell, Peter. *Canadian Marxists and the Search for a Third Way.* Kingston and Montreal: McGill-Queen's Press 1999.

– "Making Socialists: Bill Pritchard, the Socialist Party of Canada, and the Third International." *Labour/Le travail* 30 (fall 1992).

Caplan, Gerald. *The Dilemma of Canadian Socialism: The CCF in Ontario.* Toronto: McClelland & Stewart 1973.

Chown, Alice A. *The Stairway.* Toronto: University of Toronto Press 1988.

Christie, Nancy. *Engendering the State: Family, Work, and Welfare in Canada.* Toronto: University of Toronto Press 2000.

Christie, Nancy, and Michael Gauvreau. *A Full-Orbed Christianity: The Protestant Churches and Social Welfare in Canada, 1900–1940.* Montreal and Kingston: McGill-Queen's University Press 1996.

Claeys, Gregory. *The French Revolution Debate in Britain.* Houndmills, Basingstoke, Hampshire: Palgrave MacMillan 2007.

Cleverdon, Catherine. *The Woman Suffrage Movement in Canada.* Toronto: University of Toronto Press 1974.

Cline, Catherine. *E.D. Morel, 1873–1924: The Strategies of Protest.* Belfast: Blackstaff Press 1980.

Comacchio, Cynthia. *The Dominion of Youth: Adolescence and the Making of Modern Canada, 1920 to 1950.* Waterloo: Wilfrid Laurier University Press 2006.

Communist Party of Canada. *Canada's Party of Socialism: History of the Communist Party of Canada, 1921–1976.* Toronto: Progress Books 1982.

Copp, Terry. *An Anatomy of Poverty: The Condition of the Working Class in Montreal, 1897–1929.* Toronto: McClelland & Stewart 1974.

Cottrell, Peter. *The Anglo-Irish War: The Troubles of 1913–1922.* Oxford: Osprey 2006.

Crowley, Terry. *Agnes Macphail and the Politics of Equality.* Toronto: James Lorimer 1990.

Dehli, Kari. "Love and Knowledge: Adult Education in the Toronto Home and School Council, 1916–40." *Ontario History* 88, no. 3 (September 1996).

Dumont, Micheline, Michèle Jean, Marie Lavigne, and Jennifer Stoddart. *Quebec Women: A History.* Toronto: Women's Press 1987.

Dumont, Micheline, and Louise Toupin. *La Pensée féministe au Québec.* Montreal: Les Éditions de remue-ménage 2003.

Earle, Michael J. "The Coalminers and their 'Red' Union: The Amalgamated Mine Workers of Nova Scotia, 1932–1936." *Labour/Le travail* 22 (fall 1988).

Early, Frances H. *A World without War: How U.S. Feminists and Pacifists Resisted World War I*. Syracuse: Syracuse University Press 1997.

Engels, Frederick. *Socialism: Utopian and Scientific*. New York: International Publishers 1985.

English, John. *Borden: His Life and World*. Toronto and New York: McGraw-Hill Ryerson 1977.

– *The Decline of Politics: The Conservatives and the Party System, 1901–1920*. Toronto: University of Toronto Press 1977.

English, John, and Réal Bélanger, eds. *Dictionary of Canadian Biography*. Toronto: University of Toronto Press 2005.

Ewen, Geoffrey. "Quebec: Class and Ethnicity." In *The Workers' Revolt in Canada, 1917–1925*, edited by Craig Heron. Toronto: University of Toronto Press 1998.

Figes, Orlando. *A People's Tragedy: The Russian Revolution 1891–1924*. London, Pimlico 1996.

Fitzpatrick, Sheila. *The Russian Revolution, 1917–1936*. Oxford and New York: Oxford University Press, 1985.

Forsey, Eugene. *A Life on the Fringe: The Memoirs of Eugene Forsey*. Toronto: Oxford University Press 1990.

Foster, Carrie A. *The Women and the Warriors: The U.S. Section of the Women's International League for Peace and Freedom, 1915–1946*. Syracuse: Syracuse University Press 1995.

Foster, Catherine. *Women for All Seasons: The Story of the Women's International League for Peace and Freedom*. Athens: University of Georgia Press 1989.

Fowler, Robert Booth. *Carrie Catt: Feminist Politician*. Boston: Northeastern University Press 1986.

Frager, Ruth. *Sweatshop Strife: Class, Ethnicity, and Gender in the Jewish Labour Movement of Toronto, 1900–1939*. Toronto: University of Toronto Press 1992.

Frank, David. *J.B. McLachlan: A Biography*. Toronto: James Lorimer 1999.

French, Doris, and Margaret Stewart. *Ask No Quarter: A Biography of Agnes Macphail*. Toronto: Longmans, Green 1959.

Gabel, Paul. *And God Created Lenin: Marxism vs. Religion in Russia, 1917–1929*. New York: Prometheus Books 2005.

Goldman, Wendy Z. *Women, the State, and Revolution: Soviet Family Policy and Social Life, 1917–1936*. Cambridge: Cambridge University Press 1993.

Griffiths, N.E.S. *The Splendid Vision: Centennial History of the National Council of Women of Canada, 1893–1993*. Ottawa: Carleton University Press 1993.

Hannant, Larry. "'My God, Are They Sending Women?': Three Canadian Women in the Spanish Civil War, 1936–1939." *Journal of the Canadian Historical Association/Revue de la société Historique du Canada* 15, no. 1 (2004).

Harrison, Robert. *State and Society in Twentieth-Century America*. London and New York: Longman 1997.

Heller, Otto. *Prophets of Dissent: Essays on Maeterlinck, Strindberg, Nietzsche and Tolstoy*. New York: Alfred A. Knopf 1918.

Henderson, Rose. *Kids What I Knows*. Montreal: W.H. Eaton and Sons, n.d.

– *Woman and War*. Vancouver: Federated Labour Party 1925.

Heron, Craig. *Booze: A Distilled History*. Toronto: Between the Lines 2003.

– "Labourism and the Canadian Working Class." *Labour/Le travail* 13 (spring 1984).

Higashi, Sumiko. *Cecil B. De Mille and American Culture: The Silent Era*. Berkeley: University of California Press 1994.

Hobbs, Margaret, and Joan Sangster. *The Woman Worker, 1926–1929*. St John's: Canadian Committee on Labour History 1999.

Hochschild, Adam. *King Leopold's Ghost: A Story of Greed, Terror, and Heroism in Colonial Africa*. New York: Mariner Books 1999.

Hofstadter, Richard. *The Age of Reform*. New York: Vintage Books 1955.

Horn, Michiel. "Lost Causes": *"Lost Causes": The League for Social Reconstruction*. Toronto: University of Toronto Press 1981.

Horowitz, Gad. *Canadian Labour in Politics*. Toronto: University of Toronto Press 1968.

Johnston, Faith. *A Great Restlessness: The Life and Politics of Dorise Nielsen*. Winnipeg: University of Manitoba Press 2006.

Jones, Andrew, and Leonard Rutman. *In the Children's Aid: J.J. Kelso and Child Welfare in Ontario*. Toronto: University of Toronto Press 1981.

Kealey, Gregory S. "Labour and Working-Class History in Canada: Prospects in the 1980s." *Labour/Le travailleur* 7 (spring 1981).

– "1919: The Canadian Labour Revolt." In *The Character of Class Struggle: Essays in Canadian Working-Class History*, edited by Bryan D. Palmer. Toronto: McClelland & Stewart 1986.

– "Spymasters, Spies, and Their Subjects: The RCMP and Canadian State Repression, 1914–39." In *Whose National Security? Canadian State Surveillance and the Creation of Enemies*, edited by Gary Kinsman, Dieter K. Buse, and Mercedes Steedman. Toronto: Between the Lines 2000.

– "Stanley Brehaut Ryerson: Canadian Revolutionary Intellectual." *Studies in Political Economy* 9 (fall 1982).

– "Stanley Brehaut Ryerson: Marxist Historian." *Studies in Political Economy* 9 (fall 1982).

– "State Repression of Labour and the Left in Canada, 1914–20: The Impact of the First World War." *Canadian Historical Review* 73, no. 3 (September 1992).

Kealey, Gregory S., and Bryan D. Palmer. *Dreaming of What Might Be: The Knights of Labor in Ontario, 1880–1900*. Toronto: New Hogtown Press 1987.

Kealey, Gregory S., and Reg Whitaker, eds. *R.C.M.P. Security Bulletins: The Early Years, 1919–1929*. St John's: Canadian Committee on Labour History 1994.

Kealey, Linda. *Enlisting Women for the Cause: Women, Labour, and the Left in Canada, 1890–1920*. Toronto: University of Toronto Press 1998.

Kelso, J.J. "A Pension for Widowed Mothers." *Social Service* (November 1904).

Kilbourn, William, ed. *The Toronto Book*. Toronto: MacMillan 1976.

Kissane, Bill. *The Politics of the Irish Civil War*. Oxford: Oxford University Press 2005.

Kolko, Gabriel. *The Triumph of Conservatism*. New York: Free Press 1963.

Koven, Seth, and Sonya Michel, eds. *Mothers of a New World: Maternalist Politics and the Origins of Welfare States*. New York and London: Routledge 1993.

Lavigne, Marie, and Yolande Pinard. *Les Femmes dans la société québécoise: Aspects historiques*. Montreal: Éditions du Boréal Express 1977.

Lavigne, Marie, and Jennifer Stoddart. "Women's Work in Montreal at the Beginning of the Century." In *Women in Canada*, edited by Marylee Stephenson. Don Mills: General Publishing 1977.

Lévesque, Andrée. *Virage à gauche interdit: Les communistes, les socialistes, et leurs ennemis au Québec, 1929–1939*. Montreal: Boréal Express 1984.

– *Red Travellers: Jeanne Corbin and Her Comrades*. Montreal and Kingston: McGill-Queen's University Press 2006.

– *Eva Circé-Côté. Libre penseuse, 1871–1949*. Montreal: Les éditions du remue-ménage 2010.

Lewis, David. *The Good Fight: Political Memoirs, 1909–1958*. Toronto: Macmillan 1981.

Lewis, S.P. *Grace: The Life of Grace MacInnis*. Madeira Park, BC: Harbour Publishing 1993.

Linteau, Paul André. *Histoire de Montréal depuis la Confédération*. Quebec: Boréal 2000.

Lipton, Charles. *The Trade Union Movement of Canada, 1827–1959*. Montreal: Canadian Social Publications 1968.

Little, Margaret. *"No Car, No Radio, No Liquor Permit": The Moral Regulation of Single Mothers in Ontario, 1920–1997*. Toronto: Oxford University Press 1998.

Lusane, Clarence. *Hitler's Black Victims: The Historical Experience of Afro-Germans, European Blacks, Africans, and African Americans in the Nazi Era*. New York: Routledge 2002.

MacDowell, Laurel Sefton. *Renegade Lawyer: The Life of J.L. Cohen*. Toronto: University of Toronto Press 2001.

MacEwen, Paul. *Miners and Steelworkers: Labour in Cape Breton*. Toronto, 1976.

Macke, Marlene. *Take My Love to the Friends: The Story of Laura R. Davis*. St Marys, ON: Chestnut Park Press 2009.

MacQuarrie, Heath, ed. *Robert Laird Borden: His Memoirs*. Vol. 1, *1854–1915*. Toronto: McClelland & Stewart 1969.

Maeterlinck, Maurice. *The Blue Bird: A Fairy Play in Six Acts*. New York: Dodd, Mead and Co. 1914.

Manley, John. "'Audacity, Audacity, Still More Audacity': Tim Buck, the Party, and the People, 1932–1939." *Labour/Le travail* 49 (spring 2002).

– "Canadian Communists, Revolutionary Unionism, and the 'Third Period': The Workers' Unity League, 1929–1935." *Journal of the Canadian Historical Association* 5 (1994).

– "Women and the Left in the 1930s: The Case of the Toronto CCF Women's Joint Committee." *Atlantis* 5, no. 2 (spring 1980).

Mann Trofimenkoff, Susan. "Feminist Biography." *Atlantis* 10, no. 2 (spring 1985).

– *The Dream of Nation: A Social and Intellectual History of Quebec*. Toronto: Gage 1983.

Maurutto, Paula. "Private Policing and Surveillance of Catholics: Anti-Communism in the Roman Catholic Archdiocese of Toronto, 1920–1960." *Labour/Le travail* 40 (fall 1997).

May, Henry F. *The End of American Innocence: A Study in the First Years of Our Own Time, 1912–1917*. Chicago: Quadrangle Books 1959.

McClung, Nellie. *In Times Like These*. Toronto and Buffalo: University of Toronto Press 1972.

McCormack, A. Ross. *Reformers, Rebels, and Revolutionaries: The Western Canadian Radical Movement, 1899–1919*. Toronto and Buffalo: University of Toronto Press 1977.

McKay, Ian. *Reasoning Otherwise: Leftists and the People's Enlightenment in Canada, 1890–1920*. Toronto: Between the Lines 2008.

McKenty, Neil. *Mitch Hepburn*. Toronto: McClelland & Stewart 1967.

McLaren, Angus. *Our Own Master Race: Eugenics in Canada, 1885–1945*. Toronto: McClelland & Stewart 1990.

Mellor, John. *The Company Store: James Bryson McLachlan and the Cape Breton Coal Miners, 1900–1925*. Toronto: Doubleday 1983.

Mitchell, Tom. "'Legal Gentlemen Appointed by the Federal Government': The Canadian State, the Citizens' Committee of 1000, and Winnipeg's Seditious Conspiracy Trials of 1919–1920." *Labour/Le travail* 53 (spring 2004).

Morel, E.D. *The Horror on the Rhine*. London: Union of Democratic Control 1920.

Moritz, Albert, and Theresa Moritz. *The World's Most Dangerous Woman: A New Biography of Emma Goldman*. Vancouver and Toronto: Subway Books 2001.

Morley, J.T. *Secular Socialists: The CCF/NDP in Ontario, a Biography*. Kingston and Montreal: McGill-Queen's University Press 1984.

Morton, Desmond. *Working People*. Montreal and Kingston: McGill-Queen's University Press 1998.

Morton, Suzanne. *At Odds: Gambling and Canadians, 1919–1969*. Toronto: University of Toronto Press, 2003.

Morton, W.L. *The Progressive Party in Canada*. Toronto: University of Toronto Press 1967.

Myers, Tamara. *Caught: Montreal's Modern Girls and the Law, 1869–1945*. Toronto: University of Toronto Press 2006.

– "On Probation: The Rise and Fall of Jewish Women's Antidelinquency Work in Interwar Montreal." In *Negotiating Identities in 19th- and 20th-Century Montreal*, edited by Bettina Bradbury and Tamara Myers. Vancouver: UBC Press 2005.

– "The Voluntary Delinquent: Parents, Daughters, and the Montreal Juvenile Delinquents' Court in 1918." *Canadian Historical Review* 80, no. 2 (June 1999).

Naylor, James. *The New Democracy: Challenging the Social Order in Industrial Ontario, 1914–1925*. Toronto: University of Toronto Press 1991.

– "Ontario Workers and the Decline of Labourism." In *Patterns of the Past: Interpreting Ontario's History*, edited by Roger Hall, William Westfall, and Laurel Sefton MacDowell. Toronto: Dundurn Press 1988.

Newton, Janice. *The Feminist Challenge to the Canadian Left, 1900–1918*. Montreal and Kingston: McGill-Queen's University Press 1995.

Palmer, Bryan D. "Maurice Spector, James P. Cannon, and the Origins of Canadian Trotskyism." *Labour/Le travail* 56 (fall 2005).

– *Working-Class Experience: Rethinking the History of Canadian Labour, 1800–1991*. Toronto: McClelland & Stewart 1992.

Penfold, Steven. "'Have You No Manhood in You?': Gender and Class in the Cape Breton Coal Towns, 1920–1926." In *Gender and History in Canada*, edited by Joy Parr and Mark Rosenfeld. Toronto: Copp Clark 1996.

Penner, Norman. *Canadian Communism: The Stalin Years and Beyond*. Toronto: Methuen 1988.

– *The Canadian Left: A Critical Analysis*. Scarborough, ON: Prentice-Hall of Canada 1977.

Pennington, Doris. *Agnes Macphail: Reformer*. Toronto: Simon & Pierre 1989.

Phillips, Melanie. *The Ascent of Woman: A History of the Suffragette Movement and the Ideas behind It*. London: Abacus 2003.

Pierce, Lorne. *Fifty Years of Public Service: A Life of James L. Hughes*. Toronto: Oxford University Press 1924.

Reinders, Robert C. "Racialism on the Left: E.D. Morel and the 'Black Horror on the Rhine.'" *International Review of Social History* 13 (1968).

Roberts, Barbara. "Women against War, 1914–1918: Francis Beynon and Laura Hughes." In *Up and Doing: Canadian Women and Peace*, edited by Janice Williamson and Deborah Gorham. Toronto: Women's Press 1989.

Roberts, Charles G.D., and Arthur Leonard Tunnell, eds. *The Canadian Who's Who 2*. Toronto: Trans-Canada Press 1936–37.

Robin, Martin. *Radical Politics and Canadian Labour*. Kingston: Queen's University Industrial Relations Centre 1968.

Rooke, P.T., and R.L. Schnell. *Discarding the Asylum: From Child Rescue to the Welfare State in English Canada*. New York: University Press of America 1983.

Sangster, Joan. *Dreams of Equality: Women on the Canadian Left, 1920–1950*. Toronto: McClelland & Stewart 1989.

– *Girl Trouble: Female Delinquency in English Canada*. Toronto: Between the Lines 2002.

– "The Making of a Socialist-Feminist: The Early Career of Beatrice Brigden, 1888–1941." *Atlantis* 13, no. 1 (fall 1987)

– "The 1907 Bell Telephone Strike: Organizing Women Workers." *Labour/Le travailleur* 3 (1978).

Schott, Linda K. *Reconstructing Women's Thoughts: The Women's International League for Peace and Freedom before World War II*. Stanford: Stanford University Press 1997.

Schreiner, Olive. *Woman and Labor*. Mineola, NY: Dover 1998.

Schulz, Patricia. *The East York Workers' Association: A Response to the Great Depression*. Toronto: New Hogtown Press 1975.

Shaw, Rosa L. *Proud Heritage: A History of the National Council of Women of Canada*. Toronto: Ryerson Press 1957.

Socknat, Thomas. *Witness against War: Pacifism in Canada, 1900–1945*. Toronto: University of Toronto Press 1987.

Speisman, Stephen A. *The Jews of Toronto: A History to 1937*. Toronto: McClelland & Stewart 1979.

Steedman, Mercedes. *Angels of the Workplace: Women and the Construction of Gender Relations in the Canadian Clothing Industry, 1890–1940*. Toronto: Oxford University Press 1997.

Strange, Carolyn. *Toronto's Girl Problem: The Perils and Pleasures of the City, 1880–1930*. Toronto: University of Toronto Press 1995.

Strong-Boag, Veronica. *The New Day Recalled: Lives of Girls and Women in English Canada, 1919–1939*. Markham, ON: Penguin 1988.

– *The Parliament of Women: The National Council of Women of Canada, 1893–1929*. Ottawa: National Museums of Canada 1976.

– "Peace-Making Women: Canada, 1919–1939." In *Women and Peace: Theoretical, Historical and Practical Perspectives*, edited by Ruth Roach Pierson. London: Croom Helm 1987.

Struthers, James. *No Fault of Their Own: Unemployment and the Canadian Welfare State, 1914–1941*. Toronto: University of Toronto Press 1983.

Suchat, Rabbi Wilfred. *The Gate of Heaven: The Story of Congregation Shaar Hashomayim of Montreal, 1846–1996*. Montreal & Kingston: McGill-Queen's University Press 2000.

Taylor, Barbara. *Eve and the New Jerusalem: Socialism and Feminism in the Nineteenth Century*. Cambridge, MA: Harvard University Press 1993.

Tennyson, Brian. "The Ontario General Election of 1919: The Beginnings of Agrarian Revolt." *Journal of Canadian Studies* 4 (February 1969).

Thompson, John Herd, with Allen Seager. *Canada, 1922–1939: Decades of Discord*. Toronto: McClelland & Stewart 1985.

Tulchinsky, Gerald. *Taking Root: The Origins of the Canadian Jewish Community*. Toronto: Lester 1992.

Valverde, Mariana. *The Age of Light, Soap, and Water*. Toronto: McClelland &
    Stewart 1991.

van den Hoonaard, Will. "Biographical Zoning and Bahá'i Biographical
    Writing." *Bahá'i Studies Review* 12 (2004)

– *The Origins of the Bahá'i Community of Canada, 1898–1948*. Waterloo: Wilfrid
    Laurier University Press 1996.

Vigod, Bernard. *Quebec before Duplessis: The Political Career of Louis-Alexandre
    Taschereau*. Kingston and Montreal: McGill-Queen's University Press 1986.

Wagar, Samuel E.C. "Theosophical Socialists in the 1920s Okanagan: Jack
    Logie's Social Issues Summer Camps." Master's thesis, Simon Fraser
    University, 2003.

Wiebe, Robert. *The Search for Order, 1877–1920*. New York: Hill & Wang
    1967.

White, Randall. *Too Good to Be True: Toronto in the 1920s*. Toronto and Oxford:
    Dundurn Press 1993.

Whitehorn, Alan. *Canadian Socialism: Essays on the CCF-NDP*. Toronto: Oxford
    University Press 1992.

Wollstonecraft, Mary. *A Vindication of the Rights of Woman*. London: Penguin
    1992.

Young, Walter D. *The Anatomy of a Party: The National CCF, 1932–1961*.
    Toronto: University of Toronto Press 1969.

Index

264; Popular Front, 171, 219,
225–7, 239–40, 254, 269–70,
333n86; public life of Toronto,
197; relationship with CCF, 245–
6, 250, 255, 260–1; Second
Period, 171; secret Guelph meeting, 1921 308n31; SPC supporters, 81; support of CCF candidates,
228–9; tactics, 181, 213, 258;
Third Period, 169–71, 185; trade
union policy, 256; views Canada as
colony, 139, 309n52; and women's
left political activism, 230
Communist Party of Great Britain,
96, 102, 126, 248, 300n24,
328n37
Conboy, Fred, 240
Conference to Defend Arrested
Regina Trekkers, 250–1, 254,
332n75
Congo Reform Association, 97
Conner, James MacArthur, 164,
174–81, 222, 248, 251, 265, 268,
272
Conservative Party of Canada, 53,
61, 83, 119, 146–7
Cooke, Alice, 239, 252–3
Cooperative Commonwealth
Federation, 79, 90, 157, 162, 223,
226–7, 235–6, 240–2, 246, 278,
315n126, n127, n133, 318n155,
328n28, 329n40, 333n86,
333n92; CCF Clubs, 174–81, 196,
211, 214–16, 320n33, 327n27,
330n45; emergence, 162–3;
forums, 206–8, 238; founding
convention, 315n116; and

Henderson memorial fund, 274;
and Henderson's death, 269–70;
histories, 276; identity, 221;
labour base, 183–7; National
Convention, 1936, 256–61; neglect of Quebec labour movement,
258, 332n73; newspaper, 237;
Ontario convention, 215; Ontario
Provincial Council, 245, 248–9,
254, 328n39; Ontario Women's
Committee, 329n44; peace resolution, 228; principles, 179; Regina
Manifesto, 182, 209, 214, 247,
256, 317n142; reinstates mem-
bers, 255; relationship with CPC,
229–31, 250; relationship with
CYC, 219; relationship with ILP,
222; relationship with Labor
Conference, 210–13; relationship
with NLP, 172–3; support of
dressmakers' strike, 217; suspi-
cious of PWA, 253; suspicious of
WJC, 251. See also Women's Joint
Committee
Cooperative Commonwealth Youth
Movement, 218, 220, 224, 230,
249
Copithorne, John, 195
Copp, Terry, 16, 23, 53
Corbin, Jeanne, 169
Cotterill, Murray, 220, 259–60
Cotton, Lorna 255, 269. See Thomas,
Lorna Cotton
Cotton's Weekly, 68
Coulson, R.W., 239
Courtice, Ada Mary Brown, 155
CRA. See Congo Reform Association